From the Wadsworth Series in Mass Communication and Journalism

General Mass Communication

Communications Law: Liberties, Restraints, and the Modern Media, 2nd Ed.,
   by John D. Zelezny
Communications Media in the Information Society, Updated Edition, by Joseph Straubhaar
   & Robert LaRose
Ethics in Media Communications: Cases and Controversies, 2nd Ed., by Louis Day
International Communications: History, Conflict, and Control of the Global Metropolis,
   by Robert S. Fortner
The Interplay of Influence, 4th Ed., by Kathleen Hall Jamieson & Karlyn Kohrs Campbell
Media/Impact: An Introduction to Mass Media, 3rd Ed., by Shirley Biagi
Media/Reader: Perspectives on Media Industries, Effects, and Issues, 3rd Ed., by Shirley Biagi
Mediamerica, Mediaworld: Form, Content, and Consequence of Mass Communication,
   Updated 5th Ed., by Edward Jay Whetmore
Women and Media: Content, Careers, and Criticism, by Cynthia Lont

Journalism

Creative Editing for Print Media, 2nd Ed., by Dorothy Bowles & Diane L. Borden
Free-Lancer and Staff Writer, 5th Ed., by William Rivers
News Writing, by Peter Berkow
The Search: Information Gathering for the Mass Media, by Lauren Kessler & Duncan McDonald
When Words Collide: A Media Writer's Guide to Grammar and Style, 4th Ed.,
   by Lauren Kessler and Duncan McDonald
Writing and Reporting News: A Coaching Method, 2nd Ed., by Carole Rich

Photography and Design

Design Principles for Desktop Publishers, 2nd Ed., by Tom Lichty
*Desktop Computing Workbook: A Guide to Fifteen Programs in Macintosh
   and Windows Formats,* by Paul Martin Lester
Introduction to Photography, 4th Ed., by Marvin J. Rosen & David L. DeVries
Visual Communication: Images with Messages, by Paul Martin Lester

Public Relations and Advertising

Advertising and Marketing to the New Majority: A Case Study Approach, by Gail Baker Woods
Creative Strategy in Advertising, 5th Ed., by A. Jerome Jewler
Electronic Public Relations, by Eugene Marlow
International Advertising: Communicating Across Cultures, by Barbara Mueller
Public Relations Cases, 3rd Ed., by Jerry A. Hendrix
Public Relations Writing: Form and Style, 4th Ed., by Doug Newsom & Bob Carrell
This Is PR: The Realities of Public Relations, 6th Ed., by Doug Newsom, Judy VanSlyke Turk
   & Dean Kruckeberg

Research and Theory

Communication Research: Strategies and Sources, 4th Ed., by Rebecca B. Rubin,
   Alan M. Rubin & Linda J. Piele
Mass Communication Theory: Foundations, Ferment, and Future, by Stanley Baran
   & Dennis Davis
Mass Media Research: An Introduction, 5th Ed., by Roger D. Wimmer & Joseph R. Dominick
The Practice of Social Research, 7th Ed., by Earl Babbie
Surveying Public Opinion, by Sondra Miller Rubenstein

The Interplay of Influence

News, Advertising, Politics,
and the Mass Media

FOURTH EDITION

Kathleen Hall Jamieson
University of Pennsylvania

Karlyn Kohrs Campbell
University of Minnesota

Wadsworth Publishing Company
I⊤P® An International Thomson Publishing Company

Belmont, CA • Albany, NY • Bonn • Boston • Cincinnati • Detroit • Johannesburg • London • Madrid •
Melbourne • Mexico City • New York • Paris • San Francisco • Singapore • Tokyo • Toronto • Washington

To Our Grandmothers,
Myra Moore Hall Zabel and Hinke Douma Kohrs,
who loved us, indulged our eccentricities, and nurtured our dreams.

Mass Communications Editor: *Todd Robert Armstrong*
Project Development Editor: *Lewis De Simone*
Editorial Assistant: *Michael Gillespie*
Senior Project Editor: *Debby Kramer*
Production: *Scratchgravel Publishing Services*

Print Buyer: *Barbara Britton*
Permissions Editor: *Robert Kauser*
Copy Editor: *Lura Harrison*
Cover Designer: *Gary Head*
Compositor: *Scratchgravel Publishing Services*
Printer: *Quebecor Printing/Fairfield*
Cover Printer: *Phoenix Color Corp.*

Printed in the United States of America
2 3 4 5 6 7 8 9 10

For more information, contact Wadsworth Publishing Company, 10 Davis Drive, Belmont, CA 94002, or electronically at http://www.thomson.com/wadsworth.html

International Thomson Publishing Europe
Berkshire House 168-173
High Holborn
London, WC1V 7AA, England

Thomas Nelson Australia
102 Dodds Street
South Melbourne 3205
Victoria, Australia

Nelson Canada
1120 Birchmount Road
Scarborough, Ontario
Canada M1K 5G4

International Thomson Publishing GmbH
Königswinterer Strasse 418
53227 Bonn, Germany

International Thomson Editores
Campos Eliseos 385, Piso 7
Col. Polanco
11560 México D.F. México

International Thomson Publishing Asia
221 Henderson Road
#05-10 Henderson Building
Singapore 0315

International Thomson Publishing Japan
Hirakawacho Kyowa Building, 3F
2-2-1 Hirakawacho
Chiyoda-ku, Tokyo 102, Japan

International Thomson Publishing Southern Africa
Building 18, Constantia Park
240 Old Pretoria Road
Halfway House, 1685 South Africa

Library of Congress Cataloging-in-Publication Data
Jamieson, Kathleen Hall.
    The interplay of influence : news, advertising, politics, and the
mass media / Kathleen Hall Jamieson, Karlyn Kohrs Campbell. — 4th ed.
        p.   cm. — (Wadsworth series in mass communication and journalism)
    Includes bibliographical references and index.
    ISBN 0-534-51431-6
    1. Mass media—Influence.   2. Mass media—Audiences.   3. Mass
media—United States.   I. Campbell, Karlyn Kohrs.   II. Title.   III. Series.
P94.J34   1997
302.23—dc20   96-19714

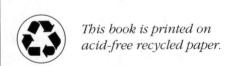

This book is printed on acid-free recycled paper.

Brief Contents

Contents

CHAPTER 2

What Is News? 39

CHAPTER 3

News as Persuasion 78

CHAPTER 4

Influencing the News Media   119

CHAPTER 5

Ratings and Revenues: The Audience in Mass Media Social Systems   153

CHAPTER 6

What Is Advertising?   190

CHAPTER 7

Persuasion Through Advertising   215

CHAPTER 8

Influencing Advertisers   246

CHAPTER 9

How to Influence the Media   272

CHAPTER 10

Political versus Product Campaigns   292

CHAPTER 11

News and Advertising in the Political Campaign   307

Preface

Since we wrote the first edition of *The Interplay of Influence,* the world of news, advertising, and politics has undergone a seismic revolution. Cable television now reaches two out of three of the nation's homes, carrying civic information on C-SPAN and round-the-clock Headline News on CNN. In many mid-sized cities, the second paper that political activists subscribe to is not a local one—for there are fewer and fewer two-newspaper towns—but *The New York Times,* which is delivered daily thanks to satellite transmission to regional printing plants. In addition, computer services have made it possible to scan stories from around the nation and even around the globe.

On the horizon with the passage of a landmark telecommunications bill in early 1996 is a new conception of media. Within the next decade we may be able to receive video from the phone company and phone service from the cable company. Congress has told television set manufacturers to include a "V-chip" in every new set, creating the possibility, if broadcasters cooperate by rating shows, that parents will be able to block sexually oriented or violent programs entirely or during certain hours. By doing so, they will be able to cast a countable "no" vote with advertisers on such shows. In the current ratings system we count who watches, not who doesn't. With the V-chip, advertisers would know the size and demographic identity of the audience offended by the sponsored programming. To no one's surprise, many broadcasters opposed the V-chip.

The world of politics has changed as well. Candidates now have Web pages that recruit volunteers, offer campaign material, and solicit funds. In newsrooms, computer databases make it easier to check candidate consistency and to monitor the flow of money reported to the Federal Election Commission. And adwatches have been added to the range of available forms of news reports.

These changes in the world of media have led us to expand the scope of issues confronted in this new edition of *The Interplay of Influence.* But even with all the changes afoot, we are pleased to note how durable are the original principles we set forth in the first edition. This edition offers new illustrations of those principles.

The other durable elements in our lives are our institutional homes. We remain happily situated at the University of Pennsylvania's Annenberg School and the University of Minnesota's Department of Speech–Communication.

We thank the following reviewers of previous editions for their helpful suggestions: Dennis C. Alexander, University of Utah; Chuck Bantz, University of Minnesota; Jane Banks, Syracuse University; Sam Becker, University of Iowa; Bob Cathcart, Quenns College; Gina Daddario, State University of New York at Cortland; Richard J. Harris, Kansas State University; Kathryn Ingle, University of Virginia; Don Kirkley, University of Maryland; Joe Lamp, Anne Arundel Community College; Margaret K. Latimer, Auburn University; Larry Lichty, University of Maryland; Val E. Limburg, Washington State University; Marin Pearson Allen, Gallaudet College; John Robinson, University of Maryland; James L. Rogers, University of North Texas; Gordon Whiting, Brigham Young University; and Eric Zonot, University of Maryland.

We also appreciate the helpful comments of the reviewers of this 4th edition: Peggy Bieber-Roberts, University of Wyoming; Gina Daddario, State University of New York at Cortland; Kate Madden, State University of New York at Brockport; and James L. Rogers, University of North Texas.

We thank our research assistants, Leila Brammer and Deborah Stinnett. In particular, we thank Kim Szpiech for her research on the Deep Dish Television Network. Finally, we thank Robert and Paul with whom we carry on an endless interplay of influence.

Kathleen Hall Jamieson
Karlyn Kohrs Campbell

CHAPTER 1

The Mass Media: An Introduction

Many Americans wake up to the sounds of music and news on a clock radio, wash and dress to the *Today* show or *Good Morning America,* breakfast with a morning paper, commute to the patter of a favorite disc jockey, dine with the evening news, relax with prime-time television, and doze to the strains of music on a clock radio. Americans, on the average, have their television sets on more than seven hours each day, listen to radios more than eighteen hours each week, and report reading some part of a daily newspaper four days each week and about fifteen books each year. The mass media are undeniably a central part of life in the United States.

This book is about the influence of the mass media, specifically television, radio, newspapers, and magazines. Many books on this subject already exist, but this book considers not only how the media influence all of us, but also how the media are, in turn, influenced by others—individuals, groups, government agencies, politicians, and other mass media. We hope to show that media persuasion works two ways: the media persuade us, but we and others can and do influence the media. This book is neither a history of nor an attack on media; it is a study of the communication and persuasion that take place through them.

Our perspective is rhetorical, focusing on how news, advertising, and political uses of the mass media shape conceptions of reality and influence attitudes and behaviors. We examine how consumer choices, individual and group protest, and regulatory mechanisms influence the mass media. As students of rhetoric, we know that any choice has an influence; whatever decisions newspeople, advertisers, or programmers make, the result will be a worldview shaped by those decisions.

We are not, then, looking for evidence that media personnel make choices—that is an inevitable part of using symbols. Rather, we examine patterns of choice. The decisions of newspeople, advertisers, and programmers are significant, as they fall into systematic patterns that consistently present a particular view of "reality." We hope to make explicit the assumptions underlying their choices. A rhetorical perspective is controversial in regard to news because we are used to

BOX 1-1

How Much Americans Say They Watch

According to the General Social Survey conducted in 1993, more than 96 percent of Americans say that they watch television for at least one hour on an average day. About half claim to watch more than three hours of television a day.[a] Heavy users of television tend to be less well-educated and working in occupations of lower prestige; however, people who are more well-off financially are increasing the amount of time they spend watching television, probably because they have access to diverse programs through cable and satellite transmissions.[b] For example, in spring 1994, 40 percent of television homes with incomes over $75,000 had pay cable whereas fewer than 25 percent of homes with incomes of less than $30,000 had this service.[c] More than 95 million, or 98.3 percent, of U.S. homes have at least one television set;[d] an average television household has 2.28 sets;[e] and 16 percent of U.S. households with television have four or more sets.[f] Of U.S. homes with television, 65.9 percent use cable services.[g] As of spring 1994, approximately 82 percent of U.S. households owned a VCR.[h] Again, income influences the rate of ownership of media technology. Nearly all people with incomes over $75,000 own a VCR in comparison with 60 percent of people with incomes under $20,000.[i]

[a]General Social Surveys, 1972–1993: Cumulative Code Book, conducted for the National Data Program for the Social Sciences at the National Opinion Research Center, University of Chicago. The Roper Center for Public Opinion Research, University of Connecticut, August 1993, p. 280.
[b]Xiaoming Hao, "Trend: Television Viewing among American Adults in the 1990s," *Journal of Broadcasting & Electronic Media*, vol. 38, no. 3 (Summer 1994): 359.
[c]"Cable Penetration by Demographic Segments," *TV Dimensions '95*, ed. Ed Papazian (New York: Media Dynamics, Inc., 1995), p. 10.
[d]"Television—Households," *Marketer's Guide to Media*, Spring/Summer 95 (New York: BPI Communications, 1995), p. 21.
[e]"Television Sets," *Marketer's Guide to Media*, Spring/Summer 95, p. 23.
[f]Simmons Market Research Bureau, 1993 Study of Media & Markets, as reported in *TV Dimensions '95*, p. 17.
[g]"Growth of Cable TV Penetration," *Marketer's Guide to Media*, Spring/Summer 95, p. 56.
[h]"VCR Basics," *TV Dimensions '95*, p. 129.
[i]"VCR Penetration by Demographic Segments, Spring 1994," *TV Dimensions '95*, p. 130.

thinking of the news as "objective," as a report of what occurs. But a rhetorical perspective is natural and common for political and product advertising and for analyzing politicians' efforts to influence the public by manipulating news coverage; these efforts are obviously and intentionally persuasive.

Because of our rhetorical perspective, we focus our attention on mass media messages that are most significant in terms of audience beliefs and attitudes: news, editorials and commentary, and advertising. Because these messages are all part of political mass communication, this book ends with a discussion of news and advertising in political campaigns. The primary news channels in our society are television, newspapers, and magazines, so most of our illustrations will be drawn from them. We pay particular attention to television, now the most pervasive and influential mass medium.

BOX 1-2

Rhetoric

The faculty of discovering, in any given case, the available means of persuasion.

Aristotle

That art or talent by which discourse is adapted to its end.

George Campbell

The use of language as a symbolic means of inducing cooperation in beings that by nature respond to symbols.

Kenneth Burke

BOX 1-3

Rhetoric Is Unavoidable

Even if a given terminology is a *reflection* of reality, by its very nature as a terminology it must be a *selection* of reality; and to this extent it must also function as a *deflection* of reality.[a]

[a]Kenneth Burke, *Language as Symbolic Action* (Berkeley: University of California Press, 1966), p. 45.

BOX 1-4

Participation/Identification

To *participate* is to take part, to join in, or to share with others. To participate is to be actively involved. Participation refers to the active role of the audience in creating meaning and sharing experience. When participation occurs, source and audience jointly create the message.

To *identify* is to associate or affiliate yourself closely with a person or group or with their values. In this process you see yourself as like someone else, imagine yourself in another's position, or empathize with others' problems and rejoice in their successes.

The ideas developed here are based on three fundamental assumptions. First, we assume that all communication is reciprocal, jointly created by the source and the audience. No one can commit an act of communication alone. It is an *inter*act (inter = between) or a *trans*act (trans = through, across) that comes into being because the participants cooperate in creating meaning and sharing experience. For this reason, participation and identification are key concepts in our analysis.

Second, we assume that each mass medium has unique resources for communication and influence because of the characteristic ways in which we receive, perceive, and interact with it. Each is a special kind of channel with distinctive capacities for inducing our participation. As a result, we contrast the communicative and persuasive potential of the various media.

Third, we assume that the nature and impact of mass-mediated messages cannot be separated from the economic and political system in which the mass media function. The mass media reflect certain cultural values and assumptions precisely because mass media outlets are large corporations supported by advertising and constrained by governmental and internal regulation and public pressure. For this reason, we explore the commercial bases of the mass media and detail the forms of regulation and the influences bearing on them.

This book is organized to examine news, advertising, and political communication, in that order. In each instance, we examine the media, first as persuaders who influence their audiences, then as entities influenced and regulated by citizens, groups, and government. In the case of the news, we look first at what news is, then examine its influence, and finally look at how the news media are influenced.

We then look at the ratings and revenues in all of the mass media before exploring the nature and types of commercial messages. We study the ways in which advertising persuades as well as the ways in which advertisers can be influenced. The final sections on political communication synthesize material from news and advertising, as both are involved in political communication.

However, continuing our earlier format, we look first at how people are influenced politically through and by the media and then at how the media are, in turn, influenced by politicians and their supporters. We hope that these chapters will increase your understanding of how mass media influence and are, in turn, influenced.

The mass media are so familiar, so much a part of our everyday lives, that we all feel we know and understand them. But it is precisely because they are so familiar that we need to study them. Familiarity, for example, may blind us to the distinctive communication that takes place through the mass media, and especially to the processes by which media influence us.

One important distinction between mass communication and other forms of communication in the United States is their commercial basis: *the primary function of the mass media is to attract and hold large audiences for advertisers.* They also inform and entertain, of course; but informing and entertaining are only means to the end of providing a mass audience for advertisers.

In more detail, here are some ways in which mass communication is unique.

Distinctive Characteristics of Mass Communication

Mass communication is affected by its context—the industrial, affluent, mass society—and mass communication differs in important ways from other forms of communication. It differs not only because it is commercial, but also in terms of its audience, its messages, and its sources.[1]

---

1. The distinctions outlined here are those described by Charles Wright in *Mass Communication: A Sociological Perspective*, 3d ed. (New York: Random House, 1986), pp. 6–9.

BOX 1-5

Anonymity

Dr. Ruth Westheimer, the pixieish sex therapist, was launched to fame by a sex advice show on New York radio. Her popularity led to a national call-in show for NBC radio and a television talk show on the Lifetime Cable Network. "Radio was crucial in giving me the opportunity to talk about sexual matters in an explicit way," she says. "Not only the power of the medium, but the anonymity it provides."[a]

[a]*Time*, 4 November 1985, p. 75.

BOX 1-6

The National Village

A young man, dubbed by the press "the mystery boy," was found crying and confused in a bus terminal in Cheyenne, Wyoming, October 26, 1985. He had neither identification nor money. Police and social workers struggled to learn anything that would help them identify the young man. On October 28, newspapers around the country printed his picture. The next day the questions were answered. The youth was Gordon Vanderberg, a convicted felon who had been treated for mental illness and a hearing impairment in New York and Los Angeles. "Basically, the media solved this mystery," police detective Marty Luna said. . . . "They did a fantastic job of blitzing his picture all over the U.S. . . . It's like the whole country was one small town. When they get the word out, you're going to find somebody who can solve these puzzles."[a]

[a]*Washington Post*, 30 October 1985, p. A2.

The Audience

The audience for mass communication is *large;* mass communication addresses massive audiences. This means that the audience is made up of so many people that it would be impossible for them to meet and interact face-to-face. The members of the audience are also *anonymous;* that is, audience members know others are watching, listening, or reading, but they do not know just who the others are. Note that the mass audience is thus the opposite of a *group,* which is defined as a small number of people who can meet and talk face-to-face, who come to know each other, and who develop attachments to each other. Finally, the mass audience is *heterogeneous;* it is made up of all sorts of people. The mass audience is so varied because nearly everyone has access to these media—you can read or watch or listen whether you are old or young; rich or poor; educated or uneducated; in a city, suburb, town, or on a farm.

There are television sets in 98.3 percent of U.S. households,[2] radios are in over 99 percent, and most Americans can afford a newspaper, a magazine, or a paperback book. This saturation of the mass media reflects our affluent society; although there is an admission fee, nearly all Americans can pay it. The print media require literacy, which narrows their audience somewhat, but electronic media can be consumed and enjoyed by nearly everyone. Some cable television channels are targeted at more specific audiences, a phenomenon called "narrowcasting," but even these audiences, although smaller, are very large. The audience for mass communication is, then, large, anonymous, and heterogeneous.

The Mediated Message

The messages of mass communication are also distinctive. In general, they are *transient* or ephemeral, here today and gone tomorrow, intended and useful only for the immediate moment. Most mass communication is tied to a particular time, place, and set of events. Morning newspapers report what happened yesterday; the episodes of soap operas and prime-time series are quickly forgotten; paperbacks and magazines are read and thrown away. In this respect, mass communication is the opposite of communication in the fine arts or in what is sometimes called "high culture." We expect to savor and cherish great paintings and sculptures; we read, reread, and study great books and plays; we listen over and over again to great pieces of music.

Obviously, some high culture is transmitted through the mass media. We can listen to opera "Live from Lincoln Center"; in the summer, we can tune in to the Boston Pops concerts; we can watch productions of great plays; and we hope to see repeated broadcasts of some mini-series, documentaries, and interviews.

But these are exceptions. The vast majority of mass communication is tied to the daily and immediate; it is temporary and forgettable—a characteristic not only of radio and television, but also of newspapers, even though they are not as ephemeral.

Mass media messages are *transmitted rapidly*. Most audience members receive them at approximately the same time, as illustrated by television. Television critics agree on at least one thing: that the best television is live coverage of sports events, such as the World Series and the Super Bowl, and of breaking news stories, such as the student demonstrations and subsequent military response in Beijing's Tiananmen Square or an earthquake's interruption of the World Series in San Francisco. No other form of communication reaches so many so quickly, and it is a given of newspapers, radio, and television that nothing is staler than yesterday's news.

Because nearly everyone has access to them, the messages of mass communication are *public;* they are addressed to everyone, and they are created to be intelligible and acceptable to all. Newspapers are written in ordinary language

2. "Television Households," *Marketer's Guide to the Media*, Spring/Summer 95, (New York: BPI Communications, 1995), p. 21.

with words chosen for their commonality and familiarity. Television and radio censor themselves to avoid giving offense to anyone. (Obviously, they do not always succeed!)

Once again, there are exceptions. Some media are specialized (sometimes called segmented or minority media). In contrast to *TV Guide, People,* and the *Reader's Digest,* some magazines aim at smaller, well-defined audiences: *Ebony* at African Americans; *Guns and Ammo* at hunters and gun enthusiasts; *Electronic Media* at those interested in radio and television programming. Similarly, although there are radio news networks that blanket the country, there are also Spanish-language stations and stations aimed just at those who love top-40 or jazz or classical music. Note, however, that all of us have access to these varied outlets, and because of their public nature, even such specialized media must take some care to avoid giving offense.

The pornography battle illustrates this problem: groups object to pornography precisely because all of us, including children, may be exposed to it. This issue is complicated and difficult, but it is the public character of pornography that arouses the most serious objections.

In summary, then, the messages of mass communication are transient, transmitted rapidly, and public.

The Source

The sources of messages in the mass media are also distinctive. Because sending such messages is costly and technologically complex, the sources must be *organizational* or institutional. Historically, the sources of mass communication have been large organizations, such as radio and television networks, newspaper chains, publishing firms, and conglomerates that own different media or a variety of industries including one or more mass media outlets. Of course, there are variations in size. Some stations are independent; some newspapers are family firms; some magazines are produced by small, cohesive groups. But even in these smaller versions, mass communication is the product of an organization. The 1995 merger of Capital Cities and ABC is a dramatic reminder that key sources of mass-mediated messages are very large organizations that not only produce programming but also distribute it. In the climate of deregulation, similar mergers will occur.

Production and distribution require a division of labor, highly trained specialists, and elaborate and expensive equipment. For this reason, very few individuals, as individuals, have direct access to the mass media. Those who speak or write through them represent teams, organizations, groups, or the public. In this sense, mass communication is *impersonal,* produced by a unit of people with varied skills.

The sources of mass communication, then, are organizational and, in that sense, impersonal or anonymous.

These characteristics of audiences, messages, and sources differentiate mass communication from other kinds of communication. But there are areas in which these distinctions blur. How is one to classify an outdoor concert by a rock group using sophisticated sound equipment to produce music for an audience of tens of thousands (which may also be sold as a record or marketed as a video)? What of a filmed theatrical production or operas and concerts televised live? Obviously, mass communication is part of and related to other kinds of communication. Although we can indicate distinctions, we must also acknowledge similarities and interrelationships.

Interpersonal and Mass Communication: Relationships

Mass communication is part of the whole process of communication going on all of the time in our lives. People watch television in their homes, and what they see and hear is affected by family attitudes and the comments of friends and relatives. Despite the importance of the mass media, we still hear live speeches, and we still talk to each other in small groups face-to-face at parties, in classes, at the grocery store, and in city council meetings.

All of these contacts influence our experience of and our reaction to mediated messages. But the messages in the mass media also affect our communication with family and friends. Mass communication needs to be studied, and for purposes of study we have to try to isolate it, but mass communication is not really separable from other kinds of communication.

Mass Media Use

The relationship between mass communication and other forms of communication is evident in our use of the mass media. With the exception of films shown in theaters, most mediated messages are consumed by individuals alone or in small groups: a family or group of friends around a television set, a carpool of fellow workers listening to a radio program, a bus rider reading a newspaper, a computer user exploring the Internet.

Thus, the mass media reach large, anonymous, heterogeneous audiences with rapid, transient, public messages generated by impersonal, organizational sources; however, most mass communication occurs in intimate, personal, small-group settings.

Some worry that our experience of the mediated message is displacing our desire to experience the real thing. Scholars debate whether low voter turnout is prompted in part by the would-be voters' sense that they already have participated fully in the campaign by watching it in ads and televised news, including debates between candidates.

Similarly, former Philadelphia Orchestra music director Riccardo Muti notes that:

Recording is changing the way some people view our art. With the continuing refinement of compact discs, and the promise of video discs, some people are beginning to suggest that electronic media could replace the live concert experience. We must never let this happen.[3]

Impact of Mass Media

Mediated messages have not just entered our lives; they have changed our patterns of living. The impact of television has been the most dramatic: Americans spend more time watching television than doing anything else except sleeping and eating!

The effect of all of this is the subject of much controversy. One recent study gathered ongoing reactions from television viewers; the research led to the following conclusions:

> Television viewing is a passive and relaxing, low concentration activity. Viewing is often driven by the wish to escape or avoid negative affective states. Viewers tend to feel passive and less alert after viewing. Heavier viewers feel worse than light viewers generally, and particularly when alone or during unstructured time.[4]

Television has also changed the way we get information. Nearly half of all Americans admit to getting their news only from television rather than from newspapers.[5] In fact, more Americans trust television as a news source (46%) than trust newspapers (31%).[6]

But our attitudes toward television and the other mass media are mixed. We Americans fear the power of the press and the power and influence of the mass media generally, as reflected in such books as *Amusing Ourselves to Death, The Electronic Nightmare: The New Communications and Freedom,* and *Networks of Power: Corporate TV's Threat to Democracy* .[7]

Some of our fear and distrust arises from a belief that the mass media are monolithic, controlled by ever-fewer people, and speak with a single voice. Such attitudes reflect a recognition of the power held by those who control our access to information. Patterns of ownership that increasingly concentrate media outlets in fewer and fewer hands are also a source of concern. Despite such concentration of power, the mass media present a varied picture, and different types can be identified.

---

3. *Philadelphia Inquirer*, 17 October 1989, p. 11A.

4. Robert Kubey and Mihaly Csikszentmihalyi, *Television and the Quality of Life: How Viewing Shapes Everyday Experience* (Hillsdale, N.J.: Lawrence Erlbaum, 1990), pp. 171–173.

5. Roper Organization, "America's Watching, Public Attitudes Towards Television," 1993.

6. Gallup Poll News Service, 2 April 1993.

7. Neil Postman, *Amusing Ourselves to Death: Public Discourse in the Age of Show Business* (New York: Viking, 1985); John Wicklein, *The Electronic Nightmare: The New Communications and Freedom* (New York: Viking, 1981); Dennis Mazzocco, *Networks of Power: Corporate TV's Threat to Democracy* (Boston: South End Press, 1994).

Kinds of Mass Media

Some mass media are international in scope, some are national, and some are segmented, addressing specialized audiences. A few form an elite of opinion leaders. The electronic media may be independently owned and unaffiliated, part of a group with common ownership, affiliated with the networks, or owned and operated by the networks. Newspapers may be independently owned or be parts of chains or media conglomerates. Finally, each medium has unique qualities because of its technology, its structure, and its function.

International Media

A medium is international if it regularly and predictably carries its messages across national boundaries. The *International Herald Tribune,* for example, is an international newspaper available throughout Europe as well as in the United States.

Broadcast signals don't recognize national boundaries. Increasingly, what was national broadcasting is becoming international as satellites make it available to people in different countries and time zones. In summer 1989, the Cable News Network (CNN) signed a five-year agreement with the Soviet Union that enabled CNN to transmit its 24-hour-a-day news on the Soviet satellite Intersputnik to the Indian subcontinent as well as to Southeast Asia and Africa. Because CNN was already carried on Pan Am Sat to Central and South America and to Europe and the Far East on Intelsat, this meant that CNN International was beamed to most of the countries on earth. Specifically, the service was available in eighty-five foreign countries and the United States.[8] The first subscribers to the service were international hotels.[9] Cable systems in the Baltic Republics, the Ukraine, and Uzbekistan also picked up the news service. In January 1995, Turner Broadcasting made CNN International available to U.S. cable subscribers. By June 1995, CNNI was accessible in 5.5 million U.S. households via cable and direct-to-home satellite.[10]

The fall of the Berlin Wall in autumn 1989 offered other prospects for transnational broadcasting. In late 1989, the 24-hour-a-day music channel, MTV Europe (now solely owned by Viacom, but then a partnership of the Mirror Group of Newspapers, Viacom International, and British Telecommunications) reached 10.8 million European homes. The channel began exploring the possibility of bringing its service to eastern Europe with the fall of the Wall. In March 1989, MTV Europe moved into Hungary where it reached 112,484 households. Those owning satellite dishes could receive MTV Europe in Poland and Czechoslovakia.[11]

---

8. *Electronic Media,* 4 December 1989, p. 38.
9. *Washington Post,* 10 August 1989, p. C10.
10. *Television Digest,* 12 June 1995, p. 4.
11. Sean Kelly, "MTV Sets Sights in Eastern Europe," *Electronic Media,* 4 December 1989, p. 34.

By 1994, MTV Europe had become one of the most successful cable networks in Europe, with over 60 million subscribers, more than in the United States. Its biggest market in Europe is Germany, where it is received in more than 18 million households. Viacom has also introduced its Nickelodeon network across Europe in partnership with British Sky Broadcasting, the satellite television company half-owned by Rupert Murdoch.[12]

In October 1990, MTV announced that it had signed an agreement with the Soviet television company Gostelradio to provide the main Soviet television channel with a weekly hour of MTV programming. At that time, the hour-long MTV show was the first program on Soviet television that was commercially sponsored. Today, the MTV program reaches 88 million households in the former Soviet Union.[13]

Political Repercussions   The ability of mediated messages to cross national boundaries changed the face of politics in the 1970s and 1980s. In the late 1970s underground radio stations originating in a suburb of Paris carried a message that was dubbed to tape recorders. These dubbed cassettes passed through the underground to Iran where the transmitted words of the Ayatollah Ruholla Khomeini helped inflame a revolution against the Shah of Iran.

In summer 1989, satellite transmission carried the pictures of demonstrating students building a Goddess of Democracy in Tiananmen Square. Countries around the world beamed back evidence of international support for the student movement. Ironically, days later the same satellite feeds were used by Beijing police to identify and capture dissidents. Had it not been for television, the students might, in the words of columnist David Broder, "have escaped into anonymity."[14]

The emergence of global media in global markets is comparatively recent. In the early 1970s, only twenty-four nations had earth-based broadcasting facilities. By that decade's end, more than 135 nations were using the Intelsat global satellite system full time.[15]

As the 1980s drew to a close, satellite transmission was changing our conception of the world and of international affairs. The Soviet protest over the U.S. invasion of Panama was not delivered first to a U.S. embassy or to the White House. Instead, a Soviet leader called the Moscow bureau of CNN.[16]

Breaking Informational Barriers   But more efficient forms of protest are not the only by-product of the new informational age. To deliver satellites into space, previously inconceivable forms of technical and economic cooperation are

---

12. Richard W. Stevenson, "Lights! Camera! Europe!" *New York Times,* 6 February 1994, sec. 3, p. 1.
13. Ibid.
14. David S. Broder, "The Limits of Modern Technology," *Philadelphia Inquirer,* 18 June 1989, p. 7C.
15. James F. Larson, *Television's Window on the World: International Affairs Coverage on the U.S. Networks* (Norwood, N.J.: Ablex Press, 1984), pp. 2–3.
16. Jonathan Alter, "Ted's Global Village," *Newsweek,* 11 June 1990, p. 49.

emerging. In 1989, the White House agreed to allow China to use its "Long March" rocket booster to launch U.S.-made satellites; China has had a series of failed launches with its Long March-1 and Long March-2 rockets.[17] Arianespace, a French-based organization owned jointly by west European governments and companies, has had more success in commercial launches and currently holds 60 percent of the new orders for the sixty-eight satellites due to be sent into orbit over the next few years. Because of the great demand for satellites in a number of communications areas—television, telephone, and other information transmitting systems—several new companies around the world are also looking into providing commercial launch services.[18]

Similarly, in July 1990, McGraw-Hill became the first large U.S. media company to publish a Russian-language newsmagazine—*Business Week/USSR*—in the Soviet Union.[19] The magazine, with a circulation of 60,000, includes translated articles from *Business Week International*. In 1991, *Reader's Digest* started a Russian-language edition to be sold in four Russian cities. That August, the journal's 50,000 copies sold out within days. Circulation increased to 80,000 for the second issue and to 100,000 for the third with the same results.[20] Between 1989 and 1991 more than two dozen U.S. publishers set up operations in eastern Europe and the former USSR; however, about half the magazines went under. For example, the upscale, nonacademic science magazine *Omni* was launched in Russia by General Media, but failed to find a sustained readership. Time Inc.'s chairman and CEO Reginald Brack, Jr., felt that eastern Europe and Russia's markets for magazines were still too uncertain to justify investment.[21]

Informational barriers have fallen more rapidly than economic barriers. This is the case in part because television's images do not require the audience to be either literate or multilingual. Words are not needed to caption the exploding shuttle Challenger as a tragedy, to comment on the significance of PLO chairman Yassir Arafat shaking hands with Yitzhak Shamir at the White House, or to explain the meaning of the pope kneeling in prayer at Auschwitz, with two prison-garbed survivors at his side. And whereas customs officials can intercept goods or books moving illegally across national boundaries, blocking a satellite feed or a fax is more difficult.

At the same time that unprecedented amounts of international information are available, state control of the media is waning. Those long denied free access to political information are eager consumers. In 1988, Mexican newspapers and radio, but not the government-dominated Televisa, gave opposition candidate Cuauhtemoc Cardenas coverage. The result was that the public turned to other channels, and Televisa's once dominant evening news ratings plummeted.

---

17. AP, "China Fails in Space, Again," *Chicago Tribune*, 26 January 1995, p. 1.
18. Peter Marsh, "Survey of Aerospace," *Financial Times*, 12 June 1995, p. ix.
19. Deirdre Carmody, "Business Week Publishing Russian-Language Edition," *New York Times*, 20 July 1990, p. D5.
20. Deirdre Carmody, "The Media Business; American Dream Turns into a Moscow Magazine," *New York Times*, 16 December 1991, p. D8.
21. Alison Gray Johnson, "Beyond the Iron Curtain; Periodical Publishing in Former Communist Countries," *Folio: The Magazine for Magazine Management*, 1 September 1993, p. 66.

State control had always been predicated on the understanding that the power of television to shape our perspective on the world is profound. In March 1985, a split screen on ABC's *Nightline* brought the U.S. audience a tense exchange between South African foreign minister Roelof Botha and Bishop Desmond Tutu, the former from Capetown, the latter in his church in Johannesburg. One analyst noted that the positioning of these two adversaries side by side provided "a striking picture by [giving] Tutu the parity on TV that he and his fellow blacks are denied in their South African homeland."[22]

Technology Casts a Spotlight   Technology magnified a hidden truth in still another world-shaping event. Careful analysis of the tapes of Romanian leader Nicolae Ceausescu's execution revealed evidence that he had not been summarily executed but probably had first been tortured; magnified portions of the tape played in slow motion carried the evidence to the world.

From the tape showing Ceausescu's execution to scenes of crowds dancing atop the Berlin Wall, international television has fashioned common global experiences. At the same time it has provided a clearer sense of the problems we share. For weeks in spring 1990, stories about the pollution of the air and water in East Germany heightened our awareness of the fragility of the ecostructure. Within the same period, international news carried a U.S. government study's warning that inadequately stored waste produced by the manufacture of nuclear weaponry was posing an environmental hazard that would require a costly response.

In what political scientists are calling a "multipolar world," the news the world sees will not necessarily reflect the perspective of the superpowers, or focus on their special interests, such as have dominated international news from the end of World War II to the fall of communism in the Soviet Union.

The trend has already begun. In 1987 CNN began a unique worldwide service that enabled television journalists or stations from any country to become contributors to CNN's *World Report* by sending in a videocassette. If it is technically possible, the film is aired uncensored. Nancy Peckenham, the executive producer of *World Report* explained CNN's philosophy about airing these 2½-minute segments: "We don't make judgment calls. We feel these reports are a reflection of life and the state of information and ideas in these countries. I don't have the right to say something is propaganda and doesn't meet the standards of journalism in the West. Everyone and every country has a bias and we don't attempt to judge that bias." CNN began the *World Report* in response to the concerns of television producers from developing countries who felt that their areas of the world were distorted by the mainstream media, which only took an interest in their countries when they were experiencing a natural disaster or political unrest. Robert Royer, producer of Jamaica Broadcasting Co., feels that "CNN's World Report allows us to present our own views to the global audience." But the reports can also have an impact on local politics. Edmund Katiti, managing director of Cabelsat TV in Uganda feels that his government's

---

22. Howard Rosenberg, "Getting South Africa Down in Black, White," *Los Angeles Times*, 20 March 1985, p. 1.

leaders "watch their step now because they are afraid we will do a CNN World Report on them."[23]

The emergence of a global village is changing the ways in which we think about ourselves and the world. What was once called "foreign" news is increasingly called "international" news, and those who habitually refer to the United States as America are increasingly aware that that is a label we share with our neighbors to the north and south.

National Media

For our purposes, a medium is considered national if it has a large audience in all regions of the United States. It is not government owned; there are no state-owned mass media in this country. The Public Broadcasting Service, although partly funded by the federal government, is an independent corporation. The United States Information Agency, an agency of the federal government, may not broadcast its material in the United States except by a special act of Congress.

National media include the four major television networks—ABC, CBS, NBC, and Fox—as well as the noncommercial Public Broadcasting Service. (Two new national networks, United Paramount and Warner Bros., do not yet have complete weekly schedules, and the Home Shopping Network does not have the range of programming that the other commercial networks offer.) National media also include the major radio networks; the major wire services, Associated Press (AP) and Reuters; magazines such as the newsweeklies *Time, Newsweek,* and *U.S. News & World Report;* and such general interest magazines as the *Reader's Digest, TV Guide,* and *People;* the *Wall Street Journal;* the *New York Times; USA Today;* and the *Christian Science Monitor* also are distributed nationally.

In March 1995, the *Wall Street Journal* had a daily circulation of 1,823,207—the largest daily circulation of any newspaper in the United States and more than one-third of the weekly circulation of *Time.*[24] Contrast this with even the largest newspaper chains, which tend to be somewhat regional in character. Most chains encourage local autonomy in newsgathering and editorial policy.

In mid-1982, the Gannett newspaper chain began publishing a national newspaper, *USA Today,* modeled on television's notions of news. The stories in *USA Today* are brief, extensively illustrated, and written to emphasize "the human interest angle." By 1989, *USA Today* had eclipsed the *New York Times* and the *Christian Science Monitor* in daily circulation, reaching more than 1.3 million individuals daily. In 1995, the average Monday through Thursday circulation of *USA Today* was 1,570,624, jumping to 1.9 million on Fridays.[25]

23. Sarah Veal, "CNN Passes Around the Mike," *International Herald Tribune,* 11 May 1994, Finance Section.

24. *Marketer's Guide to the Media,* Spring/Summer 95 (New York: BPI Communications, 1995), p. 202; "Consumer Magazine Paid Circulation," *Advertising Age,* 20 February 1995, p. 34.

25. "National Newspapers," *Marketer's Guide to the Media,* Spring/Summer 95 (New York: BPI Communications, 1995), p. 202.

BOX 1-7

The Public Broadcasting System

The Public Broadcasting System (PBS) is a loose federation of 351 local broadcasting authorities scattered across the United States. This structure emphasizes localism, but localism is costly.

Programs produced by PBS stations make up only 42 percent of all its national programming, and of these programs, 60 percent are produced by three regional stations—WGBH in Boston, WNET in New York, and WETA in Washington, D.C. An additional 16 percent of all programs are produced by the Children's Television Workshop, and most of the rest come from overseas companies like the BBC. Seventy-five cents of every PBS dollar is spent by the 351 local stations on the cost of their offices, studios, personnel, and local programming; only about 7 percent of PBS's budget is spent on making programs.

In 1993 PBS received, through its chief regulatory body, the Corporation for Public Broadcasting, some $253 million, about 13.5 percent of total revenue, which amounted to slightly less than one tax dollar per American per year. The $253 million the CPB received from Congress in 1993 generated more than $1.5 billion in investment from membership programs, matching grants, and business sponsorship.[a]

[a]Robert Hughes, "Why Watch It, Anyway?" *New York Review of Books,* 16 February, 1995, pp. 37–42.

Competitors to national network news are also emerging. In summer 1986, the Associated Press and CONUS Communications instituted a television news feed service called "TV Direct." The service provides video-formatted AP news photos and video feeds of Washington events to television stations across the country. AP serves nearly 6,000 broadcast stations nationwide; CONUS is a news cooperative of television stations. Another competitor, the Cable News Network (CNN), based in Atlanta, is a 24-hour-a-day national news operation now available in hotels throughout the world.

Specialized Media

Specialized media, also called "segmented" or "minority" media, are aimed at and limited to a geographically defined audience—*New York* and *California* magazines, for example—or by interest, for example, *Stereo Review* or *Flying.* Specialized media are defined by their special audiences, such as *Ms.* magazine, which is aimed at women with feminist leanings. Such an audience may be relatively small but spread throughout the nation. By contrast, local media are defined entirely by geography, aimed at an audience located in a particular area. They can be as small as the *West Central Minnesota Daily Tribune,* directed at those who live in Willmar and the surrounding area, or as large and prestigious as the *Philadelphia Inquirer.*

BOX 1-8

CONUS

Stanley S. Hubbard, owner of KSTP-TV, the ABC affiliate in St. Paul, Minnesota, established a satellite newsgathering service to compete with the networks. CONUS, an acronym for Continental U.S., is a consortium of some seventy network-affiliated and independent local stations. The key to the system is a fleet of mobile vans (costing $200,000–$300,000) with uplinks to satellites via dishes and capable of reaching more than 700 U.S. television stations.

At a Gannett Center for Media Studies conference, Adam Clayton Powell III, formerly with CBS News and National Public Radio, commented: "To get them [live shots] 10 years ago meant about seventeen technicians and borrowing a truck from the television network of the kind they used to cover football games and setting up microwave towers—all expensive and time consuming. Now you can do it with three and sometimes even two persons."[a]

By the mid-1990s, however, "microwave [satellite] trucks have gotten smaller and more of them have live-feed capability, so that everywhere you have a camera you can get a picture back to the station. While the microwave van used to be a mini-production studio, with editing and other capabilities, vans are now being down-sized and the editing function is being moved back to the studio."[b]

[a]Burton Benjamin, "Technology and the Bottom Line Create Profound Challenges," *New York Times*, 17 August 1986, p. 1H.
[b]"Getting the Most Out of the Latest Technology," *Broadcasting & Cable*, 3 October 1994, p. S3.

Elite Media

A third way of differentiating among the media is to recognize outlets or programs having a national impact, although their audience may be relatively small and geographically limited. These media are opinion leaders; they are an elite group that affects the decisions made in other media. The *New York Times* falls into this category. Herbert Gans, for example, writes that "The *Times* is treated as the professional setter of standards. . . . When editors and producers are uncertain about a selection decision, they will check whether, where, and how the *Times* has covered the story; and story selectors see to it that many of the *Times'* front-page stories find their way into television programs and magazines."[26] An elite medium is trusted, respected, and used by other journalists. The *Wall Street Journal* is an elite medium because of its preeminence in the financial community and because it covers stories in depth.

Some television programs also fall into this category, such as *The NewsHour with Jim Lehrer* shown weeknights on the Public Broadcasting System. To a lesser

---

26. Herbert Gans, *Deciding What's News: A Study of CBS Evening News, NBC Evening News, Newsweek and Time* (New York: Pantheon, 1979), p. 180.

BOX 1-9

PBS's "NewsHour"

New York, NY—On Friday, October 20, 1995, *The MacNeil/Lehrer NewsHour* will become *The NewsHour with Jim Lehrer* when Robert MacNeil, who announced his retirement late last year, steps down as co-anchor of the nightly newscast. The date simultaneously marks *The NewsHour's* 20th anniversary. . . .

  The NewsHour with Jim Lehrer remains the nation's only hourlong newscast, seen weeknightly on more than 300 PBS stations.

  As executive editor and sole anchor, Lehrer will guide the program. . . . *The NewsHour with Jim Lehrer* will originate from Washington DC. . . .

  The NewsHour with Jim Lehrer is funded by the Archer Daniels Midland company, New York Life Insurance company, public television stations and the Corporation for Public Broadcasting. It is produced by MacNeil/Lehrer Productions and WETA/26 Washington DC, in association with Thirteen/WNET New York.[a]

[a]Press release from *The MacNeil/Lehrer NewsHour.*

---

extent this is also true of the network programs *This Week with David Brinkley, Meet the Press,* and *Face the Nation,* which air on Sundays. Clips from these programs, featuring prominent international and national political leaders, often appear on Sunday evening newscasts or in Monday's papers. Some specialized magazines with unusually prominent and authoritative authors function in a similar way, as, for instance, the journal *Foreign Affairs.* Most elite media are specialized media that have a national impact because they act as opinion leaders for other mass media. David Broder's column in the *Washington Post* is an example of opinion-leading political analysis; the *Congressional Quarterly* is the definitive outlet for information on Congress; the *New York Review of Books* contains authoritative commentary on books.

Major News Carriers

Classifying media as international, national, specialized, or elite focuses attention on the size and location of their audience and on relationships among the media. But equally important are the technology, patterns of ownership, and organization that exist in each medium.

Television

By 1995, there were 1,520 television stations in the United States. Of these, more than 1,100 carried commercials. These television stations are divided between VHF (very high frequency, channels 2 through 13) and UHF (ultra high

CASE STUDY 1-1

Altering News Norms—The Influence of CNN

Prior to the advent of CNN, if you or I wanted to learn what had happened in the world on a given day, we would either have to locate an all-news radio station or wait until early evening to tune in to a network news broadcast. People interested in world affairs adjusted their time to that of the networks. Meals and social activities were scheduled around network news time. The availability of 24-hour-a-day news changed all that. News is now available at our convenience.

The sheer quantity of news coverage dictated some other changes in the ways in which CNN news was programmed. Instead of a single "star" anchor, CNN developed a cast of anchors; focus on the personality of the anchor decreased. The result was subtle but evident in the difference in the way Mary Alice Williams's move from CNN was treated; the flurry of national publicity that followed in the wake of Roger Mudd's departure from NBC did not ensue. Williams was one of many; the news had not been built around her in any special way.

A second difference in patterns of anchoring and reporting emerged. Women and minorities were more likely to appear in those roles on CNN than on the other networks. This pluralization of the news also was reflected in the use of tape and reporters from around the world.

By broadcasting around the clock, CNN ensured that without disrupting "commercial" programming, it could "go live." At 2:32 P.M. EST, CNN led the other networks by four minutes with the report that shots had been fired at President Ronald Reagan. Moreover, it could stay on the air with a live report as long as the news producer wished. CNN, for example, aired twenty-nine straight hours of coverage on the attempted assassination, Hinckley's motives, and Reagan's progress.

Live coverage makes us more aware of the extent to which most broadcast news is packaged by the conventions of editing discussed earlier. In the twenty-nine hours of CNN coverage of the assassination attempt, "CNN's viewers got the story in the jumbled way that a journalist receives fragments of information before transforming them into an orderly, polished report. The 'process' of gathering news determined the form in which the news was delivered. With CNN's unlimited time, the story could unfold at its own pace. With all those 'ragged edges' exposed."[a]

As the tanks moved in on the demonstrators in Tiananmen Square in Beijing, the CNN reporters could no longer sustain the calm, controlled tone that ordinarily characterizes edited news. Neither we nor they could be certain what was happening. CNN audiences around the world were encircled by the tensions and tragedies of the moment. Those who received their information in the 2-minute, predigested packages of edited news could not experience this story in the same way.

In its first decade, CNN established the importance of the function it served. CNN was the only network on "live" on January 28, 1986, when the space shuttle Challenger exploded. For hours in 1987, audiences followed CNN's coverage of efforts to rescue Baby Jessica. That programming drew the highest rating CNN had received up to that time—a 6.6.

In summer 1989, CNN's coverage of Tiananmen Square riveted audience attention on the ongoing struggle of the Chinese students to democratize their country. In May 1989, those watching CNN's coverage of Tiananmen Square heard anchor Bernard Shaw confirm the extent to which live coverage had affected world affairs:

[a]Hank Wittemore, *CNN: The Inside Story* (New York: Little, Brown, 1990), p. 192.

I am being told that the Chinese government has closed the city of Beijing and no journalists are being allowed. . . . Unbelievably, we all came here to cover a summit, and we walked into a revolution. . . . Now we are being told that if we don't stop transmitting, the Chinese government will take our equipment. It will be interesting to see what happens. . . . President Bush is being quoted by reporters covering him in Maine, and it's being relayed to us. He is saying, "Word of the news blackout is very disturbing."

By 1990, we routinely expected to see "CNN LIVE" imprinted on newspaper photos of breaking news.

As noted earlier, CNN's *World Report* has modified the ideology underlying news as well. In the $2\frac{1}{2}$-minute segments aired unedited from around the globe, we see the play of competing ideologies at work. The differences were evident in news stories following the invasion of Kuwait by Iraq. From the Palestinians came stories claiming that the U.N. sanctions against Iraq created a double standard; they pointed out that when U.N. resolutions had condemned Israeli actions, U.N. sanctions had been effectively blocked by a U.S. veto in the Security Council. Small countries dependent on Arab oil focused their stories primarily on the economic impact of the embargo; some declared they were being used as pawns in a U.S. game. One story from the Philippines emphasized the economic hardship imposed on that country by the inability of its nationals working in Kuwait to continue sending payments to their families at home. Only on CNN could audiences around the world hear the 76-minute speech that Iraq's leader Saddam Hussein sent to the United States to be broadcast to the public.

Because CNN broadcasts around the globe, it has become a vehicle for airing the competing claims of various nations and their leaders. Voices previously unlikely to be heard by U.S. audiences have received airplay. In September 1990, for example, CNN carried a speech by Jordan's King Hussein appealing for moderation by all sides in the Kuwait–Iraq crisis. King Hussein warned that the world was slipping into war in the Middle East just as it had slipped into World War I. Within days, the Saudi ambassador to the United States was on CNN delivering a rebuttal to Hussein's speech. The appropriate analogy, argued the ambassador, was the role Hitler's aggression played in starting World War II. One index of power is the ability to have one's message heard; by that measure, CNN has empowered countries and leaders that otherwise would play a smaller role on the international stage. In short, CNN has accelerated the emergence of a multipolar world.

At the same time, it has become a medium of information for world leaders themselves. Message after message from Saddam Hussein to the world indicated that he had been following world reaction. The presumed channel: CNN. And in August 1989, the *New York Times* reported a presidential aide noting that President Bush was considering ways to respond to the threat to U.S. hostages in Lebanon while in his study "watching CNN." The president's press secretary, Marlin Fitzwater, told the reporter, "CNN has opened up a whole new communications system between governments in terms of immediacy and directness. In many cases, it's the first communication we have."[b]

Because of its on-the-spot coverage of the bombing of Baghdad as the war in the Persian Gulf began, scores of CBS, NBC, and ABC affiliates dumped their

[b]Quoted in Wittemore, p. 302.

(continued on next page)

Nelson Mandela with F. W. DeKlerk.
(© 1994 CNN, Inc. All rights reserved.)

The night skyline of Baghdad, Iraq,
during the Gulf War airstrikes.
(© 1993 CNN, Inc. All rights reserved.)

A crowd of people in front of the
Berlin Wall.
(© 1989 CNN, Inc. All rights reserved.)

network coverage in favor of CNN. For example, WCCO, a CBS affiliate in Minneapolis, routinely interrupted the *CBS Evening News* to switch to CNN, and in a close three-way ratings race for number 1, WCCO's ratings clobbered its NBC and ABC affiliate rivals during the opening week of the Persian Gulf War.

CNN's dominance of news coverage of the opening days of the war may have been a turning point in television news, shifting power from ABC, NBC, and CBS and toward CNN. "The gulf crisis is a defining event," said S. Robert Lichter of the Center for Media and Public Affairs in Washington, D.C. "It's as if history is conspiring to help CNN." Larry Gerbrandt of Paul Kagan Associates, cable television analysts, agreed: "No one will ever doubt their advertising line again—that CNN is the most important network in the world. This is the greatest journalism story of the decade."[c]

EXERCISE: Examine the CNN pictures above. What is memorable about each? What is newsworthy? What facets of the news story does each picture feature? What difference, if any, does it make that the events captured in these pictures were broadcast live?

EXERCISE: How was our understanding of each of the pictured events changed by the presence of live coverage? Are some events more newsworthy than they otherwise would have been? How are traditional news norms altered by the ability to transmit images from around the globe? What effect will such coverage have on politics? on the conduct of world leaders? on issues of concern?

[c]Adapted from Bob Wisehart, "Amid the Chaos, CNN Establishes a New World Order," *Sacramento Bee*, 20 January 1991, pp. D1, D4.

frequency, channels 14 through 88). At the end of 1994, there were 559 commercial VHF television stations on the air and 598 commercial UHF.[27] They also are divided between commercial and noncommercial (educational) stations.

Most of the commercial television stations are affiliated with a network. The majority of nonaffiliated television stations are UHF stations with limited coverage areas and audiences. Until 1986, when someone said "the networks" they were referring to ABC, NBC, CBS, and, occasionally, CNN, but in that year the Fox Broadcasting Company began developing the Fox network. Owned by Media Corporation president Rupert Murdoch, the Fox network expanded its number of affiliate stations from 130 to 200 when it purchased the rights to broadcast NFL football games. Unlike ABC, CBS, and NBC, the Fox network does not offer national news shows in the morning and the evening, although several local Fox affiliates have their own news teams and local news programs. In mid-1995, Fox, in conjunction with the news service Reuters, began developing a news program that would be available 24-hours a day for Fox affiliates.[28]

More than the other commercial networks, Fox has focused on attracting younger viewers with programs such as *The X-Files, Beverly Hills, 90210,* and *Melrose Place.* One of Fox's continuing hit shows is the offbeat cartoon program *The Simpsons.* Between 1989 and 1990, this single show boosted Fox's Sunday night ratings 21 percent.[29] Brandon Tartikoff, former president of NBC's entertainment divisions, explains Fox's strategy this way:

> Fox is after the 18–34-year-old demographic. Why? Because that is the most fickle group of people on the planet today who have any sort of disposable income. They don't have lifelong habits formed, they haven't always bought a Buick, they haven't always drunk Yuban coffee, they haven't always used Tide. If you come in with a brand new splashy advertising campaign for a Nissan car or for a new brand of toothpaste, you've got a real buyer there.[30]

In the last quarter of 1994, Fox was the network with the youngest audience, with an average age of 29.6, while CBS had the oldest with an average of 50.0.[31]

Two new commercial networks, United Paramount Network (UPN) and Warner Bros. (WB), began broadcasting new entertainment shows in January 1995. WB began with one night of broadcasting and UPN started with two nights. By the end of the regular broadcast season, 7 of the UPN and WB shows occupied the lowest positions of the 142 shows rated during the year. Only UPN's *Star Trek Voyager,* which built on fans' decades-long loyalty to the show's concept, was consistently among the top 100 rated programs.[32]

Government regulations limiting media ownership are changing drastically. What had been intended to prevent concentration of ownership of television,

---

27. *Broadcasting and Cable Yearbook 1995* (R. R. Bowker, A Reed Reference Publishing Co., 1995), p. xxi.
28. "Fox 'Serious' on Free Political Time," *Television Digest,* 12 June 1995, p. 6.
29. *Electronic Media,* 9 April 1990, p. 43.
30. "Tartikoff Talks," *Broadcasting,* 4 June 1990, p. 40.
31. Jennifer DeCoursey, "Median TV Viewers Aging," *Advertising Age,* 17 April 1995, p. 30.
32. *Electronic Media,* 24 April 1995, p. 48.

BOX 1-10

A&E

Jointly owned by Capital Cities/ABC, NBC, and the Hearst Corporation, A&E went on the air on February 1, 1984, the result of a merger of the ARTS (owned by ABC and Hearst) and the Entertainment Channel (a venture of Rockefeller Center and RCA). It had 9 million subscribers and a solitary advertiser, Ford. By May 1995, A&E was the fifth most viewed cable network[a] with 64 million subscribers via more than 9,300 cable systems in the United States and Canada.[b]

To persuade cable systems around the country to carry A&E, an effort was made to make A&E part of the fabric of every community in which it operated. A National Cable Library project was initiated, and working through local cable systems, A&E offered to set up video libraries, composed of tapes of its programming, in local libraries.

The A&E network succeeded by being relentlessly frugal. It produced little original programming, instead acquiring programs, mainly from the BBC. In 1984, 60 percent of its shows came from the BBC; in 1989, less than 40 percent did. The 1995–96 schedule includes *Bob Vila's Home Again, 20th Century,* and the *A&E Mystery Movie.* By combining dance and opera with slapstick comedy and historical documentaries and programs about war, A&E attracts the viewers advertisers seek. A&E claims to offer advertisers desirable demographics: people 35 to 45 years old, with four years of college, and average annual incomes of $40,000 to $50,000.[c]

[a]N. R. Kleinfield, "A&E: A Cable Success Story," *New York Times,* 16 April 1989, p. 31H.
"A&E Television Network," *Advertising Age,* 8 May 1995, p. C6.
[b] "1995 Guide to National Cable TV Networks," *Advertising Age,* 5 May 1995, p. C43.
[c]*Advertising Age,* 5 May 1995, p. C6.

---

radio, and newspapers in a few hands is seen by the 1995 Republican Congress as restricting competition between old and new technologies. Likely to pass, despite Clinton administration opposition, are measures that permit companies to own more radio stations and permit single ownership of an unlimited number of television stations covering up to 35 percent of television homes.[33] The Telecommunications Bill passed in February 1996 also lifted the law that banned a single company from owning a TV station and cable system in one market.[34]

The Rise of Cable   In 1982, cable television had 27 million subscribers, more than one-quarter of all television homes in the United States; by mid-1986, 42 percent of all television homes subscribed. As of 1994, cable television penetration stood at 65.9 percent of all U.S. television households. In real numbers that meant that approximately 61.2 million out of a total of 94.3 million television homes have subscribed to cable.[35] In 1995, the number of homes subscribing to

---

33. *Broadcasting & Cable,* 19 June 1995, p. 6.
34. *Philadelphia Inquirer,* 2 February 1996, p. A6.
35. "Growth of Cable TV Penetration," *Marketer's Guide to the Media,* Spring/Summer 95 (New York: BPI Communications, 1995), p. 56.

BOX 1-11

BET

Black Entertainment Television, a 24-hour-a-day, Washington-based operation, was the nation's first television network aimed at an African-American audience. The network's founder and president, Robert L. Johnson, launched BET in 1980. In 1991, BET Holdings Inc. completed a $72.3 million initial public offering to become the first black-owned company traded on the New York Stock Exchange.[a] In 1989, BET was carried on just 1,825 of the nation's 7,500 cable systems and ranked 20th out of 42 basic services in terms of subscribers (with 23.8 million) and was 15th out of 20 networks in revenues, with a projected $22.4 million in 1989. Although by April 1995, BET provided programming such as news, public affairs, jazz, off-network sitcoms, gospel, music videos, and sports, for 42.3 million subscribers in the United States, the network no longer ranked among the top 20 basic services.[b] Now offered as part of the basic cable package, its revenues come from advertising and subscriber fees.

BET relies heavily on low-cost programming, although it produces more than 20 percent of the shows that it airs. Johnson explains: "Our strong cash flow is the basis of our ability to deliver a quality product at a low cost, mainly because our heavy concentration is in music videos—essentially given to us at no cost for promotional considerations—and in our ability to buy off-network product at a low cost because we are buying black-oriented sitcoms that didn't find their way out of network into any form of syndication."[c]

Company founder Johnson also has ventured into publishing with *YSB* and *Emerge* magazines, and has worked to develop home-shopping programs aimed at African Americans.[d] BET also acquired Action Pay Per View, broadcast in 7 million homes,[e] and has formed joint ventures to make family-oriented films with Blockbuster and action films with Encore.[f]

[a]Alfred Edmond, Jr., "Milestones in Black Business," *Black Enterprise*, January 1995, p. 104.
[b]"Black Entertainment Television to Explore State of the Family," *Business Wire*, 13 June 1995.
[c]Rich Brown and Don West, "Bob Johnson on the Information Revolution: All Ahead Slow," *Broadcasting & Cable*, 3 July 1995, pp. 16–19. Cited material on p. 17.
[d]"Top 50 Black Powerbrokers in Entertainment," *Black Enterprise*, December 1994, p. 66.
[e] Brown and West, p. 19.
[f]Laura M. Litvan, "A Broadcaster's Vision," *Nation's Business*, February 1995, pp. 13–14. Cited material on p. 14.

cable increased more than 3 percent to about 64 million.[36] Only 28 percent of subscribers take at least one premium channel, such as Home Box Office. In May 1995, HBO had 19.2 million subscribers.[37]

Cable systems with many channels offer the possibility of diversified programming. Channels presenting exclusively children's programs, news, sports,

36. Bill Carter, "Cable Picks up Viewers the Networks Cast Adrift," *New York Times*, 5 June 1995, p. C7. Much of this increase is believed to be a result of the movement of older viewers from network to cable programming.
37. Stephen Battaglio and Scott Hattrick, "Bewkes Takes Charge at HBO," *Hollywood Reporter*, 4 May 1995.

BOX 1-12

Shopping Electronically—Home Shopping Network and Infomercials

In 1986, Home Shopping Network Inc., which captivated bargain-hungry consumers by offering discounted merchandise through cable television, expanded into broadcast television by agreeing to purchase nine UHF stations in major markets for an estimated $150 million. The stations Home Shopping acquired were in Newark (New Jersey), Smithtown (Long Island), Boston, Baltimore, Philadelphia, Cleveland, Houston, San Francisco, and Los Angeles. By the early 1990s, HSN had become a national network, rivaling the major commercial networks for the number of stations owned in markets across the country. In May 1995, HSN and America Online launched a new area on the online service for shopping. HSN Interactive now offers Global Plaza, and will soon initiate Masterworks, another online store offering best-sellers and fine books, works of art, and music in addition to an array of jewelry and other gifts.[a]

To maximize their use of UHF stations, most of which have limited range and small viewerships, Home Shopping and the recently created Infomall cable network, owned by Paxson Communications, provide six to seven hours a day of public service and children's programming, which makes them eligible under current FCC rules to be carried by cable operators in their areas.[b]

Twelve of the nation's top cable networks now offer more than twenty hours per week of infomercial programming, according to the Cabletelevision Advertising Bureau. The CAB says those with the most paid programming hours per week are Lifetime (52), Black Entertainment Television (48), and The Nashville Network and The Discovery Channel (42) each. Top multiple-system cable operators Cox Cable Communications and Jones Intercable recently formed a joint venture to combine their fledgling infomercial networks, Consumer Information Network and Product Information Network. "As you study the infomercial industry, it is the fastest growing advertising segment in America," says Greg Liptak, president of Jones Satellite Networks and program director of Product Information Network. In the past ten years, he says, the industry's annual revenue has skyrocketed from $30 million to $900 million.[c]

In l994, 29 percent of all adults watched one of the home shopping channels but only 10 percent reported making a purchase. Home shopping viewers tend to be over age 30, are predominantly women, and are concentrated in the $30,000+ household income segments.[d] In comparison, 70 percent of all adults have seen infomercials, and 17 percent have bought infomercial products.

[a]Mark Berniker, "NBC Joins Microsoft's Multimedia Fold; Broadcaster Wants to Enter Online, CD-ROM, Interactive TV Markets," *Broadcasting & Cable,* 22 May 1995, p. 21.
[b]Julie A. Zier, "Paxson Building Infomercial Net," *Broadcasting & Cable,* 16 January 1995, p. 102.
[c]Rich Brown, "Infomercial Marketers Make Their Pitch," *Broadcasting & Cable,* 23 January 1995.
[d]"Exposure of Home Shopping/Infomercials among the U.S. Adult Population: January–February 1994," a Times Mirror survey published in *TV Dimensions '95,* ed. Ed Papazian (New York: Media Dynamics, Inc., 1995), p. 144.

BOX 1-13

Minority Ownership of Media

In 1978, the Federal Communications Commission (FCC) adopted rules to increase minority ownership. The rules created tax and other incentives to encourage purchases of radio and television stations by minorities. These regulations tripled the number of minority-owned stations to nearly 3 percent of the total. Specifically, the 300 stations owned by members of minority groups represent 2.7 percent of the 11,021 stations in the United States, but many are the weakest in their markets. Of the nation's 1,151 television stations, minorities own 27; of the 9,870 radio stations, 273 are minority owned.[a]

[a]*New York Times*, 31 May 1994, pp. C1, C2.

comedy, and first-run movies now exist. Sports network, ESPN, gained viewers in 1989, but ratings for NFL broadcasts on the other networks remained virtually unchanged. Its contract with the NFL permitted ESPN to televise one game per week during the second half of the regular football season. Nine percent more viewers watched the games on ESPN than had in 1988.[38] In 1993, ESPN started a second sports channel targeted at a younger viewing audience. By 1995, ESPN was the most frequently watched basic cable channel.[39]

Some cable systems provide nonprofit channels or public access channels that give local and minority groups and individuals access to the airwaves. Some channels are free of advertising; others cluster ads at the end of a half-hour of programming. Still others, such as in-house home shopping channels, provide two-way interactive systems allowing viewers to purchase products by calling 800 numbers. Currently, interactive technology is an $11.1 billion industry that includes a range of products and activities, such as video games, virtual reality, home shopping, CD-ROMs, Internet, interactive 800 numbers and television programs, and commercial online services.[40] An example is Windows 95, a Microsoft product. Through this system, the individual will be able to interact with a range of content providers, including American Greetings, C-SPAN, The New York Times Co., QVC, Hollywood Online, and ESP-Net SportsZone.[41] Interactive technology raises the threat of invasion of privacy because certain systems can be used to accumulate personal and otherwise inaccessible information about users.

Cable also has pioneered what some tout as the future in message delivery— pay-per-view (PPV). In 1990, between 13 and 18 million U.S. homes were capable of receiving pay-per-view events. By 1995 that number was upward of 25 million. Pay-per-view occurs on channels that carry programs to homes that have

---

38. Thomas Tyrer, "Cable Gains, Broadcast Flat in This Season's NFL Ratings," *Electronic Media*, 11 December 1989, p. 6.
39. "ESPN," *Advertising Age*, 8 May 1995, p. C17.
40. Debra Aho Williamson, "Building a New Industry," *Advertising Age*, 13 March 1995, p. S-3.
41. Scott Donaton, "The Battle for Online Content," *Advertising Age*, 15 May 1995, pp. 16–17.

BOX 1-14

Public Access Television: Deep Dish TV Network

There are some real alternatives to commercial television, but the story of the Deep Dish Television Network illustrates just what a struggle it is to create and maintain alternative programming. Originally, public, educational, and government access channels (PEG) were created to open up new outlets for local expression, promote added diversity in television programming, advance educational and instructional television, and increase information about the services and activities of local governments. Between 1979 and 1984, the federal government adopted a hands-off policy toward access, and many stations were threatened with elimination. The Cable Communications Act of 1984 saved public access cable television by asserting the basic right of all communities to have access to and representation on cable systems. In addition, in *Capital Cities, Inc. v. Crisp* (1984), the Supreme Court ruled that the state could not place content restrictions on signals sent to local cable systems. This guaranteed freedom from censorship to access channels.

Beginning in 1986, the Deep Dish Television Network became the first public access satellite network. "The First National Public Access Satellite Project" was a ten-part series that aired in hour-long shows over a ten-week period starting in April. Compiled from over 20,000 hours of locally produced programming, the series incorporated almost half of the 360 tapes received from local access stations, and it aired on at least 186 cable stations in the United States, reaching viewers in all but eight states.[a] The first program was devoted to information about public access. Those that followed each had a different subject, ranging from domestic labor and housing crises to international relations and issues of concern to women, minority groups, and children.

The 1988 season included programs about labor, Latino experiences and images, farming and agriculture, war and militarism, communication across national borders, perspectives on AIDS, the use of humor and theater to promote social change, understanding Central America, and videos produced by and about young people (mostly teenagers) and older people. Two hundred and fifty access stations in forty-three states ran the second season, and Deep Dish Television calculated that it had reached more than 12 million U.S. households.

Two series were aired in 1990. The first addressed the rise of "hate programming" on public access channels and included programs that detailed specific incidents of as well as community responses to programming by "hate groups." The second series addressed the relationship between environmental issues and racism, labor, and particular groups of socially, politically, or economically disadvantaged people. Other programming during that year aroused controversy, particularly programming concerned with U.S. propaganda illegally broadcast to Cuba, excerpts from Cuban television, and a live address by former Nicaraguan president Daniel Ortega after he lost his bid for reelection in February 1990.[b] Deep

[a]*Deep Dish Directory*, 1986. Available from Deep Dish Television Network, 339 Lafayette St., New York, NY 10012.
[b]"Censored Air," *Nation*, vol. 253, no. 2, 1991, p. 40.

Dish programs are far from neutral; they are meant to raise awareness and generate questions in the minds of viewers. Accordingly, many are offensive to some audience members. In spite of the controversy aroused in 1990, Deep Dish received an NEA grant for its 1991 spring season for a series "Behind Censorship: The Assault on Civil Liberties."

In 1991 Deep Dish members produced the "Gulf Crisis TV Project," a series of programs exploring peaceful alternatives to the military agenda of war in the Persian Gulf. The first four programs aired on more than two dozen PBS stations and on almost 300 public access channels, and were taped by at least forty other PBS stations for possible use. The series also was purchased by stations outside the country and aired in Britain, Japan, Australia, and Germany. More than 200 tapes from around the country were used to create these four programs.

The second series, "Behind Censorship," was sponsored by WYBE-Philadelphia public television for redistribution on the PBS satellite system in spring 1992. The fall 1992 season, "Rock the Boat," was advertised as alternative perspectives on the history of Native-American survival in the 500 years since Columbus arrived in the New World. Because of technical difficulties and staff turnover, the 1993 season series, "Visions of Ourselves," did not air until the fall. Although originally planned for distribution in 1993, the series "Sick and Tired of Being Sick and Tired" did not air until spring 1994, long after the Clinton administration health care reform program had gone down to defeat. Technical, staff, and financial problems caused the delay, but what might have been an important contribution to the debate came too late.

Public access television relies on individuals and organizations to create the raw materials out of which programming is created. The quality of such programming is affected by the level of technical skills of those involved, which vary greatly. Compiling these videotapes into series to be distributed by satellite requires skilled and dedicated staff, who must also do all the other tasks related to disseminating information about programming. Financing for these projects usually comes from grants and other nonprofit sources, requiring the staff to find interested sources of support and to write applications. Finally, it is difficult to reach audiences. Many of you will never have heard of Deep Dish Television or have seen any of its programming. If it is familiar, it may well be because you were exposed to its programming on a PBS station. Viewership on public access cable channels is low, in part because it is difficult to find out about the programming offered and because the quality of the programming varies, with some of it painfully similar to home movies and videotapes. Nonetheless, Deep Dish Television produced high-quality, alternative programming that expressed the views of disadvantaged groups and presented positions on controversial subjects that tend to be overlooked or underemphasized on commercial television. However, the difficulties of Deep Dish Television suggest just how hard it is to produce alternative programming on a regular and predictable schedule.

agreed to subscribe. Movies and boxing are the types of programming most frequently carried on a pay-per-view basis. Of all of the cable subscribers only 17 percent had used PPV in 1993. Those who use PPV, do so on average once every two months.[42]

In 1992, NBC offered full coverage of the 1992 Summer Olympics to cable viewers on a pay-per-view basis. This PPV service provided 600 ad-free hours of sports coverage from Barcelona, Spain, in a package costing approximately $150 per home.[43] PPV Olympic programming did not attract customers, however, and NBC lost $100 million.[44] PPV has had somewhat more success attracting viewers with musical events. The two highest grossing musical events were the Judds' Farewell concert in 1991, which earned $5.5 million, and Woodstock 1994, which earned more than $12 million in PPV revenue. However, the figures for Woodstock 1994 indicate that only 300,000 or 1.2 to 1.5 percent of the nation's 24 million addressable homes paid to have the concert brought into their living rooms.[45]

In 1984, Congress essentially deregulated cable. The legislation specified that cable rate deregulation would occur in 1987. Subsequent complaints about rate increases and poor service led to calls for re-regulation. Congress responded with the 1992 Cable TV Consumer Protection Act, which rolled back cable rates in most areas and regulated future increases. Legislation passed in February 1996 deregulated rates for those whose cable systems reached fewer than 50,000 subscribers and set deregulation of other systems for March 1999. That date can be moved up if a telephone company enters the market to compete.[46]

The Public Broadcasting Service (PBS) was once the only service dedicating itself to educational television. In 1990, PBS was programming 15 to 20 hours per week in prime time and 120 hours per week at other times. Between 1985 and 1990, PBS's prime-time ratings dropped 30 percent. Cable had begun to provide alternative educational television. CNN and C-SPAN compete with PBS's public affairs programming, its documentaries go head-to-head with the Discovery and History channels, and its children's programming is rivaled by Nickelodeon and Disney.[47]

The New Technology   Television's future depends in part on technology: direct satellite transmission to homes without the use of cable; the costs of laying cable; the carrying capacity of fiber optics cable; the potential for using existing telephone lines; the sophistication of interactive systems for purchasing programs and products. Low-power (low-band, very-high-frequency) television offers such opportunities.

---

42. *TV Dimensions '95*, ed. Ed Papazian (New York: Media Dynamics, Inc., 1995), p. 140.
43. Bill Carter, "NBC to Offer 600 Hours of Olympics, at a Price," *New York Times*, 12 February 1990, p. D10.
44. Barry Layne, "Waiting for the Future is Pastime of Sports TV," *Hollywood Reporter*, 17 December 1992.
45. Jane Dalzell, "Woodstock Sets PPV Revenue Record," *Electronic Media*, 29 August 1994, p. 14.
46. *Broadcasting & Cable*, 19 June 1995, p. 6; *Philadelphia Inquirer*, 2 February 1996, p. A6.
47. "Marketplace Won't Let Privatized CPB Die," *Electronic Media*, 20 February 1995, p. 14.

Direct Broadcast Satellite (DBS) transmits television programming via satellite directly to antennas at subscribers' homes rather than through cable. Three companies currently are spearheading efforts to develop DBS systems: Hughes' DIRECTV, Hubbard Broadcasting USSB, and Primestar, a joint venture project of Time Warner Cable, TCI, and Cox Communications. Even though customers must purchase a $700 18-inch satellite dish in order to subscribe, more than 600,000 U.S. homes had purchased the DBS service by the beginning of 1995.[48]

In the past, low-power television stations have served almost exclusively as boosters or translators, making signals available to communities that couldn't receive regular transmissions. Low-power stations that originate programming are experimental. In Washington, D.C., a low-power station beams Spanish-language programs to one particular area, an example of low-power television aiming a weak signal at a specific audience. The spring 1995 FCC list showed 1,591 licensed low-power television (LPTV) stations.[49] In the mid-1990s, LPTV stations could broadcast on more than one channel at a time. Although the new technology limited LPTVs to only 10 to 20 channels, in comparison with up to 180 with a DBS system, many communications companies continued to purchase LPTV licenses so they could offer affordable broadcasting services to rural customers who cannot readily receive cable TV.[50]

Over-the-air pay television systems are also beginning to compete with cable systems in urban areas, however. In 1982, the Microband Corporation of America urged the Federal Communications Commission to allow three such "wireless cable" systems in each of the nation's fifty largest television markets. (In fall 1989, Microband filed for bankruptcy.) Wireless cable, also known as multichannel, multipoint distribution service (MMDS), sends multiple channels of video programming by microwave transmission rather than by cable. In its compressed, digital form, MMDS provides more than 100 channels to a radius of approximately 40 miles from the transmitter tower that receives the programs via satellite. The MMDS transmitter delivers video to homes that are in its "line of sight." The microwave signal is received by an antenna on the subscriber's home; then a box usually set on top of the television decodes and decompresses the digital signal. In 1995, approximately 170 systems serviced more than 700,000 MMDS subscribers. In its early years wireless cable suffered from poor signal reception and limited offerings, often of only one channel. Today's MMDS digital technology delivers a clearer picture and CD-quality sound. The costs of MMDS and the time required to build the transmitters and antennas are far less than for laying cable. Because of its potential, large corporations are moving into this area.

Future development also depends on regulation and patterns of ownership. For example, the Federal Communications Commission formerly banned telephone companies from controlling cable systems in their service areas and television networks from controlling cable systems anywhere in the country. Legislation

---

48. Lindsey Kelley, "Primestar Ramps up for DBS Race," *Electronic Media*, 30 January 1995, p. 32.
49. *Broadcasting & Cable*, 27 March 1995, p. 54.
50. "Multichannel for Rural Areas," *Communications Daily*, 20 May 1994, p. 2.

BOX 1-15

VCR

One other factor has changed the ways in which we view television. The advent of the VCR has made it possible to rearrange television's schedule to suit our own. By spring 1994, VCR penetration had increased to 82 percent of television homes and was expected to rise to 85 percent by late 1996.[a] According to Nielsen studies, the average VCR home uses the machine 5 hours a week—1.5 hours for recording and 3.5 hours for playing tapes.[b] Despite all this, it is reported that 70 percent of all VCR owners do not know how to program their machines. Coming to the rescue is Starsight, a system available by means of a microchip placed in new televisions, VCRs, or set-top receivers. With Starsight, a viewer can call up an up-to-date schedule grid of all channels up to a week in advance, highlight program choices and program the VCR with the push of the remote button.[c]

[a]*New York Times,* 26 February 1996, p. B17.
[b] "VCR Basics," *TV Dimensions '95,* ed. Ed Papazian (New York: Media Dynamics Inc., 1995), p. 129.
[c]*New York Times,* 26 June 1995, p. D6.

---

passed in 1996 permitted the phone company to deliver video and long distance cable and related companies to offer local phone service.[51]

In response to this prospect of deregulation, the GTE Corporation, owner of telephone companies around the nation, is planning to introduce video services to about 7 million customers in the next eight years. MCI Communications and Sprint Corporation, the second and third largest long-distance carriers in the country, have each announced plans to enter the video market—MCI by building local networks and Sprint by joining with four of the largest cable companies.[52]

Radio

Radio best illustrates media specialization and segmentation. It was once dominated by national networks comparable to those we now associate with television. Originally, there were four national networks—ABC, CBS, NBC, and the Mutual Broadcasting System—but what remains of them are primarily news services. Today, however, radio has become a segmented medium. More than thirty-three national radio networks are currently in existence, compared with twenty-three in 1990 and just nine in 1974.[53] Some of them provide 24-hour-a-day adult popular, top-40, jazz, classical, or country and western music. Two things have contributed to the proliferation of networks: one is an increase in the

---

51. *Broadcasting & Cable,* 19 June 1995, p. 6; *Philadelphia Inquirer,* 2 February 1996, p. A6.
52. *New York Times,* 17 June 1995, sec. 1, p. 1.
53. "Network Radio," *Marketer's Guide to Media,* Spring/Summer 95 (New York: BPI Communications, 1995), pp. 82–83.

BOX 1-16

Formats in Radio

Those who program for radio and who buy time on this medium think of radio formats in these terms:

contemporary hits, top-40, contemporary	album-oriented rock
	classical
adult contemporary	country
oldies (1955–1987)	talk
black (75 percent or more of audience)	news
Hispanic/Spanish	Big Band
urban (majority of audience is non-Caucasian but a large segment is Caucasian)	middle-of-the-road
	jazz
	religious
easy listening	gospel

---

number of radio stations from about 4,000 in 1968 to nearly 10,000 ten years later, and to 12,000 in 1994.[54] The second is an effort to reach specialized audiences (see Chapter 5 on ratings and revenues). For example, only 30 of the 9,993 commercial radio stations in the country play classical music, yet most of them are profitable. Because there is a recognizable public demand for classical music, there are advertisers eager to reach the upscale audience such programming attracts.[55]

Although music, news, and sports constitute the bulk of network fare, the radio dial is increasingly filling up with daily, weekly, or monthly "long-form" programming, from music/variety series like NBC's *Live from the Hard Rock Cafe* to national talk/call-in shows, many inspired by the phenomenal success of Mutual Radio's *Larry King Show* and the syndicated *Rush Limbaugh Show.*

Advertisers want their commercials to reach particular consumers, and to compete with other stations for these consumers, stations need the resources of networks—particularly programming they could not afford to produce themselves. Some networks are regional, such as the New York Yankees baseball network. Others are national but aimed at a particular ethnic group, such as the Black Radio Network, a news source geared toward African Americans that has 168 affiliates. Although radio generally is considered a local medium, this claim is open to dispute. About one-fifth of all radio stations in the United States use one of the national networks for their music programming, and most stations rely on national services for their news programming.[56] As a result, although programs may be beamed from a local station, the programming can originate elsewhere.

---

54. R. Unmacht, ed., *The M Street Radio Directory* (Alexandria, Va.: M Street Corp., 1994), p. 19.
55. John von Rhein, "Bach, Beethoven and the Bottom Line: Classical Radio Is Imperiled, but Chicago's Two Stations Are Holding On," *Chicago Tribune,* 8 May 1994, Arts, p. 5.
56. R. Unmacht, ed., *The M Street Radio Directory,* p. 19.

BOX 1-17

National Public Radio (NPR)

About 25 percent of the annual appropriation to the Corporation for Public Broadcasting is set aside for radio. Approximately 60 percent of NPR's operating budget ($59 million for 1995) comes from dues paid by well over 500 member radio stations, which are funded in part by federal money. When money is tight, the stations feel the pinch, as does NPR because of its dependence on them.

The audience for NPR's news programs has grown from 4.2 million to 16 million in the last decade, and member donations to public radio have grown from $40 million in 1985 to $95 million in 1994. NPR's news budget, however, has gone from $7 million in 1985 to $22 million in 1995.

Susan Stamberg, former host of *All Things Considered,* comments that "With all the takeovers, with all the mergers, with all the bottom-lineness that has hit commercial television, this is the last bastion for electronic news reporting."

Federal budget-cutting may force NPR to become more commercial—to rely on audience research and eliminate risk-taking, experimental programs with more limited appeal. The decline in federal support also has forced NPR news to turn to private sources. NPR has raised money from foundations to hire reporters to cover such important subjects as science, religion, Japan, and the media, but the risk is that when news beats are linked to grant money, certain topics will be covered disproportionately.[a]

[a]Marc Gunther, "At NPR, All Things Reconsidered," *New York Times*, 13 August 1995, pp. H1, H27. Cited material on p. H27.

One unusual network, National Public Radio (NPR), took to the air in October 1970. Beginning with 90 member stations, it had grown to 545 in 1996. NPR produces forty-six hours a week of original national programming from its Washington, D.C., headquarters, and more than half of that is news and public affairs, including its well-known news program *All Things Considered,* which airs nationally during afternoon drive time and attracts 6.5 million listeners a week. In the early 1990s, NPR started *Talk of the Nation,* a 2-hour radio call-in program, which addresses political, social, and scientific issues. Every week, nearly 16 million listeners tune in their radios to hear NPR programming.[57]

A comparable public network, American Public Radio, was formed in 1982. Many stations carry programming from both NPR and APR. In July 1994, APR changed its name to Public Radio International. Based in Minneapolis, Minnesota, PRI has 530 affiliate stations that can subscribe to any mix of the more than 300 hours per week in programs PRI transmits each week via satellite. PRI broadcasts the business news program, *Marketplace,* the *Christian Science Monitor's Monitor Radio,* as well as variety programs such as the quiz show, *What Do You*

---

57. Interview with Kathy Gray, NPR, Washington, D.C., 7 March 1996.

Know? and the long-running *Prairie Home Companion.* Total listenership for PRI is about 18 million per week.[58]

Along with a small number of noncommercial radio stations, such as the Pacifica Radio Network, PRI and NPR are among the few sources of in-depth news on radio. Most news coverage on commercial radio is satellite-delivered headline services.

Talk Radio

The National Association of Radio Talk Hosts was founded in 1988; 75 members attended its first meeting. Today, the group has more than 3,000 members.

The importance of talk radio was clear in the last presidential campaign when both Vice-President Dan Quayle and Democratic aspirant Bill Clinton addressed the National Association's convention. In the same year, Bush and Quayle appeared on Limbaugh's program, and Clinton staged his comeback in New York on *Imus in the Morning.* Although exit polls found that talk shows were second only to debates in the help they provided voters, nearly one in five could not evaluate talk radio's role in the campaign. Politicians' belief in the influence of talk radio persisted after the election. In fall 1993, the day after Clinton's national address on health-care reform, more than sixty-five talk show hosts broadcast from the White House lawn.

Although he was talking about a television, rather than a radio call-in show, Clinton's message in 1993 was clear. "You know why I can stiff you on the press conferences?" Clinton asked at a Radio and Television Correspondents Association dinner in March 1993. "Because Larry King has liberated me from you by giving me to the American people directly."

Without a doubt the most influential individual call-in host is Rush Limbaugh, who is credited by the Republican leadership with the Republican take over of the House and Senate in 1994. Heard on over 600 stations, Limbaugh's nationally syndicated 3-hour radio show reaches a cumulative weekly audience of more than 20 million. It is the most popular talk show on radio. His half-hour television show ranks third among late night offerings and is available to 98 percent of the national audience. His 1992 book, *The Way Things Ought to Be,* was in the top spot on the *New York Times'* best-seller list for seven straight weeks and has sold over 2 million hardcover copies. "The Limbaugh Letter," a monthly publication with 170,000 subscribers, is promoted on his radio and television show. As a lecturer, Limbaugh commands $25,000 an appearance, and in so-called Limbaugh bars and Limbaugh restaurants, patrons gather to listen to his radio program. Limbaugh claims to reach a combined radio and television audience of 90 million people. His audience, he reports, is upscale and educated. The power of his message is increased as well by his invitations to supporters and opponents to communicate with him by phone, fax, and e-mail.

---

58. Interview with Dale Spear, PRI, Minneapolis, Minn., 12 July 1995.

Recent evidence suggests that talk radio is more helpful to conservatives than liberals, and to Republicans than Democrats. The *Times Mirror* survey of summer 1993 found that Republicans are twice as likely to listen as Democrats, and conservatives are more likely to listen than liberals. Half of all conservatives reported listening regularly or sometimes.

As the 1994 campaign approached, evidence was mounting that talk radio was a medium of and for but not by conservatives. In the exit polls of the 1994 election (cf. ABC), 25 percent of the Republicans said they had listened to talk radio. Republican pollster Frank Luntz reports that those who listened to ten or more hours voted Republican in 1994 by a ratio of 3 to 1.[59] Yet, according to *Times Mirror,* the hosts are about as likely to self-identify as liberals as conservatives. In the wake of the November 1994 elections, the freshman Republican members of Congress named Rush Limbaugh an honorary member. The *New York Times* called Limbaugh "an electronic precinct captain for Republicans in Congress."[60]

Talk radio is also a haven for aspiring, retiring, and out-of-office politicians. With an estimated audience of 250,000, former New York City mayor Ed Koch outdraws even Rush Limbaugh on WABC in New York City. Former governor and presidential aspirant Jerry Brown's daily show is aired by 5 large stations in major metropolitan areas. Former Chicago alderman "Fast Eddie" Vrdolyak is on the air in Chicago. Marjorie Clapprood, who lost a race for lieutenant governor in Massachusetts in 1990, is on the air in Boston. Former senator and presidential hopeful Gary Hart, until recently, had a show on KOA-AM in Denver. The 3-hour Saturday and Sunday call-in show of the former Texas agriculture commissioner Jim Hightower can be heard on 145 stations across the nation. More recent additions include former Republican gubernatorial contender Ellen Sauerbrey who is on the air on WBAL-AM in Baltimore and former Connecticut governor Lowell Weicker on CRN International. Republican Alan Keyes, a presidential candidate in 1996, is on in the morning drive time in Baltimore as well.

Talk radio can be a political springboard as well. New Jersey governor Christine Todd Whitman was a part-time radio call-in host before successfully running for governor, while Maryland's governor Donald Schaefer hosted a weekly show.

According to the Times Mirror survey, listeners believe that these shows offer a diversity of points of view. Hosts acknowledge, however, that conservatives and those angry with government are overrepresented.

With what effect? Although a *U.S. News & World Report* poll in summer 1993 found that more of Limbaugh's listeners say they listen for entertainment (28 percent) than for information (1 percent) or for opinion (10 percent), talk radio's ability to activate partisans on a topic of interest to them has been documented. For example, in February 1994, the executive director of the Home School Legal Defense Association concluded that a provision in a piece of education legislation was a threat to home schoolers. He got on the phone to talk radio hosts

---

59. Katharine Q. Seelye, "Republicans Get a Pep Talk from Rush Limbaugh," *New York Times,* 12 December 1994, p. A16.
60. Timothy Egan, "The 104th Congress: Talk Radio," *New York Times,* 2 March 1995, p. B8.

around the country, reaching almost fifty of them. Within hours, Congress was flooded with cards, calls, and faxes. A week and a half later, the offending provision had been stripped from the bill by a vote of 422-1.

In 1989, talk radio was also given credit for mobilizing the masses against a recommended congressional pay hike. Radio listeners also created public pressure against the confirmation of Clinton's attorney general nominee Zoe Baird and fueled opposition to his proposed ban on discrimination against gays in the military.

Newspapers

In 1984, there were approximately 1,688 daily newspapers in the United States with a combined circulation of 63,340,320.[61] By 1995, that number had dropped to 1,556 dailies, with a combined circulation of 59,811,594.[62] Competing with them for readers and advertising dollars were 7,176 weekly newspapers, some distributed free of charge, with a combined circulation of 78,763,120.[63] Almost all daily newspapers subscribe to a major wire service, with the result that much of the news they print, especially on national and international events, originates with the wire services.

Chain ownership of newspapers is on the increase. By 1995, 85 percent of the daily newspapers in the United States were owned by groups or chains instead of being private companies or family owned.[64] Knight-Ridder owns 27 daily newspapers with a daily circulation of 3,605,770; Gannett owns the most—81 local newspapers and *USA Today* with a daily circulation of 5,830,579, and in mid-1995, it purchased another 11 daily newspapers.[65] Despite chain ownership, reliance on wire service materials, and ownership of other media outlets, however, newspapers are basically local media.

In May 1995, *Editor & Publisher* wrote that "For the fourth consecutive six-month reporting period, most of the 25 biggest U.S. papers showed year-to-year circulation declines."[66] Only 61.5 percent of U.S. adults report reading a newspaper daily; in 1970 that percent was 77.6. But newspaper owners saw some reason for optimism. In 1994, advertising revenues were $34.2 billion, up $2.3 billion from the preceding year.[67]

To attract more readers, newspaper editors are trying various tactics to appeal to diverse audiences, including Hispanics, gays, and young people. The *Miami Herald* has added a weekly page of Brazilian news in Portuguese and a

---

61. *Electronic Media*, 16 April 1990, p. 66.
62. Newspaper Association of America, *Marketer's Guide to Media*, Spring/Summer 95 (New York: BPI Communications, 1995), p. 179.
63. Newspaper Association of America, Reston, Va.
64. Patricia Sherlock, "Borg Family Guided Record to Success," *The Bergen County Record*, 4 June 1995, p. O43.
65. William Glaberson, "The Press," *New York Times*, 30 July 1995, pp. E1, E6.
66. *Editor & Publisher*, 6 May 1995, p. 12.
67. *New York Times*, 25 April 1995, p. D4.

BOX 1-18

Competition among Newspapers

Among the more than 1,500 U.S. cities with a daily newspaper, in 1995 only 36 had at least two separately owned newspapers, while 26 cities had two newspapers published under joint ownership agreements.[a] In the six months ending September 30, 1995 the *Wall Street Journal* lost 1 percent of its daily circulation, dropping to 1,780,422; *USA Today* lost 3.9 percent for a circulation of 1,465,936; and the *New York Times* lost 2.92 percent for a circulation of 1,114,168.[b]

[a]Newspaper Association of America, Reston, Va., 12 July 1995. Telephone interview.
[b]William Glaberson, "The Media Business," *New York Times*, 31 October 1995, p. D9.

---

weekly page of Haitian news in Creole. Several newspapers are including special inserts targeted at younger readers. Newspaper chains are also interested in electronic publishing.

In response to what is perceived as a threat by computer companies and online services to the prominence of their role as providers of information, newspapers are joining the technological revolution. In April 1995, Gannett, Knight-Ridder, Times Mirror and five other corporations, representing 185 newspapers, announced the formation of New Century Network. With this network, not only will the news and classified advertising of the newspapers of one city be available to customers in another, but also services such as ordering tickets for sports and entertainment events across the country as well. "We believe it will change the face of the newspaper industry," said Peter Winter, interim head of the Network.[68] The Network aims to put 75 newspapers online in the next two years.

Magazines

Under the impact of television, both radio and magazines became specialized or segmented media. Because advertisers could reach the same mass audience more cheaply and quickly via television, many well-known mass circulation magazines, including *Look* and the *Saturday Evening Post,* went out of business. Recently, magazines targeted at special audiences have sprung up, such as *Motorcyclist* and *Fantasy* and *Science Fiction.* There are only a few national magazines, and three are newsweeklies: *Time, Newsweek,* and *U.S. News & World Report. Time* is owned by Time Inc., *Newsweek* by the Washington Post Company. These examples are typical because many magazines today are owned by chains, large corporations, and conglomerates, in part because it is very costly to start a magazine and because the survival rate for magazines is low. (By contrast, *U.S.*

---

68. *Philadelphia Inquirer*, 20 April 1995, p. C1.

BOX 1-19

Magazine Circulation for the Last Half of 1994ᵃ

Rank		Circulation
1	*Modern Maturity*	21,716,727
2	*Reader's Digest*	15,126,664
3	*TV Guide*	14,037,062
4	*National Geographic*	9,203,079
5	*Better Homes & Gardens*	7,613,661
12	*Time*	4,063,146
15	*People*	3,424,858
18	*Sports Illustrated*	3,252,641
19	*Newsweek*	3,158,617
20	*National Enquirer*	3,066,032
25	*U.S. News & World Report*	2,240,710
50	*Golf Magazine*	1,269,642
75	*Discover*	1,008,916
100	*Working Mother*	828,729
150	*Beckett Baseball Card Monthly*	546,667
200	*Car Craft*	379,219

ᵃAudit Bureau of Circulations and BPA International figures.

News is employee owned.) On average, only 10 percent of new magazines survive beyond their first year; nevertheless, as of 1994 there were 2,944 consumer, farm, and international magazines.[69]

The degree of specialization in this medium can be seen in a closer look at some of the mass circulation magazines. Many publish special editions designed to permit advertisers to reach specific audiences. *Time,* for instance, publishes regional editions, editions aimed at special groups, and an international edition. One edition goes primarily to college students, another to the 1,300,000 people living in the most affluent zip code areas within metropolitan markets, and still another to about 640,000 business and professional people. Similarly, *Sports Illustrated* publishes four regional editions and a special homeowners' edition limited to slightly over one half million subscribers located in zip code areas with the highest concentration of home ownership. Other magazines, such as *Cosmopolitan* and *Good Housekeeping,* publish Spanish-language editions. In other words, although mass circulation magazines exist, many of them publish special editions with advertising aimed at distinct audiences.

Magazines have several advantages over television for advertisers. According to data collected by the Magazine Publishers' Association, better-educated and

---

69. "Number of Consumer and Farm Magazines," *Marketer's Guide to Media,* Spring/Summer 95 (New York: BPI Communications, 1995), p. 149.

more affluent people are more apt to read magazines than to watch television. For example, in 1994, men with incomes more than $60,000 a year spent 7 percent of their daily time reading magazines whereas men earning less than $20,000 devoted only 2 percent of their time to this activity.[70] A magazine becomes a trusted and familiar source reflecting an image that the subscriber can identify with. In addition, some advertisers now banned from television, like cigarette manufacturers, must rely on print outlets.

TO SUM UP

These are some perspectives for examining the existing mass media. Despite the power and wealth of concentrated mass media ownership, few media are national in scope. Instead, most outlets aim at specialized audiences based on location, age, sex, income, education, ethnic background, or other variables important in determining a person's interests. The mass media speak with varied voices to varied audiences.

SELECTED READINGS

Barrett, Marvin, ed. *Broadcast Journalism, 1979–1981: The Eighth Alfred I. Dupont-Columbia Survey*. New York: Everest House, 1982.

Brown, Les. *Les Brown's Encyclopedia of Television*. 3d ed. Detroit: Gale Research, 1992.

Kubey, Robert, and Mihaly Csikszentmihalyi. *Television and the Quality of Life: How Viewing Shapes Everyday Experience*. Hillsdale, N.J.: Lawrence Erlbaum, 1990.

Lichty, Lawrence W., and Malachi C. Topping. *American Broadcasting: A Source Book on the History of Radio and Television*. New York: Hastings House, 1975.

Mazzocco, Dennis. *Networks of Power: Corporate TV's Threat to Democracy*. Boston, Mass.: South End Press, 1994.

Schudson, Michael. *Discovering the News: A Social History of American Newspapers*. New York: Basic Books, 1978.

———. *The Power of News*. Cambridge, Mass.: Harvard University Press, 1995.

Turow, Joseph. *Media Systems in Society: Understanding Industries, Strategies, and Power*. New York: Longman, 1992.

———. *Advertising and the New Media World*. Chicago: University of Chicago Press. Forthcoming.

Wright, Charles R. *Mass Communication: A Sociological Perspective*. 3d ed. New York: Random House, 1986.

---

70. "Distribution of Daily Time Spent with the Four Major Media," in *TV Dimensions '95*, ed. Ed Papazian (New York: Media Dynamics Inc., 1995), p. 428.

CHAPTER 2

What Is News?

Just what is news? Despite many efforts, no neat, satisfactory answer to that question has been found. Some deaths are news; many more are not. Some strikes draw headlines; others are ignored. Some protests become lead stories; others go unnoticed; still others are deliberately disregarded. The best answer seems to be that news is what reporters, editors, and producers decide is news.

That answer contradicts traditional notions that news is "out there," that reporters "just cover the story," that news is "what's happening." Instead, that answer says that news is selected, even created, by newspeople. It claims that news is not just "the facts," but also rhetoric—messages influencing how readers and viewers perceive reality. It would be surprising if this were not the case.

News is gathered, written, edited, produced, and disseminated by human beings who are part of organizations and who have beliefs and values. Organizations, such as networks, have functions and goals as well as relationships to government, to regulatory agencies, to advertisers, to their parent companies, and to the vast audiences they seek to attract. These beliefs, values, functions, and interests are bound to influence the messages these networks publish and broadcast.

On a more complex level, this answer suggests that newsgatherers and news organizations are persuaders who shape our views of reality, who induce us to believe one thing rather than another. We examine this controversial argument in the next chapter. Here, however, we treat the simpler claim. We examine the concept of "hard news" or "spot news" (everyone concedes that "soft news," such as feature stories, is not objective) in order to set up a model of the news story. We explore the criteria governing what newspeople define as news, the constraints influencing what actually will be covered, and the conventions controlling how a news event will be presented.

We begin by identifying the norms that define what is newsworthy. Then we discuss the external and internal factors that influence what is actually covered and reported. Finally, we describe considerations that affect how the news is presented.

Hard News Defined

Hard news is the report of an event that happened or that was disclosed within the previous twenty-four hours and treats an issue of ongoing concern. The crime story is the model for hard news.[1] A violent crime (murder, armed robbery, rape) is an event, a definable happening. It occurs between individuals (perpetrator and victim). It is dramatic, conflict-filled, and involves extreme physical action and emotional intensity. It disrupts legitimate order and threatens the community. Ordinarily, what happened can be told in a short, simple story, and information about the event can be verified by official sources such as the police or the district attorney. The crime scene (or its effects) is usually visual, is easily reduced to tape or photograph, and is part of the regular beat of a reporter.

A typical crime has all the qualities of a newsworthy event: it is (1) personalized—it happened to specific individuals; (2) dramatic, conflict-filled, controversial, violent; (3) actual and concrete, not theoretical or abstract; (4) novel or deviant; and (5) linked to issues of ongoing concern to the news media. These characteristics reflect the qualities of mass media messages discussed in Chapter 1.

1. Hard news is personalized, about individuals.   Mass media news must be accessible to, and interesting for, a diverse mass audience. Consequently, news stories must be clear, simple, and attention-getting. Hard news is personalized and individualized because such stories create wide audience identification. We care more about the reactions of a tornado victim than about statistics on the force of the wind, and we are eager to see the person who faced down the tank in Tiananmen Square. The human connection allows us to imagine ourselves in the situation or to create meaning out of what is puzzling and complex. Unlike stories about destruction of the ozone layer or the spread of nuclear weapons, stories about individuals have causes and consequences on a manageable scale. Individuals can act or speak in a time span that fits into a news story, and it is easier to visualize a person than an idea, a process, or a structure.

An interview can personify an abstract idea or clothe an idea in living flesh. So, for example, as former *MacNeil/Lehrer NewsHour* anchor Robert MacNeil noted, "In Somalia, it was not merely the pictures that wrung [*sic*] the hearts of the public. The pictures were made more eloquent by the words of Audrey Hepburn of UNICEF and Mary Robinson of Northern Ireland."[2] The personal and individual character of hard news reflects the use of interviews and human sources as the bases for the research underlying most news stories.

---

1. An analysis of subjects covered by urban newspapers, presented in May 1994 by Sean Aday, Christopher Ferris, and Michael Grant of the Annenberg School for Communication, University of Pennsylvania, found that crime stories were prominent. Crime, and the related categories of violence and the courts, made up 22.2 percent of Philadelphia daily newspaper stories in a one-month period.
2. Robert MacNeil, "The Flickering Images That May Drive Presidents," *Media Studies Journal* (Winter 1995), pp. 124-125.

Interviews not only personalize, but also allow reporters to draw on the expertise of others, an important advantage for reporters who are usually generalists, not specialists. The news is personalized and individualized by heavy coverage of the president; of congressional leaders; of the wealthy, powerful, and prestigious; and of sports, stage, screen, and fashion celebrities. These are the "stars" of the news who, like the star hired to lure us to a film, are intended to draw the mass audience to the news channel.

The emphasis on individuals can create distortion. In finding a spokesperson, the news media generally will choose the more flamboyant, articulate, and theatrical characters who are willing to assume that role, not necessarily the most thoughtful or most central figures. During the health care reform debate of 1994, the media gravitated toward those opponents of the Clinton plan who phrased their objections in the starkest terms. Newt Gingrich's comment that universal coverage was impossible without a police state was given coverage while more moderate statements by then House speaker Bob Michel were not. Indeed, one might argue that Gingrich's capacity to capture media attention paved his way to the House speakership.

Defining hard news as personal, as about individuals, means that it is not about processes or the exploration of ideas; it is the story of a group or a movement only to the extent that a group or movement can be personified by one member's testimony. The focus on individuals simplifies and clarifies. It creates audience identification; it reflects journalistic reliance on human sources and on the interview.

The tendency to focus on people rather than processes means that some important questions may go unanswered. Former *Washington Post* editor Ben Bagdikian recalls the experience in the 1980s of seeing for the first time the homeless begging for money. "Newspapers and television had lots of stories about the homeless," he notes. "But I kept waiting year after year for our best newspaper or broadcast journalists to ask [the] . . . right question and highlight the answers: 'Why, in the midst of this wonderful prosperity of the 1980s do we have for the first time since the Great Depression, growing numbers of men, women, and children living in the streets?'"[3]

That pattern persisted in July 1995 when a tent city erected by the homeless in Philadelphia drew a front-page photo and story from the *Philadelphia Inquirer*. Under banners reading "Philadelphia, House Your People," "We Want Houses," and "No Casas No Paz (No Houses No Peace)," the approximately thirty homeless—half of them children—had set up five donated tents in a vacant lot. When outdoor temperatures persisted in the 90-degree range, concerns about children living outside in the heat were raised by welfare workers. "Being homeless is not grounds for taking away anyone's children," a housing official is quoted as saying. "But the impact of the heat is something we're concerned about."

---

3. Ben Bagdikian, *Double Vision: Reflections on My Heritage, Life, and Profession* (Boston: Beacon Press, 1995), p. 186.

Elba Gonzalez shares the tent city with her children.
(Copyright © The Philadelphia Inquirer, Dirk Shadd.)

Those concerns are the stuff of which drama is made. At the center of the drama is a young mother shown in the picture seated on a torn couch under a small tent with her three children. At the side of the tent, the Kensington Welfare Rights Union has placed a U.S. flag, a symbol inviting readers to see irony in the plight of the small destitute family.

Conflict was added to the mix with the visit of the welfare workers to the site coupled with the fire department turning off the hydrants and the police ticketing nearby residents who were assisting the protesters. Capturing conflict, drama, and the personalizing of mothers and children camped in an otherwise vacant lot, the *Philadelphia Inquirer*'s story was headed "Camp Seeks, and Fears, City's Notice." The subhead suggested conflict: "The homeless camp is, in part, a protest. So far, it's getting only unwanted attention."

The *Inquirer*'s article admits that the camp drew press attention only when the prospect of conflict with the city arose. "For a while—as flies buzzed around their donated food, as the heat hit record highs and the rain fell in torrents, as children bathed at fire hydrants and slept in stuffy tents staked in dusty gravel— it looked as if nobody would notice," said the article. "Then, for better or worse, the homeless camp at the corner of Fourth Street and Lehigh Avenue started getting attention. The fire department turned off the hydrants. . . ."[4]

---

4. John Woestendiek, "Camp Seeks, and Fears, City's Notice," *Philadelphia Inquirer*, 26 July 1995, pp. A1, A8.

CASE STUDY 2-1

Focusing on the Individual to Make News

In spring 1990, newspaper readers read that *Outweek* had published gay rights activists' statements that a number of prominent and presumed heterosexual celebrities, newspersons, and politicians are gay. Gay rights activists Michael Petrelis and Carl Goodman held a news conference in Washington, D.C., in May 1990, to read out the names of twelve individuals in public life whom they claimed are gay. Using the opportunity provided by live television, a gay author "outed" a gubernatorial candidate in a northeastern state on a talk show.

Billboards advocating the reelection of Republican Senator Mark Hatfield were altered to read "closeted gay . . . living a lie . . . voting to oppress." And immediately after his death, supermarket tabloids carried stories claiming that business tycoon Malcolm Forbes had been gay. *Outweek,* whose national circulation is 40,000, published a detailed account of what it reported to be Forbes's activities.

Outing is controversial within the gay community. The National Gay and Lesbian Task Force, the Human Rights Campaign Fund, and the Lambda Legal Defense and Education Fund oppose outing, calling it blackmail and psychological terror. Proponents of outing argue, "If I say someone is straight, I have not revealed anything private. But if I say he is gay, there is the impression that I have." Outing for such activists is a claiming of "role-models."[a]

By featuring supposed revelations about individuals who are of ongoing news interest, those favoring outing capitalize on news norms. "Revealing," "uncovering," and "exposing" are words of honor to most reporters. But other news norms argue against coverage. Those listed as gay—including television and film stars Richard Chamberlain and John Travolta—have denied it, and those sources listing them have provided nothing that sustains the tests of proof. Additionally, even in an age obsessed with the private lives of public figures, some find such publicizing an invasion of privacy.

In the column "Press Gallery" published in the weekly *Roll Call,* a publication focused on the actions of Congress, two reporters framed the issues raised by the Petrelis and Goodman press conference this way: "Reporters were skeptical, since, among other things, Petrelis and Goodman gave no proof of the listees' alleged sexual preference. Another problem for the reporters was trying to figure out why they should be reporting this exceedingly private information or misinformation." The reporters concluded: "PG [Press Gallery] contends that in almost every case, a politician's sexual preference, fidelity, bizarre boudoir behavior, or other personal peccadilloes are not fair game unless the politician is stupid enough to invite scrutiny. . . . We also agree . . . that rank hypocrisy also qualifies a Member for disclosure."[b]

But press behavior was not that clear-cut. *The Philadelphia Inquirer* and NPR among others named Mark Hatfield as the senator whose billboards were being defaced. Some sources, *Roll Call* and the *Washington Times* among them, covered the press conference but published no names. Some outlets, the *Washington Post* and the *New York Times,* remained silent.

[a]Michael Matza, "Outrage," *Philadelphia Inquirer,* 28 June 1990, pp. 1, 8E.
[b]"How the Media Should Deal with the 'Outing' of Alleged Homosexual Members," *Roll Call,* 4 June 1990, pp. 14, 16.

With shelters overcrowded, the tent city was the Welfare Rights group's way of trying to impel city action, action predicated on the sympathetic coverage of local news outlets. The article answered the question, Why are the homeless there? with two explanations: This was a protest to draw attention to the absence of adequate housing, and the shelters were overcrowded. Unasked was, why are the shelters overcrowded? Is there an increase in homelessness in summer? Has the city reduced the number of housing units? cut shelter capacity? Is it significant that all of the homeless quoted in the article bear Hispanic surnames; is that an indication that the problem is uniquely concentrated in this group? And because the family shown in the photo has recently moved from Puerto Rico, is this a problem occasioned by immigration? As important is the absence of a larger social context: Is this a problem unique to Philadelphia or common to other large urban areas as well? Is it local or national in scope? And, if national, what is being done or can be done about it?

As this example illustrates, personalizing issues is a problem both because it diverts attention from more substantive questions and because the choice of persons to cover is frequently skewed by their class, race, ethnicity, and gender. For example, during the week of the highly publicized rape of a white investment banker in Central Park by a nonwhite gang, twenty-eight other women in New York also reported rapes. Nearly all of these were women of color, and their assaults, including at least one of comparable brutality, went largely unreported by the press.[5]

2. Hard news is dramatic, conflict-filled, and violent.   Mass media news must gain and hold audience attention. Presenting hard news as drama is a way to structure a story to do just that. Drama begins with what is called an "inciting action," an event that disrupts normal routines (this is the event that becomes the "news peg," discussed in the next section). Conflict escalates in a rising action to a climax, the high point of tension, which is followed by an unraveling or resolution. Such structure, as illustrated by jokes, plays, novels, and television series episodes, is beloved by audiences and can evoke intense participation and identification.

The typical news story is organized dramatically to identify a problem, to describe it in a narrative of rising action, to locate the protagonists and set them against each other (usually in short interviews), and to create some sort of resolution. This format gives coherence to data, and it makes an item a story in the most literal sense, a story that is likely to gain and hold an audience. Hard news is exciting, and the essence of excitement is drama.

Conflict is an intrinsic element in drama; drama's rising action unfolds through increasingly intense conflict. Conflict disrupts routine and is thus novel and unusual (another criterion discussed next). Conflicts are newsworthy events,

---

5. Helen Benedict, *Virgin or Vamp: How the Press Covers Sex Crimes* (New York: Oxford University Press, 1992), p. 219; Don Terry, "In the Week of an Infamous Rape, 28 Other Victims Suffer," *Gender and Public Policy*, ed. Kenneth Winston and Mary Jo Bane (Boulder, Colo.: Westview, 1993), p. 160.

and reporting conflict is a way to create interest. The presidential election campaign that runs for more than a year is treated as a horse race or a sports contest in part so that it can be divided into specific events—primary victories, caucus defeats, slugging it out in debates, going one-on-one with hecklers during a speech—filled with the drama and conflict characteristic of hard news. News coverage emphasizes conflict by interviewing and quoting opposing sides on an issue; such interviews not only allow a reporter to remain detached, they also create an impression of fair and balanced coverage.

This focus on conflict creates imbalance in the reporting of both international and domestic affairs. Reporting of foreign affairs tends, for example, to stress conflict whereas government officials stress accommodation.

Violence is the most dramatic form of conflict, and it is nearly always treated as newsworthy. The attraction of violence explains the relatively heavy coverage of crime news and its capacity to sell papers and attract viewers. So routine have some types of crime become, however, that they draw only perfunctory coverage. "Repeatedly bludgeoned with crime and violence by every medium," writes *Baltimore Sun* police reporter David Simon:

> our culture is now so bored with ordinary tragedy that we only become excited by those crimes that are larger, more unlikely and more bizarre. During the year I spent in the Baltimore homicide unit, the only murders to make the *Baltimore Sun's* front page involved two separate incidents of arson that claimed the lives of three and two young toddlers, respectively. The rape and murder of an 11-year-old girl, abducted as she walked home from a city library branch, made the front page of the metro section. The death of an 81-year-old woman, sodomized and then suffocated in her South Baltimore home, ran on an inside page, next to the weather chart.[6]

Still, a violent event is likely to be a matter of community concern, of great interest to many people. This is particularly true when the vulnerable have been the victims of violence.

The McMartin case is illustrative. In August 1983, a mother reported that her young son had been molested by Raymond Buckey at the Virginia McMartin Preschool. What followed were "lurid news reports of children being raped and sodomized, of dead rabbits, mutilated corpses, and a horse killing, and of blood drinking, satanic rituals, and the sacrifice of a live baby in a church."[7] Six years later, after a 30-month trial, a Los Angeles County jury rejected nearly all of the child molestation charges against Raymond Buckey and Peggy McMartin Buckey.

In the wake of the verdict, the media that had covered the charges and trial engaged in self-examination. David Shaw, who covers the media for the *Los Angeles Times,* wrote a four-part series on that paper's coverage. The series concluded that the paper consistently had favored the prosecution. In Shaw's judgment, the media's role was "pivotal and sometimes distorting."

---

6. "Cops, Killers, and Crispy Critters," *Media Studies Journal* (Winter 1992), p. 36.
7. Robert Reinhold, "McMartin Case: Swept Away by Panic about Molestation," *New York Times*, 24 January 1990, pp. 1, A18.

Some alleged that it was the news media that had "pressured authorities to push the case."[8] The first report on the case was aired on KABC-TV on February 2, 1984. Ongoing reports by KABC-TV were promoted by newspaper ads placed by the station showing a battered teddy bear. The first KABC report combined drama, violence, and disclosure. More than sixty children, it said, "have now each told authorities that he or she had been keeping a grotesque secret of being sexually abused and made to appear in pornographic films while in the preschool's care—and of having been forced to witness the mutilation and killing of animals to scare the kids into keeping silent."[9] The news norms of drama, conflict, violence, and disclosure coupled with the desire to be first and to stay competitive prompted KABC to downplay such other journalistic norms as two-sidedness and balance.

3. Hard news is action, an event, an identifiable occurrence.   Hard news relates the details of a specific occurrence that is the occasion for a news report, the "peg" on which the news story is hung. An event is concrete and discrete; ordinarily it can be explained clearly in a limited time or space. A single event is more likely to be intelligible and to be a novel, dramatic event involving specific individuals. Many events can be photographed or taped, an important consideration for both print and television journalism. Note that this norm, like the emphasis on individuals, works against coverage of processes or ideas.

Although hard news is believed to involve fast-breaking, unforeseen events, news organizations typically cover events that can be scheduled in advance, so reporters and camera crews readily can be present and record them. As a result, newspeople tend to cover news conferences and briefings, speeches, announcements, ceremonies, and other scheduled events. This is one reason that pseudo-events (events staged just for media coverage)[10] and what are called "photo opportunities" are an effective way to manipulate news coverage. The problem of needing to know in advance about the unexpected explains why reporters are tempted to ask participants to recreate what happened when faced with a situation like a riot.

In his study of a California newspaper, Mark Fishman found that journalistic concepts of newsworthy events coincided with what he called "bureaucratic phase structures," the ways various bureaucracies punctuate processes in order to divide them into stages—for example, arrests, indictments, verdicts, and sentencings in crime news. He found that journalists depended on such definitions for the meaning and relevance of what they observed, for determining which events were newsworthy, which accounts were suspicious or reliable, what was controversial, and what constituted the sides and terms of a controversy.[11] These were the bases on which journalists decided what counted as an event.

Hard news is the story of an act or an occurrence. This single, isolated event is simpler to communicate and easier to understand than a process or an idea. It

---

8. *New York Times,* 24 January 1990, p. A18.
9. Ibid.
10. Daniel Boorstin, *The Image: A Guide to Pseudo-Events in America* (New York: Atheneum, 1962).
11. Mark Fishman, *Manufacturing the News* (Austin: University of Texas Press, 1980), pp. 63–70, 134.

is likely to be dramatic and novel and to involve individuals. However, the emphasis on events reveals a contradiction at the heart of newsgathering: the desire to cover events as they happen and the need to cover events that are scheduled in advance.

As coverage of homelessness illustrates, tying news stories to a specific event limits, even prevents, the treatment of processes, structures, patterns, and systems.

4. Hard news is novel, deviant, out of the ordinary.   Hard news reports what happened today, not what happens every day. Although novel events are more likely to be covered if they are part of a current theme in the news, hard news is the opposite of the routine and accepted. The syndicated column "News of the Weird" is a flagrant example of this norm.

One study concluded that all mass media content is entertainment, in that it is conduct "outside the expected limits of routine behavior."[12] Even news stories are entertainment designed to attract and hold a mass audience. For example, during the times surveys are conducted by television rating services, local television news programs air "lurid and titillating news features, most often those with a sex or violence angle that can be heavily promoted, ideally as a weeklong series."[13]

The problems with this entertainment requirement—related to the novelty criterion in our scheme of things—are suggested by Tom Wicker: "The dull, the routine, the unexciting, is seldom seen as news, although . . . the dull, routine, unexciting management of rates and routes for the railroads, truckers, and airlines may affect far more Americans in their daily lives than some relatively more glamorous presidential directive or congressional action."[14]

Reporters, chosen partly for their nose for what is new and unusual, have a low tolerance for the long haul of a complex story that may take years to develop. This well-known media emphasis on novelty also tempts protesters to invent ever more extreme ways to dramatize their cause in order to obtain coverage.

Those protesting the development and use of nuclear power illustrate this problem. Their concerns were dramatized in 1978 with the accident at Three Mile Island, and they received substantial press coverage. Since that time, however, press interest has been low, although protesters believe that their concerns continue to be legitimate, and work on nuclear plants continues. Even the disaster at Chernobyl in 1986 did not help them, once it was established that the construction of that plant had few similarities to plants in the United States. As a result, protesters become more desperate to attract journalistic attention. For example, one antinuclear protester, participating in a demonstration marking the 36th anniversary of the first nuclear test at the Nevada Test Site, knelt in front of a bus carrying workers to the test site and poured red fluid from a baby's bottle. As sheriff's deputies lifted her from the road, she screamed: "This is the blood of the future! This is the blood of our children!"[15]

---

12. David Altheide and Robert P. Snow, *Media Logic* (Beverly Hills: Sage, 1979), p. 19.
13. Tony Schwartz, "Ratings Sweeps Boost Lurid Side of the News," *New York Times*, 25 November 1980, p. C17.
14. Tom Wicker, *On Press* (New York: Viking, 1978), p. 44.
15. "Actor and 71 Others Arrested at Nuclear Test Site," *New York Times*, 28 January 1987, p. 13Y.

BOX 2-1

The Scramble for Local News Ratings

A promotional announcement on NBC-owned-and-operated (O&O) Channel 4 in New York City, shown immediately before *L.A. Law,* said that upcoming news items on the 11 P.M. news included the death of a "star" of the show; subsequent announcements changed that to "familiar face." The announcement referred to the suicide of David Rappaport, the diminutive actor who had appeared as an aggressive but sympathetic lawyer on several episodes of the series during the previous two seasons.

A network news executive, who asked for anonymity, said, "It was unseemly but effective," and commented that such incidents demonstrated the increasing interplay between entertainment and news programs at both the network and local levels, and the declining enforcement of news standards.

Both the promotion and its placement were calculated to hold the *L.A. Law* audience for the news program. The tactic worked—the 11 P.M. news broadcast had a 19.3 rating and 37 percent of the audience, an increase of more than 30 percent over the preceding week. In New York, each rating point represents about 72,000 homes with television. The jump in ratings was particularly significant because it took place during May, a sweeps month, when ratings determine how much stations will charge for advertising.[a]

[a]Jeremy Gerard, "Station Uses Suicide Report to Hold Viewers," *New York Times,* 5 May 1990, p. 13Y.

BOX 2-2

Ratings and Revenues: Local News versus Prime-Time Entertainment

In 1989 in Los Angeles, a television trendsetter, KHJ, an independent station owned by the Walt Disney Company, announced that it would introduce in January 1990 the nation's first 3-hour local newscast, from 8 P.M. to 11 P.M. This change resulted in 14.5 hours of local news daily on seven VHF television stations in the area, the most hours in any market in the country (according to Willis Dugg, president of Audience Research and Development, Inc., a Dallas television news consulting company).

The increasing hours of local news programming was motivated by the quest for advertising profits, especially because many sponsors think news programs attract affluent viewers. Local news can be profitable even when less than 4 percent of households are watching (according to Steve Cagle, a vice-president at Frank Magid Associates, a research and consulting firm in Marion, Iowa).[a]

[a]Michael Lev, "Local News Is Challenging Prime-Time Shows," *New York Times,* 17 July 1989, p. 29Y.

BOX 2-3

Ad Too Violent and Inflammatory

A 30-second ad urging viewers to call their senators and ask them to vote against $400 million in aid to El Salvador was rejected by television stations throughout the country. The ad is polished and powerful. As a spot of blood grows on a check being written to the Internal Revenue Service, there are sounds of rifle shots and photographs of the six Jesuit priests murdered by the Salvadoran military in 1989. As the blood grows, a voice says, "Your tax dollars are putting America into the red. Tell your senator, 'vote no' on aid to El Salvador. Keep America out of the red."

The ad was produced by a coalition of peace organizations and may signal a new vehicle of expression for cause-oriented organizations that are finding it increasingly difficult to attract the attention of either the news media or the U.S. public.

All network-affiliated stations in New York and Washington rejected the ad for various reasons, some on the grounds that it was too violent. (A Planned Parenthood study of network "entertainment" discovered that elementary schoolchildren see 12,000 acts of violence a year on television programs.)

The program manager of a Los Angeles station, WJLA, rejected the ad and explained: "We make it our policy to not air material which is intended to inflame or incite unreasoned public responses rather than reasoned debate."[a]

[a]"Ad That Was Too Bloody for Most TV Stations Debuts in Twin Cities," *Star Tribune*, 25 September 1990, p. 1B.

Resource-poor groups often have to depend on deviance and disruption in order to receive media coverage. In her study of newspaper access, Edie Goldenberg concluded that "the more a group's political goals deviate from prevailing social norms, the more likely the group is to gain access to the press, other things being equal."[16] Elsewhere she writes "that the intensity of a conflict is a good predictor of coverage, . . . that 'unruly groups,' those who initiate violence or strikes, are relatively successful as compared with those that do not."[17] As these comments indicate, the emphasis on novelty in hard news is closely related to its focus on drama, conflict, and violence; the novelty of a large demonstration is likely to be overshadowed by the violent acts of a few.

Similarly, the news media are more likely to cover a protest group representative who is flamboyant and theatrical, regardless of who has the largest following.

---

16. Edie N. Goldenberg, *Making the Papers* (Lexington, Mass.: Lexington Books, 1975), p. 28.
17. "An Overview of Access to the Media," in *Women in the News*, ed. Laurily Keir Epstein (New York: Hastings House, 1978), pp. 55–56. Goldenberg also cites the work of William A. Gamson, *The Strategy of Social Protest* (Homewood, Ill.: Dorsey, 1975), in support of her claims.

In 1990, a feminist group known as Guerrilla Girls gained the attention of the *New York Times* with its consciousness-raising posters and gorilla masks. On Sunday June 17, 1990, both appeared in that paper.[18] The Guerrilla Girls are social critics of the ways in which female artists are treated. The women in the group remain anonymous. Their prime weapons are sarcasm and humor. After conservative Senator Jesse Helms protested federal funding of a photo exhibit by Robert Mapplethorpe, the group put out a poster saying, "Relax, Senator Helms, The Art World *Is* Your Kind Of Place!" The poster supported that statement with such claims as: "The number of blacks at an art opening is about the same as at one of your garden parties." Another poster asked: "How many women had one-person exhibitions at NYC museums last year?" A list followed:

Guggenheim 0
Metropolitan 0
Modern 1
Whitney 0

Another poster promulgated a tongue-in-cheek "code of ethics for art museums." The code included the commandment: "Thou shalt provide lavish funerals for Women and Artists of Color who thou planneth to exhibit only after their death." The novelty of the title "Guerrilla Girls," the play on *guerrilla* apparent in wearing gorilla masks, the anonymity of the group members (they sometimes adopt the names of women artists), and the use of humor as protest are all novel. As such, they invite media coverage.[19]

5. Hard news reports events linked to issues prevalent in the news at the time. News coverage follows certain issues at various times, such as the issue of civil rights in the 1960s, women's liberation for a period in the 1970s, and gay rights in the 1980s. For example, when the United States began its space program, each launch received detailed news coverage. Much of this coverage concerned whether or not NASA was ready to launch the rockets involved in the Mercury, Gemini, and Apollo programs and whether flights that included astronauts were safe. As years passed without disasters, however, the space program generally, as well as the shuttle launches begun in 1983, came to seem routine, and newspeople began to treat them perfunctorily.

Accordingly, reporters did not continue to probe questions of safety and were caught unaware by the Challenger disaster. Television and print reporters did not know of the imminent danger to the Challenger space shuttle, due to the likelihood that the seals—called O-rings—in the solid-rocket boosters might malfunction because of the cold weather at launch time. They had grown accustomed to successful shuttle flights and relied on NASA's assurances that all was well.

The assumption that shuttle flights were routine and safe produced a kind of reporting that put pressure on NASA to launch Challenger on January 28, 1986,

18. "Waging Guerrilla Warfare Against the Art World," p. 31.
19. *Confessions of the Guerrilla Girls* by the Guerrilla Girls with an essay by Whitney Chadwick (New York: Harper Perennial, 1995), reprints all their posters from 1985 to 1994.

despite unsafe conditions. Richard G. Smith, head of the Kennedy Space Center in Florida at the time of the Challenger explosion, argued that snide news stories about aborted launches had created "98 percent of the pressure" to go ahead with the ill-fated Challenger flight.

What Smith was referring to included statements by newscasters, such as those by Dan Rather on the *CBS Evening News*. Rather referred to news about one delay as "the latest on today's high-tech low comedy," and later said that because of postponements, the launch was now known as "Mission Impossible."[20] What became newsworthy were delays, launches aborted for reasons of safety, and these delays became an ongoing story of implied incompetence, a news perspective that may have contributed to the disaster itself.

Stories about continuing issues generate audience identification and create the comforting sense of a pattern in the complexity of modern life.

The coverage of individuals who are certifiably newsworthy reflects this concern for continuity in the news. The newsworthy are those who have made news in the past, such as elected officials; athletic champions; and film, television, or rock stars. For example, a presidential candidate labeled a "front-runner"—a status conferred on those who win early caucus or primary votes—becomes more newsworthy and consequently gets more news coverage.

Some themes are woven into the very nature of news gathering in the United States. These include: (1) *Appearance versus reality.* This reflects an emphasis on conflict and the "objective" role of skeptical newsgatherers who uncover hypocrisy. (2) *Little guys versus big guys.* This theme reflects an emphasis on the personal and individual by taking a particular interest in the underdog or outsider or exposing corrupt and self-interested actions by the powerful against the powerless. (3) *Good against evil.* The essence of drama, this theme is related to crime as a news model and to investigative journalism as a norm for reporting and the reporter's role. (4) *Efficiency versus inefficiency.* This is usually an attempt to uncover waste and mismanagement, illustrating the emphasis on politics and government in the news. (5) *The unique versus the routine.* Reflecting a stress on novelty, this is illustrated by the human interest stories appearing at the end of most newscasts or in syndicated newspaper columns, such as "News of the Weird." All of these themes presume that there are identifiable forces at work in the world, and that they usually are in conflict. News coverage influences us by defining what the sides are and what each side means.

Themes provide continuity in the news and help make sense out of a welter of happenings. They increase the potential for audience identification. Some themes reflect the journalist's role and the concept that reporters have of their function in this society.

These five criteria—ongoing issues or themes, discrete events, novelty or deviance, drama-conflict-violence, and a focus on individuals—define what newsgatherers consider newsworthy. As the following case study of a protester's hunger strike illustrates, those who meet these criteria are likely to obtain news coverage.

---

20. Neil Hickey, "It Exposed TV's Failures—as Well as NASA's," *TV Guide*, 24 January 1987, p. 3.

When Is a Hunger Strike Newsworthy?

Rick Hoye, a 28-year-old junior majoring in international relations at the University of Minnesota, began a hunger strike June 6, 1980, to dramatize his contention that the university's Board of Regents ought to reverse its earlier vote and order a boycott of Nestlé products on the campus. Prior to the hunger strike, Hoye headed a campus chapter of the Infant Formula Action Coalition, a group that had worked unsuccessfully for over a year to pass the boycott. Fifty student groups supported the boycott. In February 1980, the University Senate, a body composed of faculty and students, had passed a resolution advocating a boycott. In June 1980, the Board of Regents voted 8 to 3 against a boycott. That vote followed the recommendation of University President C. Peter Magrath, who contended that it was inappropriate for a public university to become involved in such a boycott.

The proposed boycott was designed to protest Nestlé's manufacture and promotion of infant formulas in underdeveloped countries. Because these mothers used the formula in unsanitary conditions and diluted it with impure water, they increased the likelihood that their infants would suffer from malnutrition or contract diseases. By breastfeeding the infants instead, mothers could minimize these risks.

To dramatize the hunger strike, Hoye pitched a tent outside Morrill Hall, the building housing both the Board of Regents meeting room and the office of the university's president. A large sign at the side of the tent read:

UNIVERSITY OF MINNESOTA

NESTLÉ BOYCOTT

HUNGER STRIKE BY RICK HOYE

DAY _____ · WEIGHT _____

After thirty-four days, Hoye ended his fast when a committee of the Board of Regents listened to his case. Although the university did not subsequently boycott Nestlé products, Hoye's strike was a qualified success. His dramatic "visualization" of the process of starvation drew more press coverage to his cause than had his two years of previous work. With press attention came attention from the university's Board of Regents. One of the regents, who had supported the boycott, learned of Hoye's hunger strike not through administration channels but by reading about it in a newspaper.

With press attention came access to university officials. The *Minneapolis Star* noted, for example, that "after a *Star* reporter called [President] Magrath's office Tuesday, he talked to Hoye for the first time since the fast started, and then returned the call."[a]

With press attention came the opportunity to address a committee of the Board of Regents.

With press attention came increased public awareness of the issue.

The media could have dismissed Hoye's strike as a stunt; instead, they treated it sympathetically. "He is not a nut, or a publicity-crazed radical out to topple the

[a]*Minneapolis Star*, 3 July 1980, p. 11A.

Staff Photo by Regene Radniecki

Hoye to end fast

Rick Hoye told a committee of the University of Minnesota regents Thursday that the university should be involved in ending world hunger by supporting a boycott of Nestlé Co. products. Hoye, 28, who began fasting June 6 after the regents voted against boycotting Nestlé products, plans to end the protest at 1 p.m. today. The university student, an international relations major, lost 40 pounds and will begin eating on the advice of his doctor to avoid permanent damage to his health. Hoye and other Nestlé critics object to the company's marketing of infant formula in underdeveloped countries.

The *Minneapolis Tribune,* 11 July 1980, p. 1B.
(Reprinted with permission of the *Minneapolis Tribune.*)

university administration—not even the Nestlé administration," wrote Joe Kimball of the *Minneapolis Tribune.*[b] And the *Star*'s associate editor Harold Chucker wrote, "Despite their snorts and grunts, the cynics—some of them, anyway—have a grudging admiration for the idealist. They see themselves at a younger age when they, too, believed anything was possible with the right kind of protest or demonstration."[c]

Why Did Hoye Receive Media Attention?

The cause he advocated had a following—a body of committed supporters. Groups on campus had endorsed the boycott. The campus senate, a representative body, had endorsed the boycott. The proposed boycott had met opposition. The Board of Regents had voted it down; the president opposed it. This opposition gave the story conflict, and with the conflict came a recognizable cast of

[b]Joe Kimball, "Student 'Sticks Neck Out' with Fast," *Minneapolis Tribune,* 4 July 1980, p. 5B.
[c]Harold Chucker, "Young Idealist Shouldn't Repeat Cynics' Mistakes," *Minneapolis Star,* 24 July 1980, p. 8A.

(continued on next page)

characters. The president would speak for those who opposed the boycott. By staging a dramatic hunger strike, Hoye invited the media to see the conflict as on-going and to pit him against the regents and the president.

Because Hoye had headed the coalition, he was a credible spokesperson for those on campus advocating boycott.

Because Hoye was an international relations major, his interest in world hunger seemed consistent with his reason for being a student.

Because Hoye had seen mothers feeding their infants contaminated formula in Guatemala and Honduras in 1978, his concern about the issue could be grounded in his personal experience.

Because the hunger strike could be tied to the argument that the infant formula contributed to malnutrition and disease, the dramatic act could not be casually dismissed as a gimmick.

Because Hoye suffered the effects of the fast—nausea, vomiting, light-headedness—and because his doctor warned that he risked permanent damage to his health, the media could not report the story one time and then abandon it. Once covered, the story demanded a follow-up. Would he starve to death? Would his health be damaged? Would he give up? The nature of Hoye's protest involved reporters in a dramatic narrative. One story demanded another and another until the full drama was played out and Hoye either got what he wanted or abandoned the strike.

Hoye apparently had nothing to gain from the strike personally. He would not benefit personally if Nestlé products were boycotted. This was not a way to be elected to an office, for example. Thus, his action appeared disinterested and selfless. The tent, the sign, the physical evidence of weight loss, the sign's daily report of weight dramatized and made concrete an issue that was otherwise abstract. By making it concrete, Hoye made the issue attractive to and usable by the mass media.

What Were the Risks Involved in This Dramatic Act?

Hoye's hunger strike, rather than the reason for the strike, might have become the focus of media coverage. Since Hoye no longer headed the coalition, he might not have been seen as a representative of or a spokesperson for the boycott. The significance of Hoye's act would be reduced if he was not perceived to represent those favoring the boycott.

Perhaps the relation between the tent and the hunger strike or between the hunger strike and the boycott would not have been recognized clearly.

Follow-Up

Hoye's action was part of a national effort led by Boston-based INFACT (Infant Formula Action Coalition). INFACT instigated a 7-year boycott of Nestlé products, which eventually prompted the large company to limit its marketing of possibly damaging infant formula in less-developed countries.

This case study illustrates one student's use of the principles governing what makes news. The next section of this chapter examines other factors that influence what will be covered.

What Is Covered and Reported?

Newsgathering is affected by access, costs, and limitations of time and space. News stories must attract and hold an audience and avoid offending advertisers, audiences, and media owners. These factors influence what choices newspeople make and ultimately determine which stories will be printed and aired.

External Constraints

Some of the factors influencing news coverage lie outside the event or medium itself. These are external constraints. If an event is to be covered, reporters must know it is to happen; if it is to be videotaped, there must be enough advance notice to get a camera crew to the scene. The event must happen early enough to let reporters meet their deadlines, and the cost of the coverage must seem reasonable. In addition, coverage is affected by competition from other media and from other newsworthy events.

Access   News organizations struggle to impose order in the midst of chaos. Reporters often have little or no idea when or where the news will break: when or where a crime will be committed, a riot will break out, or one country will attack another. Thus, reporters are assigned to beats so they can monitor the goings-on in places where newsworthy events often occur—the police station, city hall, the State Department, the House of Representatives, the Supreme Court, the White House. The chance that an event will be covered is increased if it is part of a reporter's regular beat, or if official sources that are regularly consulted call it to her or his attention. For instance, one study of 2,850 stories appearing in the *New York Times* and the *Washington Post* found that such routine channels accounted for 58.2 percent of the articles.[21]

Many newsworthy events fall between the cracks of assigned beats. Reporters may be assigned to substantive beats, such as energy or the environment, to overcome this problem. In addition, there are general assignment reporters who are dispatched to cover breaking stories or who try to ferret out newsworthy events. The beat system is really a pattern of access for reporters. It is a method by which reporters survey the scene to learn what is happening and by which they develop "informed, reliable sources" of information. Modern news organizations rely heavily on officials in government bureaucracies. Events on regular beats or confirmed by official sources tend to be covered and reported; events outside these beats or denied by official sources usually go unpublished.[22]

---

21. Leon V. Sigal, *Reporters and Officials: The Organization and Politics of Newsmaking* (Lexington, Mass.: D.C. Heath, 1973), p. 121, Table 6–1.
22. See David Halberstam, *The Powers That Be* (New York: Alfred A. Knopf, 1979), especially p. 434, for numerous examples of the powers of President Lyndon Johnson to suppress news stories from correspondents in Saigon.

Many news stories could not be written without the help of confidential sources. Jack Nelson, Washington bureau chief for the *Los Angeles Times,* notes that such sources help uncover information others try to conceal from the public, and that some of the most important exposés have been developed this way, including the Pentagon Papers, the My Lai massacre, and the Watergate stories. Specifically, the Pulitzer-Prize-winning My Lai stories of Seymour Hersh were made possible by the confidential involvement of three Army officers, a member of Congress, and two congressional aides.[23]

Although beats and official sources are efficient ways for reporters to obtain and check information, this system limits some kinds of coverage. For example, because early events in a developing social movement fall outside this system of beats and sources, they tend not to be noticed by the news media. Only as movements increase in size and scope and seek press coverage will reporters be assigned to cover them. Examples are the South Africa divestment movement, the antinuclear disarmament movement, feminism, and gay rights.

Cost   It costs money to bring the news to the public. Because a notepad, pencil, and tape recorder cost far less than a camera crew, it is cheaper to gather news for a newspaper or magazine than for television. The more costly a story, the more important it must be before it will be covered and published. Dan Rather, then a CBS reporter, wrote about this constraint and about how it affects investigative reporting: "A newspaper can commit a so-called 'investigative team' to a story and tie up the time and salaries of maybe a half dozen reporters. But that's all. If a television network commits to that kind of assignment, the cost can quickly run into six figures and above."[24] Such costs explain why investigative reporting is more common in the print media.

Stories that are written but not published ("overset") are not as costly for newspapers as for television. An unused set of stories costs a newspaper its overhead plus the reporter's salary. An unused taped segment can cost thousands of dollars. Consequently, although a newspaper assignment editor stores overset for possible use on a slow news day or in Sunday's larger paper, a television producer must be more certain that what is assembled can be and probably will be aired. Yet more television stories are gathered for use on the evening news than are actually aired. To cover their costs, networks try to find other places for these segments. A segment that does not air on the *ABC Evening News* may air on tomorrow's *Good Morning America* or be fed to affiliates for use on their local news shows.

The competitors to national network news mentioned in Chapter 1 have influenced newsgathering decisions. The video news services offered by CONUS, Associated Press TV, Reuters, the Cable News Network, and other similar services, are comparable to the national and international news wire services. As a result, many independent (unaffiliated) stations are using material from various satellite services to report on world and national news. The networks have re-

---

23. William E. Porter, *Assault on the Media: The Nixon Years* (Ann Arbor: University of Michigan Press, 1976), p. 227.
24. Dan Rather, *The Camera Never Blinks* (New York: William Morrow, 1977), p. 234.

sponded to such competition. In addition to establishing satellite links that allow their affiliates to share locally produced news stories with one another, the major networks have offered to help their respective affiliate stations pay for satellite vans that are like mobile television stations.

In return for subsidies, a network has the right to use its affiliate's van when a significant news event occurs in the affiliate's area. These vans, with their satellite dishes, enable local stations to cover national and international news; as affiliates' vans are used by the networks, they extend the coverage of the networks as well.

Similar factors influence the coverage of foreign news. To cover and report foreign news, a newspaper or network must support a foreign correspondent and, for same-day coverage, incur the cost of transmitting videotape or photographs by satellite. Such costs were important in the coverage of the Vietnam War, and they are one explanation for the small amount of news we receive from Africa and Central and South America, despite the frequency of newsworthy events. Once an expenditure has been built into the system, however, the more likely it is that the persons and equipment will generate news stories, no matter how newsworthy the events. For example, a network or newspaper maintaining London correspondents is more likely to report news from Great Britain and to seek British reactions to events in the United States than is a network or newspaper without a London correspondent. As the heavy coverage of the Iranian hostage crisis illustrated, however, the number of stories also is related to relevance for the U.S. audience.

In addition, the declining cost of portable, lightweight cameras and portable satellite uplinks has not only contributed to their use but also increased the likelihood that CNN would broadcast breaking news from around the world, live.

Time and Space   Like a newspaper, a network evening newscast has a certain amount of space to fill. Television time can be increased by adding news bulletins or special reports, and newspaper space can be increased by adding extra pages, a special section, or even a special edition, but to do so is costly. On days filled with newsworthy events, some stories that might otherwise be printed or aired will be omitted.

On the other hand, because a certain amount of time or space must be filled on a predictable basis, what is newsworthy on a day barren of interesting events will be different from what is newsworthy on an action-filled day. Yet because we receive a newspaper of a certain number of pages or a half-hour news telecast, we are likely to conclude that the events covered on the two days are of comparable importance. A publisher or producer has yet to announce "there was no news today, so the next twenty-one minutes or the next eighteen pages are empty." As commentator David Brinkley observes, "there are days, as we all know, when material of any kind is scarce, and we have to use what we can get, including some we know is not great, but air time has to be filled."[25]

---

25. David Brinkley, "A Question for Television Newsmen: Does Anyone Really Care?" in *Television Today: A Close-up View; Readings from TV Guide*, ed. Barry Cole (New York: Oxford, 1981), p. 139. The amount of prepaid advertising affects the number of pages in a newspaper. The more advertising, the larger the "news hole."

What is covered and published is influenced by factors outside the story itself. These include access, cost, available time or space, and the number of newsworthy events to fill them.

Internal Constraints

The characteristics of the medium itself may influence whether or not an event is covered and, more important, whether a story is printed or aired. These characteristics of the medium are what we call "internal constraints." Some of these constraints are a necessary part of the medium; some are conventions.

Use Available Footage   Television news coverage is also unique because television can replay its own past from tape and film archives, storehouses of the conventions and commonplaces that are television's memory. In the archives are televisual bits of the lives of famous persons who engaged in dramatic events during television's lifetime. The information stored in television's memory is different from that in the morgues of the nation's newspapers. For example, when Representative and former Senator Claude Pepper (D-Fla.) died in summer 1989, the broadcast networks called up the peroration of his stirring appeal to the House to pass catastrophic health insurance. Print obituaries recounted events from his entire career and included tributes from the people who had known and respected him.

Cover Visual Events   For both print and television journalism, the ability to tape or photograph an event is an important determinant of coverage and publication. The effort by a Connecticut television station to show portions of a figure-skating championship on its evening newscast illustrates the intense pull of the visual. ABC-TV had bought exclusive rights to show the 1981 World Figure Skating Championships held at the Hartford Civic Center on its *Wide World of Sports*. The Hartford station (WFSB) sued the local sponsors to stop their enforcement of a ban against all television cameras except ABC's. The case is an interesting test of First Amendment principles versus property rights to copyrighted material. However, of more interest here is the admission by the Hartford station's vice-president for news that the event would have merited "only a brief mention in the sports roundup *were it not for the visual quality of the skaters gliding gracefully across the rink.*"[26]

Television has a strong preference for visual events, but newspapers also try to accompany stories with attention-getting photographs. The 1984 famine in Ethiopia was widely reported in the newspapers beginning in late 1983 and early 1984. But it was not until late October and early November 1984, when pictures of the victims began appearing on network television news, that massive efforts were mobilized to help the starving people of that country. On October 23, 15.5 million

---

26. Jonathan Friendly, "Exclusive TV Rights vs. Covering the News," *New York Times*, 14 March 1981, p. 21. Italics added.

viewers of *NBC Nightly News* saw televised coverage of the famine. In the seven weeks following the NBC broadcast, Catholic Relief Services, one of the two charities mentioned by name in the NBC broadcast, reported 91,000 pieces of mail offering help, including $13 million in contributions.[27]

The reason for the long delay in securing and transmitting the story to television news was that the Marxist government of Ethiopia had put up roadblocks to stop the reporters. Journalists were denied permission to enter the country to get the story. The photographer and reporter who brought back the dramatic tape aired by the BBC, and picked up by NBC and others, cajoled their way into the country. An acting official had inadvertently given them access to the refugee camps.

Similarly, "After the Persian Gulf war, [President] Bush was determined not to be drawn into Iraq's internal battles, confident that the blows he had dealt Saddam Hussein would prompt his overthrow. Instead, Saddam attacked the Kurds and pictures of their misery were so affecting that Bush felt forced to intervene to protect them."[28]

Politicians respond to this bias by feeding the media's appetite for compelling visuals. The results occasionally are comic. In August 1989, President George Bush's speechwriters conceived the idea of having Bush dramatize his antidrug speech to the nation by holding up a bag of crack purchased by narcotics agents near the White House. The attorney general asked drug enforcement officials to make the buy. The *Washington Post* reported the results:

> The first time, the alleged drug dealer never showed up. On the second try, the undercover Drug Enforcement Administration agent wore a body microphone that didn't work. Then the cameraman who was supposed to be videotaping the deal missed the action because he was assaulted by a homeless person. "This is like a Keystone Kops thing," U.S. District Judge Stanley Sporkin said to the witness, DEA special agent Sam Gaye.[29]

Because television is a visual medium, it deals well with issues that can be reduced to concrete, dramatic illustrations. Some important issues, such as the economy, are not easily reduced to tangible, dramatic, 2-minute-and-35-second bites of information.

The problems involved in news coverage of economic issues were exemplified by limited and delayed coverage of widespread failures of savings and loan associations. Former *Wall Street Journal* reporter Ellen Hume writes that when Michael Gartner, president of NBC News, was asked why television hadn't covered the crisis much even after it made headlines in 1988, he commented "that the story didn't lend itself to images, and without such images, 'television can't do facts.'"[30]

---

27. *New York Times*, 16 December 1984, p. 9.
28. MacNeil, "The Flickering Images," p. 123.
29. Tracey Thompson, "Buying Drugs for the President Was No Easy Task," report from the *Washington Post* carried in the *Philadelphia Inquirer*, 16 December 1989, p. 12A.
30. Ellen Hume, "Why the Press Blew the S & L Scandal," *New York Times*, 24 May 1990, p. A19Y.

Finally, in 1990, the problem that had surfaced years earlier received wide coverage. There were several reasons for the increase in television attention: (1) it was estimated that the cost of a federal bailout might reach $500 billion; (2) respected members of Congress, including five prominent senators, were shown to have delayed measures to limit costs in response to lobbying and campaign contributions from the thrifts; and (3) President Bush's son Neil, a director of the Silverado Banking, Savings and Loan Association in Denver, was charged with a conflict of interest in its delayed closing and was sued by federal regulators who charged that "'gross negligence' had led to a collapse that could cost taxpayers more than $1 billion."[31] News coverage had been delayed by the lack of economic expertise among reporters and by the complexity and geographic spread of the story.

Specialized media outlets, whose reporters had the expertise to interpret what was occurring, broke the story earlier. In 1983, the *American Banker* linked a New York City deposit broker (later convicted of fraud) to a criminal investigation of several midwestern banks that were short of tens of millions of dollars. In 1985, the *National Mortgage News* began to detect that, in many cases, failing savings institutions had been defrauded. In 1989, two of its reporters, Stephen Pizzo and Paul Muolo, with Mary Fricker, a financial reporter at the *Santa Rosa* (Calif.) *Press Democrat,* published *Inside Job: The Looting of America's Savings and Loans.* The book won an award from the Investigative Reporters and Editorials Association at the University of Missouri, and in August 1990 appeared on the *New York Times* best-seller list.

Stan Strachan, editor and one of the founders of *National Mortgage News,* commented: "Had it [the savings crisis] reached the public consciousness a few years earlier, we could have saved a huge amount of money."[32]

Commenting on the difficulty in getting stories on this problem published, Tom Freedman, formerly legislative director to Representative Charles E. Schumer (D-N.Y.), asserts: "The nuts and bolts of banking and housing legislation were not 'sexy' issues," and adds: "In Washington, there is widespread acceptance of the idea that the public doesn't want complicated news."[33] In such cases, news norms affect political decision making. Only certain kinds of stories will attract coverage by journalists, which, in turn, creates the public concern that energizes lawmakers. When complex issues don't attract news coverage, politicians are likely to ignore them to focus on simpler, more dramatic issues whose coverage has aroused public concern.

The economy is complex. Economists speak in a language not readily intelligible to the general population. No single economic indicator, of itself, gives a complete and accurate picture of the country's economic condition. Because it is a construct, the economy can't be televised in the same way a battle or a presi-

---

31. Stephen Labaton, "F.D.I.C. Sues Neil Bush and Others at Silverado," *New York Times*, 22 September 1990, p. 17Y.

32. Kathleen Quinn, "As S. & L.'s Sink, a Trade Weekly Is Soaring," *New York Times*, 27 August 1990, p. C8.

33. Tom Freedman, "While Journalists Chase 'Sexy' Issues," *New York Times*, 16 September 1990, p. E23.

dential inauguration can. Consequently, television seeks out the human interest angle in an economic story and focuses on the rate of inflation, translated into the increased cost of a basket of groceries in representative cities; on the FHA and VA mortgage rates, translated into how much more it will cost some average citizen this month to buy an FHA- or VA-financed home; and on the unemployment rate, translated into a story of the impact of continued unemployment on a specific worker in South Succotash. Because these facets of the economy lend themselves to bar graphs plotting change from month to month and to representative illustrations, coverage of these aspects is the mainstay of the economic news a viewer can expect to see on television, along with interviews of such national figures as Alan Greenspan, head of the Federal Reserve System.

Cover Newsworthy People   An event is more likely to be covered and published if it involves people in positions of authority or people who have been newsworthy in the past. Not only are such stories personal and about individuals, but also they satisfy a deep-seated curiosity of the mass audience about how the other half lives. Newsworthy people are leaders in their professions, celebrities of all kinds, and powerful people (world leaders, politicians, the very rich). It is axiomatic, for example, that the president is news. So are past presidents— and their families—as news stories about the births of Caroline Kennedy's children and John Kennedy, Jr.'s romances indicate. Their association with a past president and a current senator (Edward M. Kennedy, D-Mass.) make such events newsworthy.

Similarly, quite trivial happenings involving movie and television stars and well-known athletes receive coverage. When Zsa Zsa Gabor was arrested for slapping a police officer, the arrest and subsequent trial made news. Past celebrities like feminist Gloria Steinem continue to command sporadic treatment from newsgatherers, doubly illustrated when Steinem drew coverage after authoring a book on Marilyn Monroe, also a former celebrity. When the celebrity is charged with a crime, two news norms converge to increase the likelihood of coverage. As a result, the trials of Senator Edward Kennedy's nephew William Kennedy Smith on rape charges and former football star O. J. Simpson on murder charges drew front-page and top-of-the-broadcast treatment. In other words, an event involving people who have been newsworthy in the past is more likely to be reported.

Avoid Giving Offense   An event is less likely to be covered and reported if it offends media owners, the government, advertisers, or the mass audience. For example, on November 30, 1989, NBC's *Today* aired a piece by investigative reporter Peter Karl of NBC-owned WMAQ-TV in Chicago. The 3-minute piece summarized a five-part series that Karl had done for WMAQ on defective airplane bolts. The report did not mention that the defective bolts were produced by General Electric Company, the parent company of NBC. After a week of public criticism, *Today* broadcast a 4-minute follow-up that identified GE by name.[34]

---

34. Diane Mermigas, "'Today' Airs Follow-up after GE Controversy," *Electronic Media*, 11 December 1989, p. 2.

BOX 2-4

The Interplay of Influence Between Stations and Advertisers

"Boston's WHDH-TV made a gutsy call in airing what it knew was dynamite: a tv spot urging a boycott of Folger's coffee because purchases contribute to 'misery, destruction and death' in El Salvador by indirectly aiding its coffee growers and right-wing government. Now it's dealing with the bang that followed, Procter and Gamble's yanking of all its ads from the station."[a]

[a]Editorial, *Advertising Age*, 21 May 1990, p. 28.

The news media also avoid offending business. Lou Cannon accounts for the weakness of journalistic business reporting in part by the newspapers' desire to shield themselves against financial disclosure. He quotes Peter Silverman, business and financial news editor of the Washington Post, as saying "newspapers themselves are among the most secretive and the most protective about the facts and figures of their own business. They are not likely to ask others to do what they are unwilling to do themselves."[35]

When the audience is offended, the media usually listen. For example, under pressures from individuals and government, all three networks adopted guidelines for the coverage of riots. There are conventions for coverage of violence that exclude graphic presentations of blood and killing because it is assumed that dinner-hour audiences would be offended.

A dramatic, newsworthy event, however, can disrupt the application of such norms. For example, on the morning of January 22, 1987, shortly after Pennsylvania State treasurer R. Budd Dwyer committed suicide at a news conference, Harrisburg television station WHTM broadcast a videotape of the event. The station did not first warn its viewers, who included children home from school because of a snowstorm. The station repeated the film on its two evening newscasts, although it added warnings. Similarly, television stations in Philadelphia and Pittsburgh also showed complete footage of the tragedy immediately after it happened, although they did not rebroadcast it on evening newscasts. Viewers protested.

Newspapers that published only pictures of Dwyer waving or holding the revolver were praised. Newspapers that used a picture of Dwyer with the barrel of the gun in his mouth, such as the *Philadelphia Inquirer,* the *Kansas City Star,* the *Sacramento Bee,* and the *Washington Post,* received numerous complaints from readers.[36]

Don't Become the News   Television is a more intrusive medium than print. In most cases, a print reporter will alter the observed environment less than a television reporter accompanied by a camera crew. Does television coverage change the nature of the story? The question was answered dramatically in June

---

35. Lou Cannon, *Reporting: An Inside View* (Sacramento: California Journal Press, 1977), pp. 134–135.

36. Lou Gelfand, "If You Ran the Paper?" [Minneapolis] *Star Tribune*, 1 February 1987, p.25A.

BOX 2-5

Self-Censorship

Failure of the news media to cover the United States's "news cartel" was the most underreported story of 1987, according to Project Censored. "The impact of this information cartel on a free society is ignored by the mass media," said a news release from project director Professor Carl Jensen.[a]

Why did the June 11, 1987 *Time* magazine cover article on the novelist-lawyer Scott Turow fail to mention three things?

1. The paperback publisher of Mr. Turow's two best-selling novels is Warner Books.
2. The producer of the $20-million movie of Mr. Turow's 1987 best-seller *Presumed Innocent* is Warner Brothers.
3. The book club that promoted Mr. Turow's new novel as an important 1990 release was the Book-of-the-Month Club.

Note: Warner Books, Warner Brothers, and the Book-of-the-Month Club are all owned by *Time*'s parent, Time Warner Inc.[b]

Time magazine's dogged coverage of the controversy involving its parent, Time Warner Inc., and gangsta rap music may burnish the publication's reputation outside the company. But it could exacerbate the strains inside Time Warner. . . . *Time* published an aggressive cover article last week about its owner. In stark black and red type, *Time* asked "Are Music and Movies Killing America's Soul?" . . . "What makes the piece terrific is that we had the guts to write about an issue so close to the company," said Henry Muller, a former managing editor of *Time* who is now the editorial director of Time Inc., the company's magazine division. . . . Several *Time* editors said it was unprecedented for an editor-in-chief to show such independence. Indeed, Mr. Pearlstine's predecessor, Jason MacManus, made what many journalists considered an infamous decision, that *Time* should not cover the merger of Time Inc. and Warner Communications the week it was announced in 1989.[c]

[a]Lou Gelfand, "If You Ran the Paper," [Minneapolis] *Star Tribune,* 26 June 1988, p. 23A.
[b]Deirdre Carmody, "The Media Business," *New York Times*, 18 June 1990, p. D10.
[c]Mark Lander, "Time Warner, Under Its Own Spotlight," *New York Times,* 12 June 1995, p. D5.

1981 when ABC's crew for the newsmagazine *20/20* was filming a story about the emergency care of infants in Arizona. The filming focused on the Air Evac Rescue Program, a program that airlifts patients to physicians or physicians to patients. On June 2, "several Air Evac officials delayed for an hour the emergency departure of an emergency flight from Phoenix to Douglas, a mining town with a population of 12,000 near the Mexican border, so that a larger plane could be outfitted for the television producers and cameramen."[37] The infant waiting for the physician was suffering from "respiratory distress," but the child's life was not in danger.

---

37. *Washington Post*, 11 June 1981, p. A38.

BOX 2-6

Who's the News?

"[E]lection news now focuses more on the journalists than on the candidates. In the 1960s, when presidential candidates appeared on television they were usually pictured speaking: 84 percent of the time, candidates' images on the screen were accompanied by their words. The average sound bite was 40 seconds in length. In contrast, the average sound bite in 1992 was less than 9 seconds, and pictures of the candidates were not usually accompanied by the sound of their voices. For every minute the candidates spoke on the network evening news in 1992, the reporters who were covering them talked 6 minutes."[a]

[a]Thomas E. Patterson, *Tomorrow's News*, Project Vote Smart, Center for National Independence in Politics (Summer 1995): 1.

The *Arizona Republic* covered the story on the front page. The director of the Air Evac service was suspended. ABC contended that it had not requested the delay; nonetheless, the delay would not have occurred if the film crew had not been covering the story. What if the infant had died as a result of the delay? Did the absence of a life-threatening situation justify delay in the name of televised coverage of the Air Evac unit? These are the sorts of troublesome questions posed by the intrusive nature of television.

In other words, news coverage and publication are influenced by the criteria of newsworthiness, the conventions of news coverage, and the characteristics of the medium itself. A story is more likely to be aired on television if there is footage available in the archive, if the event is visual, if the item concerns newsworthy people, if it is inoffensive to audience tastes, and if there is little chance that the sheer fact of coverage itself will become newsworthy.

How the Story Is Presented

When an event is covered and a decision is made to air or publish the story, the conventions governing news presentation come into play. These conventions are influenced by five factors: reporters' lack of specialized expertise; ideals of fairness and balance in publication of controversial material; story length; story structure; and the norm of objectivity in news presentations.

Reporter Expertise

Although every effort is made to enhance reporters' on-air credibility, reporters cannot be experts on all the topics they cover. For the most part, journalists are generalists who rely on the expertise of others for information.[38]

---

38. Stephen Hess, in *The Washington Reporters* (Washington, D.C.: Brookings Institution, 1981), documents this situation for journalists in the Washington press corps. According to his survey, most

Most reporters begin on general assignment beats that require coverage of a number of varied topics; many are assigned to more than one beat. Whatever the beat, they are likely to cover stories related to a number of subjects—thus, communication to a mass audience works against specialization. Reporters sometimes argue that their lack of expertise is an advantage; it puts them in the same position as their audiences.

Such attitudes can lead to selective vision. For example, despite an enormous volume of commentary attempting to account for the rape of a white investment banker in New York City's Central Park by a nonwhite gang, the most obvious gender-related explanations were notable for their absence. Almost all coverage focused on race and poverty; almost none surveyed the research on gang rape, which reveals that such crimes are frequently committed by white middle-class athletes and fraternity members. In Helen Benedict's recent survey, only one of some thirty reporters who routinely covered sex crimes had ever read a book on rape, and few had made any effort to consult experts. In explaining the *New York Times*'s selective coverage of the Central Park rape, the metropolitan editor acknowledged, "I can't imagine the range of reaction to the sexual aspect of the crime would be very strong."[39]

News organizations are also wary of acculturation. For example, the *New York Times* rotates its foreign correspondents every three to five years in the belief that greater familiarity with a country might slant reporters' stories.

A major change in the last several years has been the enormous growth in the use of computer technology and, with it, increased access to computerized databases. Whereas most reporters used to have limited research facilities and research staff and were dependent in large part on materials drawn from the news outlet's archive or morgue, this is no longer true. A reporter at a small newspaper in a rural area has access to the same "information superhighway" as the reporter at the *New York Times*. The explosion in the amount of information easily available may have led to an increase in research. In 1990, ABC News had four full-time researchers. In 1995, it had nine full-time, professional researchers in New York and three more in Washington.

Nonetheless, the research tool of most journalists is the interview rather than the library or other documents. The interview frees newsworkers from determining facts by using the sophisticated, expensive, or time-consuming methods of other kinds of investigators. On the other hand, the principle that something is so because somebody says it allows newsworkers to capitalize on the fruits of these more complex techniques by talking with those who have already used them. The person must be somebody in a position to know what

---

Washington journalists are generalists (p. 49). They use no documents in the presentation of nearly three-fourths of their stories; when used, documents are likely to be newspaper articles (p. 18). Although 93 percent of Washington reporters in 1978 were college graduates and 33 percent had graduate degrees (p. 83), a beat is considered more desirable if no documents research is required (p. 52), and, even on specialized beats such as economics or law, journalists tend to read popular rather than scholarly journals (p. 64).

39. Helen Benedict, "Covering Rape Without Feminism," *Women and Law in the Media*, ed. Martha Fineman (New York: Routledge, in press), p. 2. Survey results on p. 7.

Appearing on Television—Necessary to Be Credible in Print?

Chris Matthews, former speechwriter and spokesman for House Speaker Tip O'Neill and author of *Hardball,* wanted to be a pundit—to be a regular on political television talk shows. Larry Kramer, executive editor of the *San Francisco Examiner,* agreed to make Matthews a columnist complete with the prestigious title of "Washington bureau chief." "He needed to be a journalist," Kramer explained, "to have the kind of respectability to be on TV." Matthews had the sorts of talents that work on television; Kramer needed visibility for his afternoon newspaper, which Matthews could provide by appearing on these shows "with our name under his picture."

Matthews became such a familiar face on television talk shows that *Washingtonian* magazine named him "one of the top 50 journalists" in the city.

Matthews's story is not an isolated case. The *Chicago Tribune* employs a media consultant to coach and promote its Washington correspondents for television. Other print media have followed suit. Television commentator David Gergen became an editor at *U.S. News & World Report, Newsweek,* which gives reporters cash bonuses for television appearances, hired Morton Kondracke as its Washington bureau chief after he became a regular on television.

Some observers fear the impact of television opinion journalism on basic journalistic values of reporting, neutrality, and objectivity, as it reinforces the skills that get one and keep one on television—a knack for asserting opinions in concise, memorable, sound bites. "I need someone who is glib, colorful, whose thoughts can be condensed into a conversational style," said Karen Sughrue, when she was executive producer of *Face the Nation.*

Sue Ducat, producer of PBS's *Washington Week in Review,* reports being inundated by requests from print reporters seeking to appear on the show. Although payment for an appearance on most talk shows is small, being on television is the surest way for print reporters to get rich—it leads to book contracts and, most lucrative of all, to the lecture circuit.

The journalist-as-Washington-insider, offering advice, is an essential part of these programs. Many of the shows, such as CNN's *Capital Gang,* mix journalists, partisans, and government officials together as equals—a process likely to distance journalists from the public they are supposed to represent and to make criticism of the government policies supported by their "guests" less likely.[a]

[a]Thomas B. Rosenstiel (*Los Angeles Times*), "Some Say TV Show Culture May Change Values of Journalists," *Star Tribune,* 23 May 1989, pp. 1, 2E.

---

they say, somebody entitled to know what they say. Typically, competent knowers for journalists are bureaucrats and agency officials.[40]

Not only is an interview a research tool, but it also personalizes a story. When the interview format is used to present a story, it allows the reporter to re-

---

40. Fishman, *Manufacturing the News,* pp. 92–93; Stephen Hess reports that Washington journalists in his survey conducted close to five interviews per story (*Washington Reporters,* p. 17).

main a detached observer; and if conflicting views are presented, it is a natural way of dramatizing an issue and reporting material in a balanced manner.

Lack of expertise can allow inaccuracies or bias to creep into a reporter's work. In order to compensate, reporters, particularly those writing for elite media, check their stories with informed sources. Problems can arise here too.

"Reporters are still uncomfortable about saying things on their own authority, so they turn to the experts," writes Stephen Hess, a speechwriter in the Eisenhower White House, an urban affairs adviser to President Richard Nixon, now on the staff of the Brookings Institution and author of several books on the press. In 1989, the year Hess decided to count his own calls, he received 1,294 calls from 183 news organizations in 17 countries. Contacted recently on a July 1995 afternoon, he already had received calls that day from the BBC, Reuters, the AP, *Time,* and McClatchy.

Jack Nelson, head of the Washington bureau of the *Los Angeles Times,* agreed: "When you are going to make an opinionated kind of statement, particularly in the news columns, editors insist you attribute it to someone other than yourself—so you go shopping."[41]

Out of his experiences, Hess has come to surmise "that TV news is increasingly dishonest in that increasingly its stories gather quotes or other material to fit a hypothesis." With smaller budgets and staffs, reporters are under pressure to make every story usable and under pressure to do fewer interviews. "In other words, reporters tend to interview only those who fit a preconceived notion of what the story will be and a story's hypothesis becomes self-fulfilling." This he believes is beginning to erode a strength of journalism—its capacity to see for itself.[42]

Fairness and Balance

Presenting opposing viewpoints has become a staple of news presentation. One commentator writes: "'Objectivity,' contrary to popular belief, does not refer to the truthfulness of media interpretation, but demands merely impartiality of coverage, which is stylistically supplied by quoting two opposing sources."[43] Given the importance of the interview as a journalistic technique, this is the natural way to extend it to provide balance.

Many problems have more than two solutions, however, and many issues generate more than two opposing viewpoints. News stories almost never reflect such complexity; instead, they tend to present issues in terms of pros and cons, to look at social movements as made up of moderates and militants, to divide

---

41. Barbara Gamarekian, "In Pursuit of the Clever Quotemaster," *New York Times,* 12 May 1989, p. 10Y.

42. Stephen Hess, "New Phase Makes TV News Increasingly Dishonest," *Star Tribune,* 17 October 1989, p. 13A.

43. Gertrude Joch Robinson, "Women, Media Access and Social Control," in *Women in the News,* p. 89.

CASE STUDY 2-4

The Role of the Media in the 1994 Health Care Reform Debate

A comprehensive study of the news coverage of the 1994 health care reform debate concluded that:

- Reporters tended not to cover the very real areas of agreement between Democrats and Republicans. Consensus, although necessary for the survival and passage of a health-care bill, seemed uninteresting to reporters. Republicans and Democrats did agree on certain key issues. Senate Minority Leader Bob Dole and President Clinton agreed that reform was needed. They also agreed that insurance purchasing pools of some sort were a good idea. (The reasons were straightforward. Such groups spread risks across large groups of consumers and have the marketplace clout to hold down costs.) Unresolved were the size, composition, and management of the groups. Clinton called them "alliances" and made them mandatory; Dole called them "voluntary purchasing cooperatives."

  There was also bipartisan support for some insurance reform proposals. Each of the seven plans before Congress in February—three sponsored by Democrats, four by Republicans—would have barred insurance companies from denying policies to those with existing illnesses, and would have provided "portability" by allowing workers to keep their insurance when they switched jobs. However, these points of agreement did not receive much attention from journalists.

- Journalists focused on some plans more than others. The Clinton plan framed the debate. In print, the Clinton plan was about five times more likely to be mentioned, and in broadcast, it was about four times more likely to be mentioned than the second most-mentioned plan, which in both print and broadcast was a modification of the Clinton plan, backed by Senate Majority Leader George Mitchell. In the process, plans with substantial congressional support—Wellstone-McDermott to the Clinton plan's left, and Michel to the Clinton plan's right—were effectively denied the national stage.

---

reaction into support for or resistance to administration policy. This reflects the emphasis on conflict and drama in hard news; the distortions it creates are often criticized for treating electoral campaigns as horse races or athletic contests.

The preoccupation with winning and losing was evident in coverage of the 1984 debates between Reagan and Mondale, in which news coverage focused on Mondale's use of "There you go again," the phrase Reagan had used so effectively in 1980 in responding to Jimmy Carter. What was forgotten in the process was the issue Reagan and Mondale were discussing—Social Security. We would argue that such treatment is a natural outgrowth of the criteria for hard news and the conventions governing news presentation, which shape the resulting stories and influence the view of reality they present.

- Reporters were interested in conflict, sometimes to the exclusion of covering other health plans. Media focus on the clash between Clinton and Cooper, both Democrats with separate health plans, shunted into the shadows the four Republican plans, eclipsing from public view some very real policy options. Senator John Chafee (R., R.I.) proposed a plan that provided universal coverage, but, unlike Clinton's, did not require that employers provide it. Other plans—including those by Michel and Senator Phil Gramm of Texas—offered tax breaks to buy insurance and tax-sheltered savings accounts to pay for coverage, and other ideas.

- Viable policy options were prematurely judged "dead" by reporters, and hence, did not receive coverage. Early in the process, seven different pieces of legislation, each representing a different plan, were simmered down to two—and in the process, important ideas slipped from public view. A world traveler who returned to the United States in mid-January would have surmised from the news coverage that only Clinton's plan and the Cooper-Breaux plan were before Congress.

When researchers queried reporters about the focus on Clinton and Cooper-Breaux rather than Michel or Wellstone-McDermott, they were told that neither the Wellstone-McDermott nor the Republican alternative (Michel) had any chance of passing. That prophecy proved false. One of the five bills that emerged from committee included a single-payer provision in the form of extension of Medicare, similar to the Wellstone-McDermott bill. And the compromise proposal being crafted as the legislative process drew to a close bore more than a passing resemblance to the Michel bill.[a]

[a]From "Media in the Middle: Fairness and Accuracy in the 1994 Health Care Reform Debate." A report by the Annenberg Public Policy Center of the University of Pennsylvania, funded by The Robert Wood Johnson Foundation (February 1995).

The emphasis on opposing points of view can create another kind of distortion. It is as if the media must find an opposition and, for purposes of balance, promote it as relatively equal in size and importance to its counterpart even if the opposition is minuscule.

Story Length

The typical news story is short and simple. There are ordinarily fifteen to twenty stories on the evening network news, and each story averages slightly more than one minute in length. The "action news" approach to local newscasts, recommended by Frank N. Magid Associates of Marion, Iowa, largest of the news consulting firms, is thirty to forty short, fast-paced items in the twenty-two minutes of a typical half-hour newscast.

The nature of the television medium means that listeners cannot skip boring items, and bored listeners may switch channels or turn off the set. Broadcasters sometimes say that their stories would be longer if the nightly network newscasts were extended to forty-five minutes or an hour, but when in 1963 the networks moved from fifteen minutes to thirty minutes of news, the length of the individual stories did not increase appreciably.

The constraints of time and space force reporters to simplify. Print reporters order their material into a pyramidal structure that opens with a lead (first paragraph) identifying who, what, where, when, how, and why; material is then developed in order of decreasing importance so it can be cut from the end if space runs short. The result is that a single, discrete event is reported, and such coverage tends to separate events from their context.

Special kinds of news stories have been developed to correct for this kind of distortion: feature articles that highlight human interest, interpretive and background stories that explain the more complex event or place events in a more meaningful frame of reference, news analysis and commentary, and editorials. These appear in all media, but they are most common in the elite media, although even here they are limited. Bob Woodward and Carl Bernstein, the *Washington Post* reporters who became famous for their investigative work on the events of Watergate, remarked that during their investigative reporting they had no time or opportunity to write a synthetic piece integrating their findings into a coherent whole.[44] For the most part, this kind of news coverage appears in specialized media or programming, in newsweeklies, in weekly commentary magazines, or in documentaries. The result is that such stories are more likely to reach smaller, more specialized audiences.

Walter Cronkite, the former anchor of *CBS Evening News* and a highly respected journalist, stated repeatedly that network news simply provides a headline service. In fact, a half-hour news program provides less verbal information than the front page of the *New York Times*. The success of such public television programs as *The NewsHour with Jim Lehrer*, however, attests to television's ability to discuss ideas in depth.

But until the inception of ABC's *Nightline*, a half-hour program devoted to one to three issues, no in-depth commercial news program had attracted an audience big enough to warrant regularly scheduled in-depth news. *Nightline*, created to provide detailed coverage of the Iranian hostage crisis, continues to defy conventional wisdom by drawing a high-income audience attractive to advertisers and challenging the ratings of its late-night rivals, the *Tonight Show* and the *David Letterman Show*.

To celebrate its fifteenth anniversary in 1995, *Nightline* dedicated one hour to a special on the political and economic crisis in Mexico, instead of a retrospective

---

44. Cited in Timothy Crouse, *The Boys on the Bus: Riding with the Campaign Press Corps* (New York: Random House, 1972), p. 296.

BOX 2-7

Network Newscasts vs. Some Newspapers[a]

A study by the Freedom Forum Media Studies Center analyzed the amount of coverage, in words printed or spoken, given to national and international events from January 3 to January 27, 1995. The study compared the top three networks' evening newscasts with the national and international reports of three newspapers. The *Des Moines Register* (circulation 188,000), and the *Atlanta Constitution* (circulation 307,000) were chosen because they were typical of regional newspapers read by about 20 million Americans every day. The *New York Times* (circulation about 1.2 million) was chosen because it is a leading metropolitan newspaper that is distributed nationally.

The researchers found that the ABC, CBS, and NBC evening news provided a larger volume of reporting, measured in words, on the California floods than did some papers, and provided reports on the earthquake in Kobe, Japan, that were comparable to the newspapers' coverage. Perhaps most surprising, the researchers said, *ABC World News Tonight,* for example, offered more coverage on the complex welfare debate than any of the three newspapers whose coverage the researchers analyzed.

The volume of national and international news in the *New York Times* was more than six times that of all news on all subjects on the three networks. The amount of national and international news in the *New York Times* is more than three times that of the other two papers, the report found, adding that it provided about 25,000 words each day on national and international news. The *Atlanta Constitution* provided about 8,000 words, the *Des Moines Register* about 7,500. The network evening news broadcasts use about 4,000 words on an entire broadcast.

According to a 1993 study, 69 percent of Americans said they got most of their news from television, compared with 43 percent who said they got most from newspapers.

[a]*New York Times*, 6 April 1995, p. A10.

---

of the show's highlights. "We always do exceptionally well when we put on a serious show like that," said Ted Koppel. Executive producer, Tom Bettag, goes further, "When we do something light or frivolous, our ratings are always lower."[45]

Koppel and *Nightline* have also broken news stories. As the PTL scandal began to unfold, Koppel was the first to interview Jim Bakker—the minister charged with misusing funds donated by his viewers. After the Donna Rice story broke, presidential hopeful Gary Hart did his first explanatory interview with Koppel. Koppel was also first to interview Ferdinand Marcos after he fled the Philippines.[46]

---

45. Bill Carter, "The Media Business," *New York Times*, 27 March 1995, p. D1.
46. Ray Richmond, "A Pioneering Show's Anniversary," *Philadelphia Inquirer*, 8 November 1989, pp. 1, 8E.

The different ways in which space and time are organized in newspapers and on television affect news coverage. Television has a limited number of available commercial minutes and cannot expand the hours of the day or the time available for advertising. By contrast, as the amount of advertising sold increases, the amount of news published in a newspaper (the "news hole") increases.

Story Structure

Stories are stories. News reports, particularly televised news reports, are likely to be shaped into a narrative-dramatic structure. This kind of structure not only gives coherence to various bits of data, but is ideal for emphasizing action, drama, and conflict. Even within the conventional structure of the print story— moving from more important to less important facts—a news item is likely to begin with an action identified as a problem, develop through a narrative of increasing tension or conflict (including the identification of opposing forces, often interviewed and quoted), and close with a suggested or predicted resolution. This structure dominates coverage in television news. It is ideally suited to reporting single, dramatic events, to presenting characters (spokespersons who are quoted), to focusing on action, and to covering novel, exciting events. Conversely, it is ill-suited to coverage of an idea, concept, or process. Because journalists rely so heavily on narrative-dramatic structure, this more abstract content is not only harder to report but more likely to be distorted. An example of this technique is presented in the news account shown in Figure 2.1.

Objectivity

Some of the roles that journalists play have already been mentioned, such as the "detached observer," the "investigator," or the "objective" reporter of events. Social historian Michael Schudson points out that objectivity became an ideal in journalism rather recently and that it became an ideal "precisely when the impossibility of overcoming subjectivity in presenting the news was widely accepted and . . . precisely because subjectivity had come to be regarded as inevitable."[47] One communications researcher notes that in the role of reporter, the journalist no longer uses mainly "an intellectual skill as critic, interpreter and contemporary historian but a technical skill at writing, a capacity to translate the specialized language and purpose of government, science, art, medicine, finance into an idiom that can be understood by broader, more amorphous, less educated audiences."[48] This detaches the journalist from the events reported and has a significant impact on the style of news coverage.

---

47. Michael Schudson, *Discovering the News: A Social History of American Newspapers* (New York: Basic Books, 1978), p. 157.
48. James W. Carey, "The Communications Revolution and the Professional Communicator," in *The Sociology of Mass Media Communicators: The Sociology Review Monograph*, no. 13, ed. Paul Halmos (Keele, England: University of Keele, January 1969), p. 32.

BOX 2-8

Write a Story

In 1963, Reuven Frank, then president of NBC News, wrote a memo to his staff that read as follows:

> Every news story should, without any sacrifice of probity or responsibility display the attributes of fiction, of drama. It should have structure and conflict, problem and denouement, rising action and falling action—a beginning, a middle, and an end.[a]

[a]Cited by John Corry, "TV: The News Movie, New Form of Program," *New York Times*, 26 January 1988, p. 24Y.

Reporters rarely speak in the first person, refer to their own actions in observing events and finding facts, or reveal their perceptions of the sources' motives; nor do they ordinarily indicate the validity of quoted statements. News coverage of Senator Joseph McCarthy's charges of subversion in high places illustrates the limitations of this conception of the journalistic role. Hillier Krieghbaum commented: "It was, in a way, a nose to nose confrontation with the realistic requirements of objectivity and fairness. [Now journalists] had to face up to the reality that a prominent individual, with senatorial privilege, could make virtually any statement that he wanted to. What did a reporter do if a senator's facts were in doubt—or obviously wrong?"[49] Daniel Patrick Moynihan, now a senator from New York, wrote: "McCarthy went on . . . making such charges, and the national press, which detested and disbelieved him throughout, went on printing them. The American style of objective journalism made McCarthy."[50] Reporter Lou Cannon points to still another dimension of the problem. "As McCarthy well knew, objective reporting gives the accuser a powerful advantage over the accused. This is because the accusation usually becomes the lead and the lead becomes the headline. The denial might be carried in a sublead in newspapers that used it; otherwise the reader had to plow through the story to find the denial even though all newspaper editors are aware that many readers do not get beyond the first few paragraphs."[51]

Moreover, news stories are written in the limited vocabulary of ordinary language accessible to the mass audience; the standard style for modern newswriting removes all signs of the reporter's identity or consciousness. This is the counterpart, in newswriting, of the impersonal, organizational, virtually anonymous source characteristic of mass communication (see Chapter 1).

---

49. Hillier Krieghbaum, *Pressures on the Press* (New York: Thomas Y. Crowell, 1973), p. 11.
50. Daniel Patrick Moynihan, "The President and the Press," in *The Presidency Reappraised,* ed. Rexford G. Tugwell and Thomas E. Cronin (New York: Praeger, 1974), p. 159.
51. Cannon, *Reporting,* pp. 46–47.

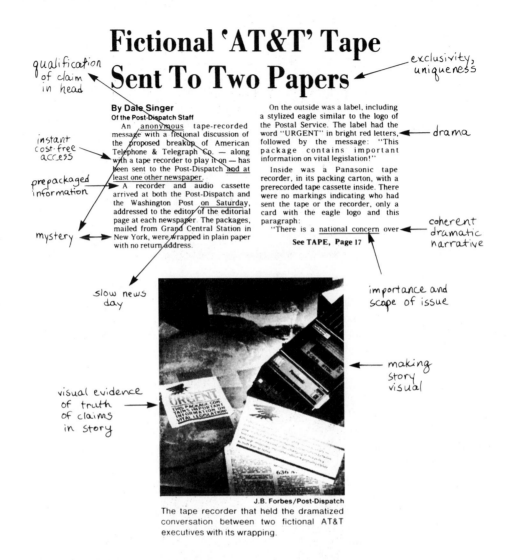

Figure 2.1   This article contains a fictional story within a nonfictional story within a news story. The story of Bill and Charlie is enveloped by the story containing its senders' purpose, which is contained within the news account.

(Reprinted by permission of J. B. Forbes/*Post-Dispatch*.)

Tape

■ FROM PAGE ONE

our nation''s telecommunications' policy, and rightly so. Here, ready to play, is a fictional and entertaining conversation between two executives involved in the changing of this policy. Although imaginary, the conversation is probably closer to truth than to fiction.''

The tape recording begins with a telephone call from a man identifying himself as "Charlie Brown," asking to speak with the president of Illinois Bell Telephone Co., who is identified only as "Bill." The chairman of AT&T is Charles L. Brown. The president of Illinois Bell is William L. Weiss.

Included on the professionally produced 10-minute tape is a discussion between Charlie and Bill about the proposed settlement worked out by AT&T and Assistant Attorney General William Baxter. The settlement was announced in January as an end to a longstanding antitrust suit against AT&T.

Under the agreement, AT&T would divest itself of its regional operating companies, which would become free-standing companies. AT&T would retain its Western Electric, Bell Laboratories and Long Lines, or long distance, operations.

As the taped discussion continues, the man portraying the president of Illinois Bell becomes increasingly disturbed as "Charlie" spells out the working details of the settlement. He makes it appear as if the parent company would be keeping all of the money-making activities, leaving the regional operating companies with unprofitable local service.

"We'll really have some rate problems," Bill tells Charlie, in a voice that sounds close to tears. "The state's going to get upset, the governor will get upset, the utility commission will get upset. Charlie, this is beginning to sound very difficult."

Later, Bill moans, "How in the world am I going to get and keep the best people?" Charlie replies, "With what we're leaving you, you won't need the best people."

The tape ridicules Baxter, saying that the assistant attorney general was in such a rush to arrange the settlement that "he called from the ski slope, then he hurried back here and we settled."

At the end, Bill pleads with Charlie not to leave him hanging, and Charlie, before hanging up, assures him he will help out, but only on an "arm's length" basis. At the beginning and the end of the tape is the famous recording by the Coasters of the song "Charlie Brown," including the refrain:

"He's gonna get caught, just you wait and see.
"Why's everybody always picking on me?"

Officials with Southwestern Bell Telephone Co. in St. Louis and with AT&T in Washington said they had no idea who sent the recording. They criticized the tape as a poor way to try to influence editorial opinion.

Pickard Wagner, an AT&T spokesman in Washington, said, "The fact that it is completely anonymous and disparages the head of AT&T and Illinois Bell illustrates the depths that whoever is behind this is sinking to."

Dana Campbell, division staff manager for media relations for Southwestern Bell, added, "It sounds like someone is trying to play games. It makes me a little angry. I get a little perturbed with anyone who sends out something in the mail without identifying himself."

The package sent to the Post-Dispatch was addressed personally to William F. Woo, head of the newspaper's editorial page since 1974. He called the tape recorder "some press agent's concept of a swell idea. I'm not at all amused by it. Inasmuch as it's anonymous, we will pay as much attention to it as we do to unsigned letters, which is to say none at all."

Woo said he could not recall ever receiving an anonymous press release before. He noted that, like the tape-recorded message, the newspaper's editorials have raised serious questions about the proposed AT&T settlement.

"This sort of anonymous attack is really disgusting," he said. "I wish I knew where it came from, and when we do find out where it came from, the tape recorder and message will be returned with a sharp note."

BOX 2-9

Is TV More Cluttered Than Ever?

"Clutter" is the television industry's term for everything that is nonprogramming time—commercials, PSAs, promos, station IDs, and program credits. Commercials make up the greatest part of clutter. The advertising industry's survey of prime-time clutter in May 1994 indicated continued increases, with Fox being the first to break the 15-minute mark.[a]

ABC	13 minutes 40 seconds
CBS	14 minutes 9 seconds
NBC	14 minutes 18 seconds
Fox	15 minutes 13 seconds

[a]*Broadcasting & Cable*, 8 May 1995, p. 82.

Whereas the ordinary reporting role requires detachment, the investigative reporter's role moves from detachment to an adversarial position that uses skepticism to uncover hypocrisy, corruption, or misuse of power. This role is epitomized by Mike Wallace's stance on *60 Minutes*. Wallace enacts the probing investigator determined to expose evil, to protect the underdog, to unearth the reality behind deceptive appearances.

Journalists who adopt this role tend to produce mildly skeptical stories, like the reporting done by CNN and ABC correspondents Bruce Morton and Sam Donaldson. Both Morton and Donaldson tend to cast doubt on motives, to debunk, to use the conventions of balance to raise objections or to suggest internal contradictions. This treatment, frustrating or infuriating to even the most powerful newsmakers, is a familiar journalistic perspective and a logical extension of the role of detached observer.

The roles of print and television reporters differ because the media themselves differ. However impersonal the style of the television reporter, "it is, above all, a personal voice that tells the day's news on the tube. One actually hears the voice; one sees the face, body, and manner of the person who speaks. This individual is constantly on view, intruding his person and personality almost continuously into the narrative."[52] This important difference between audience experience of print and television news may be one factor accounting for greater trust in television news.

TO SUM UP

This chapter has explored how news organizations define what news is. We have set out five criteria defining hard news, we have explored the external and internal constraints affecting what will be covered and reported, and we have shown

---

52. Paul Weaver, "Newspaper News and Television News," *Television as a Social Force* 87 (1975), p. 89.

how conventions of news presentation influence the character of the story that emerges. The inescapable conclusion is that through their methods of news-gathering and reporting, the news media shape our views of reality.

Reporters influence us in many ways: by choosing what to write about, by deciding which sources to consult, by selecting a particular lead and structuring a story in a given way. All of the decisions made by newsgatherers combine to create stories that are rhetorical and persuasive.

In words that paraphrase rhetorical theorist Kenneth Burke, journalism professor James Carey expresses our point of view: "All journalism, including objective reporting, is a creative and imaginative work, a symbolic strategy; journalism sizes up situations, names their elements, structure, and outstanding ingredients, and names them in a way that contains an attitude toward them."[53] In short, all journalism is rhetorical.

SELECTED READINGS

Dayan, Daniel, and Elihu Katz. *Media Events: The Live Broadcasting of History*. Cambridge, Mass.: Harvard University Press, 1992.

Ettema, James S., and Theodore L. Glasser. "Narrative Form and Moral Force: The Realization of Innocence and Guilt through Investigative Journalism." *Journal of Communication* 38 (Summer 1988): 8–26.

Hess, Stephen. *The Washington Reporters*. Washington, D.C.: Brookings Institute, 1981.

Levy, Mark, and John P. Robinson. *The Main Source: Learning from Television News*. People and Communication Series, Volume 17. Beverly Hills: Sage, 1986.

Manoff, Robert Carl, and Michael Schudson, eds. *Reading the News*. New York: Pantheon, 1987.

Meyrowitz, Joshua. *No Sense of Place: The Impact of the Electronic Media on Social Behavior*. New York: Oxford University Press, 1985.

Smith, Anthony. *Goodbye Gutenberg: The Newspaper Revolution of the 1980's*. New York: Oxford University Press, 1980.

---

53. Carey, "Communications Revolution," p. 36.

CHAPTER 3

News as Persuasion

News is persuasive not simply in what it covers, a claim we made in Chapter 2, but also in how it is presented. In this chapter we analyze the presentation of news, including dramatizing and sensationalizing coverage, inaccurate and incomplete reporting, unbalanced interpretations, and direct intervention in news events. Here we assume newspeople have decided something is newsworthy, and we examine how they present it.

In this chapter we consider the claim that media resources are used to influence our interpretations of events, to support certain perspectives and to reject others, and, in general, to function ideologically—that is, to promote "ideas which represent the interests of social groups and classes."[1] We examine this claim primarily in terms of television news, particularly network news, because it is now the most trusted news source in our society.

Dramatizing and Sensationalizing Content

The best-known statement about the mass media is probably Marshall McLuhan's "the medium is the message," later revised to "the medium is the massage." What these statements point to is the importance of technology in understanding how any medium can function persuasively. The impact of television news is, in part, a function of the screen, the camera, special effects, and the use of videotape.

The Screen

The television screen is small—very small indeed compared with a screen in a movie theater or to the size of people and objects in real life—and, therefore, it miniaturizes. Ballet dancers become tiny dolls; huge trucks are the size of toys. Within this frame, everything is tiny.

---

1. Glasgow University Media Group, *More Bad News* (London: Routledge & Kegan Paul, 1980), p. 402.

| Dramatic close-up | Medium close-up | Medium shot |

Figure 3.1   Common television camera shots.

Even cataclysms are shrunk to the size of small rectangles. ABC's Jim Wooten explained the inadequacy of television to capture the condition of the refugees in Zaire in a report for *Nightline* July 26, 1994. "Not with these pictures, or a million more" could he capture the extent of the crowd and their terror and desperation, he said. He told us what it was that the camera could not capture by telling us what the situation was not like: "It is not like the famine in Somalia. It is not like the flight of the Iraqi Kurds into the mountains of Iran and Turkey. . . . It is not like anything I've ever seen in thirty years as a reporter."

The television screen also reduces everyone and everything to the same size—an anchor is as large (or as small) as the Empire State Building. As a result, television alters our perceptions of space and proportion.

Some of what we now experience as television may no longer be true if high definition television becomes the norm. High definition television (HDTV) will provide a larger viewing screen able to carry a higher level of detail and quality. Where existing sets are one-quarter wider on their horizontal side than on their vertical, HDTV will be almost twice as long. From a distance, today's screens look square; HDTV will look rectangular. Among other things, this means that more horizontal eye movement will be required. Some scholars posit that "The combination of closer-viewing distance and wider screen will have the effect of putting the viewer 'in' the picture, because the screen will occupy a much greater proportion of the field of vision."[2] We now sit at some distance from the screen to dull the imperfections apparent at closer viewing.

The language of the television screen is the language of close-ups. Close-up shots compensate for the poor quality of the television picture. The most common camera shots used on television are illustrated in Figure 3.1. These typical close-up shots reflect the personal and social contact that is characteristic of television as a medium. The dramatic close-up reflects close personal distance or touching distance; the chest shot reflects far personal distance; and the medium shot reflects close social distance (just beyond touching distance)—the distance at which we carry on impersonal business, as with salespeople.

Distance is related to intimacy. Television simulates intimate relationships between total strangers by bringing viewers close to actors and reporters; they enter our living rooms and bedrooms; they talk to us while we eat. The reliance

2. D. Lachrenbruch, "HDTV," *TV Guide,* 5 June 1989, p. 19.

on close-ups creates new rules for our sense of interpersonal space. For example, when viewers encounter newspeople face to face, they tend to treat them as friends although they are total strangers. Because of the size of the screen and the use of close-ups, our experience of television, whether news or entertainment, involves personal and social contact and a sense of intimacy. As the last chapter noted, television news, unlike print, is personal in the sense that we see and hear a real person—an anchor or correspondent—presenting it. The television screen and the close-ups reinforce its personal character.

The Camera

The camera has a point of view; its lens becomes a viewer. Rules governing the shooting of news footage recognize the biases involved in camera angles and shots. For example, slow motion footage is considered tender, even romantic; jumpy images are considered dramatic; extreme close-ups are considered intense and dramatic.

Camera angles are also important. According to one study of journalistic practices, "For a news cameraworker, facticity is produced by meeting an event 'head on,' with camera placement fixed to simulate the angle of a person of average height confronting another person eye to eye. All else is condemned as 'distortion.'" If an interview is shot head-on, at eye level, that camera position suggests equality between the interviewer and the interviewee; if the camera looks up (worm's-eye view) at the person being interviewed, it suggests that the interviewee is more powerful and has a psychological advantage. Conversely, if the camera looks down (bird's-eye view) at the person being interviewed, it belittles the interviewee. That is why interviews and press conferences are shot head-on and from a fixed perspective.[3]

Camera shots and angles are important in television news. Reporters and anchors are shown in the medium close-up and medium shot, as are nearly all individuals in hard news stories. These distances are considered impartial and detached, the visual counterpart of journalistic objectivity. By contrast, more intimate shots are used for drama, to capture emotional reactions. Disaster victims, for example, may be shown in dramatic close-ups, but because this is an "emotional" and thus a nonobjective distance, reporters and anchors will not be shown in this way. Similarly, news programs rarely show individuals full length in longer shots at what is public distance. Such distances depersonalize and decrease the emotional involvement of the viewer. They destroy the personal and social contact that is the hallmark of television news. Only crowds (such as audiences, rioters, or groups of soldiers) or persons in establishing shots (used to identify where the event is taking place), for example, will be shown full length in longer shots.

---

3. Gaye Tuchman, *Making News: A Study in the Construction of Reality* (New York: Free Press, 1978), pp. 112, 114.

BOX 3-1

Camera Angle as Point of View

Henry Hampton, producer of "Eyes on the Prize I" (1954–1965) and "Eyes on the Prize II" (1965–1980), documentaries on the history of the civil rights movement, advised those who reviewed thousands of feet of television news footage to look for those moments when the news cameras changed position, literally and figuratively, in reporting stories about the movement. These are the shifts he identifies:

In the beginning of the movement, in stories about the Supreme Court school desegregation decision, the cameras showed the black characters sympathetically and their white antagonists as villains. As the movement heated up, the cameras moved behind the march leaders and looked outward at the hostile sheriffs and their deputies. Later, when "Black Power" became the cry of Stokely Carmichael and other activists, the cameras shifted away from the movement point of view. By the time of the 1967 riots (for the record, he notes, many African Americans still call them rebellions), the camera's point of view had shifted once again to look from behind the police lines aimed outward at the rioters.

"Millions of viewers have taken their racial lessons from the position of the lens, for the full impact of television is as much a result of by-product as it is of intent."[a]

[a]Adapted from Henry Hampton, "The Camera Lens as Two-Edged Sword," *New York Times,* 15 January 1989, p. 29H.

The camera has particular limitations and strengths. Photographic meaning is usually not self-evident; some explanation of context is required.[4] The camera eye is myopic; it cannot distinguish between trivial and important details. But photographs are powerful and dramatic visualizations of emotion. Irving Kristol puts it this way: "What television *can* do, however—and do with extraordinary power—is to mobilize the audience's emotions around a vivid, simplified, essentially melodramatic vision of the political world, in which praise and blame are the magnetic poles. What television can do, in other words, is what demagogic rhetoric used to do less efficaciously."[5] The emotional power of television is a by-product of its visual resources and the size and intimacy of the television screen.

Ordinary news footage takes advantage of the power of the camera. Correspondents reporting stories are framed against easily recognizable locations filled with symbolic significance: the White House, Big Ben, Red Square. A story about New York may be framed against its skyline; a strike is identified by a line of

---

4. William C. Adams, "Visual Analysis of Newscasts: Issues in Social Science Research," in *Television Network News: Issues in Content Research,* ed. William C. Adams and Fay Schreibman (Washington, D.C.: Television and Politics Study Program, School of Public and International Affairs, George Washington University, 1978), p. 169.

5. Irving Kristol, "Crisis for Journalists: The Missing Elite," in *Press, Politics and Popular Government,* ed. George Will (Washington, D.C.: American Enterprise Institute, 1972), p. 51.

BOX 3-2

Faraway Places and Tight Budgets

In the pursuit of pictures of events, the networks are increasingly buying and using videotape shot by stringers and by amateurs with portable videocameras. These changes raise fundamental questions about the ethical standards of television news. They include:

1. Has increasing reliance on nonstaff personnel, because of budget cuts and the difficulties in reporting stories in remote parts of the world, had an effect on the coverage of network news divisions?
2. Does the dependence of network news departments on good pictures invite abuse of journalistic standards?

Questions such as these have been raised by a number of incidents. For example, in fall 1989, the *New York Post* charged that Mike Hoover, a freelance cameraman, faked and restaged battle sequences in film used in award-winning reports for CBS newscasts and in a 1987 documentary about the war in Afghanistan. CBS staff members had questioned him on details and edited out material if any aspect of the coverage had seemed vague. But film was extremely prized by the networks trying to cover Afghanistan. It rarely turned up on any newscast, and Hoover's film was of exceedingly high quality.[a]

[a]Bill Carter, "Questions of Method and Morality in the CBS News Case," *New York Times*, 4 October 1989, p. 13Y.

---

pickets or a silent factory; a murder is indicated by a pool of blood or the outline of a corpse on a sidewalk or a drug bust by needles and a stack of plastic packets. In this way the topics of news stories are instantly identified for the viewer, and the authority of reporters is enhanced—they are there, on the spot.

Special Effects

Technology is changing the potential of the television camera and screen through Chyron machines, which superimpose text on pictures; Adda electronic graphics-storage units; and Quantel computers, which create visual excitement by manipulating television images. ABC News led in the use of such equipment. Mike Buddy, a director of ABC's *World News Tonight,* is described as spending much of his day "packaging" news stories through technological equipment that gives editorial content a visual "shampoo."

To emphasize elements in a news story, news directors can use stop action, freeze frame, slow motion, or a zoom lens to focus on a postage-stamp-sized image on the screen. With a Chyron 4 character generator, they can superimpose text in colors. The Quantel 5000 Plus, a computerized switcher, enables directors to mold electronic images. ABC director Buddy says, "This is where we add the bells and whistles."[6] He explains that ABC tries to make economic information visually interesting by using special visual effects, "We tell the story graphically: freeze a picture, shrink it, put a catchphrase underneath the picture that encapsulates a paragraph of what the correspondent is saying. We try to make our graphics move the story forward instead of being a reference mark."[7]

The 1980s produced major advances in the technological manipulation of images. For the first time, computer-generated graphics could be animated on the screen. The result has been a proliferation of increasingly intricate introductory news logos. Promised soon is the virtual reality news set. Already in use in Europe, these simulated 3-D environments are projected onto a blue screen, placing the television talent in the middle of a weather map or on a set, furnished according to the latest ratings information.[8]

The heavy use of special effects is designed to attract viewers and increase ratings. Its use by news producers is defended on the grounds that U.S. television viewers have been trained to absorb information via commercials, so news programs must apply the same techniques. The view is that, on television at least, action speaks louder than words, and that emotion-filled pictures speak loudest.

The persuasive impact of television news is directly related to the television screen, the use of close-ups, the power of the camera, and the resources of special effects. They are used not only to dramatize and sensationalize news content, but also to enhance the authority and credibility of correspondents and anchors. This credibility was diminished, however, when the versatility of digital imaging tempted an ABC News producer to broadcast a composite image, leading the watching public to believe that correspondent Cokie Roberts was reporting on the State of the Union Address from in front of the Capitol, instead of from the ABC studio.[9]

Editing

Both print and broadcast journalism compress time. Events that took days or hours to transpire are reduced to a few paragraphs or a few minutes of airtime. In shortening an event it is difficult to maintain a sense of continuity. When continuous action is broken visually, by removing a section of tape or film, the image seems to jump; this editing procedure is called a "jump cut." When an editor wants the viewer to know that segments have been lifted from different parts of a speech, for example, a jump cut is deliberately used to tell the viewer that editing has occurred.

Ordinarily, producers do not want to draw attention to such breaks in continuity. To avoid breaks, "cut aways"—shots that cut away from the main action—

---

6. Desmond Smith, "The Wide World of Roone Arledge," *New York Times Magazine*, 28 February 1980, p. 66.
7. Edward Tivnan, "The Cronkite Syndrome," *The Dial*, November 1980, p. 49.
8. Edmond Rosenthal, "Virtually a Reality in U.S.," *Electronic Media*, 1 May 1995, p. 18.
9. John Carmody, *Washington Post*, 15 February 1994, p. E4.

are used to show, for example, audience reaction. During a speech, the camera may cut away to the face of the candidate's spouse; during a football game, the camera may cut away to the scoreboard or the cheerleaders. Because the camera limits the visual field, viewers see what the camera sees and cut away from the action with it, even if they would prefer to keep watching the game.

Because of its editing capacity, television can distort by reordering events. For example, a 1984 Ronald Reagan commercial intercut Reagan on a whistle-stop train tour with clips of Reagan ads that had aired earlier. As a result, some of the people in the second ad who appeared to be watching Reagan's train were in fact nowhere in sight of it; they were actors who had filmed their segments of the ads long before the train had pulled from the station.

The ability to edit means that the character of an interview can be altered. Cut away shots are often filmed at the beginning or end of a shooting session and later edited into the tape. At the end of a news segment, for instance, the camera will shift from the interviewee to the interviewer to shoot reaction shots that will be intercut into the interview. This is the procedure routinely followed on such newsmagazines as CBS's *60 Minutes,* and it includes not only reaction shots but film of correspondents such as Mike Wallace reasking the questions. When such procedures are used, interviews can be subtly altered.

In late October 1989, television minister Pat Robertson was interviewed by Rebecca Chase of ABC News about his reaction to the sentencing of fellow televangelist Jim Bakker to forty-five years in prison for fraud. Chase asked Robertson's reaction to "the rather stiff sentence received by Bakker." Robertson responded that although the sentence was stiff, he had expected it. After all, the judge was termed "Maximum Bob" in the Carolinas. Then Chase asked whether Robertson felt that the sentence closed the era of church scandals. Robertson answered, "I am delighted to see it. I think that God really has done a job cleaning his church." When the interview aired, Robertson heard himself saying that he was delighted at the Bakker sentence. His answer to one question had been edited to follow a different question.

Because Robertson had taped the complete interview, he was able to play it on his televised *700 Club.* The night after the *700 Club* broadcast aired, ABC admitted that editing had distorted Robertson's original statement.[10]

Related charges have been made against CBS's *60 Minutes,* a Sunday night newsmagazine that has been described as "without question the most influential news program in the history of the medium."[11] The show is known for its hard-edged, often sensational investigative reporting, typified by those segments featuring correspondent Mike Wallace. Such dramatic stories have kept the program among the top ten in the Nielsen ratings, but both the confrontational or "ambush" interview (approaching the target of an investigation for an interview without warning or with a damning document or quotation) and program editing have raised journalistic and ethical questions. Bill Brown, one of the original pro-

---

10. "ABC Exposed by Pat Robertson," *Accuracy in Media, Electronic Media,* 4 December 1989, p. 6.
11. Harry Stein, "How *60 Minutes* Makes News," *New York Times Magazine,* 6 May 1979, p. 28.

ducers of *60 Minutes,* describes the confrontational device as intrinsically unfair because it is so heavily weighted in favor of the reporter.

In May 1995, those confrontational tactics were turned against ABC reporter Sam Donaldson by a reporter for the tabloid-style show *Inside Edition.* Steve Wilson accused Donaldson of hypocrisy for investigating government waste on ABC while accepting a $97,000 federal subsidy for the mohair sheep raised on his New Mexico ranch. The *Washington Post* reported this exchange:

> "Steve, I'm a rancher. You wouldn't say to me I don't have a right to buy a ranch?"
>
> Wilson tried to regain the offensive. "Are you going to keep babbling here?" he demanded.
>
> "You asked me to talk to you, Steve."
>
> "And you haven't given me a straight answer yet."
>
> "Is that—the way you accuse me of babbling, is that fair? Is that really fair?"
>
> "What's fair, Sam, is I can get out a question and you give me an honest, direct answer. . . . You make a pretty good living. A little more than $2 million a year, I'm told."
>
> "So I don't have a right to buy ranch land? . . . You're not asking questions, you're making accusations. You're going to try to hold me up as somebody who is smelly. And Steve, it's not true, and you know it. Maybe you need to make a living this way, but I don't."[12]

Throughout, Donaldson crafted sound bites that would present him in the most positive light possible, and by refusing to run from Wilson, the ABC reporter denied his pursuer footage that would make him look guilty or evasive. "The choices were to be seen to be running or to stand and answer his questions," Donaldson told the *Washington Post.*[13]

Still, evidence gathered by three North Texas State University professors challenges the assumption that such coverage necessarily hurts its subjects. In fact, companies exposed on *60 Minutes* may have benefited from the publicity. After monitoring the stock prices of the thirteen companies featured on *60 Minutes* in the past five years, they concluded that, for fifteen days after the show aired, the shares of these companies did 12 percent better on average than the rest of the market.[14]

Many questions have been raised about editing that tends to sharpen the good versus evil, appearance versus reality themes described in Chapter 2. For example, when Daniel Schorr, a former CBS correspondent, was interviewed on *60 Minutes* about his unauthorized release ("leak") of the Pike Committee report, an interview that originally lasted over an hour and a quarter was reduced to thirteen minutes. "What had been deleted in the editing . . . was material that filled out his thought processes, lending the impression of a man under stress who had

---

12. Howard Kurtz, "Can Sam Donaldson Be Made to Look Sheepish?" *Washington Post,* 12 May 1995, p. B3.

13. Ibid.

14. *Time,* 28 April 1986, p. 55.

been trying to do the right thing. The elimination of that material also reinforced the impression of Wallace as the relentless interrogator."[15]

As viewers, we are aware of the subtle manipulation possible through editing, but our awareness is rarely conscious. We test the accuracy and reliability of some material based on our perceptions of editing, however. For example, reporters who wanted to demonstrate incoherence in Reagan's extemporaneous speeches and answers had to air longer than usual segments to confirm that the segments they were showing had not been edited into incoherence.

As our examples illustrate, disputes about editing arise most frequently about television newsmagazines and documentaries, although regular newscasts are also edited. The special effects we have described increase the possibilities for manipulation of filmed and taped material in order to make it more dramatic, more sensational, and hence more appealing to viewers.

Filmed and Taped Coverage

Since 1961, most television programming has been taped or filmed. Although the electronic media, unlike print, are able to transmit news events as they occur, until the advent of CNN, live coverage was rare and noteworthy: the space shots, President Kennedy's funeral, the Kefauver, Army-McCarthy, and Watergate hearings, presidential debates and major speeches, political party conventions, royal weddings, and some coverage of breaking news—the happenings in Tiananmen Square, the aftermath of the 1989 San Francisco earthquake, and events in the war against Iraq. CNN has built its reputation as a news organization in large part on its willingness to "go live" for important events. In the 1994–95 season, the decision to carry the O. J. Simpson trial was a ratings booster for CNN.

The local anchors delivering news are generally broadcast live. The first feed of the network news is live, although segments presented within the newscast have been taped; subsequent replays of the network news are taped. Thus *CBS Evening News* is fed live from New York at 6:30 P.M., but a tape of that feed is played on Channel 9 in Washington, D.C., at 7 P.M. The quality of the tape used to store and replay information is so good that viewers cannot distinguish taped from live coverage.

In the process of transforming live events into "taped, live, edited" events, verbal and visual errors are removed and, as a result, the spontaneity characterizing early television has been lost. Until viewers contrast live and taped coverage, they are unaware of the subtle distortion created when errors are suppressed. Occasional moments in the presidency of Ronald Reagan created such awareness as when he misread his note cards and, for example, announced in his second inaugural address that he wanted to fill the world with "sand" rather than the "sound"

---

15. Harry Stein, "How *60 Minutes* Makes News," p. 80; see also Eric Barnouw, *The Sponsor: Notes on a Modern Potentate* (New York: Oxford, 1978), pp. 137–138. For a history and analysis of the series, see Stephen Zito, "Inside 'Sixty Minutes,'" *American Film* 2 (December 1976–January 1977): 31–36; 55–57.

written on his cards. A similar awareness occurred in 1988 when the nightly news carried candidate George Bush's ad-libbed comment during a speech that September 7 was the anniversary of the bombing of Pearl Harbor.

The San Francisco earthquake that occurred on October 18, 1989 demonstrated how accustomed we have become to the controlled, polished presentations of evening news. The earthquake struck at 5:04 P.M. Because ABC was prepared to carry the World Series game, Candlestick Park appeared to be the epicenter of the quake. The Goodyear blimp, also at ABC's disposal, captured the first pictures of the damaged Oakland Bay Bridge. In the absence of fresh pictures, the networks violated the norm that news must be new and repeatedly aired the same pictures: a fire burning out of control and the damaged bridge. Sources that ordinarily are not newsworthy were interviewed simply because they were in San Francisco. Tom Brokaw of NBC interviewed an NBC reporter in a Bay Area traffic jam. Ted Koppel of ABC interviewed the pilot of the blimp. Neither interviewee had any information to add to the network coverage. Local reporters appeared with information about specific San Francisco locations. But the most important questions remained unanswered for hours. Where specifically had the epicenter been? How many had been killed and injured? What was being done to rescue those trapped by falling buildings and collapsing bridges? How many buildings had been destroyed?

"The communications wonders that we all take for granted were out of service," noted Walter Goodman of the *New York Times:*

> There were pictures without sound and sound without pictures, jumpy pictures and ill-defined ones. The vulnerability of these men and the medium on which the nation depends was unsettling: matters must really be out of control when the controllers of the news are unable to deliver it.[16]

If the improvisation that characterized network coverage of the earthquake is at one end of the news continuum, the staging of events is at the other end. For the past few years, re-enactments have been a staple of the so-called tabloid news programs such as Fox's *America's Most Wanted* and NBC's *Unsolved Mysteries.*

The controversy over re-enactments in network news arose in July 1989 when ABC's *World News Tonight* hired actors to depict a supposed meeting between U.S. diplomat Felix Bloch, accused of being a spy, and a foreign agent. The camera angle, the shot through crosshairs, the shadowy scene, the black-and-white footage all suggested that ABC had scooped its competitors by being on the scene to document the transfer of a briefcase presumably containing state secrets. As controversy swirled around the ABC re-creation, ABC formally reprimanded those who had aired the piece, instituted a policy on re-creations, and required that they only be used with the permission of ABC president Roone Arledge.

---

16. Walter Goodman, "How the Networks Coped with Scant Information," *New York Times,* 19 October 1989, p. B16.

In November 1989, NBC News announced that it was banning dramatic re-enactments from all its programming.[17] CBS announced that it would not use re-creations on the *CBS Evening News with Dan Rather* but would continue their use on the now defunct *Saturday Night with Connie Chung.* Chung's program used re-creations to show such things as a day in the life of a teenage drug dealer.

On November 17, 1993, *Dateline NBC* aired a report, "Waiting to Explode," about the propensity of some General Motors pickup trucks to burst into flames in a collision. That report included film of a fiery crash that *Dateline NBC* staged to demonstrate what it said could happen in a side-impact crash involving a GM truck. Faced with a lawsuit by GM, NBC acknowledged that in the demonstration crash, conducted by a private testing company in Indiana, tiny toy rockets were attached to the underside of the truck, a 1977 Chevrolet pickup, and ignited by remote control to insure that sparks would be present when a Chevrolet Citation struck the truck's side-mounted gas tank. The retraction was delivered to forestall a costly legal process for the network. Walter Goodman, television critic of the *New York Times* commented:

> Maybe in collaborating on the embarrassing test, the producers were carried away by the virtue of their case; it would not be the first time that journalists allowed themselves liberties in behalf of some higher good. But more likely, a crash-and-fire picture was just irresistible.[18]

Goodman's comments highlight the visual bias of newsgatherers as well as their assumption that violations of journalistic norms are permissible when done for a good cause.

Editing allows television producers to exploit the potential of the screen, the camera, and special effects to dramatize and sensationalize coverage. Because nearly all television news is edited, even televised news that is not re-enacted differs from the actual event in important and predictable ways.

Anchors and On-Air Reporters

Television legitimizes the carriers of news to a greater extent than print. Walter Cronkite, until March 1981 the anchor of *CBS Evening News,* was considered the most trusted man in the United States. Cronkite's closing comment, "And that's the way it is," put him and his news team in the position of authenticators: if you saw it on the network news, it had to be important; it had to be true. In fact, some media analysts argue that the existence of a small group of individuals who regularly bring us word of happenings in the news is reassuring.

In the process of reporting, newspersons legitimize certain stories and the ways in which they frame events. Being on the news is evidence of being impor-

---

17. Adam Buckman, "NBC News Bans Using Re-Creations," *Electronic Media,* 27 November 1989, p. 3.
18. Walter Goodman, "Critic's Notebook," *New York Times,* 11 February, 1993, p. B5.

BOX 3-3

News Producers Making News[a]

In February 1993, NBC News made the front page with its infamous *Dateline NBC* episode about General Motors trucks. The news division admitted that it had strapped "sparking devices" to the bottom of a truck to make sure it would explode in a test crash. NBC News president Michael Gartner resigned after the incident.

In October 1993, the executive producer of the *NBC Nightly News,* Jeff Bralnick, made headlines by referring to the Somali faction leader, General Mohammed Farah Aidid, as an "educated jungle bunny." He made the remark, first reported in the *Daily News*, at an NBC editorial meeting.

Also in October 1993, the executive producer of ABC's *World News Tonight,* Emily Rooney, found herself in the news when she said publicly that the "old stereotype" about the liberal bias of the news media "happens to be true," a comment reported in interviews in *Electronic Media* and *TV Guide*. Peter Jennings, *World News Tonight* anchor, made similar statements to *TV Guide*. Some staff members saw the comments as an attack on their journalistic standards.

"This is a continuation of what happens when journalists become public personalities," said Bob Lichter, director of the Center for Media and Public Affairs in Washington. "The news is part of pop culture now, so the people who bring you the news are pop culture figures."

[a]Elizabeth Kolbert, "Television," *New York Times*, 18 October 1993, p. C7.

---

tant. Newspeople rarely raise questions that remain unanswered on the news; instead, they tend to speak in declarative sentences and present stories that fit neatly into problem-solution formats. Network and local newscasts legitimize an evidence-giving process that relies on their credibility as reporters and on the credibility of television as a medium; you are legitimate only if we say so and only if viewers can actually see you on the tube. Within the newscast, individuals of higher credibility legitimize less credible reporters. Cronkite, for example, invested CBS reporters with some of his credibility when he said, "Here with the story from _____ is _____." The presence of a reporter in a location near the event being reported is used to bolster credibility.

There is fierce competition for ratings dominance among the nation's local television outlets, a competition fueled by finances because stations earn a large share of their gross income (30 to 50 percent of it, usually) from their early- and late-evening local newscasts.[19]

Because anchors seem to be an important factor in ratings and because they are relatively easy to change, there is widespread use of "skin-testing" by national rating services to measure audience response to anchors, a form of testing that may measure sex appeal or empathy, but that cannot measure journalistic competence or ability. An anchor who attracts the most appealing audience for

---

19. Neil Hickey, "Have Hair Spray, Will Travel," *TV Guide*, 14 February 1981, p. 5.

BOX 3-4

Women and Newspapers: Reading and Writing

According to a study by the Newspaper Association of America, a trade group in New York, the total percentage of women reading daily newspapers has dropped from 78 to 60 during the last twenty-two years, while the percentage of male readers went from 78 to 65.

Another study conducted by the Women, Men and Media Project may explain the drop in women readers. It found that of twenty national newspapers, only 34 percent of all bylines were women's, and that women were the subjects of only 13 percent of all news stories. An estimated 82 percent of all senior editorial jobs nationwide are held by men.[a]

Columnist Ellen Goodman argues that women of all ages "are more likely than men to feel that the paper doesn't speak to them. Or about them." She quoted Nancy Woodhull, a founding editor of *USA Today* who now runs her own consulting firm, as saying, "Women around the country really notice when the press doesn't report their existence. It's like walking into a room where nobody knows you're there. If you have choices, you don't go into that room anymore."[b]

[a]Betsy Isreal, "What Do Women Want (to Read)?" *New York Times*, 4 October 1993, p. B4.
[b]*(Boston Globe) Star Tribune*, 7 April 1992, p. A10.

BOX 3-5

Minorities in Newsrooms

Minority employment at the nation's daily newspapers in 1994 rose slightly to 10.91 percent of the total newsroom workforce. In 1993, the figure was 10.49 percent.

A report showed a slight increase in the percentage of minority newsroom supervisors at daily newspapers, but it reported that 91.8 percent of newsroom managers in 1994 were white. It also found that 45.7 percent of U.S. daily newspapers employed no minority journalists at all.

This report was based on survey responses from 1,029 of the country's 1,492 daily newspapers, or 69 percent.

Minority workers constitute about 25 percent of the U.S. workforce now, a figure that is expected to rise to 30 percent by 2000.[a]

[a]*New York Times*, 5 April 1995, p. A14.

---

advertisers—viewers 18 to 54 years old—will generate premium rates for advertising even if the ratings of the news program are lower than the competition's. Equally important, a popular early-evening local news program supplies a crucial lead-in to the prime-time lineup. An appealing anchor is also a way to induce the audience to identify with a particular news program, one route to promoting loyal viewership.

Once again, producers and station owners are making news judgments that will dramatize and sensationalize coverage at the potential sacrifice of journalistic accuracy and competence. The pressure for ratings is also felt by the networks. Those who have functioned as anchors on network newscasts have thus far been journalists with impressive credentials as reporters. But Roone Arledge, president of ABC News, believes the function of the anchor is the "excitement of a lead-in voice to mobilize the passion of the audience."[20]

Like media technology, television anchors are important elements in the processes by which television news is made credible as well as the ways in which it is dramatized and sensationalized.

Inaccurate and Incomplete Reporting

Deadlines and Competition

Newspapers, television programs, and radio shows are part of our scheduled lives. We expect our favorite programs to appear at their regular times; we expect the newspaper to be at the front door by a certain hour. If those in the news media are to meet our expectations, they must also meet the deadlines that make it possible for shows to air on time or for the newspaper to arrive on schedule. Events occurring too close to the deadline or after the deadline has passed strain the abilities of journalists, and may be omitted or treated superficially. Events that happen after today's deadline must be particularly novel, dramatic, and personal if they are to be tomorrow's news.

To make the morning edition of most daily newspapers, copy must be filed by early evening. Deadlines for large Sunday papers are even earlier, often early Saturday afternoon. If meetings are scheduled for the evening or if conferences or other events take place on weekends, they are unlikely to receive coverage.

The fact of deadlines would not in itself cause journalists to scramble for the latest, freshest, most dramatic news, but in a competitive news environment deadlines create that kind of pressure. No producer or publisher wants to lose the audience to a competitor because the competitor has a scoop or a unique angle on an important story. The emphasis on being first with a story encourages superficial reporting and the publication and broadcast of inaccuracies. As *Washington Post* reporter Lou Cannon notes, speed "is a value which competes with the value of accuracy, and in competitive situations it is difficult for accuracy to gain the upper hand. We put half-baked stories that need further checking on the air or into the newspapers when the stories certainly could wait another day."[21] Competition also produces races among the networks to be the first to "call" the results of elections.

---

20. Desmond Smith, p. 66.
21. Lou Cannon, *Reporting: An Inside View* (Sacramento: California Journal Press, 1977), p. 31.

The desire to air material first sometimes causes complications. At 2 P.M. one afternoon in midsummer 1990, for example, a federal judge presiding over the drug trial of Washington, D.C. mayor Marion Barry, released a black-and-white surveillance tape showing the mayor smoking crack. The problem for broadcasters was deciding how to deal with the expletives on the tape and with the mayor's repeated attempts to seduce governmental informer "Rasheeda" Moore.

NBC-owned WRC-TV was on the air with the footage at 2:03 P.M. (EST). Because WRC had had the tape for over a month, it had had the time to edit out the potentially offensive language and scenes. For fear of influencing the trial, the station had opted to withhold the tape, an instance of self-censorship, until the judge officially released it. Starting at 2:22, CBS affiliate WUSA-TV preempted network programming with the video only. At 11:30 that evening WUSA-TV aired the complete tape with the expletives included. At 9 P.M. C-SPAN aired the entire tape.[22]

Breaking News

Breaking news is unscheduled news, a happening no one could have foreseen—an assassination attempt or a disaster. Such occurrences strain journalistic resources and pose problems for television news, despite its special ability to bring us events as they occur. First, it is very costly for television to preempt regular programming for news coverage because such preemption may affect ratings and, ordinarily, fewer commercials will be shown during breaking news. Imagine the alternative: news reports on assassination attempts against President Reagan and Pope John Paul II interrupted by commercials for soaps and soups! Roone Arledge explains the situation this way:

> Competitive factors militate against networks living up to their responsibilities. It's a major step for a network to preempt a prime-time entertainment program to do a news program, because the results are going to be that your ratings for the week or for that night are going to be lower. And huge things rise and fall on this.[23]

When the networks preempted their schedules to cover the aftermath of the San Francisco earthquake, that decision cost between $1.5 and $2 million in lost advertising revenue per network.[24]

Inaccurate reporting of breaking news events is attributable to the difficulties of on-air editing, to the desire to beat the competition to the story, and to new angles on that story. These problems are illustrated by coverage of the assassination attempt on President Reagan in April 1981. *New York Times* television critic John J. O'Connor wrote that "ABC was the first to telephone my office about the attempt on Ronald Reagan's life, naturally anxious to announce that it had beat

22. Doug Halonen, "Barry Tape Gets Wide TV Play," *Electronic Media*, 2 July 1990, p. 2.

23. "The Hottest TV News Controversies," *TV Guide*, 13 January 1979, p. 10.

24. Bill Carter, "ABC Expects No Loss from Series Suspension," *New York Times*, 19 October 1989, p. B16.

its network competitors to the air."[25] According to a report in *TV Guide,* they beat their competitors by four minutes![26]

The desire to be first with new information, combined with on-air editing, produced major errors in the coverage of the Reagan shooting. The first error was the report that the president was unhurt when he actually had been shot in the chest. The second was the report that press secretary Jim Brady had died of his wounds. CBS first made this false report, and the other networks followed. The third error was the report that Reagan was undergoing open-heart surgery, an on-air mistake made by NBC reporter Chris Wallace and picked up by the other networks. Because of competition, each network monitors the others closely; consequently, errors spread within minutes. The fourth error was the report, at 7:15 P.M., that the president was still in surgery after four hours; in fact, he had been out of surgery for more than an hour.

Similarly, during the opening days of the war against Iraq in 1991, CNN mistakenly reported that a scud missile that exploded in Tel Aviv had carried a warhead of nerve gas. Less than a half-hour later, they corrected their error.

Under deadline pressure or on-air live, reporters and commentators mistakenly attributed the April 19, 1995, bombing of the Murrah Federal Office Building in Oklahoma City to foreign agents. "The betting here is on Middle East terrorists," said CBS News's Jim Stewart. Their reliance on unnamed sources was a clue that officials were unwilling to be associated with such speculative inferences. "The fact that it was such a powerful bomb in Oklahoma City immediately drew investigators to consider deadly parallels that all have roots in the Middle East," noted ABC's John McWethy the day of the bombing. The people arrested turned out to be young midwesterners.

These errors reflect the limitations of television news coverage. It is preeminent in fast transmission of videotape of recent events, as of an assassination attempt, but it is severely limited in covering stories that take place outside the range of the camera's eye, as inside a hospital. In such circumstances, television reporters are prone to make serious errors, such as substituting "open-heart" for "open-chest" surgery—errors that print reporters avoid because they usually have time to check such stories and do not face the pressure to put hearsay on the air immediately.

Coverage of breaking news illustrates the differences between broadcast and print reporting. Print reporting may allow time to check out a story and provide complete, accurate coverage. Television reporting permits the immediate transmission of tape, events, and rumors. Tom Wicker summarized the difference this way: "When information is speedily provided by impeccable sources, the advantage is all with TV." By contrast, a newspaper can sift out rumor, mistakes, and conflicting claims "to give its readers a reasonably accurate and comprehensive report—but well after the fact."[27]

---

25. John J. O'Connor, "How the Three Networks Treat Breaking News," *New York Times,* 12 April 1981, p. D29.

26. *TV Guide,* 17 April 1981, p. A1.

27. Tom Wicker, "TV's Tough Problem," *New York Times,* 7 April 1981, p. A19.

The competition among the networks compounds the problems of coverage of breaking news. As these examples illustrate, such coverage is prone to be incomplete and inaccurate.

Story Structure

Inaccurate reporting also results from inflexible attitudes about issues and about how a story should be written. For example, newspeople reject the notion that some things, like the consequences of enacting a piece of legislation, cannot be calculated. The press has a natural desire to know what the results of a newsworthy action will be on them and their audience. Consequently, because the audience wants to know what impact the legislation will have and what it will cost, and because the press knows that unforeseen effects often are significant and newsworthy, reporters are particularly interested in gathering information about the specific effects of proposed action.

But some data simply are not available. During the debate over the bill banning mandatory retirement, for example, reporters repeatedly pressed supporters of the bill for figures on the number of older workers who would be forcibly retired if the bill did not pass, but who would opt to stay in the labor force if it was passed. The staff of the House Select Committee on Aging rebuffed press requests for such a figure on the grounds that it could not be calculated accurately. This was the case for a number of reasons: workers will stay on the job if inflation has been or is projected to remain high because inflation erodes their pensions, but these workers will not stay on for financial reasons if their pension plans contain an escalator to compensate for inflation.

Accurate data on how workers behave in periods of high inflation when given a choice about retirement did not exist, nor did data correlating types of pension plans to income and to workers facing mandatory retirement who would be protected by the bill. In addition, workers stay on the job longer if their health is good; it is difficult to predict the health of workers who face mandatory retirement or would face it in the next three to five years. In fact, data on precisely how many workers faced mandatory retirement were not exact.

A similar problem confronted reporters covering congressional arguments over raising the minimum wage. Conservatives claimed that such a move costs jobs. Liberals disputed that assertion. The studies cited on each side were contradictory and inconclusive.

Anonymous and Composite Sources, Misrepresented Tape

Early in the 1980s, four cases focused attention on journalistic practices that lead to inaccurate reporting and on the processes by which print journalism corrects for such practices. *Washington Post* reporter Janet Cooke won a 1981 Pulitzer Prize in the feature-writing category for a story, "Jimmy's World," that she later admitted was a fake. The story was a composite of fabricated quotations and events that never happened.

In a series of stories written by the *Washington Post* ombudsman Bill Green, some of the processes that produced the story were revealed. These include the pressure on reporters to write good stories in order to advance, the problem of anonymous sources, and the gaps in procedures for checking stories when reporters say that the identity of the main characters must be protected.[28]

The second case involved reporter Michael Daly of the New York *Daily News*. In a column reporting on violence in Northern Ireland, Daly told the story of a British army patrol through the eyes of gunner Christopher Spell, a name he later admitted was a pseudonym. A *Daily News* editorial said that "a number of key facts in the account proved to be erroneous, and others could not be corroborated." Like Cooke, Daly resigned, but he said that the column that cost him his job was not very different from some 300 others he had written over the previous two years, in which he had often used reconstructions and pseudonyms.[29]

The third case involved Teresa Carpenter, the *Village Voice* reporter who received the Pulitzer Prize (the one Cooke had returned) for an article about Dennis Sweeney, the killer of Allard K. Lowenstein, published on May 12, 1980. By a 13-to-1 vote, the National News Council, a policing mechanism set up by journalists, decided that complaints about the story were warranted. The council wrote that it was "disturbed by a paragraph that reads as if Carpenter had interviewed Dennis Sweeney in his cell at Rikers Island, when in fact she had not," and said that the article was "marred by the overuse of unattributed sources, by a writing style so colored and imaginative as to blur precise meanings and by . . . reckless and speculative construction." The *Voice* stood by the article, however, and said that "Ms. Carpenter's principal sources corroborated to the National News Council's staff the material that was the subject of the complaint."[30]

The fourth case concerned a December 1981 *New York Times Magazine* article by Christopher Jones, who subsequently admitted that he had lifted quotations and an entire paragraph from *Time* magazine's dispatches and had plagiarized a passage from an André Malraux novel, *The Royal Way,* in order to fabricate a fictitious trip to southwestern Cambodia. The *Times'* executive editor, Abe Rosenthal, said: "The major mistake we made is in not following our customary procedures in showing an article in a specialized subject by any writer without outstanding credentials in the field to one of our own specialists."[31] Editorially, the *Times* commented:

> When a newspaper uses precious front-page space, as the *Times* did yesterday, to expose a lie in its own columns, it is trying to do much more than confess a

---

28. Bill Green, *Washington Post*, 19 April 1981, pp. 12–15A.

29. Michael Kramer, "Just the Facts, Please," *New York*, 25 May 1981, p. 19.

30. "News Watchdog Group Scores *Voice* Pulitzer Prize Winner," *Washington Post*, 12 June 1981, p. A2.

31. James M. Markham, "Writer Admits He Fabricated an Article in *Times Magazine*," *New York Times*, 22 February 1982, pp. 1, 4Y.

procedural lapse. The point is to reaffirm a compact with the reader: that what is printed has been honestly gathered and labeled; that any credible challenge will be rigorously examined, and that serious error will get prompt and conspicuous notice.[32]

In all these cases, the pressure to write a good story led reporters to rearrange details to meet literary requirements, to use colorful language, and to create dramatic composite characters. The praise of editors and the awarding of prizes attest to such values in journalism. Bob Woodward, the former investigative reporter who was Cooke's editorial superior at the *Post,* said simply, "This story was so well-written and tied together so well that my alarm bells simply didn't go off."[33]

Subsequently, Alastair Reid, a longtime staff writer at the *New Yorker,* described how in nonfiction articles over the years, he had invented characters, rearranged events, and composed conversations. Reid claimed that these techniques made his articles truthful in spirit, if not in detail.

Reid's views were sharply criticized by other journalists. Fred Friendly, former president of CBS News and senior program adviser at the Columbia University Graduate School of Journalism, said: "A composite is a euphemism for a lie. . . . It's dishonest, and it's not journalism." Ken Auletta, a writer for the *New Yorker,* said:

> He's wrong. It is commonly agreed that we shouldn't take shortcuts without telling the reader we're taking shortcuts, and by that I mean labeling it as fiction. We cover public officials, and we expect them to tell the truth. Journalists must abide by the same standards.[34]

Newspaper readers' advocates are press efforts to prevent and expose such practices. (The *Columbia Journalism Review* and the *Washington Journalism Review* provide forums for peer review of journalistic practices.) In June 1967 the Louisville *Courier-Journal and Times* appointed an ombudsman to serve as readers' representative in adjudicating complaints about news coverage. Such major papers as the *Washington Post* and the *Los Angeles Times* added ombudsmen to their staffs in the following years.

The title of the person performing these functions varies from paper to paper. The St. Louis *Post-Dispatch's* ombudsman is called the "reader's advocate." Other titles are public affairs editor, Mr. Go-Between, editor of action-line, and reader-contact editor.[35] Readers' advocates have regular access to space and their unedited copy is printed in a prominent place, ranging from the op-ed (opinion editorial) page to the front page. To assure their independence, their contracts

---

32. "A Lie in the *Times,*" *New York Times,* 23 February 1982, p. 26Y.

33. Bill Green, "THE STORY: First the Idea, and Finally the Presses Rolled," *Washington Post,* 19 April 1981, p. 12A.

34. Maureen Dowd, "A Writer for the *New Yorker* Says He Created Composites in Reports," *New York Times,* 19 June 1984, pp. 1, 5Y.

35. Suraj Kapoor and Ralph Smith, "The Newspaper Ombudsman—A Progress Report," *Journalism Quarterly* 56 (Autumn 1979): 629.

BOX 3-6

Who's the Press For?

In response to a Gallup Poll finding that 60 percent of respondents believed the news media to be "out of touch with average Americans," Mark Jurkowitz of the *Boston Globe* came up with six ways to get back in touch:

1. *Make politics relevant to the readers*—give information about the campaign matters related to their lives, in language they can understand.
2. *Cut down on the cynicism*—go beyond the negative and confrontational news only.
3. *Make newsrooms diverse*—this includes not only racial, ethnic, and religious diversity, but also political and geographical.
4. *Avoid media celebrity*—the opinions reporters give freely at paid speaking engagements and on Sunday morning talk shows compromise their journalistic integrity in the eyes of the public.
5. *Open up the factory*—let the public know how the press works and why it is important. Admit mistakes. Allow more media criticism.
6. *Initiate news councils*—follow the lead of the Minnesota News Council, which "adjudicates disputes between citizens and the local media."

"The most crucial task facing the American press," says Jukowitz, "is convincing the public that it's on their side."

Mark Jurkowitz, "Six Ways to Reform the Media," *The Boston Globe Magazine,* 9 July, 1995, p. 18.

typically protect them from pressure and stipulate fixed terms of employment. A survey of eighteen ombudsmen revealed that they have significant reportorial experience, are well-educated, professionally active, and did not apply but were sought out for the job by the newspapers' editors.[36] In 1995, thirty-six of the nation's newspapers had ombudsmen, said John V. R. Bull, the *Philadelphia Inquirer*'s ombudsman and associate editor.

"In the recent past, too many in American journalism have been indifferent to—even contemptuous of—those who buy their newspapers. That doesn't serve anyone, in the newsroom or outside it," wrote Henry McNulty, former reader representative of the *Hartford Courant*. "As with so much else in this business, the trick is to walk a fine line. We must listen to our subscribers but not pander to them; understand their point of view but reject their prejudices; be apart from any one philosophy but not aloof from the common wisdom."[37]

Confidence in the press has been dropping. According to an April 1994 Gallup poll on Confidence in Institutions, 29 percent of the respondents said they

---

36. Ibid., pp. 629–630.
37. Phil Record, "It's Not Just Me, I See; Other Ombudsmen Have Concerns, Too," *Fort Worth Star-Telegram*, 7 May 1995, p. C6.

had "a great deal" or "quite a lot" of confidence in newspapers. This is down from the 31 percent of the year before and represents an all-time Gallup low for this question.[38] In the period from 1973 to 1993, confidence in the people running the press dropped from 23 to 11 percent. Other institutions experienced a drop as well, with Congress falling from 24 to 7 percent. During this time, however, confidence in the military rose from 32 to 42 percent.[39]

News Analysis

Television reporting is less likely than print reporting to provide in-depth analysis, establish historical context, or probe for causes. And specialized print media are more likely than daily newspapers to deal in detail with complex stories. So, for example, the *National Thrift News* carried reports of the brewing savings and loan crisis long before that story surfaced in the large dailies. Similarly, medical journals, such as the *New England Journal of Medicine,* carry detailed reports of studies of the impact of diet on health, which include the limitations on conclusions to be drawn from them. In contrast, reports in newspapers are written by nonexperts, and they tend to simplify these results, omit the limitations, and confuse readers who read reports of apparently contradictory studies and cannot decide what kinds of changes in their diets might really make a difference.[40]

Like print journalism, television news tries to present good stories. In many situations, television handles the breaking stories responsibly. However, the conventions of the medium make it difficult, if not impossible, for television news to analyze or probe the complex causes of events. When that kind of analysis appears, it is likely to be in print news.

Media Convergence

The impact of elite media outlets also can distort news coverage. For example, the sudden increase in media attention to drug use in summer 1986 was not merely a reflection of real-world happenings. Although drug use steadily increased during the 1970s, among high school seniors and young adults it actually declined between 1981 and 1986. (Most of the decline was in usage of marijuana; cocaine use remained steady.)[41]

---

38. George Gallup, Jr., *The Gallup Poll: Public Opinion 1994* (Wilmington: Scholarly Resources Inc., 1995), p. 58.

39. Timothy J. Conlan, "Federal, State, or Local? Trends in the Public's Judgment," *The Public Perspective,* January/February 1993, p. 4.

40. Lena Williams, "Studies on Diet Add to Confusion," *New York Times,* October 11, 1995, pp. B1, B7.

41. Peter Kerr, *New York Times*, 17 November 1986, pp. 1, 12.

Using data from forty-three Gallup polls reporting what Americans considered the "most important problem facing America today," Pamela Shoemaker, Wayne Wanta, and Dawn Leggett correlated public concern about drugs with fifteen years of drug coverage in three newspapers (*New York Times, Los Angeles Times,* and *Wall Street Journal*); on three networks (ABC, CBS, and NBC) and in three newsweeklies (*Time, Newsweek,* and *U.S. News & World Report*). Newspaper coverage, especially in the *New York Times* and the *Los Angeles Times,* turned out to be the best predictor of public opinion.[42]

In studying this issue, researchers developed the concept of intermedia "convergence" to describe "a process whereby the media discover issues and respond to each other in a cycle of peaking coverage." Convergence occurs most frequently when elite media discover the issue or when the story comes from the nation's capital, especially if an issue is stressed by national leaders such as the president.[43]

Unbalanced Interpretation

For years, media scholars have studied the discrepancies between events as experienced live and events as presented on television. In 1953, Gladys Engel Lang and Kurt Lang, for example, contrasted the Douglas MacArthur Day Parade as experienced by observers on the streets of Chicago with the parade as experienced via television.[44] Television dramatized the parade and exaggerated crowd responses, perhaps because television had created expectations for what the parade would be like.

The discrepancies persist. In July 1986, seventy-four evening news segments on drugs were broadcast by the three major news networks. Half of these dealt with the use of crack. In the fall of that year, CBS earned the highest Nielsen ratings of any comparable show in five years by reaching 15 million viewers with a documentary, the title: "48 Hours on Crack Street." Yet, as sociologists Craig Reinarman and Henry Levine noted in 1989, "For every one cocaine-related death in the U.S. in 1987, there were approximately 300 tobacco-related deaths and 100 alcohol-related deaths."

How then does one account for over fifteen hours of airtime and over 1,000 print stories on crack that flooded across the United States in the seven months prior to the 1986 elections? Analysts concluded that "the issue conveniently

---

42. "Drug Coverage and Public Opinion, 1972–1986," in *Communication Campaigns about Drugs: Government, Media, and the Public,* ed. Pamela J. Shoemaker (Hillsdale, N.J.: Lawrence Erlbaum, 1989), pp. 67–80.
43. Lucig H. Danielian and Stephen D. Reese, "A Closer Look at Intermedia Influences on Agenda Setting: The Cocaine Issue of 1986," in Shoemaker, pp. 57–58.
44. Gladys Engel Lang and Kurt Lang, "MacArthur Day in Chicago," *Politics and Television* (Chicago: Quadrangle Books, 1968), pp. 36–77.

served the interests of the media and politicians because it was dramatic, it afforded many opportunities for political posturing, and it reinforced stereotypes that minority groups (scapegoats) engage in deviant activities because they are fundamentally weak, uneducated, or immoral."[45]

On July 17, 1995, MTV inaugurated *MTV News Unfiltered,* a program designed to let individuals tell their stories from their own points of view. "You shot it. We air it," said host Alison Stewart on the first show. "This time if it sucks, it's your fault." Potential contributors are invited to call or send a proposal by mail, e-mail, or fax. Those selected receive a videocamera and explanatory tape. Editors pare down and polish the usable stories. The first program included an account of a househusband who objected to the absence of changing tables in men's rooms. Their absence prompted him to change his son's diaper in places such as public benches. The program also included a story by a young woman with breast cancer, a student who graduated from college in drag, and skateboarders who reported being hassled by police. This is a kind of public access television on a commercial outlet.

Insinuation

On May 6, 1990, *Washington Post* ombudsman Richard Harwood wrote that his paper's "shabby" coverage of an April 28 pro-life rally at the nation's capitol "has left a blot on this paper's professional reputation." The paper had extensively covered a pro-choice rally of approximately 125,000 the previous year. The pro-life rally of 200,000 (the crowd numbers are police estimates) was given only two short articles. The dozens of stories on the pro-choice rally had featured charts and maps and appeared on page one. The pro-life rally received no comparable attention. How did the *Post* account for the lapse? Staffers were aware of one rally and not the other. Wrote Harwood of Managing Editor Leonard Downie, "Journalists here, he [Downie] thinks, not only are not part of the anti-abortion movement but don't know anyone who is." The conservative Center for Media and Public Affairs provided another possible explanation. Stories filed in the *New York Times* and the *Washington Post* by female reporters quoted nearly three times more pro-choice sources than pro-life ones.

Following the *Post*'s lead, David Shaw of the *Los Angeles Times* wrote a four-part series arguing that Harwood was correct. Shaw's series pointed out that protesters are frequently described as militant or asked by television producers to "look angry" to fit the stereotypes of sound bites. The controversy also prompted an analysis of the biases of language. *U.S. News & World Report*'s John Leo wrote:

> About a year ago, I noticed that one of our major metropolitan newspapers had taken to using "abortion provider" as a neutral term in reporting the abortion debate. It is not neutral. "Abortion practitioner" and "doctor who performs abortions" are neutral terms. "Provider," with its overtones of nurturance and protec-

45. Charles T. Salmon, "God Understands When the Cause Is Noble," *Gannett Center Journal* (Spring 1990): 26.

tion, is a one-word argument in favor of abortion, just as "abortionist" with its overtones of back-alley sleaze, is a polemic against it.[46]

(As noted in a later chapter, all language choices are selective.)

Unbalanced interpretations also result from quite subtle inequities in press treatment. Coverage of the 1984 presidential campaign mentioned Democratic vice-presidential nominee Geraldine Ferraro's dress size but not nominee Walter Mondale's suit size; and in 1988, Barbara Bush was characterized as "grandmotherly," but George Bush was not described as grandfatherly; her white hair was noted, but his graying hair was not.

Senator Nancy Landon Kassebaum (R-Kan.) also is bothered by the way women politicians are described in the media. "Some day I'm going to hit someone over the head for calling me diminutive and soft-spoken."[47] Such insinuations may reflect prejudices in the society. Newsworthy women tend to be identified by their clothing, degree of attractiveness, size, and whether or not they are married and have children, whereas newsworthy men are not. Similarly, African Americans are more likely than whites to be identified by race. Sensitive to charges by women's rights and civil rights groups, editors have begun to change these practices in recent years.

In these cases, unbalanced interpretations result from insinuations, from the choice of language, and from the ways in which stories are routinely covered. But a case can be made that news coverage is unbalanced precisely because it develops certain themes and perspectives and suppresses others.

Ideological Bias

A common criticism of the media, especially the East Coast-based, nationally circulated *New York Times* and *Washington Post,* is that their reporting has a definite slant left of center.

Feeling this bias to have been reflected in his treatment by the press, the new Chairman of the Senate Foreign Relations Committee, Jesse Helms, wrote a response to written questions:

Q: Do you feel that you have been taken seriously as a lawmaker?
A: Absolutely—and primarily by the ultra-liberal newspapers such as the *Washington Post*. Otherwise the *Post* would not have gone to such pains to discredit me. . . .
Q: Because the chairmanship is such a high-profile position, will you be more conscious, if not restrained, about the public comments you make?
A: I'll be at least as restrained as a U.S. senator as the *Washington Post* is as a newspaper. As a matter of fact, except for your exaggerated and unjustified criticism of those with whom you have disagreed down through the years, you would today have no basis for asking such a loaded question.[48]

---

46. "Is the Press Straight on Abortion?" *U.S. News & World Report*, 16 July 1990, p. 17.
47. Bella Abzug, *Gender Gap* (Boston: Houghton Mifflin, 1984), p. 171.
48. John Monk, *Philadelphia Inquirer*, "Helms Lashes Out Over Reporter's Questions," 22 January 1995, p. A7.

The most controversial claims about distortions in news coverage are made by some contemporary sociologists and researchers who have studied the mass media intensively. They do not argue that there is a conspiracy or willful distortion in reporting and coverage. Instead, they argue that, however unintentionally, press coverage is ideological, that it reflects and promotes the interests of some groups and classes and not others, that it conceals the interrelationship between the public and the private sector, and that, in the words of *New York Times* columnist Tom Wicker, "objective journalism always favors Establishment positions and exists not least to avoid offense of them."[49]

Without a laborious reconstruction of the social and political theory underlying these claims, one example may explain this. The author is the former British journalist Henry Fairlie:

> A few years ago I attended one of these pompous week-long seminars at the Aspen Institute to discuss "investigative reporting" with a number of celebrated American editors and newspapermen. I made my point that there was an economic system that needed inquiry, and at last burst out against the imperviousness of my American colleagues by saying that I would write without payment for them a series of articles to be entitled, "I Have an Enemy at Chase Manhattan." But there were no takers; and Walter Ridder, the owner of Ridder newspapers, made a very funny speech on the final morning of the seminar, saying that he had tossed and turned all night "wondering why we don't do what Henry asks, and attack the capitalists," and that as dawn had broken across the Rockies he had found the answer: "Because I am one of them."[50]

The conclusions of researchers are remarkably similar. Erik Barnouw, a distinguished media historian, contends that commercial sponsors control all facets of television content from advertising itself to news and cultural programming on so-called public broadcasting.[51] Mark Fishman argues that the journalist's view of society is bureaucratically structured and, by definition, bureaucracies reflect the establishment—government and private corporations.[52] The Glasgow University Media Group documents a bias in favor of the powerful. Michael Schudson, a social historian, argues "that the process of news gathering itself constructs an image of reality which reinforces official viewpoints."[53] Gaye Tuchman not only contends that the news reflects the interests of those in power, but also that the news limits our knowledge of our own society.[54]

If these researchers and analysts are correct, news coverage will be informed by certain perspectives with ideological significance. First, and most important,

---

49. Wicker, *On Press* (New York: Viking, 1978), pp. 36–37.

50. Henry Fairlie, "Profit Without Honor," *New Republic* (7 May 1977): 17–18.

51. Erik Barnouw, *The Sponsor: Notes on a Modern Potentate* (New York: Oxford, 1978).

52. Mark Fishman, *Manufacturing the News* (Austin: University of Texas Press, 1980).

53. Michael Schudson, *Discovering the News: A Social History of American Newspapers* (New York: Basic Books, 1978), p. 185.

54. Tuchman, *Making News*, p. 210; elsewhere she writes of "television programming that reflects and reinforces the economic and socio-political structure of the United States" ["Introduction," *The TV Establishment: Programming for Power and Profit*, ed. Gaye Tuchman (Englewood Cliffs, N.J.: Prentice-Hall-Spectrum, 1974), p. 6].

BOX 3-7

Media Coverage Influences Foreign Policy

On August 21, 1983, opposition leader Benigno Aquino was assassinated as he arrived in Manila by plane from the United States. This dramatic, violent, public event focused media and public attention on political events in the Philippines, an important site for the United States because the Philippines had been a U.S. colony and because U.S. naval and air force bases are there.

As pressure grew on Ferdinand Marcos, the Philippine president, on November 3, 1985, he announced on U.S. television that an election would be held in mid-January 1986 and invited U.S. poll watchers to verify the fairness of the election. This second event, the announced election and campaign, a contest between Marcos and widow Corazon Aquino, to be refereed by Americans, heightened U.S. public and media interest.

Prior to these events, there had been little coverage of events there. The major U.S. networks' evening news programs had devoted fewer than three stories per year to the Philippines earlier, but one survey of the four weeks following Marcos's election announcement charted 180 minutes of coverage. "The Western media simply seized the Philippine election campaign and carried it for days at a time—with the full cooperation of both candidates."[a]

The election became headline news in newspapers, NBC and ABC anchored their evening news programs from the Philippines, and CBS sent its entire election polling team. Television cameras showed Marcos's thugs intimidating poll watchers, stealing ballots, and murdering opposition campaign workers. It was the sort of human story that viewers could appreciate: a story of unlikely heroes who formed human barricades against Marcos's soldiers and included nuns who knelt in front of tanks and recited the rosary and girls who offered flowers to soldiers— a kind of "fairy tale revolution" with a "fairy-tale heroine" [Corazon Aquino] and a happy ending.[b] In a Gallup poll in March, 76 percent of Americans said they had followed the dramatic events of February 1986 in the Philippines very or fairly closely.[c]

Although the Reagan administration continued to support Marcos, Americans were so aware of what was occurring that, as one commentator concluded, "Reagan lost much of the latitude a President has to fashion foreign policy."[d]

[a]Bryan Johnson, *The Four Days of Courage: The Untold Story of the People Who Brought Marcos Down* (New York: Free Press, 1987), pp. 91, 92.
[b]Pico Iyer, "Woman of the Year: Cory," *Time*, 4 January 1987, p. 19.
[c]*The Gallup Report*, March 1986, 246 (Princeton, N.J.: Gallup Poll, 1986), p. 16.
[d]Stewart Powell, "Playing to the TV Cameras," *U.S. News & World Report*, 10 March 1986, p. 33.

we should expect the news to tell us repeatedly that "the system works," a major theme, for example, of Watergate coverage or of the Iran-Contra arms scandal. There is evidence of such a perspective in newsgathering. Newscasts, for instance, underscore the legitimacy of the three branches of government by treating each as an identifiable entity engaged in proposing and disposing, as in the phrase "the Congress today . . . ," and television routinely covers the rituals of government, such as swearing-in ceremonies, inaugurals, welcoming addresses, and press conferences, that reinforce our sense of governmental process.

We are told not only that the system works, but that those who disrupt it in strikes or social protest are wrong or deviant—a bias that will always favor the status quo over change. Coverage of the problems of the homeless is illustrative. Researchers have found that the homeless are consistently portrayed as psychotic, disordered, and not like us. This perspective carries the corollary that "we could not be like them." As one sociologist explains:

> The notion that the homeless are largely psychotics who belong in institutions, rather than victims of displacement at the hands of enterprising realtors, spares us from the need to offer realistic solutions to the fact of deep and widening extremes of wealth and poverty in the United States. It also enables us to tell ourselves that the despair of homeless people bears no intimate connection to the privileged existence we enjoy—when, for example, we rent or purchase one of those restored townhouses that once provided shelter for people now huddled in the street.[55]

The difficulty with the view that the homeless are psychotic is that it doesn't comport with what surveys tell us about that population: "[M]ost current studies consider the mentally ill to account only for 20 to 25 percent of the total homeless population, with some estimates as low as 16 percent."[56]

Some researchers argue that news coverage systematically supports the powers that be. We have summarized their conclusions and some of the supporting evidence, but the argument also claims there is systematic self-censorship within the media, a form of internal regulation that denies the audience access to certain types of information and that mirrors the tastes of mass audiences and advertisers.

Self-Censorship

In the face of almost nightly reports of high oil company profits in 1980, Mobil sponsored an ad arguing that the profits of the networks exceeded the profits of the oil industry. All three networks refused to air it. This sort of censorship of material about media issues accompanies the self-censoring suppression of coverage of media issues on newscasts.[57] In fact, corporate struggles to air advocacy advertising on television confront the most pervasive form of self-censorship in the medium.[58]

---

55. J. Kozol, "Distancing the Homeless," *Yale Review* 77 (1986): 154–155.

56. Richard Campbell and Jimmie L. Reves, "Covering the Homeless: The Joyce Brown Story," *Critical Studies in Mass Communication* 6 (1989): 22.

57. Thomas R. Lindlof and William R. Canning, "Network News Coverage of the Broadcast Media," *Journalism Quarterly* 57 (Summer 1980): 333–338.

58. For information on issue or advocacy advertising by large corporations, see S. Prakash Sethi, *Up Against the Corporate Wall: Modern Corporations and Social Issues of the Seventies* (Englewood Cliffs, N.J.: Prentice-Hall, 1971) and *Advocacy Advertising and Large Corporations* (Lexington, Mass.: Lexington Books, 1977). In 1981, ABC accepted some issue advertising on *Nightline* on an experimental basis.

BOX 3-8

National Empowerment Television (NET)

The Free Congress Foundation, a conservative group, has launched the nation's first public affairs channel with a declared ideological spin. The channel is intended to make conservative political views a fixture of popular culture. Burton Pines, host of *Capitol Watch* and the vice chairman of NET, says: "We're going to speak to those Americans who feel they have a grievance with Washington. . . . We're going to empower Americans to hold Washington more accountable." Because the Fairness Doctrine requiring broadcasters to present opposing viewpoints on public affairs was dropped during the Reagan administration, NET does not appear to have a legal obligation to present opposing political views. NET plans to offer programming twenty-four hours a day, seven days a week.

The channel is registered as a nonprofit organization, but is still allowed to sell advertising to support its operations.[a]

[a]Elizabeth Kolbert, "And Now, All-Ideology TV, with All Talk Conservative," *New York Times*, 27 November 1993, pp. A1, A7.

The Fairness Doctrine   In 1987, the Federal Communications Commission (FCC) repealed the forty-year-old Fairness Doctrine on the grounds that it was no longer needed. In an era in which there were numerous voices in broadcasting, the public interest no longer required the doctrine, argued the Reagan-appointed commissioners. A federal appeals court subsequently ruled that the FCC had the right to eliminate the doctrine. Since then there have been several unsuccessful attempts in Congress to revive it.

The Fairness Doctrine required radio and television stations to air material on issues of public concern and to air opposing views on them. If opposing views were not broadcast, a person representing the ignored view could request response time.

Beats   Self-censorship also occurs as a result of the relationship between reporters and the sources who provide information on their beats. A symbiotic relationship develops between reporters and sources on a beat, with the result that stories having political implications may be suppressed. Reporters "can make news out of inside information that aids an agency in its competition with other agencies or helps it get its message into the White House, but they cannot so easily propose stories that can hurt the agency. Consequently, beat reporters must often practice self-censorship, keeping their most sensational stories to themselves in order to protect their beat."[59]

Reporter Seymour Hersh won a Pulitzer Prize in 1970 for his stories on the My Lai massacre. When he was asked to account for why editors missed one of

---

59. Herbert Gans, *Deciding What's News: A Study of CBS Evening News, NBC Evening News, Newsweek, and Time* (New York: Pantheon, 1979), p. 133.

the biggest stories of the year, he responded, "I honestly believe that a major problem in newspapers today is not censorship on the part of editors and publishers, but something more odious: self-censorship by the reporters."[60] Because Hersh was only able to write the story with the help of Army sources who leaked crucial information, it is possible that reporters who had to maintain good relations with Army sources felt unable to write this damaging story.

Government Support   Some self-censorship involves a predisposition to support the government line. For example, the press accepted the White House explanation that the U-2 shot down over Russia in 1959 was really a weather plane and later accepted the Johnson administration's claim that a U.S. ship had been attacked in the Gulf of Tonkin. In both instances, administration officials were lying.

The press is particularly vulnerable to government claims that revealing certain information would not be in the national interest. As former White House correspondent David Wise explains, "When the flag is attacked, or reporters are told it has been attacked, their reaction is not likely to be very different from that of any other citizen. Besides, it is vaguely unpatriotic to dispute the official version of events."[61]

Even unusual opportunities for newsgathering may be rejected on such grounds. As media historian Michael Schudson reports, "In 1956 American newspapers refused a Chinese government invitation to send correspondents to China because, as *New York Times* editor Clifton Daniel recalled, 'We did not want to embarrass our government.'"[62] Stories from China at that time would have been highly newsworthy, but this was the height of the Cold War.

The 1986 trial of a government worker charged with spying illustrates the ways in which government encourages self-censorship by the media. Ronald Pelton worked on a computer job at the National Security Agency for fourteen years. His job gave him access to secret government information. After Pelton left the NSA in 1979, he began selling secrets to the Russians. He was caught and brought to trial in 1986.

Then-CIA director William Casey was alarmed to hear on NBC's *Today* show that the spy had apparently given "away one of the NSA's most sensitive secrets—a project with the code name Ivy Bells, believed to be a top-secret underwater eavesdropping operation by American submarines inside Soviet harbors." Casey asked the Justice Department to consider prosecuting NBC under Section 798 of Title 18 of the U.S. Code, which forbids the revelation of classified information about secret codes and other communications intelligence. Meanwhile the *Washington Post* began its own coverage of the trial.

---

60. Seymour Hersh, "The Story Everyone Ignored," *Columbia Journalism Review* 8 (Winter 1969–1970): 55.

61. David Wise, *The Politics of Lying* (New York: Random House, 1973), p. 311. See also David Halberstam, "A Letter to My Daughter," *Parade*, 2 May 1982, pp. 4–7.

62. Schudson, *Discovering the News*, p. 173.

The *Post*'s coverage was the product of self-censorship. Casey had met with the editors to warn of possible prosecution. The meeting resulted in delaying a major article. President Ronald Reagan called Katherine Graham of the *Post* to stress the sensitive nature of the trial and to warn that he would back prosecution of the *Post* if the material Pelton had transmitted to the Soviets was revealed. The *Post* responded by withholding the controversial details. *Post* editor Benjamin Bradlee explained that the paper had been "unable fully to judge the validity of the national security objections of senior officials." He added "In my heart, I think the Russians already know what we kept out of the story. But I'm not absolutely sure."[63]

Support for government policies can emerge in more subtle forms. During the crisis that followed Iraq's invasion of Kuwait and the deployment of U.S. troops in Saudi Arabia, for example, some commentators pointed out that far more of those interviewed by journalists supported the government's policy than raised questions about its rationales or costs. On August 21, 1990, for example, Ted Koppel's primary guest on *Nightline* was Undersecretary of Defense Paul Wolfowitz, who was followed by John Lehman, secretary of the Navy in the Reagan administration, and Edward Luttwak, a military analyst. After describing the discussion that followed, which ignored Iraq's insistence that it has a historic claim to Kuwait—a nation created by the British as its protectorate—and which touted U.S. military strength and described Iraqi leader Saddam Hussein as insane, television analyst Noel Holston commented:

> What happened, or didn't happen, on *Nightline* is a perfect example of what watchdog groups such as Fairness and Accuracy in Reporting (FAIR) have complained about for years. On TV news and issue programs, debate and discussion too often begin at an official level where the range of options has already been decided. And they stay within narrow parameters because journalists such as Koppel allow it. They shouldn't, however, even if they run the risk of alienating their sources or some members of their audience by asking hard questions and appearing skeptical or unpatriotic (as if asking elected public officials to be forthright and accountable is unpatriotic).[64]

Holston was referring to a report released early in 1989 in which FAIR alleged a bias on ABC's *Nightline* based on who was and who was not invited as an expert participant on the central 20-minute discussion each night. As reported by its executive director Jeff Cohen, FAIR studied 865 programs with 2,498 guests and concluded that one's likelihood of appearing as a guest was enhanced by being a white male member of conservative government, military, or corporate elites. *Nightline* spokespersons responded that conservatives dominated the guest list because they have been in power lately, and that if a liberal administration were elected, the bias would shift in the other direction, a defense that FAIR

---

63. *Time*, 2 June 1986, p. 67.
64. Noel Holston, "TV Ducking the Hard Questions on Mideast," *Star Tribune*, 24 August 1990, p. 7E.

saw as self-incriminating because it presented the news program as a forum for those currently in power.[65]

In some cases, journalists also are hampered by formal types of governmental censorship. The examination reports of bank regulators, for example, are not available under the Freedom of Information Act because Congress fears that making such data available to the press and public could cause runs on banks. The inaccessibility of such data made it more difficult for reporters to document the existence of banks whose loans were undercapitalized. This made the early stages of the savings and loan crisis more difficult to cover.

Journalistic self-censorship can reflect audience tastes as well as prevailing political views.

Audience Taste The success of recent efforts by the Coalition for Better Television and the Moral Majority to pressure advertisers and the networks to eliminate sex and violence from television programming reflects the desire of television not to offend audience tastes. (See Chapter 9 for more extended treatment of how groups and individuals can influence the media.) The pressure of the audience is illustrated by coverage of racial matters. Paul Good argues that "television found it both spiritually rewarding and financially profitable to cover racism *so long as it was treated as a southern, not a national phenomenon.*"[66] His statement shows that the civil rights confrontations of the 1960s were dramatic and exciting news that, when confined to the South, were not perceived as an attack on the system.

Some contend that current coverage of racism, or lack of it, however, reflects a desire to avoid offending the white-majority audience. Media analyst Edwin Diamond describes the conditions of African Americans as "a story that many white Americans in the audience may not want to dwell upon too long, out of fear, or doubt, or guilt, or a combination of largely unexamined emotions."[67] The racially divided reactions to the not guilty verdict in the O. J. Simpson murder trial reflect wide disparities in how whites and African Americans see the world. Poll results also suggest that large numbers of whites are mistaken about basic facts about African Americans, believing that they are a larger percentage of the population (they are only 12 percent) and believing that they have made economic gains such that they have reached near parity with whites (they earn on average only 60 percent of what whites earn).[68]

The same pattern occurred in network coverage of gay rights. Once this identified audience was demonstrated to be large enough to have economic clout, networks began to respond to its sensitivities. So, for example, on February 8, 1990, CBS News suspended *60 Minutes* commentator Andy Rooney for three months

65. Jeff Cohen, "ABC's *Nightline* Serves as a Soapbox for Conservative Elite," *Star Tribune*, 28 February 1989, p. 11A.

66. Paul Good, "Is Network News Slighting the Minorities?" *TV Guide*, 5 March 1977, p. 5.

67. Edwin Diamond, "Miami Riots: Did TV Get the Real Story?" *TV Guide*, 30 August 1980, p. 20.

68. Richard Moon, *Washington Post* reprinted in *Star Tribune*, 9 October 1995, pp. A1, A9.

without pay. The action followed complaints by the 10,000-member Gay and Lesbian Alliance Against Defamation. The alliance charged that in his syndicated columns, on air, and in a letter to the *Advocate,* a gay rights publication, Rooney had made insensitive remarks about gays. But after suspending Rooney, counterpressures arose from viewers and columnists. Under the counterpressure, CBS reduced the suspension from three months to three weeks.[69]

It is, of course, very difficult to demonstrate the existence of self-censorship because much of the evidence involves the absence or omission of coverage. In addition, much of the evidence will be anecdotal reports of examples from which it is difficult to generalize. Nevertheless, as we indicate, there are powerful pressures for self-censorship and some evidence that news coverage is responsive to them.

Direct Intervention

In this final section, we detail the most extreme examples of persuasion by the news media, which involve direct intervention by journalists in news events. With few exceptions they reflect audience acceptance of journalistic participation in the events that are covered.

Breaches of Neutrality

One of the more outrageous examples of direct journalistic intervention was reported in a series of articles in the *Toronto Globe*. As other news sources have verified, a 1981 invasion of the Caribbean island of Dominica was planned by American and Canadian mercenaries and members of the Ku Klux Klan and neo-Nazi groups. According to the *Globe*'s investigative reporter Peter Moon, "details of the operation had been known for months by the Toronto radio station CFTR, which had taped interviews with participants and planned to be on the island for the invasion. The articles quoted Robert Halliday, CFTR's news director, as saying, 'If we'd gone to the police, we'd have had to work alongside them, and then we wouldn't have had the story.'"[70]

The viewing public is not prepared to accept such breaches of journalistic neutrality in the effort to get a good story. However, viewers are prepared to tolerate considerable intervention when they approve of the goals the journalist is promoting.

---

69. Jeremy Gerard, "Hurting Words, Fighting Words," *Columbia Journalism Review* (July/August 1990): 25.

70. Andrew H. Malcolm, "Toronto Paper Recounts Intrigue to Invade Dominica," *New York Times*, 17 May 1981, p. A4.

Producing Social Change

In recent decades, we have witnessed instances in which reporters were instrumental in producing social change. Bob Woodward and Carl Bernstein of the *Washington Post* uncovered many of the abuses that ultimately led to the resignation of President Richard Nixon, for example.

But not all influential investigative reporting is done by major newspapers or the networks. Lea Thompson, a consumer reporter for the Washington, D.C., affiliate of NBC, WRC-TV, was responsible for legislation mandating standards for infant formulas. Two infant formulas, Mul-Soy and Cho-Free, were missing a necessary dietary supplement, so infants fed this formula became seriously ill. The Food and Drug Administration recalled these formulas, but Thompson discovered that they were still stocked in Washington area stores.

From October 1979 to March 1980, WRC pursued the story, which was eventually carried on *NBC Nightly News* (access was made easier by WRC's status as an NBC affiliate). Members of Congress and President Carter thanked Thompson for bringing the need for stricter standards for infant formula production to the attention of Congress, and Thompson was an invited guest at the ceremony at which Carter signed the standards bill into law.

In summer 1990, news coverage was responsible for action by law enforcement agencies against puppy farms. After the television shows *20/20* and *Geraldo* broadcast indictments of the pet-breeding industry, and the Humane Society of the United States called for a national boycott of puppies bred in six midwestern states, enforcement agents in those states began cracking down. The Kansas attorney general led a raid on a Topeka kennel, seized ninety dogs, and charged their breeders with cruelty to animals. Local newspapers took up the call. "Puppy breeding should be an ideal industry for Kansas," said the Wichita *Eagle*. "This state's image for Midwestern wholesomeness could be an invaluable marketing tool. Imagine the lines at pet stores in California and other states for puppies 'raised where Toto comes from.'"[71]

Journalists as Direct Participants

In some instances, journalists have become direct participants, not merely participant-observers, in news stories. It was Walter Cronkite, for example, not a State Department official, who made Premier Anwar Sadat's trip to Israel in 1977 possible.

On September 6, 1990, CBS News moved explicitly into an advocacy posture in a 2-hour prime-time documentary titled "America's Toughest Assignment," a report on U.S. education. The program was complemented that week by special segments on all of CBS's regular news broadcasts including *Sunday Morning, 60 Minutes, CBS This Morning*, and *The CBS Evening News with Dan Rather*. On

---

71. "Dogs from 'Puppy Mills' Jam Midwestern Shelters," *Philadelphia Inquirer*, 31 July 1990, p. 6A.

BOX 3-9

Terrorism and the Press

Terrorists often seek publicity, and to that end they try to use the press. Few have been as successful as the mail bomb terrorist called the "Unabomber," who was able to induce the *New York Times* and the *Washington Post,* two of the more prestigious newspapers in the country, to publish his 35,000-word manifesto calling for a world revolution against modern technology. The eight-page insert was published in the *Post* on September 19, 1995, with both papers sharing the estimated $30,000 to $40,000 cost.

In 1978 the Unabomber began his campaign against modern industrial society by mailing bombs to university faculty associated with computer sciences or genetics. In 16 attacks, 23 have been injured and 3 killed. The writer of the manifesto promised to stop killing if the papers cooperated by publishing his work (and additional annual manifestos for the next three years).[a]

In a joint statement on their decision to publish, Donald Graham, publisher of the *Washington Post,* and Arthur Sulzberger, publisher of the *New York Times,* said that they had for three months pondered the problem of publishing "under the threat of violence," and, on the recommendation of the Attorney General and the Director of the FBI, had decided to accede to the Unabomber's demands for "public safety reasons."[b]

Not everyone thought the right decision had been made. The chairman of NYU's Department of Journalism and Mass Communication called it a "shameful episode" on two counts. Not only had the publishers given in to the demands of a terrorist, but they had also let the press be directed by the government.[c]

[a]Howard Kurtz, *Washington Post,* 19 September 1995, p. A1.
[b]Donald E. Graham and Arthur Sulzberger, Jr., *New York Times,* 19 September, 1995, p. B7.
[c]William Serrin, *Washington Post,* 24 September, 1995, p. C3.

September 6, at 11:30 P.M. (EST), a live 1-hour national exchange among parents, teachers, and education experts was aired. Said CBS correspondent Charles Kuralt, the documentary's anchor, "We're actually going to be advocates for certain changes. We are going to tell America what needs to be done."[72] The proposed changes were rooted in the recommendations of Dr. Ernest Boyer, president of the Carnegie Foundation for the Advancement of Teaching and an adviser to CBS News's Project Education. The proposals included transforming kindergarten through fourth grade into a concentrated four-year program focused on basic reading, writing, and math skills.

Neither the CBS educational initiative nor Cronkite's efforts to mediate in the Middle East drew criticism because both were consistent with bipartisan national goals and with ends approved by the U.S. public. Who, after all, opposes peace or excellence in education?

---

72. Diane Mermigas, "CBS News Takes on 'Project Education,'" *Electronic Media,* 16 July 1990, p. 16.

When their actions are not in agreement with such broad public and political consensus, journalists are criticized for becoming advocates. During coverage of the TWA hostage crisis in Lebanon, Dan Rather's pointed on-air questioning of Nabih Berri, the Islamic leader ostensibly trying to negotiate release of the hostages, prompted criticism that Rather had crossed the dividing line between journalism and personal diplomacy.

Journalists also draw criticism when they appear to be channels of propaganda for those whose views are widely condemned by the public and the politicians in the United States. "Checkbook journalism," the practice of paying for an interview, is frowned on by most reputable news organizations. In spring 1986, a related practice generated controversy in the news community. On May 5, *NBC Nightly News* featured an interview with Mohammed Abul Abbas, the terrorist suspected of planning the hijacking of the cruise ship *Achille Lauro* in October 1985. During that hijacking, a wheelchair-ridden American, Leon Klinghoffer, was killed and his body dumped overboard. Abbas had offered NBC an exclusive interview with the condition that the correspondent and crew not identify the location of the interview. During the meeting, Abbas stated that the United States was now the target of his efforts because "America is now conducting the war against us on behalf of Israel."

NBC News was careful to announce that it was not paying O. J. Simpson for a planned exclusive one-hour interview on *Dateline NBC* on October 11, 1995. Hostile audience reaction to the interview, protests by the National Organization for Women and other groups, and withdrawal of advertising by advertisers reflected the controversy aroused by this news coup. Because of advertiser resistance, NBC expected to lose $2 million in the short run from airing the interview, but the very high ratings that the interview would probably have garnered would have offset these losses. By not paying Simpson, NBC treated the planned interview as a news event.[73] On the advice of his lawyers on the day of the scheduled interview, Simpson backed out.

Intervention by the media becomes even more controversial when the media intervention benefits one person but, in the process, harms another. When officials at the Loma Linda University Medical Center refused to consider an infant for a heart transplant on the grounds that his unwed parents could not provide adequate postoperative care, the couple took their case to the media. "Baby Jesse" appeared in stories on the three major networks and in the nation's newspapers. While the couple was being interviewed on *Donahue*, a Michigan couple, whose son was brain dead at birth, agreed to donate their infant's heart to Jesse, whose story they had seen on television.

What the television coverage failed to reveal was that another infant had been waiting even longer for a heart transplant, but his parents had worked quietly through organ procurement channels instead of turning to the press for sympathy and help. After learning that Jesse had received the heart, the disappointed couple appealed through the media to Congress to "do everything possible to see

---

73. Bill Carter, "Simpson Deal Causing Angst Inside NBC and Out," *New York Times,* 11 October 1995, pp. A1, C19.

that an improved system is set up to identify donors of organs." They added, "it almost seems like publicity is the only method that's working." *Time* magazine commented, "Another ethical issue was brought to light by the baby Jesse case: the growing role of the media in determining who gets organs."[74]

The Civic Journalism Movement

In 1990, the Wichita *Eagle* introduced an election project titled "Your Vote Counts." It was, in the words of editor Davis Merritt, "an unabashed and activist effort to restore some role for citizens in the election process." The *Eagle* continued its effort in 1992 when it was joined by the Charlotte *Observer* and the Minneapolis *Star Tribune* among others. Instead of covering the horse race and in the process accounting for the tactics used by the candidates to win, civic journalism focuses on the agenda of citizens. Their agenda is determined by polls, focus groups, and discussions with citizens. "That first Voter Project, in Kansas's 1990 gubernatorial election, produced some tantalizing signs of hope," wrote Merritt. "Voter turnout in areas we reached was measurably higher than in other areas of the state. Voters within the *Eagle*'s reach felt that they understood the issues at a measurably higher level than did voters outside our area."[75]

TO SUM UP

All news coverage shapes events. In this chapter we have examined elements of news presentation that not only shape but sensationalize, distort, modify, and create events.

Media technology is used to dramatize and sensationalize news stories and to increase the authority and credibility of anchors and correspondents. The pressures of deadlines, competition, and breaking news, along with the structure of news stories, all contribute to inaccurate and incomplete reporting. News coverage becomes persuasion when language is used to create insinuations, when news coverage supports or opposes governmental policies, and when self-censorship suppresses certain kinds of news stories. Finally, on occasion newspeople become participants in the events they are covering. Such direct intervention is accepted by viewers and readers when it supports widely approved goals but rejected when reporters' actions are controversial.

In all these instances, the news media influence us, not simply by selecting what events they will cover, but by deciding how these events should be treated and interpreted. In the next chapter, we examine countervailing forces that, in turn, influence the news media.

---

74. *Time*, 23 June 1986, p. 68.
75. Davis (Buzz) Merritt, "Imagining Public Journalism: An Editor and Scholar Reflect on the Birth of an Idea," Roy W. Howard Public Lecture no. 5, April 13, 1995, p. 4.

A N A L Y S I S : Analyzing a News Item

Our analysis of news has illustrated principles with historical examples. Here we include questions that can be used to analyze a current news item.

Newsworthiness

Why was it considered newsworthy? To what event, if any, was it tied? Were drama, conflict, or violence incorporated into it? Was it personalized? Was it an extension of a continuing issue? Did it incorporate novelty, deviance?

How was its newsworthiness established in the report? Did it affect large numbers? a wide area? a celebrity? Did it have important consequences?

Was this a local, state, regional, or national story? What determined whether it would be reported in local, state, regional, or national media?

Did this story lend itself to coverage by one medium and not others, for example, a ballet on television but not on radio? If so, why?

Did the story appear in one newspaper or many? If it appeared in many, was the source of the story the same or different in different newspapers? (Did all carry it AP? UPI? *New York Times* syndicate? Or did some carry one and some another?) Did any of the accounts combine sources of information (a story based on AP and UPI accounts, for example)? If there were differences, were they significant, and, if so, how do you account for them? (local angle on national story? reaction to story event from prominent local person? informed by different political points of view?) Did the story appear on any of the network newscasts? If it appeared on some but not others, how do you account for that? How did the reports on different networks differ from each other? If it appeared in some media and not others, how do you account for that? How did national coverage differ from local coverage?

What was the angle on the story? What other angles could have been chosen? How would the story have changed if it were framed by each of these other angles? Was the story pegged to some other event? If so, what, how, and why? How newsworthy was this other event? What other pegs could have been used (piggybacking)? If another peg had been used, how would the story have changed?

Reporter

Who reported the story? Was the person given a byline? If not, why not? Why did this reporter, not another, cover this story? (regular beat? special expertise? special interest in this topic?) What are the stylistic, structural, evidentiary, and substantive predispositions of this reporter? If the story had been reported by some other specific reporter, say Lesley Stahl (CBS) rather than Bruce Morton (CNN), how would the story have differed, if at all? How did the reporter establish her or his credibility? What devices, if any, were used to suggest the reporter's "objectivity"?

The News Story

What sorts of claims were made in the story? What sort of evidence was marshaled to support the claims? Was the evidence accurate? Did the evidence warrant the claims? How was the evidence made credible? Was the source of the evidence identified? (a highly placed source?) If not, who do you think the source was? Were eyewitnesses used? Were they interviewed willingly? Did the interviews seem to be an invasion of their privacy? Was expert testimony used? If so, was the authority quoted, paraphrased, or interviewed? What determined whether the authority was quoted, paraphrased, or interviewed? Why was this authority selected rather than some other? How was the credibility of the authority established? If the story was covered on television, did the authority look credible? sound credible? Were other authorities cited? If so, what was the relationship among the authorities (pro–con; accusation–defense)?

Was a concrete example used? Were statistics used? Were governmental sources used? If so, how and why?

If the story involves an interview, what is the relationship between the reporter and the person interviewed (friendly, hostile, distant)? Were the questions asked by the reporter included in the story? If not, could you determine what the questions were from the answers? If the reporter paraphrased the questions, did the paraphrases seem consistent with the answers? Did the person interviewed seem to be facilitating coverage of the story or attempting to limit coverage? Was access to the person interviewed limited in any way? Were questions submitted in advance? Were some topics off-limits? Did the reporter agree to print or air certain parts of the interview in exchange for it? Did anyone refuse to be interviewed for this story? If so, was that fact reported? How? Was the impression created that the person who refused was guilty of something? hiding something?

Was the event reported a pseudo-event? If so, did it accomplish the purposes of the persons who staged it? If so, did the reporter note that it was a pseudo-event?

Was the story part of a series? If so, what was its function as part of the series?

Constraints

Did persons outside the media shape or try to shape the story? If so, why did they succeed or fail?

How did constraints in the media shape the story? Were media deadlines used strategically? Could the event be filmed or photographed? What were the costs of coverage? How did limitations of time and space affect coverage? How could these constraints have been overcome? (What would you have had to have argued to claim an exception?)

Did the elite media set the agenda for this story? If so, when and how? How was coverage by the elite media reflected in the story?

Framing

How was the news item introduced? (headline? prefatory statement by reporter or anchor?) What expectations did the introduction create about the story?

What other introduction could appropriately have been used? How would other introductions have reframed the report? Was there a summary statement at the end of the report? What interpretation, if any, did it impose on the report?

What values does the story support? (Problems can be solved? The system works? Legitimate authorities should solve problems? Hard work pays off? Our system of government is the best?)

Inclusion/Exclusion

What of importance about the story is not reported? Why? Were apparently trivial pieces of information included in the story? If so, why?

Setting

Where was the report situated? (dateline London? on location in Newark?) Is the setting readily accessible to the news outlet? How costly is it to cover and, if television, send a camera crew? How did cost affect likelihood of coverage? Was the reporter actually at the scene of the event reported? If so, is that fact established in the story? If so, how? If not, is that fact evident in the report? If not, what is the reporter's source of firsthand information? Is the setting used to make the report more credible (televised report about politics from the steps of the Capitol)? How, if at all, did the setting serve to dramatize the story?

Timing

When (what time of day) did the reported event occur? Did the time of occurrence mean that it was reported by some media and not others? Was the event deliberately timed to maximize or minimize coverage? On what day of the week did the event occur? Did occurrence on that day increase the likelihood that the event would be covered (slow news day), decrease the likelihood that it would be covered, or not make much difference? Did the event occur at a time of year in which there is little competition for access to the news? (4th of July weekend? post-Christmas, pre-New Year's? Thanksgiving weekend?)

If the event was not reported in a brief span of time, would it have lost its news value (for example, a presidential press conference), or could the story be stored for another day if it couldn't be fit into today's broadcast or paper (for example, a report on some ongoing struggle)?

Placement

Was it treated as hard news or soft news? Could it have been transformed from hard to soft, or soft to hard? If so, how? Where was it placed in the news broadcast, newspaper, or newsmagazine? What items were placed in a more prominent space or time? What accounts for the placement of this item in relation to other items? How much space or time was this report allotted? Was that more or less than the other reports? Account for the differences. What sorts of news stories would bump this story from the lineup?

Patterns

Are authorities appearing on this broadcast familiar faces? Have they served as authorities on this channel before? Often? If so, why? What is the apparent bias of the authority, if any? Is the authority identified as being partisan? If so, is another point of view represented? What are the similarities among authorities used in this type of media outlet? How often and in what kinds of stories do women function as authorities? African Americans? Hispanics? older persons? How often are professors used as authorities? With what schools are they associated? Are the schools located near the media outlet? Are they Ivy League schools? Are authorities from regions of the country other than that in which the media outlet is located represented?

Who is likely to cover what kind of story? Are female reporters more likely to be assigned to cover the women's movement? wives of candidates? socially significant weddings (Prince Charles's or Caroline Kennedy's)? When do African Americans, Hispanics, and older reporters appear? Are stories about some foreign countries more likely to appear than stories about other foreign countries?

Manipulation

Did those outside the media capitalize on any preexisting patterns to manipulate media coverage? Did those outside the media capitalize on extrinsic or intrinsic constraints to manipulate the story? Did the effort succeed? Were the efforts reported in the story?

How much of the report, if any, was based on press reports, actualities, or news reports provided by outsiders? How, if at all, would the report have differed if it had been prepared in its entirety by the reporter, without press releases, and so forth?

How much, if any, of the story simply recycled information from some other news source? Which source, and how do you account for the recycling?

Impact

Who, if anyone, benefited from the coverage? Who, if anyone, was damaged by the coverage? How? If someone or some organization was likely to seek news coverage to counter an impression created by the story, who would it be? What would you expect them to do? What media outlets would you expect them to use? (op-eds? letters to the editor? press conference? ads?) If the Fairness Doctrine were still in force, would they be entitled to equal time?

SELECTED READINGS

Bybee, Carl. "Constructing Women as Authorities: Local Journalism and the Microphysics of Power." *Critical Studies in Mass Communication* 7 (September 1990): 197–214.

Davis, Merritt. *Public Journalism and Public Life: Why Telling the News Is Not Enough*. Hillsdale, N.J.: Lawrence Erlbaum Associates, 1995.

Gans, Herbert. *Deciding What's News: A Study of CBS Evening News, NBC Evening News, Newsweek, and Time*. New York: Pantheon, 1979.

Glasgow University Media Group. *Bad News*. London: Routledge & Kegan Paul, 1976.

————. *More Bad News*. London: Routledge & Kegan Paul, 1980.

————. *Getting the Message: News, Truth and Power*. Ed. John Eldridge. London; New York: Routledge, 1993.

Herman, Edward S., and Noam Chomsky. *Manufacturing Consent*. New York: Pantheon, 1989.

Hess, Stephen. *International News and Foreign Correspondents*. Washington, D.C.: Brookings Institution, 1996.

Jensen, Carl. *Censored—the News That Didn't Make the News and Why*. New York: Four Walls Eight Windows, 1995.

Mann, Thomas E., and Norman J. Ornstein (eds.), *Congress, the Press and the Public*. Washington, D.C.: American Enterprise Institute and Brookings Institution, 1994.

Smith, Joel. *Understanding the Media: A Sociology of Mass Communication*. Cresskill, N.J.: Hampton Press, 1995.

Tuchman, Gaye. *Making News: A Study in the Construction of Reality*. New York: Free Press, 1978.

Wicker, Tom. *On Press*. New York: Viking, 1978.

CHAPTER 4

Influencing the News Media

The power of the news media results from their capacity to select what is reported and to shape the content of news stories. The news media are pervasive and forceful persuaders with the ability to shape our perceptions and to influence our beliefs and attitudes. But there are limits to their power, countervailing forces that, in turn, manipulate the news media. These include persons, like ourselves, and groups, like those we belong to, who capitalize on journalistic norms and routines to create newsworthy events and to shape their coverage. The commercial pressures of profits and competition, and direct pressures from the political establishment, also limit the power of the media.

Influencing Journalistic Norms and Routines

"Manipulated journalism presupposes routine journalism."[1] The ability to influence news coverage is directly related to an understanding of the journalistic norms and routines described in the preceding chapters; hence, many successful public relations consultants are former newspeople. The news media are vulnerable precisely because reporters have deadlines and beats, because they are generalists who rely on sources, and because of demands for brevity and for dramatic, visual coverage. The media's criteria for what is newsworthy and the external and internal constraints and conventions influencing what is covered and published contribute to their susceptibility.

Manipulating Deadlines

Because the news media face deadlines and are induced by competition to favor the latest details and the freshest facts, information released shortly before

---

1. Mark Fishman, *Manufacturing the News* (Austin: University of Texas Press, 1980), p. 15.

a deadline by an important person about an important matter is likely to be reported uncritically. In such cases, the event is newsworthy and the source is known and familiar. If time is taken to investigate the veracity and accuracy of the information, reporters risk having a competitor break the story first. As a result, press secretaries or news managers release controversial information as close to deadlines as possible to minimize critical scrutiny of it. This became the standard procedure of the Nixon administration in the final months of the Watergate investigation.

And, once a medium has broadcast or published the story, a second constraint comes into play, which minimizes the chance that the released information will get the scrutiny it deserves. By tomorrow, the news is stale. Fresh information is competing for space. Rehashing yesterday's news is taboo.

The news media can also be manipulated by releasing potentially damaging information when deadlines have passed or when the audience is hard to reach. For instance, once the Sunday morning papers are on the newsstands and on the breakfast tables of the U.S. public, it is difficult to reach a mass audience until the regular Monday morning channels of news begin—Monday morning drive-time radio, talk shows such as *Good Morning America,* and the Monday morning paper. Sunday evening network news is often preempted by special programming or not aired by affiliates. Consequently, President Gerald Ford's controversial decision to pardon ex-President Nixon was announced at 11 A.M. (EST) Sunday morning. The timing assured that even if the broadcast media, understaffed on weekends, turned their full attention to the pardon, few people would be reached by media news coverage.

David R. Gergen, former assistant to the president for communications; said: "If you've got some news that you don't want to be noticed, put it out Friday afternoon at 4 P.M."[2] The Reagan administration announced the formal end of our participation in the international peacekeeping force in Lebanon on a Friday at 4 P.M. Other decisions announced at that hour included restoration of tax breaks to private schools that discriminate on the basis of race; a directive, later suspended, imposing lifetime secrecy agreements on more than 100,000 government officials; and the discovery of clinically benign polyps during a routine colonoscopy on President Reagan, conducted as part of a follow-up to his rectal colon cancer surgery.

Similarly, when President George Bush decided to break his campaign pledge of "No New Taxes," he did so in a memo released to coincide with Nelson Mandela's headline-stealing speech to a joint meeting of Congress. Whereas Bush spoke in first person in making the election pledge, his memo shifted to third person. Passive voice replaced active. The simple, straightforward word *taxes* became *tax revenue increases.* At the convention he had said, "The Congress will push me to raise taxes, and I'll say no, and they'll push, and I'll say no, and they'll push again, and I'll say to them, 'Read my lips, No new taxes.'"[3] By contrast, his memo stated, "It is clear to me that both the size of the deficit problem and the need for

2. Stephen Engelberg, "The Bad News Hour: 4 P.M. Friday," *New York Times,* 6 April 1984, p. 10Y; *Washington Post,* 18 January 1986, p. A6.
3. Acceptance speech to the Republican National Convention, August 18, 1988.

a package that can be enacted require all of the following: entitlement and man-datory program reform; tax revenue increases; growth incentives; discretionary spending reductions." But Bush's efforts to minimize media scrutiny did not stop with issuing a written statement on a news-filled day. Throughout the day, Bush avoided talking to reporters, noted the *New York Times,* and "when he was asked during one brief Rose Garden appearance to expand on his written words, he re-plied, 'I'll let the statement speak for itself.'"[4]

The media also can be manipulated by releasing good news when most of the audience is watching. For example, during prime time in the opening week of the fall 1978 television season, President Carter announced unexpectedly that he had just secured an agreement between Prime Minister Menachem Begin of Israel and President Anwar Sadat of Egypt on an Egyptian-Israeli peace accord. As a result, Carter reached an unprecedented number of viewers. The announce-ment found most audience members tuned to the first television showing of a remake of the movie *King Kong* or to a new program, *Battlestar Galactica* (mis-takenly heralded as the hottest new show of the season).

Even an audience member uninterested in foreign affairs was likely to stay tuned through the peace accord announcement to see the rest of the prime-time program. And those more interested in public affairs could stay tuned for net-work news updates, read about it in the morning papers, hear about it on drive-time radio, or listen to it discussed on Monday morning talk shows. Once again, manipulation required a highly newsworthy event and a reliable source, but tim-ing was used to influence coverage to reach the largest possible audience.

Timing and speed affect the press's power to manipulate a public figure. The press manipulates the public figure if coverage of a gaffe or a problem is pro-longed; the public figure manipulates the press if she or he can quash extended coverage with a quick explanation or confession. For example, President Gerald Ford made a significant error in a debate with Jimmy Carter during the 1976 cam-paign, asserting that Poland was free. After the debate, Ford did not admit imme-diately that he had made a mistake. The news media covered the process of his aides trying to persuade him to make such a statement, and played documentary footage showing the lack of freedom in Poland. The Carter campaign treated it as a major policy error, and Carter, speaking before a Polish group, assured them that he knew how terrible things were in Poland. Finally, Ford acknowledged his error and the topic quickly disappeared from the news, but the damage had been done. Ford's momentum in the polls leveled off and his ratings began to rise again only at the end of that week. Some Ford strategists credit that error and its handling with the loss of the election.[5]

Republican strategists learned their lesson. When in a fall 1988 debate with Democratic contender Michael Dukakis, Republican nominee George Bush stated that he favored criminalizing abortion, by the early hours of the next morning aides were on the air saying that after considering it carefully overnight, Bush

---

4. Andrew Rosenthal, "Bush Now Concedes a Need for 'Tax Revenue Increases' to Reduce Deficit in Budget," *New York Times,* 27 June 1990, p. 1.
5. Jules Witcover, *Marathon: The Pursuit of the Presidency 1972–1976* (New York: Viking, 1977), pp. 606, 608.

wanted to clarify his position: only the person performing the abortion, not the woman having the abortion, should be subject to criminal prosecution.

Similarly, when British movie star Hugh Grant was charged in summer 1995 with committing a lewd act with 23-year-old prostitute Divine Brown, he promptly issued an apology, saying "Last night I did something completely insane. I have hurt people I love and embarrassed people I work with. For both things I am more sorry than I can possibly say."[6] The apology shifted news coverage from such questions as, Did he do it? Would he be convicted? and Was he sorry? to What effect would the act and apology have on his acting career, an important question since he had been arrested while in the United States promoting a new film, *Nine Months*.

Deadlines can also be used to insert questionable material into news stories, such as surveys done by interested parties using questionable methodology. Michael R. Gordon, a staff correspondent for the *National Journal,* a Washington weekly on federal policy and politics, reports such successful manipulation. A public relations firm fighting trucking deregulation arranged simultaneous press conferences in five cities to publicize the results of a poll by the Group Attitudes Company, a subsidiary of the same public relations firm. The survey, said the press handout, showed "virtually no public support for the move in Congress to deregulate the nation's trucking industry" and was cited in a number of regional papers and wire service reports. None of these reports mentioned that the company that conducted the survey was owned by the public relations firm fighting deregulation, information not included in the press releases. Facing a deadline with limited knowledge of polling and statistics, the press did not bother to question how the poll was conducted or whether its findings really supported the claim in the press release.[7]

The pressure of deadlines also makes it possible to manipulate coverage by releasing information in advance to reporters. Reporters are eager to predigest the news. This enables them to write much or all of a story in advance. Consequently, news managers delay official public release of information while making it available to the news media generally or to selected outlets or reporters. For example, in advance of the committee hearing, the communication director for a Senate committee might release the text of the chairperson's introductory statement and the testimony witnesses will give before the committee. Reporters can then compose their stories in advance and attend the hearing to insert an update into the story or to report the unexpected. Those who provide such advance information to reporters influence the perspective reporters will take in their news stories.

Manipulating Access

There is constant tension between those assigned to ferret out the news and those assigned to control press access to news sources. Press secretaries, public information officers, and public relations firms are hired to encourage press ac-

6. Cindy Pearlman, "A New Hugh?" *Philadelphia Inquirer,* 4 July 1995, p. E1.

7. Michael R. Gordon, "The Profits and Perils of Progress in P.R.," *New York Times,* 3 August 1980, p. E19.

cess to favorable information and to minimize or block press access to unfavorable information. When negative information seeps out, it is the function of news managers to prevent or lessen its spread through the media and to cast it in the best possible light.

News managers control the press by controlling press access to those who have information, for example, by limiting the number of presidential press conferences or by communicating through press releases. Control can also be exerted by providing easy access to those likely to cover an issue or program favorably and limiting the access of those thought to be opposed to the interests of the news source.

Exclusive interviews with reporters function this way. The third highest rated program of the spring 1995 season was Diane Sawyer's exclusive *PrimeTime Live* interview with music star Michael Jackson and his then wife, Lisa Marie Presley, daughter of deceased rock icon Elvis Presley. The June 14 interview was Jackson's first after his settlement of charges that he had sexually molested a young boy and after his marriage to Presley. Only the Super Bowl and the Academy Awards drew larger audiences. The agreement for the interview coincided with ABC's decision to trade ad time worth about $1 million for rights to the star's future videos. Those in ABC's news division denied that they had known of the entertainment division's talks with Jackson's managers when they scheduled the exclusive interview.

Jackson's goal was promoting his new album, "HIStory—Past, Present and Future Book I," which was released June 20. News stories reported that "in return for the rights to Jackson's videos, according to an ABC executive, ABC Entertainment aired ten, 30-second advertisements promoting the album between Diane Sawyer's interview on June 14 and the release of the album on June 21."[8] The timing led some to surmise that Jackson's managers had, in effect, given ABC the exclusive interview in return for promotional time for Jackson's new album. By airing the spots between segments of the interview, the news show became, in effect, an extended promotion for the new album.

It is also possible to manipulate coverage by leaking information favorable to one position or damaging to an opponent's position. Finally, government officials control access by refusing to respond to a specific question on the grounds that the requested information would breach national security, by asserting that the person being questioned is not empowered to reveal the information, or by answering that the matter is still under study or in litigation.

The press's desire for access is generally expressed as "the public's right to know." Problems emerge when this right conflicts with an individual's right to privacy (should a rape victim's name be included in a news story about a rape?), the right to a fair trial (does publicity minimize a defendant's ability to get a fair trial?), and national security (should the media voluntarily suppress information that may damage the nation's interests at home or abroad?).

Manipulation through control of access is best illustrated by relationships between reporters and government officials. The reporter wants information, and

---

8. "ABC Cut Ad-Video Deal with Jackson Prior to Interview," *San Francisco Examiner*, 24 June 1995, p. C3.

On the record

Backgrounder

A deep backgrounder

Off the record

Figure 4.1   Identifying the source.

the official expects something in exchange—a friendly hearing, a neutral report, or muted criticism, for example. Concealing the actual source of information is often a condition of access.

Bill Green, former *Washington Post* ombudsman, explains the "rough categories of attribution" this way: When a source speaks or holds a briefing "on the record," reporters can and do "quote the source by name." When a reporter attends a "backgrounder," he or she "can use the material but not the source." A "deep backgrounder," according to Green, "calls on the reader for an act of faith, and it produces some familiar phrases: 'it is known that' or 'it is believed that.' In other words, the fact that it came from a source cannot be revealed." When a statement is given "off the record," the reporter knows he or she "can't use it after all." Green acknowledges that this system of code phrases is necessary to elicit information that would otherwise be inaccessible but also notes that "the code and its vocabulary call credibility into question."[9] (See Figure 4.1.)

---

9. Bill Green, "That 'Unnamed' Source," *Washington Post*, 29 May 1981, p. A12.

Under such circumstances, readers and viewers are asked to trust reporters and to take their news judgments on faith, a situation that makes reporters extremely vulnerable not only to manipulation but also to backlash from the audience. UPI now has a policy of trying to help readers understand who the source is, or where his or her sympathies are, by the wording of the attribution: "sources opposed to the plan" or "Democratic sources in Congress."

Access also can be limited by denying reporters the ability to get to the scene of a news story. By expelling reporters from a country, its government ensures that internal unrest will not be transmitted, at least not by them, around the world. In 1983 during the U.S. government's invasion of Grenada, the press was kept out.

A blue-ribbon commission headed by a retired major general, Winant Sidle, concluded that this action had been improper. In the future, the report stated, military commanders should make provision for at least a pool of reporters to witness such military operations. The Pentagon adopted the Sidle recommendations as its official policy.

In December 1989, the procedure was put to the test. Reporters selected to form the pool concluded that the policy was ignored during the invasion of Panama. Noted pool television correspondent Fred Francis, "The pool was repeatedly denied or ignored when it asked for access to front-line troops, wounded soldiers—simple interviews." When pool reporters asked to observe the securing of Panama strongman Noriega's headquarters, they were told that it was "too dangerous." The army major general whose paratroops had taken the international airport informed journalists, "Sorry, my operational orders are that I cannot let you talk with any of my men. I can't speak with you."[10] By denying reporters access to the invasion itself and by permitting them in only after the territory was presumably secured, the Bush administration minimized the likelihood that the stories would focus on bureaucratic inefficiency, needless civilian deaths, or confused soldiers who did not know for what they were fighting and dying. In 1991, however, only a select pool of reporters was allowed access to information about the Persian Gulf War, and even those reports were censored.

Manipulating News Assignments

Although presidents have tried, it is difficult to manipulate reporters by attempts to change their beats; but it is possible to manipulate newspeople who are on general assignment. For example, the AP Calendar lists important events occurring in Washington. Virtually every news bureau in Washington uses it as a guide for what to cover on any given day. If an event is listed, it gets covered, whether it deserves it or not; if it's not listed, it probably won't get covered. When an event is listed, fears of competition prod the news outlets to cover it.

---

10. Arthur Lord, "Operation Just Cause—the Press in the Dark Again," *Nieman Reports* (Spring 1990): 7.

BOX 4-1

What's a Source?

Mommy, what's a source?
A thing where something comes from; the beginning of a stream.

When is a source a person?
When the person talks to a reporter.

Why do reporters always talk to a source instead of a person?
Because they think it sounds better to quote a "source" than a "person."

Can you tell the difference between a source and a person?
No. As soon as a source is finished talking with a reporter, it turns right back into a person.

Why don't source-persons use their names?
Because they're afraid or ashamed.

Why afraid?
Because they're telling the truth and that will make someone very angry—or because they're not telling the truth and that will make someone very angry.

And why would they be ashamed?
Because they may be saying something unfair, or accusing somebody without a good reason.

Why would a reporter want information that isn't true or fair?
A good reporter will only quote a source if the information is true or provable.

How does the reporter know it's true?
Because the same person told the truth before or because another dependable person agrees that it's true.

If it's true, why does a reporter have to say a source said it's true?
Because if it turns out not to be true, the reporter can blame someone else.

Someone who is just a person?
Yes.

Isn't there something else they could call a source?
Well, many reporters always call them "reliable sources" or "well-informed sources," but not in our favorite newspaper.

Why not?
Because readers might wonder why they would be going to unreliable or uninformed sources.

So what else do they call them?
Well, let's look at our favorite newspaper. Here it says: "A senior White House official," and "law-enforcement officials," and "a Clinton Administration official," and "a senior State Department official," and "a Vatican official," and "a Japanese Embassy official," and "a Housing Department official," and. . . .

But what if someone's not an official?
Well, in our favorite paper and very often *The Washington Post, The Boston Globe, The Los Angeles Times, Newsday* and other newspapers, they write about sources "familiar with" the situation. Or they quote someone "close to" the case.

Is that good?
Not if the readers get to think that some sources are not close to the case or are *un*familiar with the situation.

Why don't they just say "someone told me"?
Because "someone told me" makes it sound as if they're spreading a rumor.

What's wrong with that?
Good reporters don't spread rumors.

But how would a reporter know whether the sources or officials or people close to the case want to spread rumors?
Well, they don't. They just write that the sources who aren't named "insist on anonymity."

What does that mean?
It means the source said, "Please don't print my name," or "Don't quote me."

Why do they trust the reporter to hide their name?
Because they know the reporter is eager to get a colorful quote or fact—and may want to get information from them some other time.

Doesn't the reporter ever insist on printing their names?
I guess it happens, but you never read about it.

What would happen if reporters always insisted?
They should insist a lot more than they do. But they can't do it always. If a person—a source—can't speak with anonymity, the person might not speak at all. That means we wouldn't hear about things that could save lives or prevent bad decisions.

Like what?
Well, what if a factory is making an unsafe toy. A woman working there might want to tell about that, but not if her boss could find out and fire her. Or what if a committee chairman in Congress wanted to cut back school lunches real quick before people found out about it? Some legislative assistant might tell about that, but not if that risked being fired. And we might never hear from all those courageous students in China that the police are putting in jail just for asking too many questions.

They go to jail for asking questions?
Yes. And sometimes in our country reporters have to go to jail for not *answering* questions.

What kind of questions?
About the names of their sources.

The reporters won't say who told them about the unsafe toy?
That's right, to protect that troubled woman in the toy factory.

I get it. But if a source's name has to be secret, why even mention a source?
I told you: when reporters talk to someone who doesn't want his name in the paper, they just say a source told them. The readers are supposed to know that the reporter would never repeat what the sources said unless the reporter thought it was true.

But what if it turns out to be untrue?
Then the reporter can always say the source was wrong, not the reporter.

Oh. But if the information turns out to be right, the reporter gets the credit?
Yes. And sometimes a prize.[a]

[a]Max Frankel, "Don't Quote Me," *New York Times Magazine,* 26 March 1995, pp. 38, 40.
© 1995 by The New York Times Co. Reprinted by permission.

This is also cost efficient in the case of television, as some pooling of crews is possible under such circumstances, thus lowering costs. Arranging to have an event listed in the Calendar is one way to manipulate media news coverage.

Reporters on beats are vulnerable to manipulation. An example can be drawn from coverage of the Reagan presidential campaign. Joel Swerdlow reports some clever manipulation by Reagan news managers:

> Raw footage of a typical Reagan campaign day, for example, revealed that the crowds always seemed much larger than they actually were. To a large degree, this resulted from clever advance work by the media-sophisticated Reagan staff. At almost every stop, it was the same: they positioned a raised camera platform close to the speaker's platform, and roped off a huge "press area," designated off-limits to the public. This forced the crowd to pack tightly into the space between the candidate and the camera, ensuring that Reagan always spoke to an impressive-looking mass of humanity.[11]

In the 1950s and 1960s, some reporters acted as informants for and as channels of information from the Central Intelligence Agency. Stories initiated by the CIA found their way into major newspapers and onto the wires. Newspeople considered the CIA a trusted source of information before the revelations about the Vietnam War and Watergate cast doubt on the truthfulness of such government agencies. The CIA was able to provide reporters with access to information that they could not otherwise secure, a situation that gave those reporters a competitive edge. This information came easily and inexpensively; reporters did not have to invest time in ferreting out information, following false leads, fighting for access to sources. The CIA also provided an angle by pegging their stories to local and international events and, most important, the CIA provided stories based on beliefs and attitudes consistent with the reporters' views of the world: "us" versus "them," patriotism, the dangers of communism, the threat of communist infiltration. A variety of factors contributed to the association of the CIA with the media, and access to information was an important one.[12]

Media Competition

Chapter 3 discussed how competition and deadlines contribute to incomplete and inaccurate reporting. But competition also influences coverage, particularly competition to keep up with the elite media. Consequently, in many cases news managers focus their attention on manipulating the elite media. If a news manager gains access to an elite medium, coverage in other media follows.

Access to an elite medium works to the advantage of both the medium and the newsworthy person, in some instances. For example, in the 1988 presidential

---

11. Joel Swerdlow, "The Decline of the Boys on the Bus," *Washington Journalism Review* (January/February 1981): 16.
12. "The CIA's 3-Decade Effort to Mold the World's Views," *New York Times*, 12 December 1977, p. A12; "CIA Established Many Links to Journalists in U.S. and Abroad," *New York Times*, 27 December 1977, pp. 1, 40A.

campaign as Democratic charges that the Republicans were running a dirty campaign began to take hold, campaign manager James Baker made himself available for interviews on the Sunday afternoon news shows. There he denied the charges. Coverage by one medium influences coverage in other media. This is particularly true of the elite media, and news managers make special efforts to influence elite media coverage.

Language and Symbols

The print and electronic news media can be manipulated through the effective use of language and visual symbols. Because of its preference for the visual, television news is particularly vulnerable to the strategic use of visual symbols. For example, both print and electronic media photographed Pope John Paul II receiving flowers from former prisoners wearing striped uniforms at Auschwitz.

No explanation is needed for the ideas represented in this scene expressing a personal, pastoral papacy (the pope as a servant, as a caring, compassionate leader). It is a visual denial of anti-Semitism in the Catholic Church, a nonverbal Vatican repudiation of the view that the Jews killed Christ. John Paul II is uniquely suited to this scene. He was a member of the Polish underground that acted to save Jews, so the scene is an extension of his personal commitment. In addition, Auschwitz is in Poland, and his presence is a reminder of Polish Catholics' suffering at the hands of the Nazis and, implicitly, at the hands of the Russians. Such events rivet photographic attention because little or no commentary is required—the picture is the story. If such scenes were routine, they would not be newsworthy. It is both the freshness of the symbols and their ability to stand for more than themselves that make them attractive to news photographers. Nonverbal symbolic acts that require verbal commentary are less effective.

Similarly, in spring 1990, the wife of former Philippines' president Ferdinand Marcos, Imelda Marcos, shaped national network coverage of her acquittal on charges of misuse of state funds and at the same time secured front-page newspaper access. Marcos accomplished this by inching her way up the aisle of a church on her knees in a black mourning dress to "thank God" for the trial's outcome. The black dress reminded viewers of her widowhood, kneeling suggested that she was religious, and movement up the aisle in the posture of a penitent suggested her humility and the injustice of seeking to convict her. How, after all, could one assume the guilt of a humble, religious widow, kneeling in church?

Aware of the power of such symbols, candidates search for locations that will visually reinforce sympathetic parts of their biography. For 1996 Republican presidential hopeful Bob Dole that backdrop was Russell, Kansas, his hometown. The town is filled with places tied to Dole's humble origins, including Dawson's drugstore where the Kansan worked as a soda jerk. As reporters noted, Russell, Kansas, is "an irresistible symbol of the small-town virtues that helped Dole overcome a debilitating war injury and climb the ladder of electoral success."[13]

---

13. Howard Kurtz, "The Press in Campaignland," *Washington Post Magazine,* 16 July 1995, p. 9.

Imelda Marcos crawls on her knees to the altar at St. Patrick's
Cathedral in spring 1990, after her acquittal (UPI/Bettmann).

Nonverbal symbols are risky because sometimes they are open to more than one interpretation. At the close of the dedication ceremonies at the Nixon Library, the former president raised his arms while shaping V's with the fingers of each hand. The gesture was one characteristic of Nixon-the-campaigner and Nixon-the-president. Parodists of the former president frequently used it to cue audiences that they were about to begin their impressions of Nixon. In the context of the library ceremony, the symbol could indicate a final victory over those who invited his resignation from office. Alternatively, it could suggest that this too was a campaign event, and as such a bid for a legitimacy not yet accorded him by history. In politics, a similar problem can arise when a campaign slogan is open to more than one interpretation or when it lends itself to easy parody (see Chapter 11).

The news media can also be manipulated by the language of a statement that is artfully constructed and skillfully delivered. Ideally, such a statement should be uneditable, dramatic, concise, and synoptic. It should be capable of being delivered in under 35 seconds by a skilled speaker. If it is delivered by a credible person, about an important topic, and on an occasion accessible to the news media, it is virtually irresistible to the press. An example of such a statement was Bush's promise, "Read My Lips. No New Taxes." Another was delivered by House Minority Whip David Bonior (D., Michigan) during the summer 1995 debate over whether television manufacturers should be required to include a V-chip in new sets and broadcasters required to code violent and sexually explicit programs to enable the chip to register and block them in homes that chose to do so. "Parents should be the ones who choose what kind of shows come into their homes, not some programmers in New York," said Bonior. "We believe parents should be able to choose to let Big Bird in, and keep the 'Texas Chainsaw Massacre' out."[14] The proposal passed.

Because television is a visual medium whose natural form is the narrative, a visually evocative narrative has special power. Because news employs a story structure, narratives are particularly attractive to reporters. In summer 1995, the Democratic minority in the House of Representatives used these conventions to create a favorable context in hearings on the 1993 clash between federal officers and those within the Branch Davidian compound in Waco, Texas, that led to the deaths of those within the compound.

The clash began February 28, 1993 when seventy-five federal officers, who suspected that the Davidians were making illegal drugs and stockpiling illegal weapons tried to execute a search warrant at the compound. A shootout resulted, leaving four government officers and six cult members dead. Who shot first is contested. Despite repeated requests, their leader David Koresh refused to surrender to the agents. On April 19 the agents launched a tear gas attack, and eighty-one people within the compound died in a fire. Davidian supporters argued that the fire resulted from the ignition of the tear gas; the Clinton administration claimed that it might have been set from within the compound. On the grounds that the search warrant was unjustified and the deaths needless, Republicans set up hearings in spring 1995.

When Clinton supporters argued that the hearings had been set up and witnesses scheduled to show the administration in an unfavorable light, the Republicans agreed to permit the Democrats to choose one of the early witnesses. They chose 14-year-old Kiri Jewell, who graphically testified that she had been sexually abused by Branch Davidian leader Koresh. Front-page pictures and headlines and prominent broadcast coverage were the result. Her testimony corroborated the claim of Attorney General Janet Reno that one reason for the assault was the belief that children were being sexually abused. It also shifted the attention of the hearing and the public from questions about administration decisions to Koresh. The effectiveness of the strategy led the *New York Times* to headline a

---

14. Dennie Wharton, "V-Chip, on a Roll, Puts Industry in a Pickle," *Variety*, 17–23 July 1995, p. 21.

summary story on the hearings, "Role Reversal: Expecting Waco Hearings' Triumph, Republicans Were Instead Surprised."[15]

Language can be used to deter news coverage as well. For instance, the difficulties involved in covering highly technical, abstract material are exploited by those who want to minimize news coverage of their activities. *Politics and the Oval Office,* a report by the conservative Institute for Contemporary Studies, argues that the presidency has suffered from too much uncontrolled coverage by the media. To curb what it views as excessive coverage, the report urges the president to overwhelm media representatives with technical data: "This tactic should defuse complaints about total accessibility. It could reduce the total volume of reporting, since dry data are often defined as unnewsworthy."[16]

Adaptation to the style and perspective of specific news channels and to the interests, biases, and experiences of individual reporters is a means of manipulating the press. For example, news managers can tailor a story to the *Wall Street Journal* by filling it with technical, economic data or to *Time* magazine by providing anecdotal material and clever language.

Every reporter has special interests, biases, and experiences; for this reason, if news coverage is to be balanced, it is important to have newspeople from different ethnic backgrounds and with varied perspectives reporting stories.

In summary, language and symbols can be used to influence news coverage. Of particular force is the dramatic visual symbol, but dramatic or dull language can be used to attract or deter coverage as well. It is also possible to attract coverage by tailoring statements and events to the predispositions of the reporter or media outlet.

Manipulating Live Coverage

A special, limited opportunity to manipulate access arises with live coverage, where little or no editing occurs. The opportunities for manipulation are limited to persons who are newsworthy for some other reason—winners of awards or of major sports events, for example. In such circumstances, people can use live television coverage to make a statement they could not otherwise make; in the process they have access to an audience they could not reach if the statement were made under other circumstances and had to compete for regular news coverage. One example occurred in 1990 when profanities uttered by the heavy-metal band Guns N' Roses were heard by millions of television viewers tuned in to Monday night's American Music Awards ceremony. The profanities brought a barrage of complaints and an apology from ABC. In fall 1989, comedian Andrew Dice Clay was banned for life from MTV after making sexist remarks and using profanity on a live nationwide September 6 broadcast, the MTV Video Music Awards.[17]

Other instances have been more calculated. For example, a Native-American woman was able to read a statement on Indian rights when she refused the Os-

---

15. Neil A. Lewis, "Role Reversal," *New York Times*, 3 August 1995, p. A9.
16. "Reagan Advised to Reduce 'Imperial Media' Access," *Washington Post*, 2 February 1981, p. A2.
17. "ABC Apologizes for Rockers' Remarks," *Philadelphia Inquirer*, 24 January 1990, p. D4.

BOX 4-2

A Checklist for Creating Newsworthy Statements Likely to Be Covered and Published

To Be	*Or . . . Not to Be*
A single coherent statement	A rambling statement
clearly summarizing the issue	skirting the issue
in jargon-free English,	in gobbledygook,
written to be understood on	written to be figured out
first hearing or reading,	by a cryptographer,
which can be delivered	which could not be delivered
clearly and dramatically	effectively by Laurence Olivier
in less than 14 seconds,	in less than 35 minutes,
requiring no additional	requiring at least a paragraph of
information,	clarification,
available before deadline	available at midnight
at a convenient place for newsgatherers,	at the North Pole,
delivered in a symbolic	delivered in a setting with no
setting	apparent relationship to the
	statement
or by a person who	or by a nondescript person who
dramatizes the issue	mumbles
in a manner not subject to	in a manner that brings joy to the
parody.	hearts of Art Buchwald and
	Garry Trudeau, who hope the
	speaker will seek the presidency.

---

car won by Marlon Brando, and Vanessa Redgrave was able to make a controversial statement about Palestinian rights during her Oscar acceptance speech. Early in the 1988 primaries, presidential candidate George Bush agreed to an interview with CBS anchor Dan Rather on the condition that the interview be broadcast live. This move guaranteed that his remarks could not be edited. His success in controlling the agenda of the interview helped Bush dispel reporters' questions about his decisiveness, questions that had been summarized as "the wimp factor."

Admittedly, such opportunities are rare and special, but live coverage provides opportunities to air highly controversial messages and to reach exceptionally large and captive audiences.

Prepackaged News

Pseudo-events, news feeds, news conferences, and prepared or "canned" editorials are examples of news prepackaged for the convenience of reporters. News managers are well aware of reporters' weaknesses and endeavor to exploit

---

BOX 4-3

Ads Become News

In 1989, more than 70 million viewers, twice as many as typically watch top-rated entertainment series, saw portions of a video release in which Sears announced that it was temporarily closing its stores to switch to a new pricing policy. More than 15 million saw part of Maytag's video release announcing the retirement of its longtime commercial spokesperson, Jesse White, the "lonely repairman," according to Medialink, a New York company that distributed video news releases and, with Nielsen Media Research, monitors their use.[a]

[a]Randall Rothenberg, "Messages from Sponsors Become Harder to Detect," *New York Times*, 19 November 1989, p. E5.

---

them through prepackaged news. As one public relations and political consultant wrote, "It is much easier for a reporter to be spoon-fed than to go on a scavenger hunt in government or industry to find his next story."[18]

Reliance on prepackaged news accounts in part for the fact that most reporters missed the emergence of the savings and loan crisis. "We usually depend on governmental institutions or groups like Common Cause or Ralph Nader or General Motors or somebody to make sense out of all this data for us," explained Brooks Jackson, an award-winning Cable News Network reporter.[19]

It is legal to buy news shows off the shelf. For example, the program *Hard Copy* began airing on Channel 2 in New York in fall 1989. It was purchased from an outside vendor, Paramount, which produced it as a package for stations around the country affiliated or owned by the three largest networks. Nobody at CBS or at Channel 2 had anything to do with what the packagers put in the program, including the topics covered. Everything was decided and manufactured by the packager. Such packaged news programs are appealing because the station splits the ad revenue with the packager, making a lot more money than if they put the program together themselves. Due to the lack of a disclaimer, viewers were led to believe that reporters for the station put the stories together and were responsible for their content, even though they were not.[20] But in such instances, the packager has a wide latitude for influence.

In a process almost too bizarre to be believed, a self-confessed murderer argued in summer 1995 that he had killed and would continue to do so in order to attract sufficient media attention to ensure that a prominent media outlet would publish his 56-page, 35,000-word treatise on the ills of contemporary society. In June, the man tagged the Unabomber by the press, wrote both the *New York*

---

18. J. Kyle Goddard, "Let's Abolish News Conferences," *New York Times*, 2 December 1979, p. E12.
19. Quoted by Ellen Hume, "Why the Press Blew the S & L Scandal," *New York Times*, 24 May 1990, p. A25.
20. Anthony Lewis, "TV: Selling Off Credibility," *New York Times*, 13 October 1989, p. 23Y.

Times and the *Washington Post,* giving them until September 29 to print the tract and three annual follow-ups in return for his guarantee that he would stop trying to kill. If neither paper took up his offer, said the bomber, he would resume the killings. On August 2, both papers ran 3,000-word excerpts on page 16 as part of a report on FBI efforts to identify the bomber through analysis of his style and philosophy.

At the time that he made the original request, the killer had been blamed for sixteen bombings since 1978, which had resulted in the deaths of three and the injury of twenty-three more. His rationale suggested that he was deliberately manipulating media norms:

> To make an impression on society with words is . . . almost impossible for most individuals and small groups. Take us (FC [Freedom Club]), for example. If we had never done anything violent and had submitted the present writings to a publisher, they probably would not have been accepted. If they had been accepted and published, they probably would not have attracted many readers, because it's more fun to watch the entertainment put out by the media than to read a sober essay. Even if these writings had had many readers, most of those readers would have soon forgotten what they had read as their minds were flooded by the mass of material to which the media expose them. In order to get our message before the public with some chance of making a lasting impression, we've had to kill people.[21]

Through a joint agreement between the *Times* and *Post,* the *Post* published the terrorist's entire text in September 1995. The alleged Unabomber was apprehended when his brother read the text on the Internet and recognized the themes and the style.

Pseudo-Events An antiabortion group in Kansas City obtained several small white caskets, ordinarily used to bury very small children. After notifying the media, particularly local television stations, of their plans, they appeared with the caskets at a large local hospital requesting aborted fetuses that they hoped to bury. Shocked hospital administrators were angered at this unexpected request. Television cameras showed the heated confrontation and the poignant white caskets. As viewers watched the segment on the local news, they saw a *pseudo-event*—that is, an event created and arranged for coverage by the news media.

A pseudo-event is an arranged event, not an occurrence that happens of its own accord. Contrast this arranged event with the actual death of a baby and its removal to be buried. A pseudo-event, which takes account of newsgatherers' concepts of what is newsworthy, is arranged to exploit internal and external constraints on newsgathering and the conventions of news presentation. An ideal pseudo-event is therefore dramatic (here, the angry encounter between shocked hospital staff and the antiabortion group), personalized (abortion was reduced to individual fetuses symbolized by tiny white caskets), novel (this

---

21. Ellen O'Brien, "Newspapers Publish Unabomber Manifesto," *Philadelphia Inquirer,* 3 August 1995, p. A2.

event got coverage because it was original; if many antiabortion groups imitate it, coverage will end), an event (there was a specific encounter between hospital staff and the antiabortion group), and part of an ongoing theme in the news (national efforts to have personhood defined as beginning at the moment of conception had been getting considerable news coverage).

In addition, the encounter took place at a convenient urban location, close to most local television stations, and at a convenient time (early afternoon) well before deadlines. The event was staged by a local group at a local setting (the hospital), making it attractive to local coverage. The event is visual (the encounter occurred just outside the hospital doors in good light and was easy to tape) and made use of highly charged, poignant symbols of sorrow and death. As taped with brief statements from both sides (the antiabortion group and the shocked, angry hospital administrators) and with a reporter's wrap-up, the event fit neatly into a 99-second news segment. As a result, its appearance on the local evening news could have been predicted.

Pseudo-events are designed to transform an issue, process, person, or the like into a newsworthy event that will be covered by the mass media. Many news events are staged to an extent to surmount the problems described in Chapter 2—scheduling, deadlines, access, and so forth. In a letter to the networks evaluating charges that coverage of the 1968 Democratic Convention in Chicago had involved "staged news," the Federal Communications Commission wrote:

> In a sense, every televised press conference may be said to be staged to some extent; depictions of scenes in a television documentary—on how the poor live on a typical day in the ghetto, for example—also necessarily involve camera directions, lights, action instructions, etc. The term "pseudo-event" describes a whole class of such activities that constitute much of what journalists treat as "news."[22]

In other words, a wide range of staged events are routinely treated as news. The news media can be manipulated into coverage of these pseudo-events because of what they define as news and because of the constraints under which they operate. Because cost and the need to meet deadlines with fresh stories are important to those who produce the news, there is pressure to cover events that have the dramatic, visual, concise characteristics the media crave. Congressional hearings, news conferences, and pseudo-events have these characteristics. In covering such events the reporter minimizes the amount of background information needed and the amount of time it takes to assemble a story, and has the news peg for the story—the event itself. The problem, of course, is that by covering such an event, the reporter often accepts the assumptions of those managing the event. The well-staged event invites coverage from a certain point of view.

An important adjunct to the press conference and to other staged events is the press release. The press release attempts to create a context for viewing a

---

22. FCC Letter to the Networks (No. 69-19227767), 28 February 1969, p. 9, cited by Edward Epstein in *News from Nowhere* (New York: Random House-Vintage, 1973), p. 159.

specific event. Written to include basic information (who, what, when, where, how, why) required by editors, it is filled with dramatic, synthetic statements related to the emerging news item.

Attracting media attention carries risks if the attention has been obtained under false pretenses. A candidate's opponents are eager to bring such discrepancies to the attention of the media. For example, when Marc Holtzman, a Republican congressional candidate in Pennsylvania, announced in a news release that he had facilitated the homecoming of a Vietnamese mother of a naturalized U.S. citizen in his district, the local press carried the heartwarming story. To Holtzman's embarrassment, the press reported days later that Holtzman's role had consisted of writing a letter to Vice-President George Bush inquiring about the status of the case. Bush received Holtzman's letter a week after the State Department had issued the visa. The follow-up stories hurt Holtzman's chances for re-election in the 1986 campaign.[23]

News Feeds   News managers attempt to exercise even greater control by offering radio stations news feeds containing audio "bites" of a politician's speech complete with "wrapped around" context narrated by someone on the politician's staff. Statements recorded specifically for "feeding" are also distributed. Such news feeds are common on Capitol Hill, in political campaigns, in the executive branch, and, increasingly, are being used by business as well. A. Kent MacDougall of the *Los Angeles Times* reports:

> Business is supplying pre-recorded interviews with business advocates to television and radio stations which slip them into their newscasts, usually without reference to their source. And business is flooding small newspapers with ready-to-use canned editorials, columns, and cartoons that carry hidden corporate messages.[24]

By accepting such feeds, the broadcast producer or editor is spared the cost of gathering the material or sending a reporter to the event but sacrifices the ability to make editorial judgments. Small stations and small papers are more likely to accept such feeds than larger ones. With the exception of opinion-editorials and paid advocacy advertising, most large stations and newspapers refuse as a matter of policy to accept such prepared materials.

Cost prevents small radio and television stations from having their own correspondents in Washington or following the major campaigns, yet an interview with an important government official or candidate is a news coup. If they can make it appear that they have such desirable access, they may suppress details about how information was obtained. The FCC Code (Section 73.1212.d) requires that at both the beginning and end of a segment, broadcasters disclose the source of any such prepackaged news other than mimeographed or printed press releases. This restriction applies to feeds obtained when the station calls a

---

23. *Washington Post*, 27 May 1986, p. A4.
24. "The Credibility Gap," *Washington Journalism Review* (July/August 1981): 21.

predesignated number as well as materials sent or delivered to the station. This rule applies to political candidates and to anyone dealing with political subjects or controversial issues.

Video news releases (VNRs) were inefficient as long as they relied on video-cassettes as their means of transport. Cassettes began to clutter newsrooms, unwatched and unaired. In the mid-1980s, public relations firms began switching to satellite transmission of news feeds. Medialink, a firm specializing in VNR transmission, reported that it distributed more than 1,500 VNRs by satellite in 1989. Estimates place the number of VNRs distributed each year at between 5,000 and 15,000. When Nielsen Media Research surveyed 200 stations in 1988, it found that 93 percent had the capacity to downlink VNRs from satellite and almost three-quarters said they were willing to use such releases.[25]

To increase the likelihood that they will be used, producers of VNRs include a 90-second B-roll of visuals accompanied only by natural sound. Local announc-ers can then "voice" the narration making it appear that the station itself pro-duced the material.

Use of VNRs has enabled advertisers to circumvent bans on the advertise-ment of certain products. "In 1987, for example, the James B. Beam Distilling Company took to heart the admonition to hook an item to a news trend, and made a video news release that affirmed the patriotic preference of American dis-tillers for domestic, instead of Canadian, grain. Television viewers in some 40 cit-ies saw the report, illustrated with footage of workers packing crates with Jim Beam bourbon, on their local newscasts."[26]

Electronic press kits, the video equivalent of the written press release, now air routinely on hundreds of local television stations as coverage of entertainment news increases. Frequently, this material is neither labeled nor described as film-studio publicity. No one knows how often local reporters inject themselves into these publicity kits, but the videotapes have been carefully created to allow local reporters to do so. For example, KABC-TV, the ABC station in Los Angeles, aired what appeared to be an interview with Al Pacino and KABC-TV reporter Nancy Gould. However, Gould never talked to Pacino. She had inserted herself into a taped interview with the actor made by Universal Pictures, the producer of the feature film *Scarface* in which Pacino starred. KABC-TV suspended her and then declined to renew Gould's contract over this incident. The issue is one of jour-nalistic integrity, the responsibility to disclose to viewers that the material they are seeing is promotional and that the station's reporters have not participated in its filming.

Major studios have produced dozens of these kits. Producing the kits is ex-pensive, but far less costly than comparable advertising. George Armstrong, who developed the electronic press kit at Universal Pictures as vice-president in

25. Randall Rothenberg, "The Journalist as Maytag Repairman," *Gannett Center Journal* (Spring 1990): 105.
26. Ibid., p. 107.

BOX 4-4

The Editorial Page: What's It There For?

More than 50 percent of the 199 newspaper editors and editorial page editors surveyed in 1992 reported an increase in editorial page readership. Eighty-seven percent saw the role of editorial pages as providing assistance in making judgments. Despite this, the percentage of newspapers endorsing candidates is down for candidates on the national, state, and local levels, with a full 23 percent not endorsing any candidates at all, almost double the percentage of those surveyed in 1975 and 1983.[a]

[a]Ernest C. Hynds, "Editors at Most U.S. Dailies See Vital Roles for Editorial Page," *Journalism Quarterly,* vol. 71 (Autumn 1994): 573–582.

---

charge of advertising, noted that the kit for *E.T.* cost $125,000, but that it "brought in the equivalent of $700,000 worth of air time if we had [had] to buy it."[27]

On August 8, 1995, Sony released "Spirit of '73: Rock for Choice," a multi-artist compilation featuring fourteen female artists supporting abortion rights. One of the major marketing vehicles, said the director of marketing of the product, was a 10-minute electronic press kit featuring interviews with the artists and a behind the scenes look at the process of making the record.[28]

Public relations firms attest that television and radio stations use materials prepared by public relations firms. For example, after a Food and Drug Administration ruling favorable to a client's product, one public relations firm made a videotape for the client in the form of a news report on the FDA ruling, which was distributed to hundreds of television stations—most of whom used it. Similarly, those advising clients on how to obtain news coverage suggest that if the news media do not cover the event, do it yourself—audiotape or videotape the event, edit it into a 90-second package, attach a script for announcers, and ship it to radio or television stations in time for the evening news.

Prepared Editorials   Another kind of influence results from distributing prepared editorials and feature stories to newspapers, particularly to small, news-hungry weeklies. E. Hofer and Sons, a public relations firm, has been among the most successful in getting its prepared editorials printed in newspapers. Once again, newspapers cooperate in their own manipulation. As one commentator writes, "To publish editorials prepared by Hofer while crediting the editorial to *Industrial News Review* [the organ through which Hofer disseminates prepared editorials], of course, would not constitute publication of 'canned' editorials. It is

---

27. Sally Bedell Smith, "Electronic Press Kits Pervade TV Newscasts," *New York Times,* 30 January 1984, p. 18Y.
28. Chris Morris, "Sony's 'Spirit of '73' Rocks for Pro Choice," *Billboard,* 22 July 1995, pp. 1, 88.

when newspapers publish editorials from such sources as their own views [and hundreds do] that an ethical problem arises."[29] Editorial writing is difficult and time consuming. As a result, it is tempting to use prepared editorials, and to pretend that they were composed by the newspaper staff.

Success in attracting advertising can make newspapers more vulnerable to the manipulations of news managers and public relations consultants. This is the case because, as advertising linage increases, the size of the space to be filled by news (the "news hole") also increases. Because their news staffs are small, such newspapers tend to "rely on filler and fluff supplied by business publicists to supplement their own coverage."[30]

In other words, those who are knowledgeable about journalistic norms and routines have the ability to manipulate news coverage. By strategic use of the media's needs and constraints, public relations consultants and news managers, as well as individuals and groups, help determine what is covered and how news stories are presented.

Commercial Pressures

The news media are influenced not only by those who understand journalistic norms and routines but also by their desire for profit, by their desire to beat the competition in the ratings, and by pressures created by advertisers. News programming has become one of the most lucrative sources of revenue for both the local stations and the networks. That is true, in part, because of its low production costs and because stations and networks own and produce the news, whereas in most cases they do not own and produce entertainment programming. For example, *World News Tonight* has become one of ABC's biggest revenue producers, bigger than many of its highly rated entertainment programs. The CBS news program *60 Minutes,* among the top ten in the Nielsen ratings for thirteen consecutive years, has been the biggest moneymaker in network history, according to Don Hewitt, the program's creator: "My records tell me that we've had a net profit for CBS of over $1 billion."[31] Local news generates between 30 and 50 percent of the profits of individual television stations. As a result, there is intense pressure to achieve and maintain high ratings. Such pressures contribute to the tendencies to dramatize and sensationalize news content described in the last chapter.

What competitive pressures do not produce is an alternative news agenda. So similar is the content of most competing newspapers, for example, that one

---

29. Harry W. Stonecipher, *Editorial and Persuasive Writing: Opinion Functions of the News Media* (New York: Hastings House, 1979), p. 67.
30. A. Kent MacDougall, "Business Puffery Costs Press Credibility, Short Changes Readers," *Los Angeles Times*, 3 November 1980, sec. IV, p. 1.
31. Bill Carter, "Success of *60 Minutes* in Dollars and in Years," *New York Times*, 15 September 1990, p. 13Y.

scholar dubbed them "rivals in conformity."[32] That conclusion has weathered the tests of four decades of research.[33]

Commercial pressures on newspapers have increased as the newspaper business has become controlled by an ever-shrinking number of large corporations. In the early 1980s, media critic Ben Bagdikian estimated that just forty-six companies in the world controlled most of the global business in daily newspapers, magazines, television, books, and movies. By 1990, he said that number was twenty-three. According to William Glaberson, "the effects of that change are pervasive." He argues that one effect is that journalists think about their work differently; it makes them more flexible in response to management demands. He writes, "It is now common for publishing executives to press journalists to cooperate with their newspapers' 'business side,' breaching separation that was said in the past to be essential for journalistic integrity." Editors have become more concerned about serving the needs of advertisers. Mary Jo Meisner, editor of the Milwaukee *Journal Sentinel* created eight new neighborhood sections by examining advertisers' requirements, and Glaberson quotes her as saying, "You have to look at it from their perspective."[34]

Costs of Preempting Programming

When the news division of a network preempts regular programming for special news—such as the funeral of Winston Churchill, the visit of Pope John Paul II, or a space shuttle launch—advertisers who have paid to sponsor the regular programming are not given what they paid for and either have their money refunded or are offered alternate times to air their ads. Networks are corporations governed by boards accountable to stockholders who expect to receive dividends. The decision to preempt regular programming is a costly one. If the news interrupts or preempts a program that attracts a small audience, the network loses less money than if a popular program is interrupted. Consequently, a network whose programs are unpopular risks less by interrupting them with breaking news.

The cost of preempting entertainment programming to cover government activities was documented by a government study, which concluded that there was one major reason for the "decline in network interest in matters of government—the enormous increase in network earnings and the huge loss of profits that would result from any preemption."[35]

---

32. Stanley K. Bigman, "Rivals in Conformity: A Study of Two Competing Dailies," *Journalism Quarterly* 25 (Spring 1984): 127–131.

33. Stephen Lacy, "The Effects of Intracity Competition," *Journalism Quarterly* 64 (Summer/Autumn 1987): 281–290.

34. William Glaberson, "The Press: Bought and Sold and Gray All Over," *New York Times,* 30 July 1995, p. E1.

35. The Second Report with Recommendations of the Temporary Select Committee to Study the Senate Committee System, cited in Marvin Barrett, *Rich News, Poor News* (New York: Thomas Y. Crowell, 1978), p. 136.

Yet a network's prestige is, in part, a function of the quality of its news programming, and viewers are comforted by the assurance that if something important happens, the networks will interrupt regular programming to bring them that information. Therefore, whatever the cost, a network cannot afford to ignore important news. When John Kennedy was assassinated, for example, there was no question that the networks would preempt whatever was on the air to bring that word and ensuing developments to the audience. But most news is not as important as a presidential assassination. In such cases, profit and loss must be weighed against the gain in prestige that might result from the coverage, or the loss in prestige if the event is not covered. A network is particularly vulnerable when one of its competitors covers an event.

Television networks occasionally agree to rotate coverage of an important event to minimize loss of advertising revenue. Accordingly, the networks rotated coverage of the Iran-Contra hearings. This gave the audience a chance to choose between regular programming and coverage of the hearings. Audience members know what they have missed, or that television should have aired an event and didn't, because newspaper television critics tell them. Caught in this bind, television has sought ways to ensure audience awareness of the news without interrupting regularly scheduled programming except in extraordinary circumstances.

The "news break," sponsored by an advertiser, represents one such avenue. News breaks occur during commercial breaks in programming and are brief summaries of the day's headlines. This creates an association between news and advertising, which advertisers desire. With news breaks or news updates, advertisers, not the network, bear the cost of underwriting the time, and programming goes on as expected.

Television also runs print information across the lower third of the screen during regular programming to bring important information to the viewer. This device is used more often to tell the viewer that the local news will follow a program that is running overtime than to convey important breaking news, but it is also used to keep audiences posted on the status of hurricanes or tornadoes and to indicate disaster warnings and watches.

Not everyone agrees that live news coverage is a blessing. In 1986, for example, the ABC and NBC television networks were flooded with calls from angry viewers who tuned in to watch their favorite soap operas only to find them preempted by live coverage of congressional hearings on the Iran arms sale. All three networks preempted regular daytime programming for coverage of the hearings. ABC News spokesperson Thomas Goodman said the network received 1,330 calls. "All objected to preemption of soap operas," he said. NBC reported receiving 1,100 complaints. CBS received fewer than three dozen calls.[36] Some coverage, such as network coverage of Nixon's trip to the Soviet Union, was criticized as political propaganda. This charge was given credence when two of Nixon's re-election campaign commercials in 1972 consisted of edited news footage of his trips to Russia and China.

---

36. *New York Times*, 11 December 1986, p. 10Y.

Commercial pressures for high ratings and the revenues they assure affect judgments about what news will be covered, particularly if coverage involves the costly preemption of other lucrative programming. As a result, in 1988, all three major networks cut their coverage of the Republican and Democratic National Conventions. The extensive coverage provided by CNN and the gavel-to-gavel coverage by C-SPAN enabled viewers with cable television to see both the Democratic and Republican conventions firsthand in 1988 and 1992.

Pressures from Advertisers

The price of subscriptions does not pay the total cost of producing a newspaper or magazine. Both are underwritten by advertising revenue, and commercial television and radio are almost completely financed by advertising. Their dependence on these external sources of funding renders them vulnerable to boycotts by advertisers. For example, in spring 1986, some Detroit car dealers canceled their ads in the *Detroit Free Press* after the newspaper published an exposé detailing antitrust charges against local dealerships. The FTC had charged 105 dealers and 115 individuals with conspiracy for trying to limit showroom hours and for trying to limit competition by fixing prices.[37]

And in August 1995, the *Columbia Journalism Review* awarded a "Dart" to the *Gloucester County Times* of Woodbury, New Jersey, when the paper ran a front-page story on the twentieth anniversary of the John Wanamaker store. The paper had just gotten Wanamaker as an advertiser. When the news department told the ad department that it wouldn't run a story, the editor dispatched a reporter and ordered that the story run, complete with a photo spread.

For the first time, in early August 1995 the Federal Trade Commission acted against a group of advertisers that was boycotting a newspaper over coverage of their product. On May 22, 1994, a reporter for the *San Jose Mercury News* had written an article titled "A Car Buyer's Guide to Sanity" telling readers how to get a better buy on a car. Dealers responded by pulling about a million dollars worth of advertising. The FTC initiated an antitrust investigation that resulted in a cease-and-desist agreement by the Santa Clara County Motor Car Dealers Association.[38] The dealers' boycott raised two concerns, said the FTC official who handled the investigation. The absence of advertising deprived readers of price information while the boycott may have chilled the publication of similar articles.

Television, too, is subject to pressure from advertisers. Prior to the accident at the Three Mile Island nuclear plant, Jane Fonda appeared on a Barbara Walters ABC special to discuss her film *The China Syndrome* and its antinuclear message. General Electric, one of the four biggest builders of nuclear reactors in the world, promptly withdrew its sponsorship of the program.[39]

---

37. *Washington Post*, 28 May 1986, p. G1.
38. Anthony Ramirez, "Advertising," *New York Times*, 2 August 1995, p. D3.
39. Marvin Barrett and Zachary Sklar, *The Eye of the Storm* (New York: Lippincott and Crowell, 1980), pp. 130–131.

In addition, corporations whose environmental practices are portrayed unflatteringly on the news are striking back at the press with angry letters, point-by-point rebuttals, news releases, and paid ads. These include Hooker Chemicals and General Motors, among others.[40]

Still another example was action in early 1989 by the Washington State Fruit Commission, a growers' trade association, that withdrew $71,300 worth of television advertising for northwest cherries from CBS affiliates in St. Louis, Atlanta, and Tampa to protest a news report about Alar on CBS's *60 Minutes*. "Our association wanted to voice its displeasure over the way the CBS broadcast of the *60 Minutes* program sensationalized the Alar story," said Pat Dunlop, a spokesperson for the commission. The money budgeted for advertising was diverted to other stations in those markets.

The account, televised February 26, 1989, on *60 Minutes,* dealt with a study by the Natural Resources Defense Council on pesticides in foods that affect children and concluded that eating apples treated with Alar, a chemical used to control ripening, increased cancer risks for children. The report was disputed by the apple industry, and federal regulators have declared apples safe to eat, but the report sent apple sales into a steep decline. Growers contend they lost millions of dollars as a result. Alar is not used on cherries, but many of the group's members grow both crops.[41]

As these examples demonstrate, advertisers actively attempt to affect news coverage.

Threat of Lawsuits

The costs of defending against a lawsuit are high. Coverage of controversial subjects, hard-hitting editorials, and investigative reporting are particularly likely to attract libel suits. Consequently, local television stations, particularly those in small markets, tend to shy away from such reporting, according to a survey by the National Association of Broadcasters. Who threatens to sue? Businesspeople threaten to sue over consumer reporting on pollution, car defects, and the like. Politicians threaten to sue over politically damaging material.[42]

In recent years, the Supreme Court has let stand awards of more than $2 million each in punitive damages awarded to individuals who sued a daily newspaper and a network-owned television station. Punitive damages are now awarded in 60 percent of the cases won by plaintiffs against the media. Average awards exceed one million dollars. In early 1990, in *Sprague v. Walter,* a jury in Pennsylvania awarded $31.5 million in punitive damages against the *Philadelphia Inquirer* for a story written in the early 1970s questioning a local prosecutor's han-

---

40. A. Kent MacDougall, "Reporting Environmental Hazards, Job Dangers Pose Risks for Media," *Los Angeles Times*, 23 November 1980, sec. V, pp. 1, 2.

41. "Fruit Growers Kill Ads in Protest to CBS," *New York Times*, 7 May 1989, p. 15Y.

42. Steve Winberg, "New Coverage for TV News," *Panorama*, March 1981, p. 14.

dling of a homicide case. In *CBS Inc. v. Brown and Williamson Tobacco Corp.,* the tobacco company sued a Chicago-owned CBS affiliate for libel arguing that its advertisements had been misrepresented. CBS countered that the piece in question was commentary and as such protected by the First Amendment. The court held that the station had falsely accused the tobacco firm of soliciting young smokers as customers.[43]

Private individuals and corporations are not the only ones able to bring legal pressure to bear on the media. As we mentioned in Chapter 3, in May 1986 then CIA Director William J. Casey suggested that the Department of Justice consider prosecuting NBC News for violation of the 1950 law prohibiting disclosure of "communications intelligence." The NBC News report that Casey was objecting to concerned the trial of accused spy Ronald W. Pelton.

Another example of the power of lawsuits came in August 1995, when ABC News agreed to apologize twice in prime time, during halftime of the broadcast of *Monday Night Football* and on *Day One,* for a report broadcast on the latter that contended that Philip Morris and R. J. Reynolds controlled and manipulated nicotine levels in cigarettes in order to addict smokers. The apology was the settlement of two lawsuits by the tobacco companies charging ABC News with libel. The case against ABC News turned on a single word, "spike." In its report on how Philip Morris makes cigarettes, ABC contended that the company "spiked" cigarettes by adding nicotine in the manufacturing process. Because the production process removes nicotine from tobacco leaves used for filler, Philip Morris contends that it is "recombining" the ingredients, not spiking. The settlement aroused fears among employees that ABC might no longer be as vigilant in protecting news, particularly since Capital Cities had been acquired by the Walt Disney Company. Both the correspondent on the *Day One* segment and its producer refused to sign the settlement.

John P. Coale, one of a consortium of lawyers that has mounted the largest class action suit in history against the tobacco companies, said that ABC was intimidated by the huge damages, $10 billion, that Philip Morris was seeking in its suit. Dr. Richard A. Daynard, a professor at the Northeastern University School of Law and chair of the Tobacco Products Liability Project, a nonprofit antismoking group, said, "Philip Morris has bullied a major television network into apologizing for what was essentially a true story."[44] Cliff Douglas, executive director of Tobacco Control, Law and Policy Consulting, an antismoking research group, said, "There is no question that the documents ABC obtained from Philip Morris [as part of the libel suit] directly contradict ABC's apology." He and other critics cite this as proof that ABC's decision to settle was made by the network's parent, Capital Cities/ABC Inc., for purely financial reasons.[45] Reuven Frank, a former

43. Lee Levine and David L. Perry, "No Way to Celebrate the Bill of Rights," *Columbia Journalism Review* (July/August 1990): 38.
44. Mark Landler, "ABC News Settles Suits on Tobacco," *New York Times,* 22 August 1995, pp. A1, C6.
45. Mark Landler, "Critic Presses Tobacco Case Despite Settlement by ABC," *New York Times,* 24 August 1995, p. C2.

television news producer and former president of NBC News, which is owned by General Electric, put the decision in a slightly different light. "This is called the pay-the-$5-fine syndrome. Philip Morris could have tied up ABC in court for months."[46] Philip Morris took out full-page ads in many newspapers (for example, *Washington Post, New York Times, Wall Street Journal, Star Tribune*) trumpeting its success in forcing ABC to apologize. By obtaining an apology, particularly in a period when tobacco companies are under attack, Philip Morris achieved what no amount of ordinary advertising could have done. Moreover, their success will make other news outlets more cautious in their coverage of these issues.

The limited amount of editorializing on radio and television stations also reflects fears of legal reprisals. And when broadcasters do editorialize, they tend to take noncontroversial stands, such as "support your local blood bank" or "welcome the former hostages home." In many cases, the positions taken are vague and ambiguous. Threats of lawsuits contribute to such neutrality.

In June 1986 the Supreme Court made it easier for the news media to gain dismissal of libel suits without the high costs of trials. In a 6–3 ruling, the Court held for columnist Jack Anderson and against the conservative Liberty Lobby. A magazine edited by Anderson had called the group neo-Nazi, anti-Semitic, racist, and fascist. The Court held that judges should dismiss cases unless evidence of "actual malice" by the media was "clear and convincing." To establish actual malice, a complainant must show that the media knew the material was false or published with reckless disregard for whether it was false.

Political Pressure

Anthony Smith reports that "during the Carter Administration, government was spending $1 billion a year on its own information services (the Pentagon alone had 1,500 press officers, spending $25 million a year)."[47] That expenditure reflects the magnitude of the government effort to influence what and how information is disseminated. But the government has resources far more important than money.

The president is always news and has great power to influence press coverage through leaks, exclusive interviews, pseudo-events (like White House Rose Garden activities), and appeals to national security, among other means. Some of the ways campaigners manipulate the press are treated in Chapter 11. Here we consider the political pressure created by the federal government, particularly the executive branch.

46. Mark Landler, "Philip Morris Revels in Rare ABC News Apology for Report on Nicotine," *New York Times*, 28 August 1995, p. C5.
47. Anthony Smith, *Goodbye Gutenberg: The Newspaper Revolution of the 1980's* (New York: Oxford, 1980), p. 175.

Presidential Newsworthiness

The president is always able to make news. He can call a press conference, announce a forthcoming event (an agreement or a future summit meeting), or schedule a ritual (awarding a medal, for instance). As the *New York Times'* former White House correspondent, John Herbers, notes:

> No other institution can demand space and attention throughout the media when there is no news there. The White House does every day. The President can demand front-page coverage by holding a press conference in which he says nothing that has not been said before. He can command prime television time by granting an exclusive interview to one of the networks, and newspapers feel compelled to write about it at length because millions saw it on television.[48]

Facts that would not be newsworthy about anyone else become newsworthy when tied to the president. For example, network television as well as newspapers carried major stories on George Bush's declaration, "I do not like broccoli and I haven't liked it since I was a little kid and my mother made me eat it and I'm president of the United States and I'm not going to eat any more broccoli." By providing a moment of comic relief in an otherwise serious day, the comment humanized Bush. To laughter, he then added, "Wait a minute. For the broccoli vote out there, Barbara loves broccoli. She's tried to make me eat it; she eats it all the time herself. So she can go out and meet the caravan of [trucks bringing] broccoli." With that as a tease, the story continued. On March 26, 1990, Barbara Bush's picture appeared in newspapers. In front of her was a table of broccoli.

A focus on "the human side" of the White House can displace other forms of coverage. Inviting such coverage is itself a form of manipulation of the news agenda. By early 1990, the Bushs' dog Millie had entered the annals of U.S. history along with Franklin Roosevelt's Fala and Richard Nixon's Checkers. When Millie delivered puppies, network stories followed. A survey for the Center for the Media and Public Affairs concluded that from Bush's first day as president until November 30, 1989, Millie had appeared more frequently on network news than Bush's education secretary, his agricultural secretary, or his secretary for veterans affairs. "Let me give you a little serious, political, inside advice," Bush told a Republican fundraiser. "One single word. 'Puppies.' Worth ten points [in the polls], believe me."[49]

Such newsworthiness gives the executive enormous powers of manipulation. The Reagan administration proved highly adept at managing presidential press contacts. As one reporter noted:

> The President delivers the good news, usually in situations that insulate him from questions, while aides deal with controversial matters. . . . Few White House

---

48. John Herbers, *No Thank You, Mr. President* (New York: Norton, 1976), p. 41.
49. David Hoffman, "The Frictionless Presidency," *Gannett Center Journal* (Spring 1990): 92.

teams have exhibited such expertise in associating an executive only with the popular decisions and dramatic moments of his Presidency.[50]

Such control maintains the president's personal popularity, protects him from situations in which gaffes might be made, and allows the anger generated by unpopular decisions to be deflected onto presidential assistants. Given such control of access, press coverage is inevitably limited and manipulated. More readily than any other politician or citizen, the president also can take to the airwaves to speak directly to the American people.

When the networks judge the topic to be newsworthy, the president is granted what amounts to automatic access. After former House Democratic leader Tip O'Neill denied Ronald Reagan's June 1986 request to address the House on the issue of aid to the Contras in Nicaragua, Reagan asked for network time to speak directly to the American people. The three major networks declined on the grounds that the president's speech would not make news. Cable News Network, which carries news twenty-four hours a day, aired the speech.

National Security

Because information about foreign relations is more difficult to corroborate and because they are citizens as well as reporters, members of the press are susceptible to the administration's line on foreign policy. David Halberstam's *The Powers That Be* documents how the government sustained press support for Vietnam policy. Appeals to support presidential policies are made in the name of "national security" and "protection of vital interests." Such appeals usually prove irresistible.

Appeals to national security are complicated by competition among news outlets. In some cases, journalists keep a story off the air or out of the papers, only to see it broken by someone else. For example, for nearly a year the Carter and Reagan administrations tried to prevent publication of the existence of two secret listening posts operating in China with American equipment and Chinese personnel.

The story was finally reported in June 1981 on *NBC Nightly News*. Earlier, when they had learned of the posts' existence, two *New York Times* reporters were talked out of publishing the story—first by Carter's national security advisor, Zbigniew Brzezinski, and later by Reagan's CIA director, William J. Casey. NBC News, last in the ratings, had a strong incentive to break the story. However, the existence of the listening posts had been hinted at in the *Washington Post* several days earlier, and China's offer to replace posts lost in Iran after the revolution had been reported as early as April 1979. What gave the story such impact was the recent Reagan administration decision to authorize the first sale of "lethal" U.S. military equipment to China.[51]

---

50. Howell Raines, "Reporter's Notebook: Insulating a President," *New York Times*, 5 August 1981, p. A12.

51. Murrey Marder, "Monitoring Not-So-Secret," *Washington Post*, 19 June 1981, p. A10.

Government Manipulation

Strategic leaks of classified material are also used to manipulate the press. Just how common this practice is became clear during lawsuits over publication of the *Pentagon Papers*. In answer to claims by the Nixon administration, the *New York Times* responded "with 15 affidavits which laid out some of the ways in which government officials had selectively leaked classified material to the *Times* in the past to achieve their ends. . . . The *Post* also argued . . . that government officials had for years leaked classified material for their own purposes and introduced affidavits from staff members including Ben Bradlee, the newspaper's editor, and its foreign affairs specialist Chalmers Roberts."[52]

Stephen Hess, an analyst at the Brookings Institution, has identified six types of leaks. Each is based on a different motive: (1) policy leaks are "a straightforward pitch for or against a proposal using some document or insider's information"; (2) trial balloon leaks are an attempt to assess a proposal's strengths and weaknesses, assets and liabilities; (3) ego leaks satisfy the source's sense of self-importance; (4) goodwill leaks attempt to cultivate credit with a reporter; (5) animus leaks are designed to embarrass someone else; and (6) whistleblower leaks are the last resort of a frustrated civil servant who feels that he or she has exhausted remedies within the government.[53]

The political use of strategic leaks illustrates the symbiotic relationship between the press and the government. The government needs the press to disseminate information and to support its policies. The press needs the government as a major source of information.

This close relationship was illustrated by the Reagan administration's use of the press during trade talks held to persuade the Japanese to limit voluntarily automobile exports to the United States. The situation arose because the Reagan administration did not want to make any overt effort to restrict Japanese exports. However, the press was used to put pressure on the Japanese through a news release from "sources close to U.S. trade officials" indicating that talks were going badly and that it was hoped that other proposals would be forthcoming from the Japanese. Reporters who were induced to print that story "later concluded that they had been gulled in a U.S. scheme to put overnight pressure on the Japanese." In effect, the Reagan administration used the press as a conduit for its negotiations while maintaining the fiction that it was making no attempt to restrict Japanese exports.[54]

In August 1995, when human rights activist Harry Wu was being held on charges of spying by the Chinese government, no formal offer of a quid pro quo for his release was made. But informal contacts through the media suggested that

---

52. William E. Porter, *Assault on the Media: The Nixon Years* (Ann Arbor: University of Michigan Press, 1976), pp. 97–98.

53. Stephen Hess, *The Government/Press Connection: Press Officers and Their Offices* (Washington, D.C.: Brookings Institution, 1984), pp. 75–94.

54. William Chapmen, "Reporters Gulled into Being a Channel for Auto-Imports Haggling," *Washington Post*, 7 May 1981, p. A31.

if Wu were released, First Lady Hillary Rodham Clinton would attend the U.N.-sponsored Decade of Women Conference being held in Beijing. Wu was convicted, but sentenced to exile to the United States and released, and the First Lady announced that she would attend the conference.

Cooperation between press and government is increased by movements from press jobs to government jobs, and vice versa. For example, NBC reporter Ron Nessen, who had covered Ford as vice president, became President Ford's press secretary. Eileen Shanahan, economic reporter for the *New York Times,* took a position in the Department of Education during the Carter administration and then became a reporter for the *Washington Star.* Leslie Gelb first worked in government for Secretary of Defense McNamara, then became a reporter at the *New York Times* after a breather at the Brookings Institution. After four years at the *Times,* he moved to the State Department as Cyrus Vance's assistant secretary for politico-military affairs. Two-and-a-half years later he left the State Department, paused at the Brookings Institution, and returned to the *Times.* Meanwhile, Richard Burt, who had taken Gelb's job at the *Times,* left his position to take Gelb's former job in the State Department under Alexander Haig. NBC legal reporter Carl Stern left his position to become spokesperson for the Clinton Justice Department. Such musical chairs between government and press raise questions of journalistic integrity. Can a reporter write objectively about a person now doing her or his former job or about policies or programs that she or he once defended? Can a reporter write without bias about those who have the power to advance his or her prospects for a government job?[55]

There is considerable evidence of the power of government to manipulate press coverage. Government agencies spend huge sums of money to disseminate their messages through the mass media. The power of the presidency is also used manipulatively. By managing the president's ability to make news, to control access to information, to plead national security, to schedule staged news events, and to leak material strategically, the executive branch can gain implicit news media endorsement for administration policies. For example, when asked how the administration would respond to Soviet leader Mikhail Gorbachev's televised speech on the Chernobyl nuclear accident, former White House spokesperson Larry Speakes responded, "If it's something really big, the President would say it. . . . If it was semi-big, I'd come out and say something. If it was teeny-tiny, we'd give out a piece of paper. And if it was teeny-tinier than that, we'd let the State Department do it."[56]

The resignation of Bernard Kalb as chief spokesperson for the State Department climaxed allegations of blatant press manipulation by the Reagan administration. Kalb described his resignation as a protest against the deception and disinformation campaign launched in August against Libyan leader Muammar Qaddafi. "You face a choice—as an American, as a spokesman, as a journalist—whether to allow oneself to be absorbed in the ranks of silence, whether to vanish into unopposed acquiescence or to enter a modest dissent." He added, "Faith

---

55. Philip Nobile, "Covering Yourself: From Bureaucrat to Beat," *New York,* 30 March 1981, pp. 8–9.
56. *Washington Post,* 15 May 1986, p. A19.

in the word of America is the pulse beat of our democracy. Anything that hurts America's credibility hurts America."[57] Before accepting the post of assistant secretary of state for public affairs, Kalb had been a correspondent for the *New York Times,* CBS, and NBC for almost forty years.

Charges that the Reagan administration had engaged in a disinformation campaign about Libya and its leader arose after a story by Bob Woodward appeared in the *Washington Post.* The story disclosed details of a memorandum by Vice-Admiral John M. Poindexter, then White House national security advisor, reportedly urging a campaign against Qaddafi involving "real and illusory events— through a disinformation program."

The White House denied that the administration had planted false reports with news organizations in the United States, but former presidential spokesperson Larry Speakes had no comment on whether the administration had tried to conduct such a disinformation campaign against Libya in foreign news organizations.

According to the *Post* story, major newspapers had carried erroneous news reports generated by this plan. A front-page article appeared on August 25 in the *Wall Street Journal* saying Libya was planning new terrorist attacks. Citing unidentified "U.S. and West European intelligence officials," the story said that the United States was on a "collision course" with Libya, that "growing evidence suggests" new Libyan terrorist attacks were being planned, and that "the Pentagon is completing plans for a new and larger bombing of Libya in case the President orders it." All three network television evening news programs repeated the substance of the *Journal's* report the night after it appeared, and on August 26 many major newspapers quoted identified and unidentified officials who seemed to confirm the *Journal* article. Some newspapers, including the conservative *Washington Times,* began to question the reports and to suggest that a disinformation campaign was underway.

In a news conference, Secretary of State George Shultz refused to comment on whether or not such a campaign of disinformation had been undertaken, but seemed to confirm the report through his answers, which praised the use of deception if it would cause problems for the Libyan leader. An unidentified White House official was quoted making similar statements:

> We think for domestic consumption there will be no problems. It's Qaddafi. After all, whatever it takes to get rid of him is all right with us—that's the feeling, we think, in the country. On the foreign scene it will cause problems, though. We're constantly talking about the Soviets doing disinformation. It's going to cause difficulties for us. We don't think it's a major, lasting firestorm, but there will be some ripples.[58]

As these comments suggest, public attitudes about the proper roles of the press and the government are an important factor in setting the parameters of government manipulation of the press and press interference in political events.

---

57. Minneapolis *Star and Tribune*, 9 October 1986, p. 1A.
58. Bernard Weinraub, "White House and Its News," *New York Times*, 3 October 1986, p. 4Y.

It may seem peculiar that this chapter contains no discussion of influence exerted by the Federal Communications Commission. In our judgment, that influence ranges from minuscule to nonexistent. Network executives frequently express fears of licensing nonrenewal, but no such fears are warranted by past FCC action, at least in regard to news programming. "A renewal application has never been denied solely because of a failure to meet community needs and problems, an excess of commercials, a lack of public service announcements, or an inadequate amount of news, public affairs, or other nonentertainment material."[59]

TO SUM UP

The news media influence and are, in turn, influenced. The most effective manipulators of media news are those who understand journalistic norms and routines and use them to gain media access and to influence the nature of coverage. The news media are influenced by highly paid news managers and their clients and by other individuals and groups. The news media are also affected by commercial pressures for ratings and revenues and by the protests of those offended by news coverage. Finally, they respond to pressures from those in position of political power.

The next chapter explores the roles of ratings and revenues in mass media social systems.

SELECTED READINGS

Cole, Barry, and Mal Oettinger. *Reluctant Regulators: The FCC and the Broadcast Audience*. Reading, Mass.: Addison-Wesley, 1978.

Gitlin, Todd. *The Whole World Is Watching: Mass Media in the Making and Unmaking of the New Left*. Berkeley: University of California Press, 1980.

Glasser, Theodore L., and Charles T. Salmon. *Public Opinion and the Communication of Consent*. New York: Guilford, 1995.

Goldenberg, Edie N. *Making the Papers*. Lexington, Mass.: Lexington Books, 1975.

Hess, Stephen. *The Government/Press Connection: Press Officers and Their Offices*. Washington, D.C.: Brookings Institution, 1984.

———. *News and Newsmaking*. Washington, D.C.: Brookings Institution, 1995.

———. *The Rise of the Professional Specialist in Washington Journalism*. Washington, D.C.: Brookings Institution, 1986.

Pearce, David D. *Wary Partners: Diplomats and the Media*. Washington, D.C.: Congressional Quarterly, 1995.

Ranney, Austin. *Channels of Power*. New York: Basic Books, 1983.

Schmidt, Benno C., Jr. *Freedom of the Press vs. Public Access*. New York: Praeger, 1976.

Schwartz, Bernard. *Freedom of the Press*. New York: Facts on File, 1992.

---

59. Barry Cole and Mal Oettinger, *Reluctant Regulators: The FCC and the Broadcast Audience* (Reading, Mass.: Addison-Wesley, 1978), p. 134.

CHAPTER 5

Ratings and Revenues: The Audience in Mass Media Social Systems

This chapter is about money. Specifically, it is about how sellers (the mass media) and buyers (advertisers) determine the price to be paid for advertising in the print or broadcast media. This chapter is also about how mass media systems function. As we discussed in Chapter 1, *the primary function of the mass media is to attract and hold large audiences for advertisers.*

Here we examine how audiences are measured and how advertising rates are set. Because the price of an ad is determined by the size and makeup of the audience, this chapter is also about ratings. Ratings services measure and describe the audiences of radio and television programming and the readership of magazines; circulation size and intensity serve a similar function for newspapers.

The Mass Media: Social Systems

Wherever they exist, the mass media are complex systems composed of interrelated elements or parts.[1] Because mass media in the United States are wholly or partially commercial, measures of audience behavior (what audiences watch, hear, or read and what they buy) and revenues (the results of audience behaviors) are central to the system.

Audiences, as measured by ratings, determine the success or failure of *programming* or *content.* Content reaches the audience through *distributors*—outlets such as the networks, individual stations, wire services, theaters, magazines, and newspapers. *Producers* of content (including subsystems of reporters, actors, camera crews, labor unions, and publishers) are financed by *advertisers* or backers who, in turn, depend on advertisers for their money.

---

1. The ideas in this section are drawn from the work of Melvin L. De Fleur. (See Melvin L. De Fleur and Sandra Ball-Rokeach, *Theories of Mass Communication,* 3d ed. [New York: Longman, 1975], pp. 156–172.)

Advertising agencies connect advertisers with distributors (outlets), with content producers, and with *audience-* and *market-research organizations* such as Nielsen and Arbitron, which gather data on audience behavior (ratings and purchasing patterns).

Government regulators include the Federal Communications Commission (FCC), which licenses distributors, and the Federal Trade Commission (FTC) and the courts, which set limits on advertising, news, and program content.

Citizen regulators, which generate political pressure, include watchdog groups such as Action for Children's Television, the Gray Panthers Media Watch, and the Coalition for Better Television. *Self-regulatory mechanisms* arise to forestall government or legal regulation, or to defuse political pressure; some of these are newspaper ombudsmen and -women, the National Association of Broadcasters, the Electronic Media Ratings Council, the National Advertising Division of the Better Business Bureau, and the National Advertising Review Board.

As social systems, the mass media are part of the larger social system of our society. U.S. social norms are expressed in laws, moral codes, conventions (what we find entertaining, appropriate, or offensive), and values (what we believe in, such as the efficacy of free enterprise, the legitimacy of the profit motive, and the importance of freedom of speech). These norms influence audience behavior and underlie all forms of regulation.

All social systems seek to survive, to maintain their stability and equilibrium. In the United States, the chief requirement is commercial: in order to survive, mass media must generate profits or adequate financing, which requires attracting substantial audiences. Ratings measure how well the mass media do this, and revenues depend on such ratings. Audience behavior (what is listened to, watched, read, and bought) and audience norms (what entertains, what offends) are fundamental to mass media systems. These, in turn, reflect how the mass media have developed in the history of this society.

A Brief History of the Mass Media

Many older Americans remember a time when there were no radios; many more of us remember a time before television. The brevity of film history was underlined when Lillian Gish, who as a young woman was a star of the earliest silent films, made a presentation at the 1981 Academy Award ceremonies. Only the print media date back beyond living memory, and even their current forms are quite recent. Today's newspaper was born in the nineteenth century with the advent of the "penny press"; the pocket-sized paperback book, making all kinds of books accessible to nearly everyone, is a twentieth-century creation.

The development of the mass media coincides with U.S. growth into an industrial, mass, affluent society. This societal transformation means that nearly all of us now depend on a system called "the market" for producing, distributing, and selling goods to satisfy our needs. We do not produce what we consume; instead we sell our labor for wages and buy goods produced by others.

If such a marketing system is to work well, we need to get information about available goods and services, their location, price, and comparative advantages. Making that information known is advertising's central function.

Even this brief description shows that an industrial society is highly organized. In addition to market dependence, such a society fosters and depends on a division of labor so goods can be produced more cheaply and efficiently. Carried to its obvious conclusion, this division of labor created the assembly lines that transformed cars from rare, luxury items for the wealthy into Model T Fords most Americans could afford.

Such a society also depends on technology. As the cost of both labor and raw materials rises, items like ready-to-wear clothes can be kept within the price ranges of most Americans only when machines speed up and simplify the processes of production, enabling industries to mass produce the items. The elements of mass media systems reflect this division of labor and this reliance on technology.

Industrial societies are mass societies. If an industrial system is to work, there must be a large market for goods because the savings that come from machines and assembly lines can only be realized if many cars or dresses can be produced and sold to many people. Industrial societies also tend to be affluent societies. Industries require large amounts of capital, and successful industries must sell their goods to many individuals who must have the money to buy them. Like other industries, the media reach large audiences who must be able to afford newspapers, magazines, radios, and television sets, and the products they advertise.

The Role of Mass Media Advertising

Mass media are central to such industrial, mass, affluent societies. We depend on them to know what jobs are available, what goods we can buy, where, and for how much. The essential role of mass media advertising under such conditions is described by David Potter:

> It is when potential supply outstrips demand—that is, when abundance prevails—that advertising begins to fulfill a really essential economic function. In this situation the producer knows that the limitation upon his [sic] growth no longer lies, as it lay historically, in his productive capacity, for he can always produce as much as the market will absorb; the limitation has shifted to the market, and its selling capacity which controls his growth.[2]

The advertising Potter describes is done through the mass media—their primary function is to attract and hold large audiences for advertisers. Mass media in the

---

2. David Potter, *People of Plenty: Economic Abundance and the American Character* (Chicago: University of Chicago Press, 1954), pp. 172–173.

United States are commercial media; their job is to gather audiences for persuaders. They also inform and entertain, of course, but informing and entertaining are only means to the end of delivering mass audiences to advertisers.

The Audience

As central elements in mass media systems and the mass society, advertisers have two related purposes: to reach the largest possible audience, and to reach the ideal (target) audience for their products. An "efficient advertising buy" (reaching the largest number of the ideal or target audience at the lowest price) is measured in terms of cost per thousand (CPT) persons reached and in terms of audience desirability—the age, sex, income, education, occupation, region, location (urban, suburban, rural), and ethnic background of audience members reached.

In 1990, for example, *CBS Evening News* had two financial problems. First, it had been displaced by ABC as the most watched evening news show. This meant that whereas ABC could command up to $85,000 for thirty seconds of ad time, in the second quarter of 1990, CBS could only sell that amount of time for around $45,000. The drop in audience also meant that CBS had to offer more "make-goods" (additional ad slots at no extra charge) to compensate for not delivering the promised audience.

The second problem for CBS was that its audience had been and continued to be older overall than the audiences of its two prime competitors, and as *Electronic Media* commented, "older viewer demographics . . . are less marketable."[3] By 1995, *Variety* was noting that "Even CBS has backed off trying to convince Madison Avenue that mature Americans do spend money and is now programming young."[4] A shift in programming was underway designed to attract the younger viewers that advertisers prefer.

There is some evidence that the bulk of those viewers who abandoned CBS after its shift in programming did not go to other networks but instead found their way to cable television channels such as Discovery, Lifetime, American Movie Classics, and Arts and Entertainment, which provide programming more attractive to over-50 Americans. In 1995, cable subscriptions were up 3 percent, and differences in programming may be one explanation. Moreover, the one cable channel that lost more than 15 percent of its audience during 1994 was MTV.[5]

In spring 1978 when one of us coordinated hearings on age discrimination and television for the House Committee on Aging, broadcasters testified that as the baby boom generation aged, the size and disposable income of that large group would increase the desirability of programming for and advertising to the older market. Some signs that this was beginning to happen were evident in

---

3. "Network News Cost-Cutting Spreads," *Electronic Media*, 9 April 1990, p. 46.
4. Joe Flint, "Seniors Get Wired as Cablers Pay for Gray," *Variety*, 24 July 1995, p. 1.
5. Bill Carter, "Cable Picks up Viewers the Networks Cast Adrift," *New York Times*, 5 June 1995, p. C7.

BOX 5-1

VALS—State of the Art Advertising

The newest marketing techniques hone in on a consumer's lifestyle (marital status, education, region, sex) and attitudes (religion, ambition, optimism, and so on), which are considered better bases for appeal than income.

VALS, short for "values and lifestyles," generates a series of categories: survivors (poor, old), sustainers (struggling, young), belongers (traditional conformists), emulators (macho yuppies), achievers (familial workaholics), and "I-am-Me's" (young 1980s individualists), experientials (menopausal new-agers), and the societally conscious (1960s nostalgics). The most prestigious are the "integrated": mature, intelligent, sensitive, successful—and 2 percent of the population.

The categories sell: they're used by Time Mirror, AT&T, Procter & Gamble, Tupperware, as well as the British Conservative Party—institutions not known for romantic delusion. They assume a certain self-consciousness on the part of the consumer, an increasing awareness of personal as well as socioeconomic identity. They succeed by flattering individuals' fantasies about themselves, not by expressly relating identity to a class. They work because they play more on our fantasies about the future than on any reality about our past.[a]

[a]Andrew Sullivan, "Buying and Nothingness," *New Republic*, 8 May 1989, p. 37.

---

summer 1995 when executives announced that the Prime Life Network and an AARP network would be launched in 1996. In 1995, Nielsen reported that there were 28.9 million women and 22.5 million men over 55, and 61.9 million 18-to-49-year-old women and 60.2 million men; however, the older cohort was growing much more rapidly than the younger.[6]

Demographic shifts have influenced advertising. In the 1970s there was a shift away from "shotgun" advertising, aimed at the largest possible audience, to advertising targeted at specific audiences, such as homeowners, children, teenagers, Hispanics, or working women. For large national advertisers, the most desirable audience is women between the ages of 18 and 49 who make the largest number of consumption decisions, followed closely by men of the same ages, who are believed to make more of the decisions about such durable goods as automobiles.[7]

Advertisers speak of "upscale" and "downscale" audiences. An audience is upscale if its members are above average in education and disposable income and in the prime age group. An audience is downscale if it is older, less affluent, less well-educated, rural, and in blue-collar occupations. In 1990, the publication that attracted the largest number of readers with incomes over $60,000 was *National*

---

6. Joe Flint, p. 82.

7. The accuracy of this perception may be open to question. In "Sex, Lies & Advertising," *Ms.*, July/August 1990, Gloria Steinem indicates that "long after figures showed a third, even a half, of many car models being bought by women, U.S. carmakers continue to be uncomfortable addressing women" (p. 20).

BOX 5-2

Targeting Virile Females

On February 16, 1990, the *Washington Post* revealed R. J. Reynolds' plans for Project V.F. for "Virile Female." "The marketing plan's chief goal is to capture the market among 18-to-24-year-old women, the only group of Americans whose rate of smoking continues to increase. . . . The advertising campaign focuses on women whose favorite pastimes include cruising, partying, and attending hot-rod shows and tractor pulls with their boyfriends. . . ." The marketing recommendations dated September 21, 1989, describe the preferred Dakota (the brand name) smoker as a woman with no education beyond high school, whose chief aspiration is "to get married in her early twenties" and spend her free time "with her boyfriend doing whatever he is doing."[a]

[a]Michael Spector, "Reynolds Plan Taps 'Virile' Female Smokers," *Philadelphia Inquirer*, 18 February 1990, p. 3A.

Geographic, followed by *Better Homes and Gardens,* and *Reader's Digest.* The newspaper that reached the largest number of wealthy readers was the *Wall Street Journal,* followed by *USA Today,* and the *Sunday New York Times.* The newsmagazine with the largest number of wealthy readers was *Time,* followed by *Newsweek.*[8]

The averages for 1989–90 reveal how the viewing preferences of the audience differ by age. Among adults 18 to 24, the most popular prime-time program was Fox's *Simpsons.* Among adults 25 to 54, it was *Roseanne.* But those 55 and older preferred *60 Minutes,* which didn't make the top ten shows viewed in either of the two younger age categories.[9]

Psychodemographics—the study of the interests, attitudes, and activities of specific population groups—is becoming increasingly important, although such ratings are still relatively new. For instance, Ronald Frank and Marshall Greenberg have done an extensive study of television viewers; they divide them into fourteen different audiences based on interests and activities. As they demonstrate, there is little relationship between traditional demographic analysis of television viewers and the fourteen interest groups that they identify.[10] Advertisers and programmers are very interested in such studies because activities and interests may be better predictors of viewing habits and consumption patterns than age, sex, income, or location.

Many advertisers advertise in more than one medium; they buy a "mix," which may be composed of billboards, direct mail, newspapers, magazines, radio, or television. Because ratings are subject to error, advertisers frequently shift

---

8. Mendelsohn Media Research reported in *Advertising Age,* 19 July 1990, p. S-1.

9. "TV Favorites Affected by Audience Age," *Advertising Age,* 21 May 1990, p. 46.

10. Ronald E. Frank and Marshall G. Greenberg, *The Public's Use of Television* (Beverly Hills: Sage, 1980), pp. 215–216.

their mix to discover, for example, if advertising in newspapers and regional magazines is more effective than in national newsmagazines. Some advertisers, though, are limited to certain media; for instance, cigarettes may not be advertised on television.

Media cross-advertise themselves and their products, as well. In 1988, newspapers spent $4.5 million heralding their accomplishments on billboards.[11] Radio stations promoted themselves to television viewers.[12] Television also used advertising to promote their prime-time and daytime programming to viewers of news, and vice versa. For example, when CBS fell from first place in news viewership, the network responded by creating and airing a half dozen promotional spots on news anchor Dan Rather. The spots showed Rather addressing high school audiences across the country and bore the tag, "More Than Just an Anchorman."

Cable television and videocassettes expanded the number of options for advertisers. The advent of these outlets and the decline in network audience levels translated roughly into a 5 percent decline in network ad revenues in 1989 over 1988.[13]

Each medium differs in terms of its system of ratings and revenues. In this chapter we examine the ratings and revenues of television (commercial and public), radio, newspapers, and magazines. Once again, we focus on the dominant media and on those media most directly involved in news and political communication.

Technology

The nature of the media and their relationship with their audiences can be profoundly influenced by changes in technology. In 1975 SATCOM I, the first domestic communications satellite, was launched. Up to that time most broadcast messages were transmitted through landlines. By the mid-1980s, most radio, broadcast, and cable signals were delivered by satellite. Satellites multiply the quantity of programming to which the typical viewer has access and make possible direct and almost immediate transmission of broadcast information from one point on the globe to another.

The advent of home video recorders also altered the media environment. VCRs increased the viewer's control over what was watched and when it was watched. The concept of "daypart" (a segment of a broadcast day), once a mainstay of media planners, potentially is rendered obsolete by VCRs. Viewers who are not even home when the program originally aired can now view it at their leisure. VCR tracking by Nielsen in November 1989 revealed that VCR owners

---

11. Pamela M. Terrell, "Newspaper Advertising in the Great Outdoors," *Presstime*, August 1989, p. 608.
12. "Using TV to Build Radio Station Identity," *Broadcasting*, 18 June 1990, p. 42.
13. "Media Firms Facing Turbulent Economy," *Electronic Media*, 13 August 1990, p. 38.

spent approximately 2 hours, 11 minutes recording. The households spent 3 hours, 45 minutes a week in playback.[14]

VCRs also made it possible for viewers to eliminate commercials from programming by fast-forwarding through them. Such "zipping" (fast-forwarding through commercials) is a major concern of advertisers who are eager to learn the extent to which VCRs are whittling down the size of their audiences. Barry Kaplan, chairperson of the Advertising Research Foundation Video Electronics Media Council, believes that up to a quarter of the programming recorded is never played back and that as many as two-thirds of the commercials are "zipped" when playback does occur.[15]

Computers have altered newsgathering techniques as well. Reporters now use computers to scan archives and to reduce large amounts of data to manageable form. Inequities are found and reported. In 1984, reporters at *Newsday* used a computer to search every state-awarded highway contract and county-awarded sewer contract for an eleven-year period. The computer parsed out a pattern that would otherwise have been difficult to see. As it turned out, five firms had collected a disproportionate amount of government business.[16] In April 1990, *Los Angeles Times'* reporters Sara Fritz and Dwight Morris used computers to search the disclosure files of candidates to track political contributions by more than 100 wealthy individuals. Donald Trump was among those found to have contributed more than the legal $25,000 limit.[17]

The increased use of computer data by political reporters is a function of their increased comfort with computers and the existence of purchasable magnetic tapes containing all of the federal election data for a political cycle. Additionally, Federal Election Commission data are now accessible through computer-tied phone lines at a low charge of $25 an hour.

The advent of the World Wide Web made it possible for individuals to program their own "home pages" and at the same time created the option for advertisers to sell products online. Whereas advertisers have tried to reach demographic groups through the mass media, the interactive capacity of the computer means that companies can now adapt their messages to the individual. So, for example, Chrysler Corporation asked Web site visitors to provide some demographic information before being given a "virtual" tour of the Chrysler Technology Center. In the text, the viewer is then addressed by name. Eventually, such information may be used to tailor a message from Chrysler to the individual computer operator.[18] Such possibilities led the Magazine Publishers of America in early July 1995 to call for a standard means of measuring advertising on the

---

14. *Nielsen Media News*, April 1990, p. 3.
15. "Industry Pushing for Accurate Measure of Commercial Zipping," *Television/Radio Age*, 28 April 1986, p. 96.
16. *Time*, 7 July 1986, p. 56.
17. "At FEC, Reporters Are Finally Getting Their PCs On-Line," *Roll Call*, 25 June 1990, p. 11.
18. Charles Waltner, "'Tell Us a Little about Yourself,'" *Advertising Age*, 17 July 1995, p. 13.

World Wide Web. Each click of the computer mouse now registers as a hit. The problem with that is that the same viewer may "click" many times.

A 1995 survey found that 37 million people have Internet access while 24 million are actual Internet users and 18 million Web users.[19]

Commercial Television

When television networks solicit the attention of advertisers, they do so in terms that make plain that what they are selling is their audience. For example, in *Electronic Media,* CBS promoted the *Late Show with David Letterman* by noting "America's #1 Late Night Entertainment" and added, "From coast to coast, Dave is America's late night favorite. He dominates the demos with young, upscale influential viewers and he's tops in households, too."[20]

Audiences are drawn to news in times of perceived crisis. The result is a revenue windfall for news networks. For example, when in summer 1990 Iraq moved into Kuwait, coverage of the resulting Middle East crisis pushed network news ratings up by 19 percent. This meant that in early August 1990, the network news programs had a larger average audience than did prime-time entertainment.

Commercial television is almost entirely financed by advertising. Network and station profits are the difference between programming costs (including salaries, equipment, and facilities) and the prices advertisers are charged to air commercials. For example, if the price of producing the network evening news is $100,000, but $400,000 worth of advertising can be sold, the network's profit is $300,000.

The prices charged for advertising on individual television programs are determined by Nielsen ratings.

Audience Ratings

Nielsen Ratings   The A. C. Nielsen Company is the biggest marketing research firm in the world, and it operates in twenty-two countries. Most of its income comes from research checking supermarket and drugstore shelves to find out how well certain products, brands, and sizes are selling. The Media Research Division, which computes the ratings, is only a small part of the Nielsen Company.

The Nielsen Company developed and patented a device called an "audimeter" that could be attached to television sets to record set-on, set-off information and the channel to which the set was tuned. In 1974, Nielsen began nationwide use of the Storage Instantaneous Audimeter (SIA), capable of reading up to four sets in a household, including battery-operated portables.

---

19. Peter H. Lewis, "Technology," *New York Times*, 30 October 1995, p. D5.
20. *Electronic Media*, 24 July 1995, p. 16.

Field representatives, offering a small fee, tried to persuade families to join the ratings panel for five-year periods. During any biweekly rating period, not all Nielsen homes were counted. Some had not yet been hooked up; others were lost because of malfunctions in audimeters or telephone lines. Sets that burned out or went dark because of power failures and families out for the evening or away on vacation were all counted as "no viewing for that day." Thus, on a typical ratings day in 1977, Nielsen reported viewing information from about 993 homes.

In 1986, there were approximately 1,700 SIA households in the national Nielsen sample, each connected to a special telephone line. At least twice a day a central computer dialed the audimeters and retrieved the stored viewing information. Network Nielsen ratings, reported in the Nielsen Television Index (NTI), were based on this secret sample of homes across the country picked randomly from a Census Bureau list but with a geographic spread. Major markets, including New York, Los Angeles, and Chicago, were metered with SIAs for overnight ratings. In actuality, ratings could be delivered to customers two days after programming was aired, allowing networks to make rapid programming decisions.

The Nielsen meters recorded only what was being watched—not who, if anyone, was doing the watching. For all the meters knew, the family dog may have been tuned attentively to reruns of *Lassie*. Ratings based on meters were supplemented by ratings from diaries, which were the basis for demographic breakdowns, showing how many men, women, and children in different age groups, by area, watched each program on the air; they provided the data for local market reports. The Nielsen Company reported that about half the people they asked to keep a diary refused.[21] Keeping a diary indicating program, channel, station, number of persons watching by age and sex for each quarter hour is tedious work, as one of the authors knows from personal experience!

The national Nielsen ratings, collected in the Nielsen National TV Ratings Report, statistically estimate the number of homes viewing a program projected from the viewing patterns of the homes with audimeters, combined with data from viewer diaries. There is an acknowledged 3 percent margin of error in the Nielsen ratings with the present sample size.[22] To halve the margin of error, thus doubling the precision of the ratings, would require a sample four times as large as the one Nielsen now uses. The networks, the ad agencies, the advertisers, and the program suppliers have not been willing to pay the price for greater accuracy.

A national rating represents the percentage of sample homes tuned in to the same show. For instance, if a program scores a 20 rating for the week, that means that 20 percent of the sample homes had that show turned in for at least six minutes (about 199 sets out of the average 993 reporting). A rating is the estimated percentage of television homes (households with television sets) that watched a program. In 1995, one rating point represented 954,000 homes.

---

21. David Chagall, "The Viewers Who Go Uncounted," *TV Guide*, 1 July 1978, p. 21.

22. For an indication of what this can mean for programming decisions, see David Chagall, "Can You Believe the Ratings?" *TV Guide*, 24 June 1978, especially p. 13.

BOX 5-3

Television Ratings and Shares

TV Set Off   Channel A   Channel B

Both ratings and shares measure how many people watch a given program. Ratings measure the percentage of people viewing a program out of all U.S. households with television sets, whether turned on or not. Shares measure the percentage of people viewing a program out of those U.S. households watching television at any given time.

Rating = % of U.S. households with television tuned to channel x.
Share = % of U.S. households watching television tuned to channel x.

	Rating	Share
Channel A	40	66.6
Channel B	20	33.3

Nielsen also reports what percentage of households actually watching television is tuned in to a particular program. This number is called "share of audience."[23] In August 1990, HBO's presentation of the Madonna concert "Madonna—Live! Blonde Ambition World Tour 90" became the highest rated program,

---

23. The required share for a program to survive has been declining as the total share of viewers watching network television has declined; it will continue to decline as public and cable television, video games, and videotaped programs attract larger shares of the total audience.

BOX 5-4

In Defense of Network Television Advertising

Citing A. C. Nielsen Company figures, Richard Kostyra, executive vice-president and director of media services for J. Walter Thompson, USA, points out that during the prime-time hours in the first quarter of 1989, the three major networks reached 94 percent of U.S. homes with television sets. Audiences for the five most highly rated series exceeded 30 million people, with the top-rated *Cosby Show* watched by 36.6 million people on average each week during the 1988–89 season. "You read article after article saying that network TV is going down the tubes because of all the new media coming up," Mr. Kostyra said in an interview. "It's not completely untrue. But network TV is still the biggest and most popular form of communications to product users."[a]

[a]Randall Rothenberg, "A Ringing Defense of Mass Media," *New York Times*, 25 August 1989, p. 27Y.

---

excluding sports, in the history of cable. The show drew a 21.5 Nielsen Media Research rating, and a 31 share—numbers that translated into an audience of 4.3 million households.[24] In spring 1995, CNN's coverage of the Oklahoma City bombing raised its ratings to their highest level since the Persian Gulf War in 1991, eclipsing the record previously set by CNN viewership of the O. J. Simpson trial.[25]

Several hundred companies (advertising agencies, advertisers, program suppliers, and the networks) subscribe to the Nielsen ratings, but the networks are the largest customers in terms of the prices they pay for the service. Networks rely on Nielsen for about 90 percent of their information, and each pays Nielsen roughly $10 million a year for its services.

One weakness in the ratings is that they measure viewing demographically—by age, income, education, and family size—which has little to do with interests, tastes, attitudes, or activities. The ratings are distorted to an extent because they do not reflect viewing in hotels, hospitals, bars, prisons, clubs, summer camps, military bases, college dormitories, or homes for the elderly.

Audience measurement changed dramatically with the introduction of a device known as the "people meter." Originally marketed in Europe by the London-based AGB Research, this device instantly analyzes the age, sex, and income of viewers. These are the demographics of greatest interest to advertisers. The people meter resembles the handheld remote control devices that many people now own. The meter has buttons assigned to individual members of a family. A watcher punches in when starting to view a program and punches out when leaving. A central computer monitors who is watching what and when. The people meter not only indicates more accurately who is watching but also provides better data than diaries on what is being watched. With the proliferation of

---

24. *Electronic Media*, 13 August 1990, p. 32.
25. "High TV Ratings for Bomb," *New York Times*, 28 April 1995, p. A24.

cable channels and other independent stations, it became increasingly difficult for diary keepers to record their own viewing. The meter eliminates that problem. Moreover, because it gives a minute-by-minute account of viewing, rather than the diary report every fifteen minutes, the people meter is better able to tell specific advertisers who is watching their ads. Nielsen began using such meters in the fall of 1987.[26]

The Nielsen meters are push-button, handheld devices on which viewers record viewing in the 4,000 homes that have agreed to participate in each two-year cycle. When Nielsen replaced other forms of monitoring with meters, reported network viewership dropped by 6 percent in the first year. By 1990 the falloff had reached 10 percent. Nielsen argued that the meters were more accurate than previous measures.

By summer 1990, the audience shares of the three major networks (NBC, ABC, CBS) had fallen to 53 percent. This meant that Fox, whose rise we noted in Chapter 1, independent stations, and cable commanded 47 percent of the viewers watching in July 1990.[27]

But ad revenue didn't follow the same pattern. In May 1995, the "upfronts"—the purchase of a season's worth of advertising in advance to control prime periods—were going for record highs.[28]

Facing the decline in advertising revenues in early 1988, the networks commissioned a twenty-two-month study through the Committee on Nationwide Television Audience Measurement, a group created by the networks in 1963. The study, completed by Statistical Research Inc., cost $1 million and was reported in seven volumes. Just before the winter holidays in 1989, the report was released, with several recommendations:

Nielsen should appoint an ombudsman to monitor measurement. Small sets and sets in unusual places such as garages and hotel rooms should be monitored.

People away from home should be monitored as well.

Households should be replaced more than once every two years (the report found that fatigue reduces the reliability of the reports after the first year).

The meters should be simplified to encourage use by children.

Techniques for encouraging participation should be found (only 55 percent of those asked agree).

Multiple sets in the same home should be followed.[29]

---

26. For a brief time, AGB, a British company, and Nielsen faced off in the U.S. market. But after losing $67 million and failing to sign up two of the three networks, AGB withdrew from the U.S. market.

27. "Networks Face Higher Risk of Being Shot Down in Fall," *New York Times*, 30 July 1990, p. D10.

28. Robin Schatz, "Advertisers Prepared to Shell Out Big Money," *Philadelphia Inquirer*, 16 May 1995, p. C1.

29. Jeremy Gerard, "TV Networks Want Nielsen to Change Ratings Methods," *New York Times*, 14 December 1989, p. D1.

BOX 5-5

The Nielsen Sample

According to a study by the Committee on Nationwide Television Audience Measurement, in June 1989 only 47 percent of the households Nielsen had chosen for its sample agreed to take its "people meter," forcing the company to go to alternative homes. Eleven years earlier, 68 percent of Nielsen's first-choice homes took its meters.

The study attributed the steady decline to "an increasing societal tendency to refuse participation in surveys."[a]

[a]Randall Rothenberg, "Surveys Proliferate, but Answers Dwindle," *New York Times*, 5 October 1990, p. A6Y.

From January through the end of July 1995, ABC had a prime-time share of 19 as did NBC; CBS followed with 17 and Fox with 12.[30]

ABC, NBC, and ESPN commissioned the A. C. Nielsen Company to study viewing outside homes, and a survey was conducted from November 2 to November 29, 1989. More than 4,000 people 12 years of age and older participated, filling out diaries that logged all their viewing over the period, inside and outside the home. The results indicated than an average of 500,000 to 1.3 million people were watching television somewhere other than in their homes during some part of the day. Thirty-five percent reported viewing at work. Twenty-one percent took place in college dorms, 16 percent in hotel rooms, 9 percent in bars and restaurants, and 4 percent in second homes; 15 percent fell into other categories. The overall increase in viewing averaged 2 to 3 percent, equivalent to three-tenths to seven-tenths of a rating point, as much as the average rating for most cable channels, and an increase in audience that would be worth almost $225 million to network television.[31]

In summer 1995, Nielsen reported that "More than 23 million adult viewers watch in excess of five hours of television in out-of-home locations each week. . . . Settings include offices, college buildings, hotels, restaurants/bars and second homes, all of which are not counted in Nielsen's standard ratings."[32]

The very rich, the well-educated, the poor, and minority groups—particularly poorer African-American and Hispanic families—were traditionally underrepresented in the Nielsen samples. Minorities and poorer Americans were underrepresented because Nielsen field representatives tended to be whites who encounter hostility when they knock on doors in ghettos or barrios. It was difficult to find African-American and Hispanic families who would agree to fill out diaries, and Nielsen only began distributing Spanish-language diaries in 1978. The high level of literacy required and the tediousness of the task limited all diary

---

30. *New York Times*, 1 August 1995, p. D1.
31. Bill Carter, "TV Viewing Cited Outside of Homes," *New York Times*, 10 May 1990, p. C15Y.
32. *Variety*, 17–23 July 1995, p. 26.

BOX 5-6

The Hispanic Audience

For years only a sliver of the advertising dollar pie addressed the audiences of Hispanic media, in spite of Hispanics comprising 10 percent of the U.S. population and in some markets considerably more—Miami, 63 percent; San Antonio, 57 percent; Los Angeles, 40 percent; and New York, 24 percent. Several factors have recently conspired to produce what has been referred to as an "explosion" in this market. There have been an increase in the number of media outlets catering to Hispanic interests and a surge in marketing research on this population (led by Nielson), revealing demographics appealing to advertisers. Also significant was the size of the audience for Univision network's coverage of World Cup soccer in 1994. This drew many advertisers' attention to the market potential for the first time.[a]

Hispanic Business reports that in 1995 advertisers spent about $186.5 million on print ads to reach the Hispanic market.[b]

[a]Christy Fisher, "Telcos Lead Hispanic Ad Stampede," *Advertising Age,* 23 January 1995, p. 30.
[b]Jeffrey D. Zbar, "Marketing to Hispanics," *Advertising Age,* 18 March, 1996, p. 27.

participation to the better-educated and middle class; thus African Americans and Hispanics who agreed to fill out diaries tended to be those whose viewing patterns resembled the viewing of white middle-class audiences. The dissemination of people meters faced similar problems.

The underrepresentation of African Americans and other minorities created significant problems for television stations that appealed to such audiences. Because their primary viewership was underrepresented in the ratings sample, such outlets got lower ratings and therefore found it difficult to attract advertisers. This, in turn, made it harder for minority programming or minority outlets to survive.[33]

By November 1989, Nielsen was able to show that 11 percent of its respondents were African American.[34] Census figures in 1990 indicated that 11.3 percent of the U.S. population is African American. In early June 1990, Nielsen announced that it was "enhancing" the methods it uses to collect and report on African-American and Hispanic audiences.

Starting in 1991, Nielsen expanded its monthly National Audience Demographic Report to include African-American households and about twenty African-American demographic categories. At the same time, a number of organizations, including Tribune Entertainment and Burrell Uniworld, pledged to launch educational campaigns designed to increase the cooperation rate among African-American and Hispanic households.

---

33. Chagall, "The Viewers," pp. 20–22, 24, 26. See also Edwin Diamond, *The Tin Kazoo: Television, Politics and the News* (Cambridge, Mass.: MIT Press, 1975), pp. 152–153, for evidence gathered by the A.C. Nielsen Company that African-American households watch television "significantly more" than households generally.
34. Michael Couzens, "Berating the Raters," *Channels,* 7 May 1990, p. 17.

Still, some felt that audience estimates remained skewed in favor of white viewers. In 1994, at the urging of African-American television producers and advertising agencies, Nielson once again announced revisions in its collecting and reporting methods. It would increase the representation of African Americans in its sample and consider the creation of a separate sample and report for African Americans.[35]

This attention was driven, in part, by demography. U.S. census figures show that "the African American population is expected to swell to 39 million by 2010, 50% faster growth than the rest of the population." The publisher of *Target Market News* reports that markets spent $834 million to reach African Americans in 1994, double the $411 million of a decade ago.[36]

In summer 1990, the three major networks agreed on a new uniform policy for providing guarantees that the advertisers reach the size of audience for which they have paid. Fluctuations in the people-using-television (PUT) numbers and what the networks view as "inexplicable falloff" in audience viewing have prompted the networks to base the guarantees on trends since the 1982–83 viewing season. A PUT number is the combined ratings of all stations and channels available for viewers at a specified time. Since the people meters showed a falloff in audience, the networks have viewed the Nielsen PUT numbers with suspicion; 1982–83 was set as the starting point because that was the first year in which viewing stopped increasing. In the fourth quarter of 1989–90, Nielsen set the PUT level for one prime-time minute for women 18 to 49 at 39.3 percent. The new network methodology set the number at 39.9 percent.[37]

Utilizing the Ratings

Nielsen ratings, which are actually percentage figures for the number of television households that have tuned in a program, are used to estimate the size of the total audience. As a result, they determine how much an advertiser will pay to air a commercial at various times and, thus, determine how large a network's or station's profits will be. Networks and stations base their charges for commercial time on ratings. Advertisers buy time in terms of ratings, total cost, and the number of target-audience members among viewers. Ratings are the only bases for all of these.

From the data gathered by the ratings services, the networks have learned that although 98 percent of U.S. households have television sets, only one-third of that potential audience does two-thirds of the daily viewing. These are the habitual watchers.

---

35. "Nielson Will Change the Way it Gathers Ratings on Black TV Viewers," *Jet,* 7 November 1994, p. 40.

36. Adrienne Ward Fawcett, "Marketing African-Americans," *Advertising Age,* 17 July 1995, p. S1.

37. "Three TV Networks Line up Behind PUT Plan," *Broadcasting,* 18 June 1990, p. 22.

BOX 5-7

TV News Magazines' Average Ratings[a]

Day	Show	Time	Network	Rating/Share
Sunday	60 Minutes	7 P.M.	CBS	8.7/32
Monday	Day One	8 P.M.	ABC	8.8/14
Tuesday	Dateline NBC	10 P.M.	NBC	10.4/17
Wednesday	Now	9 P.M.	NBC	10.8/16
Thursday	Eye-to-Eye	9 P.M.	CBS	9.8/15
	PrimeTime Live	10 P.M.	ABC	14.4/25
Friday	20/20	10 P.M.	ABC	15.6/29

[a]The ratings are for the fall 1993 season as of mid-October, 1993. Nielsen Media Research, reported in the *New York Times*, 25 October 1993, p. C6.

In 1989, one prime-time rating point (1 percent of the nation's 90 million households) was worth as much as $140 million a year.[38] One percentage point in prime-time audience share means more than $30 million to a network in a year.[39]

Mini-Series   Mini-series are an attempt to gain an audience with a compelling story and hold it through subsequent prime-time evenings as the story winds to a conclusion. CBS's 8-hour "Lonesome Dove" was the highest rated mini-series not only of 1988–89 but of any mini-series in the five previous years. "Lonesome Dove" generated over $30 million in ad revenue for CBS. By contrast, "War and Remembrance," another widely promoted mini-series, lost nearly $40 million for its network.

Competition for Time Periods   Networks not only compete for overall ratings, they compete for ratings and revenues in various time periods.

For example, in spring 1990, *ABC World News Tonight* was the number-one-rated evening news broadcast with a rating of 11. Whereas thirty seconds on ABC's news cost $58,100, the same amount of time on CBS sold for $46,700.[40]

There is also competition over "late fringe time," the period from 11 P.M. to 1 A.M. In 1989, the number one late-night show was NBC's *The Tonight Show*, which had a rating of 5.6, sold advertising at $38,700 for a 30-second spot, and had a CPT of $7.31. ABC's *Nightline* followed with a rating of 4.6, but since its demographics were those upscale ones prized by advertisers, *Nightline* was able to sell 30 seconds of ad time at $39,500 for a CPT of $9.68.[41]

---

38. Jay Sharbutt, "Network-backed Study Urges Changes in Nielsen Rating System," *Philadelphia Inquirer*, 16 December 1989, p. 8D.

39. Ben H. Bagdikian, "Global Media Corporations Control What We Watch (and Read)," *Utne Reader*, June/August 1990, p. 88.

40. *Advertising Age*, 28 May 1990, p. 39.

41. Ibid., p. 40.

BOX 5-8

Less "M" in MTV

There's less music on MTV these days, at least in prime time. MTV has been showing its version of *The Dating Game* (*Singled Out*), documentaries on 20-something sex, real-life soap operas (*The Real World* and *Road Rules*), comedy (*The State*), sports shows (*Sandblast* and *MTV Sports*), an animation program (*Aeon Flux*), and reruns of *My So-Called Life,* the high-school drama canceled by ABC. In fact, two-thirds of its prime-time programs do not directly involve music. What's the reason?

According to Neil Strauss, a *New York Times* television critic, the problem is that music-video channels don't fit neatly into television's infrastructure. A station needs viewer commitment if it wants good ratings and big sponsors, and it achieves this with hour and half-hour shows that run daily or weekly. Three-and-a-half-minute music videos are an ideal length only for channel surfers who are trying to avoid commercials during a program on another station.[a]

[a]Neil Strauss, "The 'M' in MTV Loses a Little of Its Standing," *New York Times,* 13 August 1995, p. H27.

The demographic shifts in the audience are mirrored in the advertising. The company spending the most on network news ads in 1989 was Kellogg's, followed by American Home Products. The company spending the most on ads in late-night time was Anheuser-Busch.[42]

Network Affiliation

Network affiliation is very profitable for television stations and for the networks. Advertisers pay the network to air commercials according to the number of viewers. The network pays a set station rate per ad, regardless of the price paid by the advertisers. If a program increases in popularity, advertisers must pay more to the network, but the network has no obligation to pay more to the stations. Network compensation is negotiated, however, and more desirable affiliates are paid more.

The broadcasting schedule is divided between network time, in which network programming is aired, and affiliate time. Affiliate time is divided between locally originated programming, including news, and syndicated programming. Profits from these go directly to affiliates. The evening news broadcasts on all three networks are scheduled during affiliate time, which is one reason affiliates

---

42. Ibid., pp. 39–40.

BOX 5-9

The Complexities of Television Economics

Turner Broadcasting System promised "advertisers an average 5 Nielsen Television Index rating over the [1990 Goodwill] games' span ending August 5, yet in ratings from the first six days of telecasts through July 25, TBS was 50 percent behind that place with a 2.5 rating. . . . Usually, the superstation penetrates 53 million homes, yet cable operators serving 10 million viewers refused to sign up subscribers at a cost of $1.10 each for the Goodwill Games telecast. Should TBS fail to improve on its initial ratings, it will again have to offer advertisers make-goods as it had with the first games in 1986."[a]

[a]*Electronic Media*, 30 July 1990, p. 3.

BOX 5-10

The Super Bowl

Attracting the "largest audience in U.S. Television history," Super Bowl XXX in 1996 achieved a Nielsen rating of 46.1, with an estimated 138.5 million viewers. (The 1983 final episode of "MASH" received a higher rating, but the rating represented a smaller number of people.)[a]

NBC received between $1.1 million and $1.3 million per 30-second advertising unit. Among those lining up to pay these rates were Anheuser-Bush, Nike, MasterCard, and Pepsi-Cola. Big spender Oscar Mayer paid more than $2.5 million to sponsor the Diana Ross half-time show.[b]

[a]Lee Margulies, "Super Bowl XXX Breaks Record for Audience Size," *Los Angeles Times*, 30 January 1996, p. F2.
[b]Jeff Jensen, "Oscar Mayer Scores Super Bowl Halftime," *Advertising Age*, 8 January 1996, p. 1.

---

resist network efforts to extend these newscasts to forty-five minutes or one hour. One commentator explains:

> When the networks scheduled their 15-minute news broadcasts and later the 30-minute broadcasts in the affiliates' time slots, each network gained 2 minutes and 30 seconds of advertising time per 15-minute block. These extra 5 minutes of commercials bring in $30 million to $40 million a year in added revenues to each network. But they [affiliates] aren't likely to give up any more time; when they do their own local news programming, they can keep 100 percent of the revenues.[43]

Affiliates have resisted such encroachments energetically, arguing that the networks should program news in the evening hours they already control.[44]

---

43. Diamond, *Tin Kazoo*, p. 77.
44. Marvin Barrett, *Rich News, Poor News* (New York: Thomas Y. Crowell, 1978), p. 33; cited from a fifty-five-page petition filed with the FCC by Donald McGannon, president of Group W, requesting an inquiry into network practices in response to the threat of expanded network news.

The same problem occurs at other times in the day. In spring 1990, Phil Beuth, senior vice president, ABC Network Group, noted that affiliate resistance was the largest barrier to expanding the number-one-rated *Good Morning America* to weekends. "It's hard to get the stations to give up that time," noted Beuth, "which is profitable and also used as [community] service time. Some of our [network-] owned stations are even reluctant to give up the time."[45]

The relationships between networks and affiliates is complex. No network can compel an affiliate to air or clear any network program, but there are strong inducements to do so. For all the networks, compensation to affiliates is relatively low for the weekly program base of 21 to 24 hours. Program time taken over that base brings a higher rate of compensation. This encourages higher levels of program clearance by affiliates. Most affiliates clear 95 percent of the network programs they are offered, and this programming makes up about 65 percent of their total programming time.[46]

Network ownership of twelve stations ("owned and operated" by the networks, thus known as "O&Os") in major markets, and their relationship to affiliates, made the development of new networks difficult. Network O&Os usually clear network programming, and they control over 20 percent of the total television market. Similarly, affiliate patterns of clearing such large amounts of network programming work against the development of ad hoc networks formed to present special programs. Until the advent of CNN and Fox, there were few exceptions. David Frost's interviews with former president Richard Nixon were one such exception.

The success of CNN changed the network-affiliate equation. By summer 1990, CNN had created profitable relationships with 122 network affiliates. These affiliates pay CNN to receive its 24-hour-a-day news feed and provide CNN with material they have produced for their own programs.

The competition from CNN and from such independent services as CONUS prompted the major networks to consider increasing their news programming. In spring 1990, CBS was producing 41 hours of news programming a week, almost twice the amount of NBC and ABC. By January 1, 1991, NBC was providing its 209 affiliates with a 24-hour enhanced news feed.[47]

In December 1995, ABC announced and then later postponed a 24-hour televised news service on cable. Microsoft and NBC have announced similar plans. When MSNBC begins, probably in summer 1996, it will take over the time currently used by America's Talking, the NBC service begun in 1994. By the year 2000, MSNBC is expected to reach 35 million households. Fox also has announced that it is getting into the 24-hour news business in an enterprise headed by former CNBC head and former Bush campaign adviser Roger Ailes. In an attempt to stay ahead of the competition, CNN added a business news service at the end of December 1995.[48]

---

45. "Resistance to Weekend *GMA*," *Broadcasting*, 4 June 1990, p. 56.
46. Christopher H. Sterling, "Television and Radio Broadcasting," in *Who Owns the Media?* ed. Benjamin M. Compaine (New York: Harmony Books, 1979), pp. 108, 112.
47. J. Max Robins, "Network News Explodes in Off Hours," *Variety*, 1 August 1990, p. 1.
48. William Spain, "Cable Out to Feed News Junkies," *Advertising Age*, 25 March 1996, p. 30.

BOX 5-11

News and More News

The number of all-news radio stations has grown from one in 1961 to dozens, perhaps as many as ninety, in 1995, plus several hundred stations devoted to news and talk or all-talk. The time devoted to news by ABC has increased from 2 hours and 15 minutes in 1960 to 35 hours in 1994; the total of all networks is now about 110 hours, not counting CNN, Headline News, C-SPAN, Court TV, sports and weather news networks, or breaking news stories like the bombing in Oklahoma City.[a]

[a]Max Frankel, "Summer Musings," *New York Times Magazine,* 25 June 1995, p. 24.

Public Television

Ratings and revenues are also important to public (educational, nonprofit) television, which is heavily dependent for support on the same U.S. corporations that advertise on commercial television. The funding for public television comes from three sources: government appropriations, contributions from viewers, and corporate sponsors of programming.

Corporations often transform sponsorship of public television programming into image ads with the goal of demonstrating that the corporation is a good citizen. Such promotion not only ensures that large audiences in the commercial media are aware of corporate good deeds, it also increases the size of the upscale audience reached by the program itself.

Reaching this audience is a second reason for corporate largess. One of public television's main selling points is the quality of its audience, "made up largely of well-educated, affluent adults who are often in a position to influence your business," writes KCET-TV's director of development to prospective corporate clients. Thus, although the cost per thousand viewers is very high, it is a good investment, illustrated, for example, by Mobil Oil Company's continued underwriting of PBS's *Masterpiece Theater,* now renamed *Mobil Masterpiece Theater.*

When advertising agencies and corporations argued successfully that corporate funding could only be maintained or increased if the FCC were persuaded to change its rule prohibiting institutional advertising and corporate logos on public television, new regulations were adopted permitting the use of corporate logos and the identification of the products that underwriters produce.[49] In other words, public television has become much more commercial. Some limitations exist because two-thirds of all public television stations are licensed to educational institutions prohibited from running advertisements, but some stations currently sell advertising in their program guides—an action that has aroused controversy.[50]

---

49. John Weisman, "How Creeping Commercialism Is Sneaking up on Public Television," *TV Guide,* 27 June 1981, p. 44.
50. Tony Schwartz, "Four Possible Ways Out of Public TV's Crisis," *New York Times,* 17 May 1981, p. D39.

BOX 5-12

Cable Television Advertising

Cable television, once considered the stepchild of the industry by advertisers, is quickly improving its financial position. Between 1991 and 1995, cable ad revenues more than doubled, reaching $3.4 billion. The quick increase is explained by the growth in new cable channels, the bargain advertising rates, and the potential for targeting a specific audience. This is still a long distance from the $12.4 billion advertising revenue figure for broadcast television in 1995.[a]

[a]"U.S. Tightens Screws on Cable TV to Screen Out Fast and Loose Ads," *Chicago Tribune,* 24 March 1996, p. 8 Business.

Despite the important role of corporate underwriting, the need for the Public Broadcasting Service (PBS) programming to appear untainted by commercial control was evident in the controversy surrounding the firing of *This Old House* host Bob Vila. Commercial suppliers of the materials used in rebuilding houses had become so prominent that one might have mistaken the PBS program for an extended advertisement. The conflict that led to Vila's ouster occurred when the underwriter of seventeen local stations' broadcast of the show complained that Vila was a paid promoter of a home supply chain that competed head to head with the underwriter. When the underwriter pulled its $750,000 funding from the program, WGBH, the producing station, fired Vila.[51] Within months Vila reappeared in ads for Sears.

As noted in Chapter 1, competition from cable, among other factors, caused a decline in viewership of public television in the last half of the 1980s; member donations leveled off simultaneously. Since 1984, viewing of public television in cable households has declined, particularly in homes that subscribe to pay television, according to the Public Broadcasting Service. In the 1984–85 season the average monthly average-minute prime-time ratings in pay television households averaged 2.2; in the 1988–89 season the average monthly rating had plummeted to 1.6. Overall monthly prime-time ratings dropped 8 percent—from 2.7 to 2.5, according to PBS.[52]

PBS has responded by exploring the introduction of a new cable channel. Under the proposal, PBS and its New York and Boston stations, WNET-TV and WGBH-TV, would run a noncommercial cable channel in conjunction with Discovery, an existing cable channel. The new channel would operate with Discovery during the day. Discovery alone would program for prime time and night. Neil Mahrer, PBS executive vice-president, explained that the advantages include subscriber fees for PBS.

---

51. "A Rude Education in Competition," *Channels/Field Guide* 1990, p. 84.
52. Ibid.

BOX 5-13

Give the Viewers What They Want

Jonathan Schmitz, a 24-year-old from Orion Township, Michigan, was invited to appear on the *Jenny Jones* television talk show in early March 1995. Producers told him he would meet a secret admirer onstage; they did not tell him that the admirer was a male, Scott Amedure. Three days after the show was taped, Schmitz went to Amedure's home and killed him.

Talk shows like *Jenny Jones, Jerry Springer Show, Montel Williams,* and *Ricki Lake* specialize in titillating, lurid subjects and emotional, embarrassing confrontations—in the process attracting viewers away from shows hosted by Oprah Winfrey and Phil Donahue.

Initially, advertisers were nervous about being associated with such shows, but their hesitation has faded in the face of rising ratings. Such major television advertisers as Procter & Gamble and Sears, Roebuck were among those advertising on *Jenny Jones* broadcasts after the murder.

Because a successful show, such as those hosted by Jenny Jones and Ricki Lake, earns profits that range from $50 to $60 million a year, efforts to change these shows are not expected. Dennis McAlpine, a media analyst with Josephthal, Lyon and Ross, commented: "These shows make huge amounts of money. They're doing so well, I can't imagine any of these companies deciding to tone them down." Time Warner is the parent company for *Jenny Jones.*[a]

Prime-time entertainment shows on the major networks are screened by advertisers in advance; syndicated shows such as these, which are bought by an individual station in each city, are not. Descriptions sent out by the shows themselves, which are often rather vague, are the only information advertisers have about them. Graphic discussions of sex and highly abusive language, which would be unacceptable in prime time, are routine on daytime talk shows. These shows are supported by such prominent advertisers as Procter & Gamble, General Mills, Sears, Roebuck, and American Home Products. Some of the same advertisers initially refused to buy time on *N.Y.P.D. Blue,* an award-winning and prime-time ratings success on ABC, which broke precedent by including brief glimpses of nudity and occasional crude language.

Because these talk shows are on during the day, many children are in the viewing audience. According to Nielsen figures, 11 percent of the audience for *Jerry Springer* was made up of children between the ages of 2 and 17. On one typical show four young women discussed the methods they would use to relieve a young man of his virginity. On *Montel Williams,* 17 percent of the audience is under 17; *Ricki Lake* has the largest nonadult audience with 22 percent of its viewers between 2 and 17. For a typical *Ricki Lake* show, more than 600,000 underage children are tuned in.[b]

One reason for the proliferation of these shows, in addition to high ratings and profits, is that the networks have returned more daytime hours back to local stations, which use syndicated programming. Syndicators now offer almost nothing but talk shows for daytime programming.

[a]Bill Carter, "After Killing, Hard Questions for Talk Shows," *New York Times,* 14 March 1995, pp. A1, A8.
[b]Bill Carter, "Television," *New York Times,* 20 March 1995, p. C5.

From PBS affiliates' standpoint, the problem, of course, is competition. PBS supplies one-third of each of its affiliates' broadcast slate. The rest is programmed locally or obtained elsewhere. Mahrer acknowledged the concern but argued that "the cable channel's content would be designed to augment that of PBS's broadcast affiliates and wouldn't compete directly for either viewers or possible funding sources." And even if the two did experience some crossover, "at least they wouldn't surrender any ground to other alternatives. 'If we don't take one or two or three of those cable channels, someone else will, and we'd be better off competing with ourselves rather than having others compete with us.'"[53]

In spring 1990, the Television Ratings Analysis Consortium (TRAC) reported the results of a study of public television use. The study confirmed the traditional profile of public broadcasting. Homes whose household head graduated from college watch more public television than homes headed by those with lower educational levels. Approximately one-third of the public television audience reported being attracted to public television by children's programming. Interestingly, however, homes with older children watch less public television than do homes with younger children. In the past decade, the amount that young children have viewed public television has declined.[54]

The educated audience is attracted to high-quality programming, illustrated by the high viewership for the documentary series, "The Civil War," aired in 1991. In the last half of the 1980s, PBS-produced programming took more news and documentary Emmys than its competitors. Emmy-award winners included "National Geographic Specials," *Nova, Frontline,* and *The American Experience.*

Radio

Radio receives less advertising revenue than its audience would appear to warrant. Industry figures indicate that radio accounts for 40 percent of the public's consumption of media but receives only 7 percent of the available ad revenue.[55]

To a greater extent than television, radio reaches its largest audiences outside the home. The times during which we drive to work (morning drive time), drive from work (afternoon drive time), and listen in the office while working are what attract advertisers.

Radio divides into AM and FM. FM offers superior fidelity and is preferred by those who have grown up on FM stereo. Twenty years ago, 75 percent of the radio stations in the country were AM. By 1990, the percentages had reversed with 75 percent now FM. Moreover, FM stations received 77 percent of advertis-

---

53. Thomas Tyrer, "PBS to Centralize Programming," *Electronic Media,* 30 July 1990, p. 4.
54. *CPB Report,* vol. 9, no. 7 (26 March 1990): p. 3.
55. "Counting Radio's Assets," *Broadcasting,* 4 June 1990, p. 70.

ing revenues.[56] Some radio manufacturers are now producing radios without an AM band.

Because FM sound quality is generally superior to that on AM, most AM stations deliver news and talk; a few, such as the news station WINS-AM in New York, are very profitable. Many surviving AM stations are institutions in their communities. WGN-AM, which airs Chicago Cubs baseball games, is one such station. In 1989, it generated $37.4 million in advertising revenue, leading all other radio stations in the United States.

The ratings system for radio is very similar to the local market and demographics ratings systems for television. However, radio ratings measure individual, not household, listenership, and they include out-of-home listening.

Arbitron ratings dominate radio in the same way that Nielsen ratings dominate television. Radio stations charge advertisers on the basis of how many listeners Arbitron determines they have (measured in terms of listening five minutes out of a quarter hour). Drive time (6 to 10 A.M. and 3 to 7 P.M.) is radio's equivalent of prime time for advertising, and delivers an audience that cannot readily switch to television.

ABC, CBS, National Black, Sheridan, Satellite Music, Unistar, Westwood One Radio Networks, advertisers, and agencies jointly sponsor what are known as RADAR studies. These studies report radio usage. The RADAR report for spring 1990 found that more than 96 percent of those 12 or older listened to the radio during the course of a week. In an average quarter hour, nearly 24 million individuals are listening to radio. The FM share of this audience is 77 percent. Between 1985 and 1990, the FM share grew by about 1 percent a year.[57] In March 1995, RADAR reported that ABC had 43.6 percent of the listeners of network radio over 12 years of age; Westwood One, 39.5 percent; CBS, 13.9 percent; and the American Urban Radio Network (AURN), 3 percent.[58]

Just as prophets speak of HDTV as the future of television, so, too, they speak of digital audio broadcasting (DAB) as the future of radio. DAB promises "to deliver noise-free, interference-immune, compact-disc-quality audio with a vastly more spectrum-efficient scheme than is possible with the current analog (AM and FM) systems."[59]

Arbitron Ratings

The Arbitron Company is a research company specializing in measuring consumers' local media use and buying habits. Arbitron Radio, the company's largest division, compiles radio station rating reports, measuring audiences in 261 local markets and serving 2,200 radio stations and 3,500 agencies and advertisers.

---

56. Geraldine Fabrikant, "Struggling Stations in Search of a Niche," *New York Times*, 20 May 1990, p. 10F.
57. "Radar Readings," *Broadcasting*, 18 June 1990, p. 43.
58. "AURN Ratings, Audience Size Grow," *Broadcasting & Cable*, 27 March 1995, p. 13.
59. "DAB: The Next Generation of Radio Broadcasting?" *Broadcasting*, 4 June 1990, p. 62.

Restricted Formats

Like the content in other media, radio programming has been influenced by the desire to maximize profits. One illustration of this is the Drake format (named for its originator), used in top-40 radio. The Drake format or variations on it are designed for maximum efficiency in holding listeners and for standardizing music selection.

It is also ideally suited to Arbitron ratings because it is planned in terms of quarter-hour periods. Each quarter hour is organized into specific categories of record popularity, such as a current hit, an "up-and-comer," a "golden oldie," and so on. "With this format a station could use as few as thirty records for an entire broadcast day. . . . Program directors now had absolute control over what records were played and when they were scheduled."[60]

The Drake format maximizes profits because it is a proven means of attracting and holding audiences. The format functions rhetorically; listeners are introduced to new selections in the context of music that is familiar. Such a format creates and exploits audience identification.

Except for all-news and public radio, as noted previously in Chapter 1, radio is a headline news service in a form even more abbreviated than that of television. Most newscasts range from three to five minutes in length. Because it is a relatively inexpensive advertising medium, ideally suited to reaching specific target audiences, however, radio is an important medium for political mass communication.

Just as it is difficult for most cities to sustain two major newspapers, however, it is difficult to sustain two all-news radio stations.

Newspapers

The circulation of most newspapers is small, with the median circulation under 25,000. In this pool are a few very large circulation papers—the *Wall Street Journal,* with a 1995 circulation of 1,823,207—among them.[61] More than 60 percent of the daily newspapers in the United States are owned by chains. More than 97 percent of the cities that have a daily newspaper have only one, making most newspapers monopolies.[62]

The demise of the *Washington Star,* the *Philadelphia Bulletin,* the *Los Angeles Herald Examiner,* the *Baltimore Evening Sun,* and the mergers of the *Minneapolis Star* and the *Minneapolis Tribune* and the evening *Kansas City Star* with the morning *Times* are dramatic examples of changes occurring in U.S. newspa-

---

60. David L. Altheide and Robert P. Snow, *Media Logic* (Beverly Hills: Sage, 1979), p. 27.
61. Mark Fitzgerald, "Newspaper Circulation Report," *Editor & Publisher,* 6 May 1995, p. 13.
62. John Sokoski, "Sources and Channels of Local News," *Journalism Quarterly* (Winter 1989): 864–865.

pers. There is less competition in general and fewer afternoon or evening papers in particular. There are now only about fifty cities in the United States with two or more separately owned, competing newspapers. Until summer 1995 when *Newsday* folded, only one city, New York, had four—the *Daily News, Post, Times,* and *Newsday.*

Independently owned afternoon newspapers that compete with a morning newspaper are particularly vulnerable, as they must also compete with more up-to-date network and local television news and the problems of rush-hour delivery to suburban readers. In most cases, this has been fatal. Surviving afternoon papers tend to be in smaller markets. "More than 500 evening newspapers have ceased publication or switched to morning circulation in the last 35 years," *Editor & Publisher* reported in June 1995.[63]

Economic forces have created a situation in which 97 percent of the nation's daily newspapers enjoy a local newspaper monopoly, and nearly half are owned by some group or national chain.[64] Competition among alternative media has taken the place of competition among newspapers.

This trend continued in 1995 with the nation's biggest newspaper company, Gannett, purchasing another eleven dailies. To that point, Gannett had owned eighty-two dailies whose daily circulation exceeded 5.8 million. The result, wrote a reporter for the *New York Times,* was "newspapers in most cities looking more and more alike, as though stamped from some giant corporate cookie cutter, many no longer play[ing] the vibrant role they played when there were more of them and they answered to more different kinds of owners."[65]

Cross-media ownership is increasing as well. When Gannett purchased Multimedia Inc. in 1995 it added to its holdings the businesses that syndicate the shows of Phil Donahue, Sally Jessy Raphael, and Rush Limbaugh.[66]

In September 1994, Gannett owned 82 newspapers; Knight-Ridder, 27; Newhouse, 26; Times Mirror, 11; the New York Times Company, 25; and Dow Jones and Company, 22.[67] In March 1995, the Sunday *New York Times* had a circulation of 1,762,015; the *Los Angeles Times,* a Sunday circulation of 1,576,425; and the *Detroit News and Free Press,* a Sunday circulation of 1,202,604.[68]

In 1970, Congress passed the Newspaper Preservation Act, which permitted newspapers threatened with bankruptcy to share manufacturing plants and commercial operations that would otherwise violate the antitrust laws. The *Washington Post* estimates that from 1970, when the law was enacted, until 1986, newspapers in at least twenty-one cities were spared extinction by being able to share

---

63. *"Baltimore Evening Sun* to Close," *Editor & Publisher,* 3 June 1995, p. 15.

64. Raymond B. Nixon, "Trends in U.S. Newspaper Ownership: Concentration with Competition," in *Mass Media and Society,* 3d ed., ed. Alan Wells, (Palo Alto: Mayfield Publishing, 1979), p. 35.

65. William Glaberson, "The Press: Bought and Sold and Gray All Over," *New York Times,* 30 July 1995, sec. 4, p. 1.

66. Geraldine Fabrikant, "1.7 Billion Gannett Deal to Acquire Multimedia," *New York Times,* 25 July 1995, p. D1.

67. Ibid., p. 6.

68. Figures compiled by the Audit Bureau of Circulation, *Philadelphia City Paper,* 30 June–7 July 1995, p. 15.

BOX 5-14

Newspaper Companies' Revenue, 1992[a]

Gannett Company	$2,689,000
Times Mirror Company	$1,943,000
Knight-Ridder	$2,050,000
New York Times Company	$1,307,000

[a]*Advertising Age*, 3 January 1994, p. 16.

---

facilities with other papers.[69] Although two papers may share printing, advertising, and circulation functions, the act stipulates that the papers' newsrooms and editorial pages must remain separate and independent. In winter 1989, Joint Operating Agreements (JOAs) were in place in nineteen cities with three other cities pending.[70]

The results of this act are controversial. Its critics charge that such mergers hike advertising rates. Advertisers who must use the newspapers to reach readers, such as supermarkets, for example, must pay the price. Such costs are passed on to the consumer.

Defenders of the act note that it has preserved two editorial voices in some major cities. These include Albuquerque, Honolulu, Madison (Wisconsin), Miami, Pittsburgh, Salt Lake City, San Francisco, and Tucson, among others. In 1983, for example, Seattle's two major papers—the morning *Post-Intelligencer* and the evening *Times*—combined. The *Post-Intelligencer,* which appeared to be failing before the venture, is now prospering.

The ongoing existence of the Newspaper Preservation Act is uncertain. In 1989, the Supreme Court voted 4–4 to let a JOA agreement go forward between two Detroit papers. In the same year the House Committee on the Judiciary's Economic and Commercial Law Subcommittee held hearings to determine, among other things, whether the act should be repealed. Although the act withstood both of these encounters with opponents, the existence of a narrow court win and of increased congressional scrutiny means that its continuing existence is no longer assured.

Newspaper advertising revenues rise and fall with the economy. Revenues for 1994 were $34.2 billion, an increase from the year before, but the continued increase necessary to offset the rising cost of newsprint was uncertain.[71] In major newspaper markets, advertising is 53 percent retail, 35 percent classified, and 12 percent national. A drop in consumer spending or employment opportunities directly affects revenues.[72]

---

69. *Washington Post*, 13 July 1986, p. 1.
70. Stephen Lacy, "Impact of Repealing the Newspaper Preservation Act," *Newspaper Research Journal* (Winter 1990): 2.
71. David Lieberman, "Newspaper Publishers Face 1–2 Punch," *USA Today*, 5 July 1995, p. 7B.
72. Laura Loro, "Customized Info Leads Classified Rush Database . . ." *Advertising Age*, 24 April 1995, p. S8.

BOX 5-15

The African-American Press

The total circulation of all African-American newspapers is perhaps more than 5 million, but no reliable numbers exist because the papers do not all count their circulation the same way.

African-American newspapers arose in the South and in many cities of the North after the adoption of Jim Crow laws and the rise in racial violence in the 1890s. The newspapers often were the only medium available for the dissemination of news about such subjects as lynchings and education and health care for African Americans.

After the victories of the civil rights movement in the 1960s, many older newspapers suffered sharp declines in circulation. In the meantime, younger African-American publishers introduced newspapers like the *City Sun* in Brooklyn that were more aggressive in demanding equal rights and economic change than many established publications.

"We have never managed to capture a share of advertising revenue proportionate to what black consumers spend," said Steve G. Davis, the executive director of the National Newspaper Publishing Association, a trade group representing the African-American press. "Thanks to some of our work, appealing directly to corporate chairmen and other executives, we are beginning to attract some national advertising for our members, but many major corporations do not even know that a black press exists."

But editors and publishers say the African-American press still has an important role to play. "Black people are largely not accepted as a part of the American family, and until we are, we have to be able to communicate with each other in our own way."[a]

[a]Albert Scardino, "Black Papers Retain a Local Niche," *New York Times*, 24 July 1989, p. 21Y.

The relationship between readership and advertising is complex. When a paper begins to lose circulation, a downward cycle begins. Readers purchase the paper for its news content and its advertising information. The newspaper with the larger circulation gets the greater share of advertising. Increased advertising increases the news hole, which in turn attracts more readers and with them more advertisers. A newspaper trailing another in a market may find itself with 40 percent of the readership but, because of this cycle, only 25 percent of the advertising. Because advertising accounts for up to 80 percent of a newspaper's revenue, decreases in advertising can spell a paper's demise.[73]

---

73. For a lucid discussion of this downward cycle, see James N. Rosse, "The Evolution of One Newspaper Cities," in the FTC's *Proceedings of the Symposium on Media Concentration*, December 14–15, 1978 (Washington, D.C.: Government Printing Office, 1978), pp. 429–471.

Impact of Television

Although some disconfirming studies exist, in general scholars have found that those who rely on newspapers for political information are better informed than those who rely on television. The two audiences start with different dispositions. The better educated are more likely to rely on newspapers for information.[74]

Currently, paid daily newspaper circulation is 59.8 million, rising to 62.6 million on Sundays. Household penetration of dailies is 62.1 percent; Sundays, 64.9 percent.[75] More people still read a newspaper on a daily basis than don't. In general, those who do not read newspapers fall at "the lower end of the socio-economic ladder; [they] lack resources and cognitive skills due to low education, and lack of social contacts and lack of leisure time."[76] Those more involved in their community tend to be regular newspaper readers.

Television has replaced newspapers as the prime source of information for the U.S. public. Researchers account for this decline by noting the increased mobility of the population, a mobility that works against the community involvement and familiarity with coverage and layout that characterize newspaper subscribers.

Local retail advertising, the largest slice of newspaper ad revenues, comes primarily from food and drugs, entertainment and hobbies, housing and decoration, and clothing and general merchandise. Clothing and general merchandise represent nearly half of all retail advertising in newspapers, which makes newspapers vulnerable to any new medium able to provide a large audience for advertising from department and clothing stores.[77]

Cable television may pose such a threat because it can carry advertising to selected audiences, and when it is interactive, consumers can order products without leaving their living rooms.

Many national advertisers have chosen television over newspapers as their commercial outlet. Such choices, plus regulation of cigarette advertising, mean that only six industries provide two-thirds of all national advertising in newspapers: transportation, automobiles, tobacco, publishing, foods, and hotels. Because the newsstand price provides only about one-quarter and advertising three-quarters of a newspaper's revenues, newspapers are vulnerable to pressures from major advertisers.[78]

Separation of News and Advertising

Newspaper advertisers feel their messages are more believable and persuasive when they are printed next to news reports; hence, advertising charges are

---

74. Jack M. McLeod and Daniel G. McDonald, "Beyond Simple Exposure: Media Orientations and Their Impact on Political Processes," *Communication Research* 12 (1985): 3–33.

75. *Marketer's Guide to Media—Spring/Summer 1995* (New York: BPI Communications, 1995), p. 179.

76. Steven H. Chaffee and Sun Yuel Choe, "Newspaper Reading in Longitudinal Perspective: Beyond Structural Constraints," *Journalism Quarterly* 58 (Summer 1981): 201.

77. Anthony Smith, *Goodbye Gutenberg: The Newspaper Revolution of the 1980's* (New York: Oxford, 1980), pp. 65–66.

78. Ibid., p. 65.

higher for such positioning. On the other hand, journalists wish to protect the credibility of the news by separating it clearly from advertising.

Advertisers have made ingenious proposals to circumvent this journalistic concern. For example, R. J. Reynolds Industries (now RJR Nabisco), the nation's largest cigarette manufacturer and the country's largest newspaper advertiser, in 1981 offered to sponsor the sports results most papers publish on Mondays.

The proposal was analogous to television's news updates that are sponsored by product advertisers. The format had "Camel Scoreboard" in 3-inch letters across the top of the sports page. Below it appeared the usual box scores and sports statistics. Pillars similar to those on the Camel package were drawn down each side of the page, and a picture of the Camel cigarette package, the Camel slogan, and the mandatory health warning appeared at the bottom of the page.[79] The "Marlboro Sports Calendar," a variant of this, appeared in the sports section of the (Minneapolis) *Star Tribune* of Monday, August 22, 1988, listing September events, including the Summer Games in Seoul, with dates, location, and the schedule of television coverage.[80]

Some newspapers rejected this proposal on the grounds that it would look as if a tobacco company, rather than the newspaper, were providing the news. Others, including the *New York Post* and most newspapers in the Newhouse chain, have accepted it primarily out of a need for revenues. The format raises serious questions about journalistic ethics and the ability of newspapers to withstand pressures from advertisers who spend hundreds of thousands, even millions, of dollars on newspaper advertising.

This blurring of the distinctions between news and advertising is sometimes tried by politicians, as discussed in Chapter 11.

The rise of *advertorials* poses similar questions. Advertorials are "advertiser paid blocks that combine clearly identifiable advertising with simulated editorial text." Travel, food/cooking, sports, and health are among the recurring themes of advertorials. Since the early 1980s, use of advertorials has steadily increased, in part because print media have become increasingly specialized, in part because magazines have offered such blocked space at a discount.[81] Advertorials are the print version of television's infomercials.

Local Advertising

Advertisers are not attracted by total circulation but by the density of penetration in a locality: once a newspaper reaches 50 percent of the households in an area, it becomes indispensable to most kinds of advertisers. "Analysts say the crucial factor in newspaper competition is 'dominance' of the market. 'When you get 51 percent of the circulation, you get 70 percent of the advertising,' said one

79. Jonathan Friendly, "R. J. Reynolds Ad Format to Sponsor Newspaper Sports Data," *New York Times*, 7 August 1981, p. A13.

80. *Star Tribune*, 22 August 1988, p. 3C.

81. Patricia Stout, Gary B. Wilcox, and Lorrie Greer, "Trends in Magazine Advertorial Use," *Journalism Quarterly* (Winter 1989): 960–964.

financier who specializes in newspaper operations."[82] In other words, patterns of local advertising are directly related to the high percentage of localities with only a single newspaper. Thus, despite the impact of television, newspapers are by and large profitable.[83]

One analyst contrasts newspapers and television this way: "The typical newspaper audience of today has been constructed on the opposite, but in a sense complementary, principle from that of the television networks. The newspaper is local, uncompetitive, reliant on small advertisers; the television network is widespread, highly competitive, dependent upon large national advertisers."[84]

Magazines

On August 6, 1990, the Media Business section of the *New York Times* illustrated one of its purposes for existence. Page D13 contained ads for *Newsweek* and *Time* touting their coverage of the crisis in the Middle East. The goal of the ads plainly was to entice readers of the *New York Times* to buy those issues and to persuade advertisers to advertise in these two newsweeklies.

The same page contained an ad for *Ebony*. In this ad, the publisher appealed to would-be advertisers:

> This November the *Ebony* Magazine 45th Anniversary Issue is the biggest in our history offering a chance for your ad message to reach 9,519,000 consumers with a 43 percent penetration of the Black consumer market. The closing date is August 24th. The November *Ebony* 45th Anniversary Issue offers the single largest concentration of the estimated $260 billion Black consumer market ever available. Be a part of it by calling. . . .

The ad then provided telephone numbers in New York, Chicago, and Los Angeles.

Like television and radio, but unlike newspapers, magazine advertising prices are determined by ratings. Magazines are rated by Simmons Market Research Bureau, the Media Research Institute, and the Magazine Publishers' Association. Surveys by Simmons determine the number of readers per magazine copy. A very high rating is 6—meaning that, on the average, six persons read one copy of the magazine—and 1.8 is a very low rating. Simmons gathers data through interviews and questionnaires. Such surveys provide advertisers with information about how long readers look at the ads in a particular magazine, as well as how much it costs to reach a target audience.

Advertising is what makes most magazines financially viable. The exceptions are noteworthy. *Consumer Reports,* whose assessment of products would be ques-

82. Jonathan Friendly, "Requiem for a View," *New York Times*, 24 July 1981, p. A12.

83. Arnold H. Ismach, "The Economic Connection: Mass Media Profits, Ownership, and Performance," in *Enduring Issues in Mass Communication*, ed. E. E. Dennis, D. M. Gillmor, and A. Ismach (St. Paul, Minn.: West Publishing, 1978), pp. 243–259.

84. Anthony Smith, *Goodbye Gutenberg*, p. 302.

tioned if it accepted ads, does not. It has a readership of 3.8 million. In late July 1990, *Ms.* reappeared, this time ad-free. Founded as a feminist mass medium in 1973, *Ms.* lost money for most of its 17-year existence. When it suspended publication in 1989, its circulation was 543,000 with $5 million in advertising revenue.

In the lead article of the first ad-free issue, Gloria Steinem, one of the magazine's founders, detailed the frustrations of publishing an ad-reliant magazine. For example, a cover story on Afghanistan cost *Ms.* a long-term contract with Revlon, notes Steinem; the women on the cover had worn no makeup. Steinem's lead article, "Sex, Lies & Advertising," indicated that she could not previously have published the article in *Ms.* for fear of alienating advertisers.

The ad-free move was risky. Whereas its competitors sell for $1.75 or $2.00, *Ms.* now costs $4.50 an issue. The first issue contained 96 pages. In 1988, twelve issues of *Ms.* carried 382 pages of advertising.[85] In 1996, however, *Ms.* was still thriving.

Casualties of Competition

Like newspapers, magazine profits are a combination of advertising and circulation revenues, and like newspapers, magazines are dependent on certain kinds of advertising—chiefly from the tobacco, liquor, and automobile industries.[86] A magazine's health is measured by the number of its advertising pages. Compared with the first half of 1989, the number of magazine ad pages had dropped 3.3 percent in 1990.[87] "Automotive, the largest category, dropped 12.6 percent in the first half (of 1990) to $415 million. Cigarette and tobacco advertising showed the steepest first-half decline, 27.2 percent to $154.6 million."[88] Two explanations were given, "tighter ad budgets resulting from the skittish economy" and "increasing competition from other media." Highly specialized magazines are more attractive to advertisers when they seek to reach specific markets. The same advertising director said, "We're not crazy about broad-based publications [like the women's service magazines]. We would rather take a rifle shot in *Parents, Self,* or *Working Woman.*"[89] The competition among media is acute, and television is generally more attractive for major national advertising.

It is difficult for magazines to compete with television for national advertising. In fact, by the end of the 1950s, national magazines had discovered it was too expensive for their advertisers to buy pages in all copies of the magazine; therefore, different editions were created to reach different regions, occupational groups, and income levels.[90]

---

85. Deirdre Carmody, "Ms. Magazine Returns with New Spirit, but Without Ads," *New York Times,* 30 July 1990, p. D10.

86. N. R. Kleinfield, "Recharging Saturday Review," *New York Times,* 8 August 1979, p. D1.

87. "Ad Industry Fears Falloff," *Advertising Age,* 23 July 1990, p. 1.

88. Wayne Walley, "Magazine Declines Mount," *Advertising Age,* 23 July 1990, p. 32.

89. Philip Nobile, "Worry Lines at the Women's Magazines," *New York,* 18 May 1981, pp. 19–20.

90. Anthony Smith, *Goodbye Gutenberg,* p. 137. See also Chapter 1.

BOX 5-16

Health Newsletters[a]

Medical information from research studies reported in the news media is often complex and confusing. One study reports one result; another contradicts it. Increasing concern about health as the U.S. population ages has created a niche for by-subscription-only health and nutrition newsletters, several of which have circulations of 400,000 or more, larger than many metropolitan newspapers. The majority of subscribers are affluent, well educated, and older (50 and above). Most health letters have no photographs or advertising, and at an average of $30 for twelve slim (8–16 pages) issues a year, they cost more per issue than the *New Yorker.* None is sold on newsstands.

[a]*New York Times*, 9 August 1995, pp. B1, B5.

A form of network has been created in magazine advertising in order to overcome some of these problems, however. Advertisers are offered a discount for placing ads in several specialized magazines. For instance, it is difficult to convince a cigarette manufacturer to promote its brand in *Stereo Review* with a possible CPT (cost per thousand readers) of $22.84 on a circulation base of 525,000. By selling a package with *Boating* and *Skiing,* however, Ziff-Davis offers over 1 million circulation and a CPT of $14.49. A black-and-white page in *Boating, Car and Driver, Cycle, Flying,* and *Skiing* offering the equivalent of a 2.2 million circulation, yields a CPT that begins to be competitive with *Playboy.*[91] Such networks combine the best of national advertising (low rates and large audiences) with the best of demographic pinpointing to attract large advertisers.

At the same time, a growing number of magazines, including *U.S. News & World Report,* are beginning "selective binding" programs for advertisers. In 1989, as publishers were searching for new ways to attract advertisers, Time-Warner, publisher of *Time, Sports Illustrated,* and *People,* among others, introduced its TargetSelect program. The program enables the magazine to tailor ads to a specific group of subscribers while not paying to reach the rest. Ink-jet printing processes make it possible to include the name of the reader in the ad. The service enabled Isuzu to run ads in *Time, Sports Illustrated,* and *People* in January 1990. The ads not only addressed the consumer by name but after inviting the reader to take a test drive, listed the address of the nearest Isuzu dealer.

"Selective editing" has appeared as another source of new revenue. Targeted subscribers receive special editorial inserts for a fee. *Sports Illustrated* introduced a four-page "N.F.L. Plus" insert during the 1994 football season for 800,000 sub-

---

91. Benjamin M. Compaine, "Magazines," in *Who Owns the Media?,* ed. B. M. Compaine (New York: Harmony Books, 1979), p. 158.

scribers willing to pay an additional $5.20 per year. Several months earlier, "Golf Plus" was sent free of charge to 400,000 subscribers identified as golf aficionados. This weekly 16-page insert was supported by advertisers interested in reaching the golfing public.[92]

Newsweeklies

Before the advent of the national television networks and of such national newspapers as the *Wall Street Journal* and *USA Today,* the newsweeklies were the only mass circulation publications bringing news to the whole country. Although their impact has diminished, it is still great.

The covers and cover stories of *Time* and *Newsweek* are important to the magazines and to newsmakers. "A good cover can significantly increase the normal total of 300,000 copies a week each sells at the newsstands. Even though street sales are less than 10 percent of the magazines' total circulations, advertisers tend to look at the figures as a measure of which is the 'hot book' that lures a nonsubscriber."[93]

A cover story can also be influential. President Lyndon Johnson was allegedly influenced not to run for a second full term by the appearance of Bobby Kennedy on the covers of *Time* and *Newsweek,* and David Halberstam reports that President Richard Nixon agreed to grant an interview to Hugh Sidey in exchange for his appearance on *Time*'s cover.[94] *Time*'s selection of a man or woman of the year has become a news event in its own right, attesting to the continued influence of newsweeklies.

The national newsweeklies are important because their weekly publication forces them to emphasize analysis and features. Their leading stories, which interpret major news events, can influence public opinion about administrative policies because they are written for a mass popular audience (despite advertising targeted to specific audiences). They provide the news background and analyses that are precluded by the brevity of television network news and that are more difficult for newspapers with daily deadline pressure.

Like the networks, newsweeklies follow political campaigns closely; their coverage of campaigns influences public opinion about the political fortunes of aspiring presidential and vice-presidential candidates.

Time and *Newsweek* are both owned by large corporations or conglomerates. By contrast, *U.S. News & World Report* is employee owned. *Newsweek* is owned by the Washington Post Company, which also owns several television stations and ranks among the Fortune 500 with sales of nearly a half-billion dollars a year.

---

92. Deirdre Carmody, "Magazines Go Niche-Hunting with Custom-Made Sections," *New York Times,* 26 June 1995, p. D7.
93. Jonathan Friendly, "When News Magazine Covers Match, Is It a Coincidence?" *New York Times,* 22 March 1981, p. A56.
94. David Halberstam, *The Powers That Be* (New York: Alfred A. Knopf, 1979), p. 666.

Time Inc. has revenues of over $1 billion a year, but only a small part of its revenues come from sales of *Time*. Robert Sherrill indicates some of the implications of *Time*'s conglomerate ownership:

> A majority of its income is from the sale of corrugated containers and lumber; its forest products company, Temple-Eastex, is the biggest private landowner in Texas, with a million acres of timberland—which readers might want to bear in mind when they judge *Time*'s position on environmental legislation and housing prices.[95]

Media Consolidation

The 1980s produced a new trend: media consolidation. Time Inc. and Warner Communications merged to form the world's largest media organization worth $18 billion. Gulf & Western, owners of Simon & Schuster books and Paramount Pictures, divested itself of its nonmedia industries and changed its name to Paramount Communications, Inc. Until recently, the world's largest agency was Saatchi and Saatchi of London which bought 20 percent of the world's broadcast ads for clients such as Procter & Gamble. Saatchi and Saatchi had offices in eighty countries. Analyst Ben Bagdikian observes that, "A handful of mammoth private organizations have begun to dominate the world's mass media. Most of them confidently announce that by the mid-1990s they—five to ten corporate giants—will control most of the world's important newspapers, magazines, books, broadcast stations, movies, recordings, and videocassettes."[96]

The trend continued in 1995 when the Westinghouse Electric Corporation offered $5.4 billion to purchase CBS Inc. and the Walt Disney Company agreed to purchase Capital Cities/ABC Inc. for $19 million. The ABC/Disney alliance created the world's largest entertainment company.[97] At the time of the acquisition, Capital Cities/ABC owned the ABC Television Network with its top-rated prime-time comedy *Home Improvement* and its number-one newscast *World News Tonight with Peter Jennings,* as well as ten television stations; twenty-one radio stations; a controlling interest in the cable channels ESPN and ESPN2; Fairchild Publications, the publisher of *Women's Wear Daily;* newspapers including the *Kansas City Star;* and partial interests in cable programming in Japan, Germany, and Scandinavia. Disney owned the Disney Channel, Walt Disney Pictures, Hollywood Records, Buena Vista Distribution, Touchstone Television, and Disney Interactive.[98]

---

95. Robert Sherrill, *Why They Call It Politics* (New York: Harcourt Brace Jovanovich, 1979), pp. 273–274.
96. Bagdikian, p. 84.
97. Geraldine Fabrikant, "CBS Accepts Bid by Westinghouse; $5.4 Billion Deal," *New York Times,* 2 August 1995, p. 1.
98. "Who Owns What," *Philadelphia Inquirer,* 1 August 1995, p. A6.

The business page of the *Washington Post* described the new media world by noting that "Viacom's 'Forest Gump' blitz exemplifies the cross-marketing 'synergies' that companies are trying to achieve by owning the movie studio that makes the hit, the video stores that rent it and the TV networks that advertise it."[99]

TO SUM UP

These facts about ratings and revenues in television, radio, newspapers, and magazines demonstrate the importance of commercial considerations in the operation of the mass media. These processes are reflected directly in advertising— discussed in the next three chapters—and indirectly in mass political communication—the subject of the last two chapters.

SELECTED READINGS

Beville, Hugh M., Jr. *Audience Ratings: Radio, Television, and Cable.* Rev. ed. Hillsdale, N.J.: Lawrence Erlbaum, 1988.

Compaine, Benjamin M., ed. *Who Owns the Media? Concentration of Ownership in the Mass Communication Industry.* 2d ed., rev. and enl. White Plains, N.Y.: Knowledge Industry Publications, 1982.

Greenfield, Thomas. *Radio: A Reference Guide.* Westport, Conn.: Greenwood Press, 1989.

Montgomery, Kathryn C. *Target Prime Time: Advocacy Groups and the Struggle over Entertainment Television.* New York: Oxford University Press, 1989.

Reel, A. Frank. *The Networks: How They Stole the Show.* New York: Charles Scribner's, 1979.

Steinbeck, Dan. *Triumph and Erosion in the American Media and Entertainment Industries.* Westport, Conn.: Quorum Books, 1995. [economic aspects]

---

99. Paul Farhi, "Selling Is as Selling Does," *Washington Post,* 30 April 1995, p. H1. See also "The National Entertainment State" (centerfold), *The Nation,* 3 June 1996.

CHAPTER 6

What Is Advertising?

In 1990 alone, 13,300 new products were introduced. Of these, 74 percent were food products.[1] What we knew of them was the by-product of some form of advertising.

When the woman who edits this book for Wadsworth sits down at her nationally advertised computer, she wears clothes advertised both by local retailers and through national ad campaigns. We have never seen her office, but we would bet that the paint on the walls, the desk on which the computer rests, the lamp on the desk, and the pens in the drawer are as familiar to us as they are to you, although we may live thousands of miles apart. All probably have been nationally advertised.

In a sense advertising through the mass media has given us a world in common—you are familiar with the products we purchase, we are familiar with the products you purchase, and that familiarity transcends large geographical distances. In other words, we live in a world filled with advertised products; often the presence of one of these products rather than another in our lives is determined by the effect of the ad campaigns for competing products.

In this chapter we examine what advertising is and what advertising through the mass media does.

Defining Advertising

The Romans identified three goals of rhetoric: to teach, to delight, and to move. Of course, these goals rarely occur in complete isolation from one another. As we argued in our discussion of news, the process of choosing a topic, narrowing it, and selecting evidence in its support gives all messages a persuasive component.

---

1. *Advertising Age*, 16 July 1990, p. 39.

Taken at face value, news professes to inform or teach, and ads profess to move—to advocate one purchasing decision rather than another. By contrast, most prime-time programming (sitcoms, crime shows) professes to delight.

In contrast to news or other types of programming, the end of advertising is more likely to be explicit action. Here ads are more akin to editorials, which urge action, than to the other sorts of content surrounding them. An ad asks us to go somewhere, do something, try something, buy something, accept some single idea, add a new word—generally a product's trade name—to our vocabulary, and associate positive images with that word. In order to accomplish any of these objectives the ad will contain a simple, highly repetitious message. So, in general terms, we can sort the ad from its surrounding content by its simplicity, its re-dundancy, and by the clarity with which it urges adoption, choice, or action.

A broadcast commercial is to some extent that unit of content that appears in 10-, 15-, 20-, 30-, 60-, or 120-second time units and breaks unapologetically into the narrative line of some content. Televised programming usually consists of larger units of 30, 60, or 120 minutes, interrupted by commercials. The smaller, 10- to 120-second units of information appear at regular and predictable intervals within the 30- to 120-minute units of content.

Because, unlike the early days of radio and television, television programs today are rarely sponsored by just one advertiser, the subjects discussed in the 30- to 120-minute units may differ drastically from those discussed in the adja-cent 10- to 120-second blocks. For example, the evening news may report on the president's trip to Europe and cut to commercials for a shampoo, a laxative, an automobile, and to a promotional ad for a prime-time program on the same net-work that evening, and then cut back to the news, where the anchor introduces a report about a hearing on organized crime.

This segmentation and aggregation of discrete, often incompatible thematic units violate all of the rules by which we normally judge communicated content. Suppose you heard a speech discussing the president's trip, an upcoming prime-time program, a hearing on organized crime, as well as the merits of a shampoo, a laxative, and a car. Such a potpourri of topics could not be blended into a co-herent speech. As an audience member you would doubt the speaker's grasp of the rules governing public communication, and possibly question the speaker's sanity as well. After all, the ability to address a subject coherently is one sign of a person's command of the environment.

Yet we do not react negatively when television and radio break our train of thought, disrupt the story line, and introduce a series of unrelated messages. In-deed, we expect it. Consequently, *Sesame Street* built "commercials" ("This part of *Sesame Street* is brought to you by the letter A") into the program.

In the first half of 1995 all top ten magazine ad categories were showing revenue gains over the previous year. Specifically, $319.4 million had been spent on food ads in magazines, $361.1 million on consumer and business products, and $727.9 million in the top category—automotive ads.[2] Whereas in 1992 thirty

---

2. *Advertising Age,* 10 July 1995, p. 29.

Table 6-1   How the Advertising Pie Divided, 1994[a]

Magazines	5.4%
Cable television	2.0%
Network television	20.7%
Radio	6.9%
Newspapers	21.1%
Direct mail	19.7%
Other	24.20%

[a]*Marketer's Guide to Media, Spring/Summer 1995,* vol. 18, no. 1, p. 12.

seconds of broadcast ad time on top-rated *Murphy Brown* cost $310,000, in 1994 the same amount of time on top-rated *Seinfeld* sold for $390,000.[3]

Unless we plan to spend our lives in a darkened room, wearing earmuffs to block the sound of radio, and shunning television, magazines, and newspapers, we will be exposed to advertisers' efforts to persuade us. Even those who do not subscribe to a newspaper pass newsstands as they move from place to place and see discarded newspapers and magazines on buses, subways, planes, in cabs, or on coffee tables in homes they are visiting. In order of their frequency, what they will see and hear are ads for passenger cars, nonfood retail products, restaurants, cereals, beer, airlines, movies, trucks and vans, cigarettes, and telephone companies.[4] Leading the pack in spending to get your attention is Procter & Gamble. In 1994 it spent $2.69 billion in the United States advertising such products as Tide, Crest, Pampers, Noxema, Pepto-Bismol, Cover Girl cosmetics, Crisco, Bounty paper towels, Hawaiian Punch, Pringles chips, and many others.[5]

People who want to avoid radio commercials have to ignore the ads being played over the portable radios carried down the street or at the beach, over car radios when they are carpooling, or over the P.A. system in the supermarket or shopping mall.

The mass media pervade our environment, and with the mass media come the advertisements that underwrite them. A message tailored to persuade an audience to accept a product is not, of itself, advertising. But when the people selling the product pay for time or space to enable them to *bring the message in a specific unalterable form to that audience,* we call the message advertising. An advertiser, within the bounds of taste and the law, controls what the message says, how it says it, and where and how frequently it appears.

The mass media have rules of conduct guaranteeing that the advertisers are able to communicate what they want at the time or in the space purchased. For example, when a television ad is cut short due to technical malfunction, or the programming in which the ad is embedded fails to reach an audience of the size

---

3. Joe Mandese, "The Buying and Selling," *Advertising Age,* 28 February 1995, p. 20.

4. LNA/Arbitron Multi-Media Service in *Advertising Age,* 21 May 1990, p. 25.

5. *Advertising Age,* 27 September 1995, pp. 2, 56.

guaranteed by the network, the advertiser is entitled to a "make-good," a re-broadcast of the commercial at a comparable time at no additional charge. Similarly, when a newspaper transposes two prices in an ad, the newspaper will, at no cost to the advertiser, run a correction in the next edition or in the next day's paper.

Some forms of advertising do not fit neatly into this definition because they reach their audiences without the purchase of time or space. The dividing bar that separates your groceries from the next customer's at the checkout counter of the supermarket, for example, may carry a message from a cigarette manufacturer: "For a light smoke—try X." The cigarette manufacturer has given the dividers to the store free, in the hope or with the agreement that they will be used. Their use functions as advertising. When your groceries are bagged, you may notice a message about the store on the bag. When you carry the groceries from the store or use the bag as a garbage bag in your home, you have become the carrier of an ad for the store, just as you have become a walking ad for Calvin Klein when you wear jeans with his name stitched onto the hip pocket.

A movie hero may drink a certain soft drink—a form of advertising purchased by the soft drink manufacturer in exchange for supplying cast and crew with the product, or in exchange for what is called a "promotional consideration." You may have noticed, for example, that the characters in *Moonstruck* always celebrated with the same brand of champagne. Similarly, Forrest Gump drank Dr. Pepper throughout the movie that bore the character's name.

"Tie-in" campaigns are now big business. To enhance each other's markets, a number of major companies tied promotions to the summer 1995 box office hit *Apollo 13*. Omega Watch linked the product to the film in four page 'advertorials' in *Vanity Fair* and *GQ*. USA Network and the Sci Fi Channel held sweepstakes with winners getting a trip to the U.S. Space Camp. Lego asked children to build a perfect space vehicle. Hardee's gave away a toy rocket. The assumption of such tie-ins is that those who like the movie will be disposed toward the product and vice versa.[6]

Video rentals too have become carriers of advertising, often for other movies by the same company or for movies trying to reach the same target audience. For example, the introduction to the video of *The Fabulous Baker Boys* urges viewers not to rewind when the movie ends. Following the credits, they will see a video of the star singing one of the movie's songs. The promoters obviously hope that this extra plug will entice us into purchasing that compact disc.

Realizing that movie cassettes reach a predictable local audience—those living within a specifiable distance of the rental store—an inventive local marketer began placing local ads on video rentals. Those in Wichita, Kansas, renting *She's Having a Baby* saw ads for a local tire service. Because Paramount had released the film, it sued, charging copyright infringement. A Kansas circuit court judge dismissed the suit saying, "This court is frankly skeptical that viewers actually care whether Paramount is the source or sponsor of the advertisements." But the

---

6. Jeff Jensen, "Lucky '13' Fuels Studio's Hot Streak," *Advertising Age,* 31 July 1995, p. 34.

local firm lost anyway. Fearful that they would be taken to court by Paramount, his customers returned to more traditional advertising channels.[7]

Marketers also are giving away videocassettes containing their messages. In November 1990, major toy companies gave away 1.5 million copies of *The Video Toy Chest,* a 35-minute videocassette that includes 28 minutes of ads for toys. The remaining 7 minutes contain trivia contests and games. Companies whose toys were advertised on the videocassette include Milton Bradley, Playskool, and Fisher-Price. The promotion was an attempt to increase the companies' share of the $13.5 billion toy market. The target audience: boys from 4 to 14. The motivation: competition from video games and products tied to the Teenage Mutant Ninja Turtles.[8]

Kids aren't the only market for free home video ads. In October 1989, R. J. Reynolds, then the nation's second largest cigarette maker, announced that it was mailing 78-second video ads to thousands of U.S. smokers. At a cost of less than $3.00 apiece, the mailing compared favorably with a national time buy. The difference, of course, is that cigarettes can't be advertised on the nation's airwaves.[9]

Ads are also included in faxed newspapers, which usually are two- or three-page summaries of the day's top stories sent to businesses that can't get same day delivery. The *Hartford Courant,* the first of these, started in April 1989, continues to produce its faxpaper which now has a readership of several thousand, but has discontinued the sale of its bottom-of-the-page $100 ads. The *New York Times'* "TimesFax," however, sent all over the world, to seventy-eight Caribbean resorts and to sixty-four cruise ships, considers advertising a big part of its publication and offers various special editions as vehicles for its advertisers.

Some advertising is faxed directly and without invitation to the fax machines of those owning them. But unlike junk mail, whose cost is borne by the sender, the cost of junk faxes is absorbed involuntarily by the receiver who actually winds up paying in paper and toner costs for the printing of often unwanted messages. In December 1991, President Bush signed legislation that would permit those who do not wish to receive junk faxes to enter their name on a list. Advertisers who transmit to the fax machines on that list would be violating the law.

Telephones too have become conduits of unwanted advertising. We assume that most of our readers have at one time or another rushed to their phone expecting a call from a friend only to hear a recorded voice telling them that they have won a trip or prize or were eligible to receive a deep discount on magazines. Such intrusive use of the telephone can be life endangering when the numbers reached are those of the fire station, the police department, or a hospital's emergency line. By tying up the line, the advertiser blocks the access of those who need to reach quickly the hospital or the fire or police station.

Some also contend that such calls are an invasion of personal privacy, particularly when, through random digit dialing, they reach individuals who have

7. Joanne Lipman, "Local Video-Ad Business Goes on Blink," *Wall Street Journal,* 23 August 1990, p. B6.
8. Kate Fitzgerald, "'Video Toy Chest' Brimming with Ads," *Advertising Age,* 23 July 1990, p. 49.
9. John Cleghorn, "Cigarette Makers Bypass TV Ban," *Philadelphia Inquirer,* 31 October 1989, p. E1.

paid to have their phone numbers unlisted. A 1990 U.S. Congress Energy and Commerce Committee report revealed that "more than 180,000 solicitors call more than 7 million Americans every day with recorded messages sent by automatic dialers, and more than 2 million businesses send more than 30 billion pages of information by fax each year."[10] The legislation in 1991 greatly restricted the use of automated dialing devices with recorded messages.[11]

In other words, television, radio, and newspapers are not the only conduits of advertising, and many forms of advertising do not appear in purchased time or space. This chapter focuses on advertising found in the mass media, however, because without this advertising the mass media as we know them in the United States would not exist.

Mediated Advertising

Before the advent of the mass media, salespersons would often be the carriers of their own advertising, repeating the same message and carrying the same products from door to door. With the rise of mass media, such door-to-door advertising has become prohibitively expensive for most nationally sold products. Even with products like Avon cosmetics that are still sold door to door and person to person, television ads are used to predispose residents to open their doors and purchase the product.

When the door-to-door salesperson was replaced by a mediated one, the ability of the salesperson to tailor the message to each individual receiver or adapt the message in response to audience reaction was reduced. The producer of an ad carried by the mass media, rather than in person, must create a message that speaks to what a mass audience shares rather than to the individual differences of the millions who will hear or see the message.

A second major shift occurred when television, radio, and print became the conduits of advertising. None of these media could bring a real product into your home. Instead, each carried a representation of the product. So, although the traveling salesperson could show you that the product worked and could actually sell you the product, the mass-mediated ad was forced to add an additional step in the persuasive process. The ad needed to persuade you to go where the product could be found and buy the product. But first the ad would often attempt to give you a vicarious experience of using the product satisfactorily, so the next time you had the option to buy the product it would already seem comfortable and familiar. Thus, the seller who would throw dirt onto a cloth stretched out on your carpet in order to demonstrate that the vacuum cleaner would efficiently pick it up was replaced with a mediated salesperson

10. "House Considers Restriction on Advertising by Telephone and Fax," *New York Times*, 31 July 1990, p. A13.

11. *New York Times*, 22 December 1991, sec. 1, part 1, p. 28.

in an ad who showed you what the producer hoped would be something comparable. But in your home you could see the dirt, see the vacuum, and testify that there were no tricks. The door-to-door salesperson offered firsthand experience of the performance of the product. In the ad, all sorts of tricks could be employed to make it appear that the vacuum was more effective than it really was. Consequently, a need arose for rules governing what an advertiser could and could not do in ads.

Kinds of Mass Media Advertising

As we argue in the next chapter, all advertising identifies a product, service, or idea; differentiates it from related products, services, or ideas; associates it with things we value; induces us to participate in the creation of its claims; and repeats its key concepts. Most ads also are part of a campaign, and all employ slogans in some form. Yet despite these similarities, ads can be divided by type.

The regulations governing some ads (for example, political) differ from others (commercial and PSAs—public service announcements); the space or time to air some ads must be purchased (commercial, political, and advocacy or issue ads), but others (PSAs) are aired at no cost to the producer; and the objectives of different types of ads range from marketing a corporate image to electing a candidate. Therefore, here we differentiate in general terms the different kinds of advertising.

Obviously, some of these types overlap. Some ads sell both a product and a service, for example, and some PSAs urge us to vote, an appeal that may benefit one candidate or party more than another. Distinctions are also complicated by advertisers' deliberate blurring of image-building ads and PSAs.

Similarly, product ads occasionally incorporate actors playing politicians whose re-election is ensured by judicious use of a certain brand of toothpaste or mouthwash. But, in general, these distinctions are a useful way of understanding the special forms an ad can take.

Ads can be classified by the product they sell (service, goodwill, or special product ads); whether the time or space in which they run is purchased (commercials) or provided by the outlet as a community service (public service announcements); or the type of information they provide, the types of appeals they make, and the types of regulations that govern them (advocacy and political ads).

Product Ads

Some ads market a product or a product line. Ads for Dairy Queen, for example, create a world filled with Dairy Queen products and their ingredients. Mountains of chocolate, fields of fresh strawberries, pineapple, and bananas are all part of this world. Some of the ads argue that we ought to participate in this world without identifying specific products. Others tell us about a special kind of sundae or a banana split.

The televised ads for Dairy Queen illustrate well the purpose of an ad for a product or product line. By showing us the texture of the fresh fruit, the vibrant colors of the strawberries, the rich "rivers" of chocolate, the ads preview the product, familiarize us with the product's name, and induce us to experience the sensations of eating the product. Although the actual world is a miniature one, the close-up shots create the illusion that there is actually a tropical retreat with larger-than-life fruit and mountains of chocolate. The world in close-up is the size of our television screen.

A food is a consumable commodity with which we've all had experience. The function of food is clear. Consequently, the strategy of an ad for food is generally to make the food appear as delectable as possible. But what is the function of a camera or of a specific type of film? Ads for Kodak cameras and Kodak film define and clarify the function of photography and at the same time personalize it. Kodak's ads tell us that Kodak is a means of preserving the best of the past by making it possible to save and treasure memories. Ads for Kodak show us symbolically important events in the lives of believable people and demonstrate the way in which film makes it possible to preserve those events. In the ads for Dairy Queen, the product is an end in itself. We see the product. We want the product. We buy and consume the product. Kodak could, of course, show us an unexposed roll of Kodak film, but such a strategy would be impersonal and would provide no rationale for purchasing the product. So, instead, Kodak shows us what the film and the camera make possible.

The Product as Ad

When a small box of cereal, deodorant, or laundry detergent appears in our mailboxes along with a coupon toward the purchase of more of the product, the product itself is functioning as an ad. So, too, when a person behind a small table at the supermarket offers shoppers a free taste of a product and a discount coupon. The free sample has been a staple of product advertising since the inception of the profession.

When the product can be hazardous, such promotions cause controversy. Under threat of government action barring advertising to children, a major cigarette advertiser in summer 1995 announced an end to the sample as ad. Philip Morris "said it will no longer send out 4 million to 5 million packs of cigarettes by mail nor will it give away 15 million to 20 million at events annually." However, the company indicated that it would continue distributing coupons that could be redeemed for free packs.[12] Because nicotine is potentially addictive, the pack of cigarettes as sample is a particularly insidious practice.

---

12. Ira Teinowitz, "Philip Morris Hits Youth Smoking," *Advertising Age*, 10 July 1995, p. 31.

Service Ads

The ads for Kodak make the product personal by showing the intimate important moments Kodak film can capture for us. But how does an advertiser personify a service? An ad for First Bank positions a bank official on camera looking at us, the banking customers. As the bank officer entangles himself in the esoteric jargon of his profession, his image is blurred on the screen and his voice muted. Everyone in the audience who has experienced institutional double-talk has a frame of reference for this type of institutional officer. The camera is reacting for us; we make little sense of such presentations. The audio track becomes our ears as we tune the message out. The ad has induced us to re-create a familiar experience. The announcer now can tell us that First Bank has simplified the banking process; the simplification brings the bank official back into focus. The ad has told us that this bank provides a service. Our past experience is used to help us make that service seem desirable.

Ads for a service often show us what it is like without, and then with, the service. An ad for an airline, for example, shows a large person crammed into a small seat being elbowed by the passengers on either side. The service? Wider seats, fewer persons per row. In the second scene the same person is in an uncrowded seat with ample room.

Goodwill Ads

The ads we have described are clearly intent on selling something—a product, a product line, or a service. One type of ad is noteworthy for the absence of a specific sales pitch for a tangible profit-making item.

In the late 1970s it was difficult to find an ad for a gas company that was selling gasoline or the services a gas station provides. Instead, oil companies were selling their concern for the environment, their conviction that we ought to conserve energy, or their safe driving tips. These ads were an attempt to alter the public image of the oil companies in the wake of rising gasoline prices, the long lines at the pumps, the oil spills that had endangered wildlife here and abroad, and accusations of influence peddling that had pervaded the political climate during the Watergate investigations.

This type of ad falls under the general heading of "image advertising." Related forms are more specific in relating their appeals to a product. IBM, for example, does not want to be associated with the notion that computers are dehumanizing and threatening. Consequently, ads for IBM show the humane uses of computers. IBM computers are instrumental in saving lives, argues one ad. Weyerhauser, "the tree-growing people," shows planned tree planting that, the ads argue, will make it possible for today's children to build houses tomorrow.

Such image advertising can produce substantial results. After sponsoring the 1984 coast-to-coast Olympic torch relay, AT&T conducted a survey to assess the relay's results. Every potential long-distance customer in this crucial time of di-

BOX 6-1

Interplay: News and Ads

News and advertising have been encroaching on each other's territory for years. Some memorable news photographs seem to belong to everyone; whole populations have the same mental-image files, which constitute a large part of our common culture. Thus, flashing key images in ads guarantees instant connection and social commentary. For example, in December 1989, Pepsi showed video clips of the Berlin Wall as it came down, with the words "Peace on Earth" and the company logo.

Advertising feeds on news photography because news imagery is so strong it does not entirely lose its meaning when radically displaced. Manufacturers can turn the familiarity of dire images to their advantage by spoofing them. For example, Kenneth Cole, the shoe company, ran a picture of former Panamanian dictator General Manuel Noriega with the tag line, "One heel you definitely won't see at our semi-annual sale."

Most news is commercially sponsored. Unwritten rules decree that there should be a separation between news and ads, but the dividing line can be thin. Local newscasts sometimes include interviews with the condemned criminal whose story provides the plot for the docudrama to be shown later in prime time—a public relations campaign pretending to be news. In 1991, Joan Lunden, co-host of ABC's *Good Morning America,* appeared in a Vaseline commercial masquerading as a news program and delivered what sounded like a news report on skin care.[a]

[a]Vicki Goldberg, "Images of Catastrophe as Corporate Ballyhoo," *New York Times,* 3 May, 1994, pp. H33, H35.

vestiture was aware of the relay. Half were aware of AT&T's sponsorship. More important for the phone company, those who recognized that AT&T had sponsored the event were, by a statistically significant margin, more disposed to choose AT&T as their long-distance phone company.[13]

In 1986, the growing awareness of such potential rewards prompted major companies, from Eastman Kodak to American Express, to tie their corporate identities to the reconstruction of the Statue of Liberty.

In 1990, the images with which products tended to identify were environmental. Crest toothpaste's print ad read: "Turn this page back into a tree. Simply send in this certificate with proofs-of-purchase from two Crest cartons. And, together with The National Arbor Day Foundation, we'll plant a seedling in a Yellowstone-area National Forest on your behalf." An IBM spot showed the corporation working with the United Nations to solve environmental problems. The spot contrasted gridlocked traffic with a swarm of beetles. Pictures of nature were intercut with topographical maps on computer screens. We saw nature, then nature through the computer. IBM and nature conjoined.

---

13. *New York Times,* 6 July 1986, p. 6E.

BOX 6-2

Guilt by Association

The latest ad for People for the Ethical Treatment of Animals (PETA) is, according to an editorial in *Advertising Age,* a clunker.

> It does a takeoff on the "Milk, what a surprise" campaign. In it, PETA put a yellow mustache on comedian Sandra Bernhard above the line, "Urine, what a surprise." PETA's beef is that Wyeth-Ayerst Labs uses urine from pregnant horses in its post-menopause drug, to the detriment of the horses and their foals.

The milk industry becomes an innocent bystander here. It's not the object of PETA's wrath, unless milking machines are on their hate list. Yet PETA makes the association of milk with urine, surely not a milk marketer's dream.[a]

[a]"End Ad Hijacks," *Advertising Age,* 25 March 1996, p. 18.

The causes to which goodwill advertising are tied are noncontroversial. No one opposes use of a designated driver to reduce traffic fatalities. Accordingly, Coca-Cola distributes free products to those identified as designated drivers who attend the home games of the Milwaukee Brewers. And because beer companies don't want to be associated with traffic fatalities, it is not surprising that one of the corporate sponsors of the baseball team's Designated Driver Program is the Miller Brewing Company of Milwaukee.

Image advertising is designed to identify a company and its products with a positive image and to dissociate them from any negative images that may have been created in news channels.

Companies that sponsor programming on Public Broadcasting Service stations are also engaging in image advertising. Instead of linking their name with some socially approved idea (conservation, for example), sponsorship links the company with bringing culture or quality programming at no direct cost to American homes. Such sponsorship argues that the company is a good citizen of the community. We are less likely to believe evil of a good citizen. Consequently, such sponsorship insulates the company from criticism and creates positive associations for the company's products.

The benefits of event sponsorship were dramatically illustrated by the results of a survey conducted in summer 1995 on the 1996 Summer Olympics, held in Atlanta. The surveyors found that "23% of consumers would definitely or probably switch from their current brand to a brand offered by an Olympic Sponsor. And of the 64% who will be following the Olympic Games, 29% said they would definitely or probably switch to an Olympic-sponsored brand."[14]

---

14. Leah Rickard, "'96 Olympics Capture Consumer Awareness," *Advertising Age,* 10 July 1995, p. 21.

Advocacy Ads

When the company as good citizen takes a position on a public policy in an ad, the ad becomes an advocacy ad. Many stations refuse advocacy ads out of fear that they will then be bound to air the other side as well. Determining what is and is not an advocacy ad is difficult. In 1981, ABC became the first of the networks to agree to air advocacy ads, but stipulated that the ads could only run on late-night television, a less-than-desirable time for most advertisers and a time when advertising space is more difficult to sell. By October 1990, NBC, CBS, and ABC's owned-and-operated stations were all being permitted the latitude of determining whether or not to accept such ads. The change in policy was prompted by the willingness of the stations' cable competitors to accept advocacy ads and by the demise of the Fairness Doctrine. Airing such an ad no longer carries an obligation to provide free airtime for opposing points of view.

In summer 1990, Anheuser-Busch aired a 30-second advocacy ad that opened by showing workers at lunch and farmers in their fields. The announcer noted that America was built by individuals willing to give their fair share. The ad then said that Congress now wanted Americans (note, not Anheuser-Busch), who already were paying about $3 billion in excise taxes on beer, to pay more than their fair share. As a foaming stein of beer appeared on the screen, the tag said, "Can the Beer Tax. 1-800-33-Taxes." When viewers called, they were asked if they would like to have a letter of protest over a proposed hike in the excise tax sent for them to their congressional representative. In the campaign's first month, 110,000 callers asked to have the letters sent.

To magnify the power of the campaign, beer industry officials hinted that if the tax were increased, their companies might reduce sponsorship of sporting events and decrease advertising spending on television. Increasing the economic impact should increase the number of groups supporting the beer industry's position. However, critics noted that reduction of advertising was unlikely because that is the industry's major means of sustaining sales and introducing such new products as ice beer.[15]

Still, controversies over advocacy ads persist. In spring 1986, J. Peter Grace, chairman of W. R. Grace and Co., protested to the press and public that one of his ads had been rejected by the networks. Set in the year 2017, the ad showed an elderly man in a witness cage. The man is being cross-examined by a child who wants to know how the man could have let federal deficits reach $2 trillion. The networks refused to show the ad. In so doing, they were within their rights. In *Democratic National Committee v. CBS,* the Supreme Court held that the editorial judgment about what to air and what not to air belongs to the broadcaster.

Maintaining their ban on advocacy ads, in the 1993-94 season, the three major broadcast networks all rejected advocacy ads on health care reform. As a result the only "national" ads that aired for and against the Clinton reform plan appeared

---

15. "Busch Spots Fight Rise in Beer Tax," *New York Times*, 30 July 1990, p. D11.

on CNN, an outlet available in 1995 in about two out of three homes in the United States. During the health care reform debate, more money was spent on advocacy ads than had been spent to elect Bill Clinton president in 1992.

Infomercials

The infomercial is a 30-minute ad that looks like a program but is instead selling a product. Throughout the program, a toll-free number appears. By calling it, viewers can order the product. On January 1, 1990, when the Federal Communications Commission's regulation called "Syndex" went into effect, use of infomercials by cable stations rose. Syndex, an abbreviation of "syndication exclusivity," means that cable stations cannot show syndicated programs if the same programs are being shown on local television in the market. During the time that is now blocked out by Syndex, cable can, if it chooses, pick up infomercials beamed to them twenty-four hours a day at no charge via satellite. In the first quarter of 1995, $55.7 million of infomercial billings were registered in the health and fitness area, $38.4 million in beauty products, and $33.2 million in personal development.[16]

One infomercial had the look of a rock 'n roll special. For that infomercial, one producer gathered the rights to 150 past hits and packaged them on twenty cassettes. He then paid disc jockey Wolfman Jack to endorse the product as "Wolfman Jack's favorite all time hits"; $200,000 of production costs later, the infomercial offering the cassettes was ready to air. Another infomercial featuring chef Arnold Morris resembles a Julia Child cooking show. Its title: "Arnold's Gourmet Kitchen."[17]

By producing programming to go with its commercials, companies create a kin to the infomercial and also ensure that their ads will not be lost in the clutter of other messages. Valvoline, Inc., makers of Valvoline motor oil had its advertising agency, Bozell, create both the Second Annual Valvoline National Driving Test and the ads for it. Because the program bore the sponsor's name, it too was a form of advertising. The Valvoline Driving Test, which aired in late August 1990, harks back to an earlier age in broadcasting. The *Dinah Shore Show* was sponsored by Chevrolet and featured the tune "See the USA in Your Chevrolet." During the 1940s and 1950s, radio shows routinely carried the names of their sponsors.

Public Service Announcements

Unlike the advertising we have discussed so far, public service announcements (PSAs) are not aired in purchased time or space. Television stations meet part of their FCC-stipulated obligation to be responsive to the needs of the com-

---

16. *Advertising Age*, 10 July 1995, p. 29.
17. Anthony Gnoffo, Jr., "The Ad That Looks Like a Show," *Philadelphia Inquirer*, 27 November 1989, p. E1.

munity by airing public service ads. A public service ad is generally created and sponsored by a nonprofit organization to convey noncontroversial information to the public.

Ads for charities such as United Way and the Children's Hospital of Washington are PSAs. The National Institutes of Health sponsors PSAs to remind hypertensives to take their medicine, to warn us to watch for cancer's early warning signals, and to discourage us from smoking. During election years, the League of Women Voters, the networks themselves, and specially created committees use PSAs to urge us to register and vote.

The PSAs most likely to be aired are sponsored either by an agency of the government or by the Advertising Council. The Advertising Council, which accepts a limited number of campaign assignments each year, is sponsored by ad agencies. It costs a nonprofit agency from $100,000 to $300,000 to pay the production costs for an Ad Council campaign. Ad Council campaigns have been criticized for their pro-industry bias. In one often-run ad, for example, a Native American is shown paddling his canoe down a polluted stream. As he steps to the shore someone throws a bag of garbage from a passing car and a tear runs down his cheek. Critics of this ad argue that littering is a minor form of pollution. Significant air and water pollution is industry caused. Littering could be reduced by banning nonreturnable bottles—a proposal industries have fought bitterly.

Critics raised similar objections to an Ad Council campaign showing an older person in a rocker that said, "Get Off Your Rocker." The appeal urged the audience to examine its stereotypes about aging. Of course, the elderly person was the victim of many social policies over which she had no control. Getting off her rocker would not end age-based mandatory retirement, eliminate government policies that encourage institutionalization of the elderly, or end age discrimination in employment. Those problems were the fault of industry and government; changing the attitudes of older people about them would not produce institutional change. Under fire for embodying stereotypical assumptions, the ad campaign was changed to show an empty rocker, and an appeal urged all of us to examine our attitudes about aging. These two Ad Council campaigns provide some support for the contention that the Ad Council deflects criticism from industry and shifts blame and responsibility to individuals who are often powerless to correct the problems isolated in the ads.

The major advantage of an Ad Council campaign is the ability of the ad industry to place its PSAs in desirable free time. In 1990, the president of the Media-Advertising Partnership for a Drug-Free America, a partnership that includes the Ad Council, reported, "The donated media time and space have included a large percentage of prime-time, drive-time and full-page, high-visibility levels that compare favorably to paid advertising campaigns."[18] In 1994 the Ad Council produced over thirty-three ad campaigns. The media donated $891,000,000 worth of space to these ads. In 1995 the Ad Council announced that it would concentrate its campaigns on issues of particular concern to children.

---

18. Thomas A. Hedrick, Jr., "Pro Bono Anti-Drug Ad Campaign Is Working," *Advertising Age*, 25 June 1990, p. 22.

Many effective PSAs are not sponsored by the Ad Council. A Clio-award-winning ad for the Humane Society shows the violence that occurs at rodeos in slow motion, while a Strauss waltz plays in the background. The ad focuses our attention on an often-ignored facet of the rodeo. The ad argues persuasively that rodeos are inhumane. Similarly, Mothers Against Drunk Driving (MADD) sponsored a series of PSAs encouraging youths and the public at large to consider the cost in human life that is exacted by those who drive while intoxicated.

One $2 million PSA radio campaign is privately funded. Martin Himmel, former president of Jeffrey Martin Inc., commissioned media guru Tony Schwartz to produce an antismoking campaign. In one of Schwartz's spots, Patrick Reynolds, grandson of the founder of the R. J. Reynolds Tobacco Co., reveals that his grandfather, a tobacco chewer, died of cancer as did his heavy-smoking father. His mother and three brothers all have emphysema, says Reynolds. "Now tell me," the ad concludes, "do you think the cigarette companies are truthful when they tell you that smoking isn't harmful? What do you think?"

Because its producers do not pay for the time in which the PSA is aired, they cannot control its placement. Stations tend to place PSAs in times no one has purchased. Consequently, PSAs often air early in the morning or late at night, when few viewers are watching, or in documentaries for which the network could not find enough sponsors.

Political Ads

Some ads argue that we should elect one person rather than another or urge us to vote a specific way on a resolution or referendum. These ads, which differ in some important ways from other types of ads, will be discussed in Chapter 10.

How to Determine Whether It's an Ad

Advertising can also be defined by distinguishing it from the content that surrounds it. In the mass media, advertisers pay for access to the audiences attracted by programming. How does the ad itself differ from that programming?

How Ads Reveal the Advertiser

What distinguishes a televised soft news story about Jamaica, presented from a human interest angle, from a televised commercial brought to you by the Tourist Bureau of Jamaica? The commercial will identify itself as a commercial by disclosing its source. This disclosure, called a "tag," generally takes a visual form and usually is placed at the end of the commercial.

What distinguishes a televised view of a candidate's day, broadcast as a news segment on the evening news, from a slice-of-life commercial paid for by the candidate's campaign committee? The commercial is required to contain a tag identifying the committee paying for the ad. Again, the tag generally occurs at the end.

Because we are less likely to be manipulated by a message that warns us that it is manipulating us, as a commercial warns us by identifying itself as a commercial, producers of commercials try to incorporate the identifying tag in an inconspicuous way. Political committees, for example, are often legally incorporated under such titles as "Friends of Reuben Spellman," precisely because the commercial can then legally be tagged ". . . and that's why this message was paid for by Friends of Reuben Spellman." Such a tag is called a "no-tag."

How Ads Reveal the Intended Audience

The biblical injunction "seek and you shall find" takes on a new meaning when we are in the market for a product or have a problem that potentially could be remedied by a product. Have you ever noticed that when you have a cold, television and radio are filled with ads for cold remedies? And when you are trying to determine which car to buy, the number of automobile ads seems to increase? When we are troubled by a problem or an unmet need, we become information seekers about that problem or need. Communication that was always in our environment suddenly becomes relevant, and we recognize it and attend to it. We seek information to help us make a decision. At the same time the presence of the information assures us that our problem is not an imaginary one and that the problem is important. Ads about our problem tell us that it is a real one, that it is significant, and that we are justified in being concerned about it.

We also seek information once the decision to purchase has been made. But after the decision, the reasons for seeking the information change. Before the decision we seek information comparing products, arguing the unique benefits of one over the other. After we have purchased the product, we seek information to assure ourselves that the decision was a wise one. In these two instances, we function as active communication participants: we seek information.

Often, however, we are passive receivers of information. We are frequently receptive to information and willing to become involved in the creation of messages about products when we are not deliberately seeking certain types of information. How do advertisers alert the passive receivers that a product is designed for them?

Often ads tell us verbally that we are the intended audience. In summer 1990, Campbell-Taggart introduced a soft white bread labeled "IronKids." Ads for IronKids claim that it's "as wholesome as whole wheat but has the look, taste and feel of white bread." Other products that identify children as the intended market include Kids Deli, Kid Cuisine, and Kidstuff pizza. (The focus on this market is a by-product of the realization that children 6 to 14 have approximately $6 billion in discretionary income.)[19]

---

19. Trish Hall, "Younger Consumers: More to Spend, More to Want," *New York Times*, 23 August 1990, p. C1.

In other cases the identification is visual. In 1995, Domino's tried to increase its share of the $18.6 billion a year pizza market with ads featuring three thirtyish male football fanatics. At the center of the ads is Gus, his baseball cap backward on his head, who is both a wiseguy football expert and an expert at ordering and eating pizza. The ad indicates not only that it is seeking thirty-something male customers but that it is trying to increase the number of orders it gets during football games. The ads were slated as part of the chain's sponsorship of the *NFL Live* "Halftime Report."[20]

Other ads telegraph their audience both visually and verbally. If an ad says, "Trabo, the fun game for the whole family," and shows a mother, a father, a boy, and a girl playing a board game, that ad is not soliciting the attention of single adults. Although single adults might buy the product, the ad is picturing youngsters and their parents as its prime audience. The tone of the ad—the laughter, the upbeat music, the good-natured comments among participants—may also be speaking to those in the audience who view recreation as a social rather than solitary activity, whether they identify themselves with the family in the ad or not. But the ad is clearly not speaking to the single adult whose idea of an enjoyable evening is dancing into the wee hours of the morning at the hottest nightspot.

By showing the game being played by children with adults, the advertiser is also establishing that this is a game better suited for both children and adults than for adults alone. It is not a game too difficult for children; moreover it is not rated X. Yet it can be played satisfyingly by adults and children. Many products from toothpaste to breakfast cereal can be used both by children and adults.

A major sports figure, such as basketball star Michael Jordan, appeals to sports fans in general and the market of young males in particular. The products endorsed by Jordan include Gatorade, Nike, McDonald's Corporation, Rayovac, and Sara Lee Corporation. Expect to see these products featured in Jordan's first film, titled *Space Jam,* to be released in 1996.[21]

When Pepsi-Cola signed Grammy-winner M. C. Hammer to promote its "cool cans" in rap's rhythmic chants, it was targeting the younger market. Similarly Coca-Cola hired Heavy D & the Boyz to turn Sprite's "I like the Sprite in you" into rap ads for radio and TV. In addition to its clear attraction to younger viewers and listeners, rap has a number of persuasive advantages. Rhyme is memorable. Moreover, as the senior vice-president group creative director of J. Walter Thompson, USA, notes, "You can, without being untrue to the form of rap, get more lyrics per 30 seconds than with any other form of music."[22] In summer 1990, four of the country's top albums were by rap groups. And one of MTV's top-rated shows was *Yo! MTV Raps.*

Comparatively few products dictate use exclusively by either adults or children, as diapers and aftershave do. Yet many products are marketed to the whole family with the argument that the product is good for the children. One toothpaste, for example, is advertised with the appeal that if this product is used, the children will brush longer because they will like the taste of the

20. Melania Wells, "Domino's Ads Play on Football," *USA Today,* 4 August 1995, p. 10B.
21. Jeff Jensen, "Sports Marketing," *Advertising Age,* 16 October 1995, p. S24.
22. Patricia Winters, "A Trend, Friend: Is Rap 4 U, 2?" *Advertising Age,* 25 June 1990, p. 3.

toothpaste. The assumption, of course, is that Mom or Dad will buy the same brand for the whole family. Another toothpaste promises that it gives your mouth sex appeal—a claim that reveals that its target audience is very different from the ad featuring 6-year-old Johnny who brushes longer with the better-tasting toothpaste.

Indeed, if the advertiser used children as spokespersons to claim that the toothpaste gives your mouth sex appeal, the ad would be offensive. Both of these ads identify an intended audience implicitly. An explicit identification of intended audience is made in ads for Gleem toothpaste that say, "If you're an adult you have an adult set of dental problems." Gleem, according to the ad, is for the "care of your adult mouth."

Ads not only reveal the likely age of those targeted by the advertiser but also reveal whether the ad is designed to reach men or women or both. Again, some ads do this explicitly. One deodorant ad, for example, tells us that the product was specially formulated for women. In another ad for a deodorant soap, a male character tells us that the product is strong enough for a man. Then an attractive woman adds that she likes it too.

The ways in which ads signal the gender of the intended purchaser can be seen by turning off the sound on the television set and comparing the visual texts of ads for aftershaves and for perfumes. Without hearing the verbal pitch we can tell whether the product is being sold to men or women by determining whether a man or a woman is the visual focus of the ad. Is she turning to look at him or is he turning to look at her? Are a number of men in pursuit of one woman or a number of women in pursuit of one man?

An ad can also solicit the attention of the intended audience by re-creating the lifestyle that the audience member either has or desires. Why do ads for beer show groups of people rather than individuals? Why are men rather than women shown in most beer ads? In what sorts of environments are the people in beer ads shown? How are the people in ads for beer dressed—formally or casually? Are the people in beer ads middle class or upper class?

Now consider the same questions about an expensive scotch (Chivas Regal) or gin. The lifestyle created in beer ads is different from the lifestyle portrayed in ads for more expensive hard liquor. The ads tell us that beer is an out-of-doors as well as an indoor drink, that beer drinkers are active, often in sports, and that beer is a drink for people who are comfortable in casual clothes with groups of friends; it is not a drink for the solitary drinker or for the man in the tux. Within these general lifestyles the advertisers single out their market by preference for certain sorts of activities. One beer urges us to grab all the gusto you can get; the appeal is assertive, rugged. Another beer tells us that it is the beer for "when it's time to relax."

The mood of the two ads will be different because the basic appeal is different. One is more active than the other and one is more individualistic than the other. Beer ads also single out their audience by the types of environments in which the ad situates the product. Some ads place the beer drinkers in a bar; others place their beer drinkers outdoors. One beer's advertising tactic has been to show appropriate and inappropriate times for enjoying a beer, with the slogan "It's the right beer now."

Many beer ads appeal to sports enthusiasts by including famous hockey, baseball, or football professionals in the ads. Some beers set themselves apart by appealing to an upper-class market. They do this by adopting an exotic name (Michelob rather than Pabst, Schlitz, Budweiser), by packaging in a bottle with foil wrap, by implying that they're made by more expensive processes, by charging more for the product, by labeling themselves "premium" beer, and by stressing that they are imported or that the recipe is imported. So, ads themselves provide some of the clues about the identity of the intended audience.

The place in which we find the ad also provides clues. Ads targeted to children appear during certain types of television programming, such as children's specials or cartoons, and at the hours at which children's programming occurs—early morning, especially Saturday. They also appear in magazines such as *Boy's Life*. Ads designed for homemakers are seen at all hours, particularly during soap operas in the afternoon and during morning talk shows; they appear in so-called women's magazines such as *McCall*. Ads for older persons appear more often during news and public affairs programming, the types of programming older adults are most likely to watch. Ads for men appear during sports events or in so-called men's magazines; ads for adults appear during prime time.

An image-building ad for a corporation will appear adjacent to a prestigious public affairs program such as *Meet the Press* because highly educated persons, opinion leaders, and those who control the other media are more likely to attend to such programs.

Some targeting is controversial. When R. J. Reynolds announced that it was introducing a new cigarette called Uptown, directed primarily at African Americans, protests from the African-American community and from then U.S. Health and Human Services Secretary Louis Sullivan followed. The cigarette, which was to have been test-marketed in Philadelphia in December 1989, was withdrawn.

Advertising can also reduce confusion about a product. When *Newsday*'s sister publication *New York Newsday* was shut down, *Newsday* worried that it would lose both readers and advertisers. To minimize that likelihood, the paper took out ads in trade papers in late July 1995 announcing "*Newsday*'s Alive. Alive with over 1.8 million readers on Long Island and in Queens." The ad went on to assure readers that the paper was alive and well, "[r]ead by over 1.8 million adults daily and more than 2 million adults on Sunday, *Newsday* readers are educated, affluent, sophisticated and loyal. More than one million *Newsday* readers have a household income of over $50,000. And 60% read no other newspaper."

Advertising and Reality

Stereotypes

Stereotypes are simplified, inaccurate conceptions or images that have become standardized and are widely held. A stereotype can idealize or demean the group it types. If a depiction of a group reflects reality, we do not consider that depiction a stereotype.

Stereotypes make it possible for us to form generalizations about a person or advertised character without requiring a great deal of information or evidence. The less time we have to process information, the more likely we are to rely on stereotypes in drawing conclusions. The less time television producers have to communicate a message, the more likely they are to rely on stereotypes.

For example, in a 30-second commercial, a writer cannot create three-dimensional characters but must instead deal in the shorthand of stereotypes. The Harried Housewife, the Bumbling Husband in the Kitchen, the Archetypal Grandmother, the Nosy Neighbor are stock characters in commercials whose type we recognize immediately. Consequently, the writer can introduce a limited number of cues about them in a few seconds and proceed to deliver the message through them because we fill in the appropriate characteristics for this type of character.

Often the stereotypes found in commercials are so ridiculous or so harmless that they provoke no protest. "Mr. Whipple," the storekeeper who lurked behind the display cases waiting to ensnare shoppers for squeezing the Charmin, and Aunt Bluebell, who arrived at the homes of relatives with toilet paper hidden in her purse, were two such eccentrics. These characters were so implausible that if we identified with them at all, it was as comic foils.

By contrast, when a lazy, greasy, conniving thief in a sombrero and gun belt speaking in a parody of a Mexican dialect was chosen as the trade character for Frito's corn chips, Hispanic groups protested. The Frito Bandito embodied and consequently reinforced negative stereotypes about Latin Americans in general and Mexicans in particular. By drawing public attention to the stereotypes on which the Frito Bandito was based, the protest made it more difficult for the ads to use the stereotype to convey a commercial message. The protests also demonstrated that the Bandito offended a large, vocal group of potential customers, a result no advertiser desires. Consequently, the Frito Bandito disappeared from the ads.

Stereotypes that are universally held do not draw protests because we are unable to see them as stereotypes. For decades the public tolerated ads predicated on the senility of older characters. Then gerontological research established that senility among older persons is rare, and the gray rights movement focused attention on ads that embodied the myth of pervasive senility. As a result, the number of ads decreased in which older characters' seeming inability to hear, understand, or recall the product's name provided an excuse for repetition of that name.

Stereotypes are powerful means of reinforcing societal attitudes about groups of people because the process of stereotyping involves the receiver in creating the message. When the negative attitude that is reinforced is about a large, politically and economically important group such as Hispanics, African Americans, women, or elders, and is recognized by spokespersons for that group as destructive (such as, a woman's life is fulfilled if her floors shine, older persons are senile, Hispanics are lazy and dishonest), protest will follow because representatives of the stereotyped group fear that the stereotype will reinforce undesirable role models and will perpetuate discrimination against the group. Some groups have used the media to change the way in which they are portrayed by the media, as we will show in Chapter 9.

Advertising Values

Often we are unaware that advertising embeds assumptions not directly related to the products being advertised. These assumptions are diagrammed in Figure 6.1.

Television transports people to a middle-, upper-middle, and upper-class world. In the process television creates expectations in us all, expectations based on the assumption that the norm or standard in this country is a middle-class existence—or better. People in ads have spacious kitchens, large lawns, expensive appliances, and cars; they travel worldwide. Ads take for granted that the audience routinely buys soaps, deodorants, makeup, and cologne, and that the audience is not making a decision about whether to buy the product but rather is deciding *which* brand to buy.

The World According to Commercials

In the process of being urged to purchase the multitude of products that ads advocate, we are also being persuaded to a certain style of living. Contrast, for example, our standards of personal hygiene with those of our great-grandparents at the turn of the century. Underarm deodorants, in the forms we know them, did not exist and no one seemed to mind. Advertising has persuaded us that certain types of body odors are offensive and ought to be camouflaged or altered. Embedded in the argument that we ought to use a specific mouthwash is the assumption that we ought to use a mouthwash.

Similarly, the argument that we ought to use a specific floor wax assumes that we ought to wax our floors. Embedded in the argument that we ought to use a specific room deodorant is the assumption that we ought to use one.

Reliance on packaged products has contributed to the growing problem of waste disposal in the United States. If we didn't use so many packaged products and such heavily packaged products, the problem would be smaller. Because advertisers want us to continue to use their products, they reassure us that doing so is environmentally responsible, a responsibility newly found in a climate in which the public is expressing concerns about the vulnerabilities of the planet.

Accordingly, in 1990, a number of companies began using and touting their use of recycled materials in their packaging. Lever Brothers announced in July 1990 that the plastic bottles containing Wisk, All, and Snuggle would contain "up to" (note the careful use of language) 35 percent recycled resins. Procter & Gamble announced that it would include at least 25 percent recycled high-density polyethylene in bottles of Tide, Cheer, Era, Dash, and Downy. Spic 'n Span liquid cleaner bottles would be made entirely of materials that have been recycled. The scope of the industry's contribution to the landfill problem is evident in its claim that "in the first year of P & G's bottle recycling program, the company will produce 110 million containers that use the recycled plastics, keeping about 80 million bottles out of the nation's waste stream."[23] By Earth Day in April

---

23. Laurie Freeman, "Lever, P & G Green Plans Differ," *Advertising Age*, 23 July 1990, p. 46.

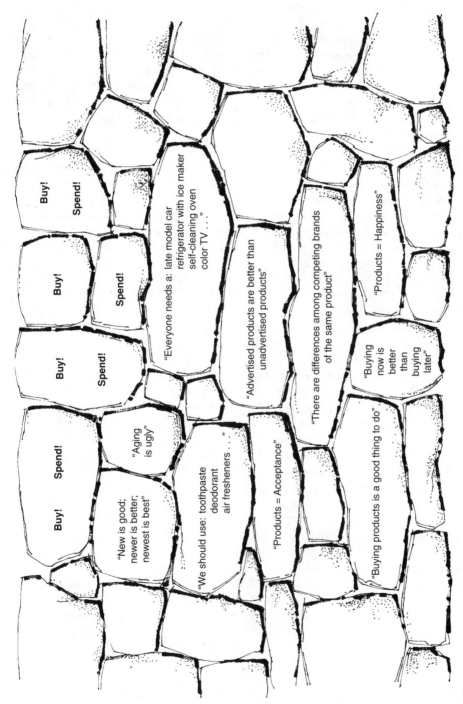

Figure 6.1 Assumptions embedded in advertising.

1995, Procter & Gamble could claim to have reduced the amount of waste it produced by 1 billion pounds.[24]

In the process of embedding these assumptions, advertising has created norms governing our sense of the acceptable home: a home in which the faucets, floors, furniture, mirrors, dishes—but not the faces of the women—shine; a home that is odor-free—no smell of cat, fish, cigars, feet—and filled with artificial, chemically created outdoor scents—lilac, rose, herbs, evergreen.

The home is filled with subtle deceptions. Spouses marvel at the cleanliness, unaware of how little effort it took with the new product to achieve that effect; and they assume that foods created from chemically enhanced mixes are homemade.

In the world of commercials, avenging guardians of the social order exist to ferret out those who fail to use the sanctioned products. Nosy neighbors and socially superior guests are ever alert to spot the smell of a cat or a cigar, or to comment snidely about spots on glasses, dull dishes, or dust on the furniture.

The characters who live out their lives in the 30- to 60-second world of the broadcast ads and in the pages of print ads seek and obtain almost instant gratification. Problems arise and are met. Promises of product performance are made and kept. All of this occurs in a very brief time span. The answer to all of the problems, needs, and expectations in the ads is ultimately found in the purchase of some product. The link between problem and solution is clear and unequivocal. Not only is the gratification instant, but it also occurs as a result of the product advertised. In contrast, our lives are more complicated and more ambiguous than the lives of advertising's population.

Characters in ads are also what psychologists would define as "other-directed." Characters seek the approval of others in ads. When that approval is withheld, it provokes crises. Neighbors detect odors in the house and crisis ensues; an air freshener is the answer. Parents detect spots on drinking glasses and a crisis occurs; a new dishwashing product eases the tension. Acquaintances spot "ring around the collar" and the family is thrown into turmoil. A clothes washing product resolves the crisis. In each of these instances, the others disapprove not only of the condition (the ring, the odor, the spots) but also implicitly, if not explicitly, disapprove of the ad's protagonist *because* of the condition. It is not only the product that ultimately wins approval in the ad but also the person who uses the product.

The need for social approval is strongly felt by all of us. It is a need that advertising exploits. In the process of exploiting the need, advertising reinforces it, legitimizes it, and enhances it.

In one sense, advertising is powerfully conservative—it is loath to offend; it reinforces institutional values. In another sense, advertising is radical because it holds out a world full of products and promises the good life to those who buy them. Yet the mass media reach many who lack the money to buy the products. Ads are materialistic. Purchase and consumption of material goods are glorified

---

24. Don Hopey, "Earth Day Message Is Clear," *Pittsburgh Post-Gazette,* 22 April 1995, p. A3.

in commercial ads. Our assumptions that ads are merchandising products are so deeply ingrained that we distrust ads created to enhance the image of a corporation, which claim "this corporation is a good citizen of the community." The notion that a manufacturer might pay to bring us a noncommercial message is suspect because until recently we had seen few such ads. In fact, the manufacturer is still merchandising a product. The product here is the company's good name, and when we respect it, the advertiser can link it to the product line and urge us to buy.

The acquisition of material goods brings happiness in the ads; material goods are satisfying. Because the ads simplify, we do not see other factors that make a happy ending possible; we do not see those factors that make the happy ending impossible even with the product or see the unhappiness that may be caused by the product.

Seeing the Other Side

Although it is generally true that ads reinforce the assumption that consumption of products is good, there is at least one major exception. In the name of fairness, the FCC required stations that broadcast cigarette ads also to run free of charge a certain number of antismoking ads. During the period in which both procigarette and anticigarette ads were aired, audiences were exposed to messages that argued that consumption of a product (cigarettes) was not only not good (as the procigarette ads claimed) but harmful and should be avoided or stopped. The antismoking campaign challenged an unspoken premise in commercial advertising—the premise that consumption of products is a good. By challenging the premise, the antismoking ads made us aware of it. In a sense, the counterads were not merely countering smoking but also countering advertising.

The Interplay of News and Advertising

We live in a complex world in which messages interact with each other to form impressions. Because people pay attention to information on topics of importance to them, public recall of news about health is high. When scientific studies seemed to confirm that oat bran had the potential to lower cholesterol, advertisers hurried to capitalize with new products such as Ralston Purina's Oat Bran Option, and with new claims for old products, such as General Mills's Cheerios and Quaker Oats. Kellogg's brought Common Sense onto the market achieving national distribution in late 1988. By mid-1989, Common Sense had attracted a 2.5 percent market share in the ready-to-eat cereal market.

But the legitimacy that news can endow, news also can take away. In mid-January 1990, the prestigious *New England Journal of Medicine* published a major study downplaying the ability of oat bran to reduce cholesterol. The study was carried in print and broadcast media reports. In March, Arbitron/SAMI scanner

reports showed that oat bran cereals, which had peaked at 4.9 percent of the cereals market in January, had plunged to a 3.18 market share. Common Sense had
dropped from attracting 2.5 percent of the cereal eaters to occupying a place on
the breakfast tables of only 1 percent.

TO SUM UP

It is more common to see the premises underlying a given ad campaign challenged in news and public affairs programming. News programs carry word of
recalls, of FTC investigations, of court cases in which advertisers' claims are challenged; consumer advocates in newspapers and on television investigate harmful effects of products. These exposés constitute a form of counteradvertising.
They make us aware that ads do not tell the "whole truth" about a product and
that ads ought to be evaluated critically. In the next chapter we focus on the critical evaluation of advertising's claims and evidence.

SELECTED READING

Turow, Joseph. *Breaking Up America: Advertisers and the New Media World*. Chicago:
    University of Chicago Press, 1997.

CHAPTER 7

Persuasion Through Advertising

The Advertiser's Aims

If we are to be persuaded to buy a product or service, we must be able to recognize it, distinguish it from its competitors, conclude that we want it or need it, and remember our desire for that product when the opportunity to obtain it arises or when we create that opportunity. To accomplish these goals, advertisers create product *recognition* through use of trademarks, packaging, and slogans; *differentiate* the product from others by creating a unique selling proposition; encourage us to want the product by enveloping it in a set of favorable *associations;* commit us to the product and its associated promises by inducing our *participation* in the creation of the ad's meaning; and ensure that we recall the product and our need for it by capsulizing these means of identification and differentiation and these associations and acts of participation in *redundant* messages—messages that are repeated again and again. In this chapter we examine the function served by advertisers' messages and expose some of the ways in which ads can entice the unwary consumer into false conclusions about products.

Creating Product Recognition

Trademarks

A trademark identifies a company's product. A trademark is a symbol—sometimes verbal, sometimes visual, sometimes both—that tells the consumer who makes the product. Trademarks do not have to be words found in the language, although once a trademark has been widely advertised, it may find its way into the dictionary. *Exxon* and *Xerox* are words created specifically to serve as trademarks.

215

BOX 7-1

Generic Murphy Bed

The United States Court of Appeals for the Second Circuit in Manhattan declared that anyone who might wish to manufacture a bed of the type that stumped the likes of Charlie Chaplin and Jackie Gleason can call it, if they want to, a Murphy bed. The judges, reversing a lower-court decision, said that many people had come to use the term *Murphy bed* "to designate generally a type of bed." The dictionary says a Murphy is "a bed that may be folded or swung into a closet." Thus, the judges said, "Murphy bed" has become a generic part of the language that cannot be owned by anyone.[a]

[a]William Glaverson, "Open and Shut Case? Generic Murphy Bed," *New York Times*, 2 May 1989, p. 13Y.

Sometimes advertisers are so successful in identifying the trademark with the product that the trademark becomes a common equivalent for the product. *Cellophane, aspirin, escalator, trampoline, nylon, linoleum,* and *thermos* were once trademarks held by individual companies. Because the manufacturers of these products and their advertisers did not protect these names adequately, the trademarks slipped into the public vocabulary and the public domain. To protect a trademark, manufacturers insist that it be used with the term for the generic product. So, for example, ads do not promote Kleenex but Kleenex *tissues*. In addition, the trademark is always capitalized.

A product may also be identified by a trade character who personifies the product's important characteristics. Often the trade character speaks for the product and functions visually as a substitute for the product, as, for example, the Pillsbury Doughboy personifies and speaks for Pillsbury Biscuits. The Doughboy resembles the biscuits—he's white in color, responds to touch by bouncing back (as freshly baked biscuits do), is immaculately clean (he wears a white baker's hat), and he's called Poppin' Fresh, suggesting that the biscuits rise, bake quickly, and taste fresh.

The vigilance with which companies protect their trademarks was evident in summer 1995 when the Hormel Foods Corporation, the producer of the pork-based luncheon meat Spam sued the makers of the movie *Muppet Treasure Island* over the presence in the film of an evil boar named "Spa'am." "Hormel officials," reported the *New York Times,* "also objected in the lawsuit to plans by the movie makers to feature the Spa-am character in Happy Meals at McDonald's restaurant and on boxes of Cheerios cereal boxes."[1]

Some trade characters are a clear and simple extension of the name of the company. The greyhound of Greyhound buses symbolizes the company's name and at the same time suggests the buses are fast, sleek, and efficient.

---

1. James C. McKinley, Jr., "Unamused, Hormel Sues Over Spa'am the Muppet," *New York Times,* 26 July 1995, p. B3.

BOX 7-2

Packaging

"Changes in packaging can increase an ad's effectiveness by more than 45 percent," Elliot Young, president, Perception Research Services, told a Cosmo/Expo packaging session. . . . "The new Diet Rite package . . . contributed to sales gains of more than 35 percent."[a]

[a]"Packaging Linked to Ad's Effect," *Advertising Age*, 3 May 1982, p. 63.

And in March 1995, the Supreme Court held that a color, such as the pink of fiberglass insulation or the blue identified with a sugar substitute, can have trademark protection. Prior to that ruling, companies could obtain federal protection for "words, names, symbols, or devices" that distinguish their products. More than fifty companies claim trademarked colors. At issue in the court case was whether Qualitex Company, which had trademark protection for its gold-green Sun Glow pads used in dry cleaning, could claim unfair competition from the Jacobson Products Company, which had begun selling a competing pad in green-gold. Color is among the characteristics consistently associated with products. So, for example, we recognize Campbell soups in part by the use of red and white on the can and identify Dr. Pepper in part by its maroon labels.

Packaging

Packaging is another potent means of providing product identification. For example, we associate Quaker Oats with the smiling Quaker on a cylindrical box, and L'eggs pantyhose with their plastic egg-shaped containers. Ideally, the name of the product and the package will reinforce each other the way the picture of the Quaker underscores Quaker Oats and the egglike container is a reminder of the name L'eggs. Similarly, the Coca-Cola bottle is recognizable both by shape and by touch.

Study after study verifies the power of packaging. In one test, the same deodorant was packaged in three different color combinations. The participants were told that they were testing three different formulations. "In this case," notes Thomas Hine author of *The Total Package*, "color scheme B was the one considered 'just right.' Those tested praised its pleasant, yet unobtrusive fragrance and its ability to stop wetness and odor for as much as 12 hours. Color scheme C was found to have a strong aroma, but not really very much effectiveness. And color scheme A was downright threatening. Several users developed skin rashes after using it, and three had severe enough problems to consult dermatologists."[2]

2. Thomas Hine, "What You See Is What You Buy," *Philadelphia Inquirer Magazine*, 2 April 1995, p. 21.

BOX 7-3

A Cracker in Another Box

"When RJR Nabisco introduced a bite-size version of graham crackers last fall, the company was abuzz. . . . But to the company's dismay, sales were sluggish. As it turns out, looks—at least the looks of the box—were the problem. So, in a crash program, Nabisco's marketing people changed the logo and changed the name to Graham Bites from Honeycomb Graham Snacks. And perhaps most important, in their eyes, from a subdued blue to a bright yellow. As a result, sales of the six-sided snack . . . are strong and getting stronger."[a]

[a]Anthony Ramirez, "Lessons in the Cracker Market," *New York Times,* 5 July 1990, p. D1.

BOX 7-4

Not Wanting to Offend . . .

Darkie toothpaste will start disappearing from Hong Kong bathrooms next month as its manufacturer attempts to end charges of racism. Bowing to international criticism, Hawley and Hazel Chemical Co., Ltd., said yesterday that its popular product would be marketed as Darlie in Hong Kong.

"We want the name of our toothpaste to be internationally acceptable. However, some people consider the word *Darkie* racially offensive, particularly in America," said Alvin Au, regional commercial director for Hawley and Hazel.[a]

[a]Reuters, 20 February 1990.

Selecting an appropriate name and appropriate packaging generally precedes selection of the slogan. The slogan describes either the product or the reasons people will want or need the product; like the name and the package, it is usually repeated in all major forms of advertising for the product.

Slogans

An effective slogan summarizes the ad and provides a memory peg on which the name of the product is hung. So, for example, we associate "Pizza" spoken by a cartoon Caesar with Little Caesar Pizza; "Sometimes you feel like a nut, sometimes you don't" with Almond Joy and Mounds candy bars; and "Get a Little Taste of French Culture" with the yogurt Yoplait. And if someone says "when you care enough to send the very best," we think "Hallmark cards" because the trademark and the slogan are now fused in our minds.

Although identifying a product and helping to differentiate one from another, a slogan may transcend the ad and enter the vocabulary through which we think about and discuss our lives. For example, one college student surprised his parents by arriving home unexpectedly. When his mother opened the door, he said, "I cared enough to send the very best," a meaning Hallmark had not intended when it created that slogan.

Similarly, at your last birthday party, someone probably said "you're not getting older, you're getting better." That statement formed the core of an extended ad campaign for Clairol hair coloring. As a slogan it capitalized on our fears of aging to reassure us implicitly that if we used the product we would look younger and better. But the slogan also underscores age stereotypes. It is, after all, possible both to get older and better. In addition the slogan promises the impossible; unless we've died we are getting older. Aging is an inexorable biological process. Moreover, there is no reason to assume that we should not want to get older. The ad plays on common fears that are unfounded. Most people, for example, report that youth was a more troublesome and traumatic time than older age. When the statement "you're not getting older, you're getting better" is made, it is no longer a statement about a hair coloring. It is a linguistic convention—an expression both parties know is only partially true. You may indeed be getting better.

Some slogans are more susceptible to parody than others. In 1964, for example, Republican presidential candidate Barry Goldwater erred in selecting the slogan, "In your heart, you know he's right." Billboards bearing the slogan were quickly defaced to read "extremely right," "but in your head you know he's wrong," or "but in your guts you know he's nuts." The parallel construction invited reconstruction.

Long after a product has abandoned a slogan, the slogan retains currency because we tend to store highly redundant messages in our memories for later retrieval. Consequently, chicken producer Frank Perdue says in one of his ads that "golden yellow is the natural color of a chicken. . . . So don't wonder why my chickens are so yellow, wonder why some chickens are so white [lifting up a competitor's white chicken]. I wonder where the yellow went?" That last sentence becomes a barometer of the age of the auditor. Those of us old enough to remember the Pepsodent toothpaste slogan, "You'll wonder where the yellow went when you brush your teeth with Pepsodent," hear the line as a clever reconstruction of an old claim and also as a literal statement. Those unexposed to the campaign hear only the literal statement.

As our discussion so far indicates, any trademark, package, or slogan that identifies a product also distinguishes that product from those employing a different trademark, package, and slogan. Indeed, the package may be all that distinguishes one product from another.

Differentiation

Rosser Reeves, one of the pioneers of advertising, coined the phrase "unique selling proposition." The unique selling proposition is a claim that differentiates one ad from another. In an era when advertising floods the environment, the unique

---

BOX 7-5

Differentiation

"'All the cosmetics companies use basically the same chemicals. It is all the same quality stuff,' says Heinz J. Eiermann, a former cosmetics chemist and industry executive who directs the Food and Drug Administration's division of cosmetics technology. 'The art of cosmetics is as much in marketing as in chemistry. Much of what you pay for is make-believe.'"[a]

"'I've never worked on a product that was better than another. They hardly . . . exist. So what I have to do is create an imagery about that product,' said George Lois, chairman of Lois Pitts Gershon Pon/GGK on *60 Minutes* in 1981."[b]

[a]Blaine Harden, "Vanity Fare," *Washington Post Magazine*, 30 May 1982, p. 10.
[b]Quoted by Roger Draper, "The Faithless Shepherd," *New York Review of Books*, 26 June 1986, p. 16.

---

selling proposition is even more important than it was when there were fewer products of the same kind and less advertising.

Crest toothpaste, for example, contains fluoride. When it was introduced, Crest was distinguished from other toothpastes by the claim, certified by a major dental association, that it would reduce the number of new cavities. Once the other products were able to make the claim that they too could reduce the number of new cavities, Crest lost its unique selling proposition. Other competitors then entered the market claiming that they whitened teeth; some claimed to freshen breath. Once the unique selling propositions of a product such as toothpaste are well known and accepted, a competitor can combine the unique selling propositions of all the others. So, a toothpaste was marketed that promised fluoride *and* fresher breath: "Double Protection AquaFresh."

It is also possible to adopt and extend a competitor's claim. A long-distance phone company, for example, urges you to use the phone to keep in touch. An airline extends the claim, arguing that flying there is the best way to keep in touch—which assumes that you have granted that keeping in touch is a good thing.

A competitor can counter a unique selling proposition by coopting it, as AquaFresh did in coopting the claims of its rivals. Alternatively, it can undercut the selling proposition by granting that it is unique but implying that that uniqueness is a disadvantage. Dove soap claimed as its unique advantage that it is one-quarter cleansing cream. A competitor responded by claiming that its product doesn't contain any greasy cream. The unique selling proposition had been recontextualized by a competitor, and in the new context it was a negative, rather than a positive, attribute of the product.

The package may be the product's major selling point. When a deodorant is advertised as "a convenient roll-on," when a frozen dinner is advertised as "oven-to-table service," it is the package, not the product being packaged, that we are being sold. *Once a mode of packaging has been widely adopted, it loses its utility as a unique selling point for any single product.* We now take for granted, for example, that rolls of waxed paper, foil, or plastic wrap will come in a box with a serrated edge so we can cleanly cut off the amount needed. By contrast, the use of plastic containers for products once bottled in glass is sufficiently new that the "unbreakable" or "squeezable" bottle is still advertised.

Association

Advertisers attempt to associate their products with a slogan, a trademark or trade character, and a package; then they try to associate the product, slogan, package, trademark, and trade character with positive experiences. Ads create wants and transform wants into needs by associating products with desirable experiences. If the ad is to succeed, it must create a strong associative link between the experience portrayed in the ad and the product. That experience must be one we would like to share, and the experience portrayed must be different from and better than that promised by competitors.

When one product evokes more positive associations than competing products, the intended audience will tell surveyors that brand is an important factor in determining which to buy. A study released in July 1995 by the International Mass Retail Association reflected the power of advertising when it reported that 60 percent of consumers ages 8 through 17 said that brand was important when buying sneakers; 58 percent said it was important when purchasing radios, CD players, and so on; 54 percent indicated its centrality in deciding on video games; and 37 percent identified it as important in purchasing jeans.[3]

Participation

By involving us in the creation of the meaning of the ad, an advertiser can increase the likelihood that we will identify with the experience portrayed in the ad. At the same time, this involvement ensures that our experience of this product as portrayed through the experience in the ad will be different from and better than that portrayed in other ads.

Identification with Ad Characters

Ads establish commonality with us by creating characters and situations with which we identify. Some of the characters represent the sorts of people advertisers think we would like to be (rich, famous, glamorous); some represent the persons advertisers think we think we are (unappreciated, overworked).

---

3. "USA Snapshots," *USA Today,* 21 July 1995, p. B1.

Some ads represent persons advertisers think we do not want to be. The purpose of such ads is to tell us that if we use the product, we will not become like that person (old, ugly, irritable, pain-ridden, covered with dandruff, disfigured by acne).

Significant Experiences

Some experiences, such as birth, are universal. Others—such as weddings, graduations, or anniversaries—are more culture-bound. But in this culture all of these moments of change function as important elements in our lives. Memorable, culturally significant moments are awaited expectantly—as a boy waits eagerly for the opportunity to shave (an activity greeted with less enthusiasm after years of confronting the need for it daily). Retirement is another such moment, although it is one more dreaded than embraced by many.

When advertisers re-create such important moments for us, they invite us to identify with their creation, to invest it with our own experience or the experience we hope to have. If an advertiser can induce us to invest the ad and, by implication, the product with our own positive feelings and experiences, we ought to emerge with a positive feeling about the product. It will not have the desired effect, of course, if we feel manipulated by the ad and feel that it cheapens our memories or projections for the future.

Some moments in our lives are almost off limits for advertisers because the associations we bring to those events are not happy but sad. Death is one such moment. Consequently, life insurance ads seek to minimize the trauma. Indeed, one life insurance ad features an escalator to the sky. The man being escorted up the escalator (presumably to heaven) is protesting that he's not ready to go yet. The ad reassures us that he is indeed ready because his life insurance is in order; he need not worry about the well-being of his survivors. Another ad for life insurance shows a man with his family, and then simply removes him from the picture as the narrative tells what their lives will be like if he's not there.

Because we fear our own death and grieve when a person we love dies, death is almost taboo as a basis for ads. The indirect treatment of death in the ads for life insurance testifies to this. Yet an ad for the Catholic Church of Maryland fractures that taboo deliberately by showing a baptism and then making a transition to a funeral, with the narrator saying "You only live once, shouldn't you go to church more than twice?" The ad is jarring, in part because it has capsulized two moments, birth and death, which we all confront. In part it is jarring also because such bold, direct treatment of death in an ad shatters expectations about ads that we are not even aware that we have until they are violated.

Making the Audience an Accomplice

Verbal and visual commonality forms the base from which the advertiser builds the ad's claims. If the advertiser then can lure us into the role of accomplice in endorsing the product, the ad will succeed. To do this, the advertiser de-

---

BOX 7-6

Brand Recall

The Newspaper Advertising Bureau, in its 1986 study of the recall of television commercials, found that 7 percent of respondents could recall the brand advertised in a commercial seen an average of 4.5 minutes earlier.[a]

[a]William F. Gloede, "TV Ad Recall Still Low: NAB Study," *Advertising Age*, 4 August 1986, p. 50.

---

termines what content we are willing to invest in the ad and then creates a structure that links that invested content to the product.

The ad may do this with a rhetorical question, as a 1968 presidential campaign ad for Democratic candidate Hubert Humphrey did when it asked, "Who is your choice to be a heartbeat away from the president?" The Humphrey-Muskie campaign knew from polling data that when the choice was reduced to Edmund Muskie (Humphrey's running mate) and Spiro Agnew (Nixon's running mate), the audience would be more likely to answer "Muskie" than "Agnew." So the rhetorical question was designed to elicit a response favorable to Humphrey. When the audience answered "Muskie," that answer made it more difficult to vote for Nixon, because in the process of accepting the question as legitimate, the auditor had accepted the assumption of the importance of the vice-president. If the vice-presidential candidate could be made a salient element in the determination of voting behavior, then Humphrey would gain an advantage because Muskie was viewed as the better vice-presidential candidate—even by a proportion of Nixon supporters. The ad itself did not tell us that Muskie was the right answer. The advertisers knew that many would fill in Muskie's name. In the process of answering the question by saying to ourselves "Muskie," we participated in creating a pro-Humphrey-Muskie message, and the strategy underlying the ad succeeded.

In addition to the use of resonant symbols such as weddings and the construction of rhetorical questions for which the audience has a ready answer, advertisers also induce participation by:

1. Juxtaposing images that have no necessary relation to one another but that, when associatively linked, lead the audience to infer a relationship ("Have a Coke and a smile").
2. Employing double entendres that prompt the audience to fill in a second meaning ("My men wear English Leather or they wear nothing at all"). So, for example, when Johns Hopkins Medicine took out an ad that said to *US News* "Thanks to you, our condition remains stable," it invited readers to ask what the five pictured issues of the newsmagazine could have to do with the stability of the medical complex in Baltimore. The answer is in the ad: "For the fifth straight year, *US News & World Report* ranked Johns Hopkins the #1 hospital in America."[4]

---

4. *New York Times*, 23 July 1995, p. 18.

The Humane Society of the United States

2100 L St., N.W. Washington, DC 20037

:30 TV P.S.A. "Rodeo"

16mm Color

VO: The following "sport" is brought to you by today's rodeos.

MUSIC UP (Strauss Waltz)

MUSIC UNDER
VO: The suggestion that this really isn't sport but cruelty

is brought to you by The Humane Society of the United States.

This commercial has won first place in both the 1980 Clio Awards and 1980 Andy Awards for BEST PUBLIC SERVICE TELEVISION.

Figure 7.1   This award-winning PSA, created for the Humane Society of the United States by the Earle Palmer Brown Advertising Agency, attracts attention by its use of slow-motion scenes of a calf-roping at a rodeo. Because we are unaccustomed to slow-motion footage in television ads, this technique focuses our attention on the content of the shots. The ad also grabs attention by violating our expectations because it substitutes a Strauss waltz for the shouting crowds we expect to hear. But as the ad progresses, we sense that a tension is building between the grace and gentleness of the waltz and the wrenching, agonized animals we see on the screen. The visual message is not aesthetically pleasing, although the music tells us it ought to be. If we are accustomed to viewing rodeos as sport, as a spec-

3. Employing a phrase outside its normal context to induce the audience to ask how, if at all, that phrase can be applied to the product. For example, automobile dealers appropriate a phrase from the film *The Godfather* to assert, "We'll make you an offer you can't refuse." And Crest headlines an ad "Years of Crest Cavity Protection and Nothing to Show for It." In smaller print, the reason is given: "No cavities: It's what every mom wants for her kids . . ."

4. Creating a questionable grammatical construction such that, in the process of untangling the statement's meaning, the audience draws a new meaning from the words. For example, an automobile ad claims that "we" not only make the car "*well*, we make it *good*."

5. Using explicit content that triggers unarticulated audience predispositions. In summer 1990, a black glossy insert in *Advertising Age* declared "*Playboy* has put me in the hearts of 10 million men." The fold-in was designed to look like the *Playboy* centerfold fold-out. Anticipating a nude female centerfold, readers opened the page to find a three-page pullout, similar to *Playboy*'s in form, but of a fully clothed businessman. The data sheet, also a carryover from *Playboy*, revealed that this was David Warren, president of Jordache. In the data sheet, Warren plugs *Playboy*. "Our previous print campaign didn't consist of major menswear publications. A big mistake. To correct it, we chose *Playboy* because it's got the largest readership among the men's magazines. And their reader is our customer: affluent, younger, contemporary with a disposable income. A perfect fit—pardon the pun."

6. Manipulating by suggesting that, unlike other ads, this one isn't manipulative. On the assumption that younger audiences are likely to see through traditional ad ploys, the ads of the 1990s are increasingly anti-ads. "We considered showing an NBA star drinking our soda," says a print ad for Sprite, "but we figured basketball players should stick to what they do best—endorsing sneakers." A television ad shows a glass of cod liver oil that looks like a glass of a carmel cola as the announcer urges viewers to "Drink what tastes good because television can make anything look delicious." The theme of the Sprite campaign asks the audience to reject ad claims and simply "Obey Your Thirst."

By luring us into participating in the creation of the ad's meaning, the advertiser increases the persuasive power of the ad. But unless the message is repeated often, it is unlikely that we will either be exposed to it or persuaded by it. The ad in Figure 7.1 is highly creative in its selection of means to induce participation.

---

tacle to be appreciated and enjoyed, or as a form of relaxation and entertainment, the ad forces us to re-evaluate our attitude. The jarring contrast between the music and the visual message forces that re-evaluation. The ad induces participation by placing the viewer in the position of a judge who must determine whether the activities shown are "sport" or "cruelty." The claim that this is sport is offered by the announcer on behalf of "today's rodeos" in the opening frame. The alternative claim is offered on behalf of the Humane Society of the United States in the fifth and sixth frames. The visual and audio content of the ad biases the viewer in favor of the second interpretation. (Reprinted by permission of the Humane Society of the United States.)

Redundancy

Repetition

We are more likely to remember a message we have heard often. Consequently, most ads are highly redundant; they repeat the same claim visually and verbally, underscoring the claim in the slogan and whenever possible in the packaging and in the name of the product as well. A radio ad for Sprite played on the notion that ads require repetition by promising, "Here's a soda jingle that'll stick in your head. We'll play it day and night until you'll wish you were dead."

Note the number of times the name of the product and its chief selling point, capsulized in the slogan, are repeated in this ad:

> *MERIT* ANNOUNCES NEW *MERIT* ULTRA LIGHTS. NOW THE *MERIT* IDEA HAS BEEN INTRODUCED AT ONLY 4 MG. TAR—NEW *MERIT* ULTRA LIGHTS. A MILDER *MERIT* FOR THOSE WHO PREFER AN ULTRA LOW TAR CIGARETTE. NEW *MERIT* ULTRA LIGHTS. IT'S GOING TO SET A WHOLE NEW TASTE STANDARD FOR ULTRA LOW TAR SMOKING.

Once the product's name and its slogan have been deeply embedded in the audience, the advertiser can enlist the audience as an accomplice in filling one or the other into the ad—thus heightening audience participation and the persuasive impact of the message. In one ad for Coke, for example, the announcer did not utter the word *Coke*. Instead the chorus sang "It's the real thing," and where the ad would ordinarily have said "Coke" we heard instead the sound of the bottle being opened and the soda fizzing. Meanwhile, bottles of Coke were shown to encourage us to fill in our part of the slogan.

Repeated Exposure

Ads also are aired repeatedly, or printed again and again, in the hope that sooner or later we will be reading, listening, or watching when they occur and will pay attention. The likelihood that we will remember a part of the ad increases as exposure to the ad increases. For this reason, advertisers often create radio ads from their televised ads' audio tracks and use pictures from television ads in magazine ads. If the advertiser is successful, repetition ensures that the ad reaches the consumer with a message that creates product *recognition, differentiates* the product from its competitors, *associates* the product with favorable experiences, and *repeatedly involves* the audience in creating the ad's meaning. In this way ads create or underscore wants and transform them into needs to be satisfied by purchase of the advertised product.

Often, as a result of this process, we purchase products with which we are satisfied. Our experience with the product and the experience promised in the ad are comparable. But sometimes, after purchase of the product, we realize that the ad led us astray. On examination, we realize that the deception did not re-

The Tobacco Industry Can't be Trusted with America's Children

They say there is no proof that smoking and smokeless tobacco cause disease and death.

They claim nicotine isn't addictive.

They swear they don't market to kids.

They claim to be taking care of the problem of underage tobacco use.

Do you believe them? 3,000 children begin smoking every day, and the rate is increasing, especially among younger kids. Almost all of them smoke one of the three most heavily advertised brands. One third will eventually die of their addiction.

President Clinton and the Food & Drug Administration, joined by many members of Congress—Republicans and Democrats—have proposed new limits on sales and marketing of tobacco to children.

Please give your support. Write to the FDA, Dockets Management Branch, Docket 95N-0253, Room 1-23, 12420 Parklawn Drive, Rockville, MD 20857. Don't trust the tobacco industry to do the right thing. They never have. They never will.

This ad is sponsored by the American Cancer Society, the American Academy of Pediatrics, the American Heart Association, the American Lung Association, the American Medical Association and over 100 other organizations that support the **Campaign for Tobacco-Free Kids.**

For additional information, or to contribute to more ads like this: **1-800-284-KIDS.**

CAMPAIGN for TOBACCO-FREE Kids

Figure 7.2 This advertisement for the Campaign for Tobacco-Free Kids is analyzed in the case study. The advertisement was created in-house by the campaign staff.

side explicitly in the ad but in our eagerness to make faulty inferences, an eagerness abetted by the advertiser.

To recap the functions served by name recognition, differentiation, association, participation, and redundancy, we will analyze in the following case study an ad (Figure 7.2) created to market the Campaign for Tobacco-Free Kids.

Analysis of "Tobacco-Free Kids"

The Campaign for Tobacco-Free Kids is a privately funded, national organization designed to reduce tobacco use among children. The Center's mandate is changing the social climate as well as public policies to decrease youth tobacco use, to limit the marketing and sales of tobacco to children, and to serve as a counterforce to the tobacco industry and its special interests.

Identification

Both the picture and the text communicate that the key ideas in this ad are kids and tobacco. The closely cropped picture focuses attention on the girl's youth and on the cigarette she holds. She looks innocent, the cigarette menacing. While her face is shaded, the cigarette is a bright white matching the white of the words in the headline and in the process making the connection between picture and words.

Differentiation

The product the ad is advancing is the tobacco-free child. The enemy: the tobacco industry. One presumably wants the child to be tobacco free; the tobacco industry, implies the ad, has a vested interest in addicting her. One tells the truth— captured in claims to be taken as fact. "3,000 children begin smoking every day, and the rate is increasing, especially among younger kids. Almost all of them smoke one of the three most heavily advertised brands." The tobacco industry makes implausible claims. "They claim nicotine isn't addictive."

Association

The sight of a child awkwardly holding a cigarette to her lips is startling. It also evokes immediate associations—with the children in our lives as well as children in general. By suggesting that the girl is being threatened both by the cigarette and by the tobacco industry, the headline "The Tobacco Industry Can't Be

Advertisers' Strategies for Persuasion

We are culturally conditioned to recognize and respect certain argumentative forms and to accept certain forms of evidence. Advertisers can exploit this training by couching their claims in forms of argument and evidence we are inclined to trust. So, for example, instead of simply urging you to use our product, we might adopt the language of social science research and claim that "four out of five professors surveyed recommended that you read this book." We are hoping, of course, that our use of social scientific language will lull you into uncritical acceptance of the claim. The four professors in question are close friends who recommended it after we bought them an expensive dinner. Because you might be suspicious if we said that 100 percent of those surveyed supported one side, we didn't pressure the fifth professor. If she'd endorsed the book, we would have

Trusted with America's Children" increases readers' identification with the young girl. The ad then invites the reader to identify with the bi-partisan political forces and respected associations that support the campaign.

Participation

The ad does not say, "The tobacco industry is lying about the dangers of tobacco and about its marketing strategies." Instead it invites the reader to draw that conclusion on his or her own. "They say there is no proof . . . They claim nicotine . . . They swear . . . They claim to be taking care of the problem of underage tobacco use."

Are the claims true or false? The indirect relation between the verb asserting their position (*claim, swear, say*) and the verb that suggests direct action ("there is no proof . . . nicotine isn't addictive . . . they don't market to kids") implies that the saying, claiming, and swearing are untrustworthy. The ad explicitly invites that inference with the question, "Do you believe them?"

To help answer that question, the ad offers evidence on tobacco use and an indication that there is political sentiment to legislate against the tobacco industry. Assuming the audience has agreed that the tobacco industry is lying, the ad then reinforces that conclusion by saying "Don't trust the tobacco industry to do the right thing. They never have. They never will."

The ad invites participation at another level. By including a 1-800 number, the ad makes it possible for the reader to call to get additional information or to contribute to the publication of more ads.

Redundancy

The ad repeats the refrain, don't trust the tobacco industry. It also uses alliteration to increase the memorability of its message. The *tobacco* industry cannot be *trusted*. Tobacco causes *disease and death*. "They never have" forecasts "They never will."

found a hostile sixth professor, ensuring that the claim would be phrased in a familiar manner. We used exactly five, but implied that "four out of *every* five" professors in a large-scale survey recommended our book. Similarly, in visual ads we might show glamorous, wise media moguls holding the book, in the hope that potential consumers would assume a necessary connection between the juxtaposed images.

Content analysis of 2,000 print ads from ten major magazines from 1900 to 1980, however, found that the informational content of ads has been decreasing. Ads have become more focused and present a more limited amount of information more dramatically than they did in the past.[5]

---

5. Cited by Michael Schudson in *Advertising: The Uneasy Persuasion* (New York: Basic Books, 1984), p. 60.

BOX 7-7

Advertisers' Influence on Women's Magazines

"Advertisers' control over the editorial content of women's magazines has become so institutionalized that it is . . . dictated to ad salespeople as official policy," writes Gloria Steinem. She gives these examples:

> Dow's Cleaning Products stipulates that ads for its Vivid and Spray 'n Wash products should be adjacent to "children or fashion editorial"; ads for Bathroom Cleaner should be next to "home furnishing/family" features.

> The De Beers diamond company, a big seller of engagement rings, prohibits magazines from placing its ads with "adjacencies to hard news or anti-love/romance theme editorial."

> Procter & Gamble products were not to be placed in any issue that included any material on gun control, abortion, the occult, cults, or the disparagement of religion.

Steinem picked random issues of women's magazines and counted the number of pages, including letters to the editors and the like, that were not ads and/or copy complementary to ads. Some examples were:

Magazine and Issue	Total Pages	Non-Ad or Non-Ad-Related
Glamour, April 1990	339	65
Vogue, May 1990	319	38
Redbook, April 1990	173	44
Family Circle, 13 March 1990	180	33
Elle, May 1990	326	39
Lear's, November 1989	173	65

Steinem quotes Sey Chassler, former editor-in-chief of *Redbook*, as saying, "I also think advertisers do this to women's magazines especially because of the general disrespect they have for women."[a]

[a]Gloria Steinem, "Sex, Lies and Advertising," *Ms.*, July/August 1990, pp. 20, 21, 25, 27.

In this section we will examine some of the ways in which advertisers use claims and evidence to prompt us to make the desired inferences about the product, its competitors, and its promises.

Naming the Product

The name of a product may be misleading. Butterball turkeys, for example, contain no butter. Similarly, McDonald's Quarter Pounder, as served, does not weigh a quarter of a pound. McDonald's ads now reveal that the meat weighed a quarter of a pound before it was cooked. This disclosure appeared only after consumer groups protested that the name was misleading.

BOX 7-8

Television Ad Strategies

Most of the ads you see on television are terribly, terribly phony. They have to be, because you're trying to cram into 30 seconds something that people would never say in their lives, and if they did, it would take half an hour. I think good advertising today doesn't try to tell people exactly what they're supposed to think. It lets them make up their own minds. Which takes realism, . . .

So said Hal Riney, of Hal Riney & Partners, an advertising agency with branches in San Francisco, Chicago, and New York; this agency created the series of ads for Bartles & Jaymes Premium Wine Coolers.

Riney also produced three ads for President Reagan's 1984 campaign. In one of them viewers saw images of a grizzly bear in the forest as Riney narrated: "Some people say the bear is tame. Others say it's vicious and dangerous. Since no one can really be sure who's right, isn't it smart to be as strong as the bear—if there is a bear?" At the end, a silhouetted rifleman stood facing the bear.

The commercial was in response to an ad for Democratic presidential candidate Walter Mondale that suggested that Reagan was trigger-happy. The shrewdness of the ad was that it sidestepped Mondale's argument.

Riney explained, "I was . . . trying to figure out how to show the Republican views on armament in a 30-second spot, without having to get into a lot of laborious details. So this parable form occurred to me. And it seemed to work very well for a controversial theme, because it didn't force you into committing to any particular point of view."[a]

[a]Art Kleiner, "Master of the Sentimental Sell," *New York Times Magazine*, 14 December 1986, pp. 58, 72.

BOX 7-9

The Enthymeme

Enthymeme is a Greek word for the special kinds of arguments found in rhetoric. Enthymemes are arguments that rely on the knowledge, values, attitudes, and experiences of the audience. An enthymeme is a partial or incomplete argument that prompts the audience to complete it with whatever the audience already knows, believes, or values. An argument that invites you to fill in your own experience or to draw a conclusion when no claim is made explicitly is an enthymeme.

Enthymemes are described in Aristotle's *Rhetoric* [translator W. Rhys Roberts (New York: Modern Library, 1954)]. Although he doesn't use the word, Tony Schwartz describes the enthymematic process in *The Responsive Chord* (New York: Doubleday, 1974).

Best Western is the name of a motel chain. By what criterion or standard are these motels the best? Who says so? Easy-Off is an oven cleaner. The name implies that the product makes cleaning your oven easy. The ads carry through this theme: "Don't put it off, use Easy-Off. Easy-Off makes oven cleaning easier."

Easier than what? Some other product? If so, which one? Who found that Easy-Off made the job easier? When? Where? Or is it easier than using no oven cleaner at all? The ad has not disclosed the criteria for assessing its claim. If the claim means that it is easier to clean your oven using this cleaner than using no cleaner at all, then it is a weak claim. But if it means easier than with other products, then the claim is considerably stronger, and the burden of proof on the advertiser is correspondingly heavier. Without specifics, we must assume only the weaker claim. Of course, that is not what the advertisers hope we will do. They hope we will interpret this ad as a statement from some unseen authority about the comparative efficiency of Easy-Off.

Differentiating Products

In his book *Confessions of an Advertising Man,* David Ogilvy, founder of one of America's most successful advertising agencies, admits that he is "continuously guilty of *suppressio veri* [suppression of truth]." "Surely," he notes, "it is asking too much to expect the advertiser to describe the shortcomings of his product? One must be forgiven for putting one's best foot forward."[6] But advertisers are often guilty not only of suppressing a product's shortcomings but of concealing the criteria and the evidence on which their claims are based. Such suppression makes it difficult to use advertising as a basis for comparing one product with another.

Pseudo-Claims   The problems involved in interpreting misleading slogans often involve meaning. What does it mean, for example, to say that product X "fights" bad breath or product Y "fights" dandruff? A promise to control is stronger than a promise to fight, but neither claim promises to eliminate the problem. What is a consumer supposed to hear when an advertiser says that a certain shampoo "controls" dandruff with regular use?

Helps is another word used to weaken claims subtly. What does it mean to say, "Vaseline Intensive Care *helps* heal roughness, dryness"? Take *helps* out and the statement claims that this lotion, acting alone, heals. Its action is direct, not indirect. The claim to "control" or "help" suggests that using the product will produce positive results. The promise to "fight" is a promise that the product will try to produce results, that it will oppose the negative condition (the dryness, the dandruff) but may not overcome it.

"And Texaco's coal gasification process could mean you won't have to worry about how it affects the environment." But what *does* that mean? "Could" suggests possibility without making a specific promise that any given outcome will occur.

Comparison with an Unidentified Other   Ads often promise "more" cleaning power, "better" cleaning action, "stronger" whitening power, or that a product has more or better ingredients. But more, better, whiter, stronger than what? No

---

6. David Ogilvy, *Confessions of an Advertising Man* (New York: Ballantine Books, 1963), p. 140.

product at all? Some specific product? When an advertiser says that product X is better than product Y, a comparative claim has been made. Of course, advertisers often do not tell us what product this product exceeds and on what grounds the performance of one is superior to another. Nonetheless, "better" implies comparison. The rules of grammar would suggest that a product that is the "best" has no superiors. But what if all of the products in a class are essentially equal? Then all are both "the best" and "the worst" because there is no basis for distinguishing one from another. (Such essentially identical products are called "parity" products.) However, we incorrectly interpret a claim that a product is the "best" to mean that it is better than all others. Similarly, we hear the claim that "Crest is unsurpassed in reducing new cavities" to mean that Crest is the best when instead the claim literally means that there are no products that are better at reducing new cavities. Others are *as good as* Crest, but none is better.

Ads often compare their product with an unnamed other product. "This trash bag is stronger than the cheap bargain bag." It probably is stronger than some cheaper bargain bag, but which one, and is the comparison a fair one? One ad claims that wine experts (which experts, and by what standards are they experts?) prefer one brand of wine over another, but the ad does not reveal that the price of the advertised brand is higher than that of its competitor. In effect, a top-of-the-line product has been compared with a middle-of-the-line product and the middle product has been found wanting. But what if similar products had been compared?

In 1971 the FTC began encouraging comparative advertising. In 1972, the networks lifted their bans on mentioning a competitive product by name.

Comparison of the Product with Its Earlier Form   "Lysol deodorizing cleanser has a great new fresh scent." New improved product X has 50 percent more cleaning power. In order to maintain their share of the market against competitors who are continually introducing new products with new additives, advertisers adjust the familiar image of a comfortable product to include something new or improved. In the process, they hope that they will not undercut our reasons for buying the product in the first place. The promise that a familiar product is now new or better—a claim that must be backed by an actual change in the product—aims to reinforce the buying habits of those who already use the product and to insulate them from the claims of more recent market entries. At the same time, it aims to attract new customers.

Irrelevant Comparisons   We tend to assume that the best seller is the best product. Instead, the best seller may be inferior to another product but have better distribution, a big early lead in the market, or better advertising than its competitors. Yet advertisers capitalize on our best-seller-is-best assumption by telling us when a product is outselling others of its type. Claims of this sort invite the audience to infer that the product's high quality accounts for its status as the best seller.

Irrelevant criteria are often applied to establish uniqueness. Because we have been taught that you get what you pay for, advertisers can persuade us that costlier is better. Of course, cost may reflect factors other than quality, including inefficient production techniques, high tariffs, high profit-taking, or even a large advertising budget. Nonetheless, a product can be made to seem unique by having a higher price than its competitors. So, for example, Boodles gin is advertised as "the ultra-refined British gin that only the world's costliest methods could produce. Boodles. The world's costliest *British* gin." Note the qualifier. It is not the *world's* costliest gin but the costliest British gin. If we accept the assumption that costliness is next to godliness, perhaps we should scan the liquor store shelves to see if there is a more expensive gin, British or not.

The Pseudo-Survey   We live in a society impressed by the natural and social sciences and accustomed to trusting their authoritative, quantitative claims. Surveys appear regularly in the news media telling us how we plan to vote, what we think about specific issues, and whom we trust. By wrapping their claims in scientific language, by expressing claims in the style of valid surveys, by placing actors in the settings we associate with the medical and scientific professions, advertisers increase the chance that we will mistakenly attach scientific validity to the claims they make.

When an ad claims that "four out of five dentists surveyed recommend sugarless gum for their patients who chew gum," it is using the familiar language of the survey report. A legitimate survey will disclose the population sampled (from what group were the dentists drawn—all dentists in the United States, dentists in a single state, dentists in a certain association or at a certain meeting?), how the survey population was chosen (random sample?), the total number of dentists asked, and the error we can expect in generalizing from this sample to the whole population. But the ad tells us *only* that four out of five dentists surveyed recommended a certain product for patients likely to engage in a certain activity. Conceivably, only five dentists were asked the question. Alternatively, the question may have been asked only of dentists already predisposed to the product. From the evidence offered in the ad, we simply don't know.

In addition, there is an important qualifier in the ad. Do the dentists who recommend sugarless gum for their gum-chewing patients recommend gum chewing? Perhaps the dentists would say, if asked, that gum chewing is foolish. Because the claim carries the qualifier "for their patients who chew gum," the dentists may not have recommended gum chewing at all. So we don't know how representative these dentists' views are, and we don't know whether they endorse gum chewing.

Creating Associations

In this section we examine the promises implied by the associations created in ads and the sources on which ads draw to build associations.

Associations with Celebrities and Authorities

Use It. Be Like Me.   When celebrities appear in commercials, they are often there to testify to the worth of a product. Sometimes they function as pseudo-authorities. What qualifies Ed McMahon as an expert on mayonnaise, motorcycles, or sunglasses? At best, celebrities speaking outside their field of achievement give testimony about their ordinary experience, experience no more authoritative than yours and mine, about how coffee tastes, or how well a detergent works. Often, the celebrity not only tells us why he or she uses the product but also hints that if we want to be like him or her, we ought to use this product.

Actors also attempt to transfer the trust we have in their characters to products. John Houseman, who played a curmudgeonly law professor in the series *Paper Chase,* carried that role with him in his endorsement of a brokerage firm that makes its "money the old-fashioned way. They earn it." After pleading guilty to 2,000 counts of wire and mail fraud, another brokerage firm, E. F. Hutton, hired Bill Cosby, the star of NBC's top-rated show of the 1985–86 season, to appear in ads designed to mend its image.

In 1995, Candice Bergen of *Murphy Brown* fame touted the value of the long distance carrier Sprint, Janine Turner who played Maggie on *Northern Exposure* spoke for Chevrolet, and Jerry Seinfeld star of *Seinfeld* promoted American Express.

Use It. I'm Doctorlike.   Advertisers associate their products with persons we are likely to trust. We are culturally conditioned to trust older white males, for example, a cultural predisposition reinforced by the leadership positions held by older white males in government and in the major religions. Consequently, it is not surprising that older white males appear more often as authority figures in ads than older women. We are also conditioned to respect the advice and information provided by certain types of professionals such as doctors, nurses, and pharmacists, who are also common figures in ads.

Cannibalizing the Past for Associations

The pervasive presence of claims that this or that product is "new" or, in the advertising cliché, "new and improved," tells us that advertisers regard new as a positive term. Indeed, they must. If we repaired small appliances rather than replacing them, if we faithfully repaired our cars instead of changing models, if we wore clothes until they became unpatchable, sales of new appliances, cars, and clothes would drop precipitously—and so would the advertising budgets of their manufacturers. Advertisers must persuade us that new is better if they are to survive in the manner to which they have become accustomed.

In order to wed us to the new, advertisers adopt the commercial equivalent of Social Darwinism: change is improvement. Because we hold the distant past in nostalgic reverence, advertisers often argue for change in the name of recapturing something we have never experienced firsthand. This reverence for the mythic past is consistent with the cult of the new insofar as what is old-fashioned is identified not with our experienced past (if the new product isn't better we stay with the old) but with a past that predates us. For example, Country Time, which is not lemonade, claims that it tastes just like good old-fashioned lemonade. The key characters in the Country Time ad are old and speak of real lemonade—the kind made by squeezing lemons—as a memory from their youth, a time clearly beyond the recall of anyone under 80. The ad implies that Country Time is better than anything else available now. Of course, we can still buy and squeeze fresh lemons, but in the world created by the ad that activity ceased at about the time the first Model T approached a highway.

In an ad for Xerox copiers, a monk miraculously made multiple copies of a rare manuscript faster than his superior imagines possible. The contrast between the ancient manuscript and the modern copies underlines our contentions that advertisers venerate newness and change, and that advertisers are committed to the sale of large quantities of mass-produced, identical products.

Before the advent of the printing press and its cousin, the photocopying machine, monks and others copied books by hand. Treasured texts were beautifully written and ornamented by gold or illuminated letters, borders, and delicate illustrations. The process took years, but the result was often a magnificent work of art. Each manuscript was unique. Because the manuscripts were usually sacred texts, the monk's work was a labor of love and service to God. The painstaking labor of such monks made possible the transmission of learning during the Dark Ages; many classic texts survived because they had been copied and hidden in cloisters. The monk, laboring by candlelight, quill in hand, evokes images of the quality and artistic value of the hand-lettered manuscript.

The ad for Xerox copiers would have us believe that the copier increased the speed with which the monk could produce manuscripts but did not diminish their quality. In place of a unique product, we now have a standardized product in as many units as we want. But the copier cannot produce the gold leaf of the original, the colors of the illuminated letters, or the intricate patterns drawn into the margins.

The copier can produce a readable copy of the text itself. Is this better? The ad implied that it is. By the end of the ad, the monk was no longer hand-copying manuscripts. Xerox copiers had made the monk who could produce a beautiful manuscript obsolete. The subtext of this ad told us that new is better than old, change brings improvement, uniqueness is neither necessary nor desirable, faster and more are better. Here, as in the ad for Country Time, the commercial identified the product with the kind of quality that you and I have not experienced directly. Such quality presumably existed only in the distant past.

Because our memory of the distant past is based on historical reconstruction, we have no primary experience with which to test claims about it. Yet the distant past is the source of powerful and evocative symbols. Advertisers cannibalize the past in order to link their products with those symbols. In the process, advertisers desacralize the sacred and trivialize the historically significant.

BOX 7-10

Philip Morris Sponsors the Bill of Rights

The Philip Morris Company paid $600,000 for the right to link itself in televised and printed promotions with the National Archives, the official custodian of the United States' historic documents. The ad read: "Join Philip Morris and the National Archives in celebrating the 200th anniversary of the Bill of Rights. For a free copy of this historic document, call [an 800 number] or write Bill of Rights, Philip Morris Companies Inc. [followed by a Washington, D.C., address]."

The law forbids Philip Morris to sell cigarettes on television. The company insisted that it was selling its diversified corporate image, not cigarettes. The association with the archives lent the company great prestige, but spokespersons for the archives insisted that the deal was a good way "to stretch the taxpayers' dollars." Congress made the National Archives an independent agency in 1984, and authorized the agency to solicit and receive gifts to enhance its role as "keeper of the nation's history."[a]

[a]"The Bill of Rights, for Rent," *New York Times*, 19 November 1989, p. 22E.

Appropriating Historical Persons and Events   The only widely accepted ritual employed to commemorate Presidents' Day, honoring the birthdays of Washington and Lincoln, is the Presidents' Day Sale. In order to draw us into stores, advertisers reduce George and Martha Washington to cartoonlike hucksters. Actors in white "Washington" wigs hector us about unbelievable bargains and swear that, like George Washington, they would never tell a lie. Similarly, ads for Fourth of July sales urge us to "declare our independence" from everything—from an old car to a malfunctioning air conditioner—and Thanksgiving Day sales imply that what we have to be thankful for are the "fantastic buys."

Another version of this tactic is employed in televised ads for Calvin Klein's Obsession. In the ads the fragrance is associated with passages from the world's great love stories including Hemingway's *The Sun Also Rises,* D. H. Lawrence's *Women in Love,* and Gustave Flaubert's *Madame Bovary.* In one of the spots, a young woman is shown running her fingers over a man's face as the announcer reads from D. H. Lawrence, "How perfect and foreign he was, how dangerous. . . . This was the glistening forbidden apple. . . ."

Just as advertisers are eager to associate with positive moments in the past and present, they are loath to be associated with traumatic ones. During network coverage of the Persian Gulf War in 1991, Procter & Gamble, Sears, Pizza Hut, and major airlines refused to place spots. As a result NBC reported a loss of $45 million in ad revenue.[7]

Trading on Someone's Good Name   Companies appropriate the names of respected historical figures, such as Lincoln and Jefferson, to trade on the truth

---

7. *Advertising Age*, 28 February 1995, p. 53.

BOX 7-11

Bush and Gorbachev for Drixoral

CBS and ABC announced that they would not broadcast a cold remedy commercial using pictures of President Bush and Soviet President Mikhail S. Gorbachev unless the drug company got permission from the two heads of state.

Schering-Plough Corporation was promoting Drixoral, its own weapon against the cold war, which included shipping boxes of Drixoral to the heads of state of East Germany, Poland, Hungary, Czechoslovakia, Romania, and Bulgaria "to ease the effects of their treacherous winter," the pharmaceutical company said in its news release. NBC planned to run the ads, and Schering was considering placing them on cable television channels.

In the past, the White House has sent stiff cease-and-desist warnings to companies using the president's picture to endorse a product. Schering said it had not asked Bush's permission before making the ads. Matthew Margo, a vice-president for program practices at CBS, said that it is "not appropriate" to use the presidency to sell products.[a]

[a]Marcy Gordon (AP), "Two Networks Bar Cold-Medicine Ads with Bush, Gorbachev," *Star Tribune*, 28 December 1989, p. 8D.

---

associated with those names. Service companies are more likely to adopt such names than manufacturers of more tangible products. Life insurance companies and banks are called Lincoln Life or Jefferson Trust, not because they were founded by Lincoln or Jefferson, but because the names themselves have residual credibility. Customers take the name, whether consciously or not, as a promise of the honesty and reliability associated with the historical person. Although the company may be only twenty or thirty years old, a name from the past suggests that the company has been providing that reliable, trustworthy service for a long time.

Appropriating a Famous Phrase   We carry about with us a repertoire of phrases identified with important persons or occasions from the past. For example, when someone says "of the people, by the people, for the people," we call up an image of Abe Lincoln. Such phrases gain our attention by drawing from that common repertoire and proceed to make us accomplices in creating the ad's meaning.

However, each of the strategies we have identified will backfire if the audience is offended by the linking of the product and the phrase, person, or event. The following two instances, in our opinion, overstep the bounds of acceptable use of the past and become tasteless. An ad for a light beer included a photograph identified as that of Goethe—the German poet, scientist, and novelist—on his deathbed. In the ad, Goethe is calling—as he actually did just before he died—for "more light!" By twisting the last words of a great man into an appeal for a beer, the advertisers have trivialized his death and reduced an important historical figure to a huckster.

The strategy in a print ad for a motel is similar. That ad rephrased the invitation on the Statue of Liberty ("Give me your tired, your poor, your huddled masses yearning to breathe free. . . . Send these the homeless, tempest-tossed to me") to a come-on for the motel: "Give us your tired, your homeless, your weary, your thirsty." The motel did not invite "your poor." By reducing Emma Lazarus's stirring words to an invitation to choose one motel over another, the ad misappropriated a phrase we respect, a phrase that forms part of our cultural heritage.

Creating a Memorable Phrase   "Where's the beef?" asked Clara Peller in a Wendy's ad that added the phrase to the nation's vocabulary in the early 1980s. A Bud Light ad created a comparable catch phrase in the early 1990s. In the Bud Light ads, a nervy young man (Eddie Jemison) talks his way into places well stocked with Bud Light by pretending to be someone he obviously is not. In the first ad of the series, after determining that the reserved limousine is well stocked with Bud Light, Eddie works his way into it by claiming to be the man for whom it is being held—Dr. Galazkiewicz. When asked if he is indeed the intended person, Eddie replies "Yes . . . I AM!" PSAs have also carried phrases that moved beyond the ad into the culture at large as did the U.S. National Highway Traffic Safety Administration's slogan "Drinking and Driving Can Kill a Friendship" and the United Negro College Fund's "A mind is a terrible thing to waste."

Exploiting Social Movements   We learn the meaning of words from their use. Many words and phrases have gained especially rich meanings for some segments of the audience because they have been identified with an important social movement.

Because advertisements face severe time and space constraints, they tend to use symbols rich with cultural meaning. Using symbols drawn from social movements with which members of the audience still identify, however, is risky. A cookware manufacturer created the message, "Black is Beautiful; White is Beautiful," to accompany a print ad showing a black and a white pot. Remove the pots from the ad and the statement "Black is beautiful" reflects the ideology of the civil rights movement. Add the pots to the ad and the ideological statement is trivialized. People who hear the statement "Black is beautiful" as a commitment to civil rights are likely to respond to this ad with anger. The statement used to express an ideological position can no longer express that position if it gains currency as a slogan to sell kettles.

Feminist reaction to the slogan for Virginia Slims cigarettes is similar. "You've come a long way, baby" combines affirmation of progress for women with a complete denial of that progress. If those of us in the audience who are women have come such a long way, then why are you still calling us "baby"? By using "you" rather than "we" in the slogan, the advertiser dissociates himself from the woman in the ad and assumes a superior position to her. At the same time, the

---

BOX 7-12

What Is Degradable?

"Packaging that claims to be made of biodegradable plastic material may in fact be a technically true claim, because the plastic may break up due to biological action," said Procter & Gamble associate ad manager Robert Viney. "But if placed side by side with a non-degradable plastic material in a landfill, there is no real difference in how quickly the landfill fills up. Then we believe such a claim would be misleading."[a]

[a]Testimony at a Senate Commerce Subcommittee Hearing, cited in *Advertising Age*, 21 May 1990, p. 2.

---

photographs occupying the upper third of the print ads reduce women's struggle for equality to a fight with some man over the right to smoke. This trivializes women's demands for the vote, for equal pay, for equal access to job opportunity, for equal access to housing and credit. If equal access to lung cancer is all the women's movement has accomplished, then the "you" in the ad hasn't come very far. However, by identifying itself with independent women and by implying that smoking this product controls weight (Virginia *Slims*), this brand has captured a sizable share of the women's market. This suggests that the campaign has not alienated its target audience.

In the 1990s, the social cause most exploited by advertising is environmental. Advertising has capitalized on a powerful public sentiment. As concerns about pollution of the water and air spread around the globe, they took political form. The green movement was launched in Europe. Environmental summits of world leaders were held. Within an environment saturated with claims that this package was environmentally better than that, this detergent more biodegradable, *National Geographic* set itself apart with an ad campaign claiming, "Only one magazine covered the environment before it was an issue."

No sector of marketing has been left untouched by environmental claims. In summer 1990, Estée Lauder announced, for example, that it would "become the first major U.S. beauty company to bring natural, non-animal-tested products packaged in recyclable containers into department stores."[8]

Nationalistic Associations   Some nations are associated with certain products, often as the product's place of birth or most notable manufacturer. So when I say "whiskey" and ask for a high-quality nationality, you might say "Irish," "Scotch," or "Canadian," but probably not "French." An advertiser can capitalize on these associations by creating an image consistent with them. In order to capitalize on the national identification of some products, advertisers give a name evoking the

---

8. Pat Sloan, "Cosmetics: Color It Green," *Advertising Age*, 23 July 1990, p. 1.

original country to a product of that type made elsewhere. Consequently, perfumes are often given French or French-sounding names, and beers are often
given German or German-sounding names.

Sponsorship of the Olympics creates international associations and implicitly
suggests that the sponsoring product has helped produce international harmony
in a spirit of friendly competition. The 1996 Summer Olympics in Atlanta have
an official courier (UPS), an official soft drink (Coke), an official beer (Budweiser), an official credit card (Visa), an official fast food (McDonalds), an offi-
cial contact lens (Bausch and Lomb), and an official watch (Swatch).

Exploiting Argumentative Forms to Create Associations and Participation

Implying Causality   Many ads imply a cause-and-effect relationship: use this
product, get that desirable effect. Critics of advertising ask if the effect occurs at
all, if the effect is a result of using this product, if the effect is a necessary result
of using the product, and if the effect is a result of using the product in conjunction with other factors or of the other factors alone. When a toothpaste claims,
for example, that brushing with it regularly will give you brighter teeth, fresher
breath, and fewer cavities, are these good things the result of the brushing or of
the toothpaste? If you substitute baking soda for the toothpaste, for example,
would you achieve the same result? When a breakfast cereal, bar, or drink claims
that when served with milk, toast, and juice it gives you a completely balanced
and nutritionally sound breakfast, would the milk, toast, and juice alone have the
same result? What does the advertised product contribute to the total nutrition of
the breakfast?

Juxtaposition   Ads commonly juxtapose products and smiling people. Are
the people smiling because they are using the product? (They're probably smiling because they are being paid to smile and will earn a lot of money in residu-
als when the ad is repeatedly aired.) Juxtaposed images encourage us to infer a
relationship between the images, in this case between the smile and the product.
Often we assume a causal relationship. Scenes that would not otherwise be juxtaposed can be edited together for television, and we accept such editing as part
of the grammar of television and are comparatively uncritical of it. Televised ads
can therefore create arguments by association more readily than print ads or
speeches. The relationships between the juxtaposed images imply arguments.
When an ad says, "Gimme sunshine . . . gimme a Dew" (Mountain Dew, a soft
drink), as scenes of young people are intercut with pictures of the soft drink, we
need to ask what the relationship is between the product and the other scene.
The relationship is not inherent; the ad has simply juxtaposed two images. The
audience fills in the relationship. If we assume a causal relationship, then the ad
comes to mean either that drinking Mountain Dew gives the drinker sunshine,
friends, and fun—or that having sunshine, friends, and fun gives us Mountain

Dew. Since the last relationship makes no sense, we will probably conclude that those who drink Mountain Dew are more likely to have the fun shown in the ad than those who do not.

We may also see the relationship as one of identity. In this case sunshine and Mountain Dew would function as synonyms, and the relationship we read into the ad is described with the simile "drinking Mountain Dew is like experiencing sunshine." The ad may also be expressing a list of things important to us: give us friends, sunshine, fun, Mountain Dew.

Exploiting Coincidental Relationships   There is no necessary relationship between use of a product and status, taste, or love. If these characteristics are related to the product at all, the relationship is coincidental. Advertisers would like us to believe the relationship is a necessary one and to infer causality where none exists.

Did Mom make the Skippy peanut butter sandwich "because she knew peanut butter is more nutritious than salami or ham or liverwurst and has no cholesterol?" "No," responds the child in the ad, "she made it because she loves me." For years Pillsbury's ads claimed that "nothin' says lovin' like somethin' from the oven and Pillsbury says it best." Some ads are indirect in their claim that purchase or use of a product is a sign of love. If we accept the Hallmark slogan, "when you care enough to send the very best," sending the card becomes a sign of caring.

Because ads have allied products with status and taste, and because we are aware that this is a manipulative ploy, other advertisers capitalize on our awareness of the ploy by inverting it: "this product is for people who don't need to establish that they have taste or for people who don't need to demonstrate to the world that they have high status." One manufacturer of small cars, for example, employed the stock background (an estate with a mansion and circular drive) and the stock foreground (an elegantly dressed couple) for an ad making a claim of status or taste, but claimed instead that theirs was the car for those who don't need to prove that they have status. Of course, the claim is the same as the claims in the other ads; that the car is a sign of status. But here the car is more—it is also a sign that the buyer does not have to prove that he or she has status. By implication, then, the other cars making the status claim are for insecure people, but this car is for the truly secure (in itself, a kind of status claim).

Implying "If . . . Then"   Ads make promises visually as well as verbally. This is possible because we invest juxtaposed visuals with an "if . . . then" link. A beautiful woman uses a certain brand of lipstick in the ad, and men follow her everywhere. Without making the argument explicit, the ad implies that if you use this product you will be beautiful, and if you are beautiful (or if you use this product), you will be more attractive to men. One could as readily take the visuals to mean that if you are already beautiful, why bother?

The "before and after" ad is the advertiser's way of countering this interpretation. In its classic form, a person or place is shown before using the product and then after: eyelashes before application of mascara, eyelashes after application of mascara. Argument: if you use this mascara then you will obtain this difference. But look carefully at the before and after pictures. Is the mascara the only thing about the model that has changed? Has other makeup, a new hairstyle or clothing, a more pleasant expression, more dynamic action, different lighting, been added to the after segment? In other words, the critic asks, is the "if" necessary and sufficient to produce the promised "then"?

Implying "If Not . . . Then Not"   Ads often imply that if you buy and use the product, you will be happier, more likable, and so forth. The converse of this strategy is used in ads designed to make us feel guilty if we don't buy the product. For example, the Hallmark slogan "when you care enough to send the very best," uses "when" to imply there are times when you don't care enough. Sometimes you don't. Sometimes you care but not enough—a very personal indictment when the person you care about is someone you ought to care about a great deal. In case you are having trouble envisioning someone you care enough about, the visual portion of the ad will fill in a son or daughter, mother or father, grandparent, or best friend in an environment or on an occasion (Christmas, birthday, graduation) at which remembering is expected social behavior.

Now that the ad has encouraged you to conclude that this is one of those times when you do care enough, it needs to legitimize sending as the appropriate expression of caring. By contrast, AT&T wants you to believe that phoning is the best expression of caring; the FTD floral delivery company wants you to think that sending flowers is the best expression of caring. So "sending" is slipped into the Hallmark slogan, and the joy the recipient experiences in the ad at "receiving" provides reinforcement for the claim that sending was the correct choice. But in case AT&T and FTD have made equally plausible claims, the ad will probably show the loved person enjoying the card again and again (its unique selling point)—unlike phone calls, which are brief and fleeting, and flowers, which wilt and die, a card, if you believe the ad, will be saved and cherished forever. Indeed, one ad shows an older person going through a trunk filled with loving cards.

Now that the slogan has us sending, it must differentiate its card from its competitors. It does this with the claim that you are sending, not just the best, but the very best.

Why not send a letter instead? It would be more personal, equally permanent, and more thoughtful. To counter this option, the ads also show people whose exact feelings are better expressed by the card than by their own words, persons too shy or too inarticulate about their feelings to be willing or able to write a letter. So, the slogan has positioned the product against its competitors, one of which is the personal letter, and has done so memorably.

But the real genius of the slogan is its implied "if not . . . then not." If you don't send Hallmark, and you accept the assumptions inherent in the slogan, then you don't care enough to send the very best. Within the terms of this slogan, not sending Hallmark cards is a sign of not caring.

BOX 7-13

Print Ad Comprehension

At a cost of more than $250,000, Jacob Jacoby, professor of consumer behavior and retail management at New York University, conducted a study sponsored by the Advertising Educational Foundation that found that 37 percent of the people exposed to magazine ads and articles don't comprehend them. The study involved 1,347 respondents over the age of 18 living in forty-eight states who were questioned on 108 advertising and editorial communications taken from eighteen magazines. Ads were understood better than editorial material, and facts were understood better than inferences, although the differences were slight. Miscomprehension rises as age increases and decreases as income increases.

This study followed an earlier study of television viewers with similar results. The results of Jacoby's study have been presented to the FTC, which is intensely interested in misleading advertising, and its results are important for advertising educators and government regulators alike.[a]

[a]Philip H. Dougherty, "Cold Water at Florida Gathering," *New York Times,* 27 March 1987, p. 42Y.

But Does Advertising Work?

By the time the class of 1996 college students had finished their senior finals, the typical student had seen an average of half a million commercials. What this generation finds persuasive differs from that which moves its parents. The 18-to-25-year-old market differs from the older markets, advertisers argue. Psycho-demographic research reveals that the old hard sell doesn't work with those reared on television. Accordingly, in an ad for Pepsi featuring performer Michael Jackson, the word *Pepsi* was never spoken by the star.

The appeals that do work are discernibly different as well. Because surveys show this group to be more preoccupied with making money, more willing to take risks, and more eager to venture into its own businesses, a Pepsi ad showed a young person establishing his own vending operation on a beach.

The generation raised on television and attuned to the fast-paced visuals and music of MTV expects rapid cuts and edits in ads. Peter Kim of J. Walter Thompson believes that this younger generation's attention span is decreasing while its ability simultaneously to grasp many bits of information is increasing.[9]

Still, in this generation as in others, ads seldom create needs. Instead, they guide our selection from among competing products. And, as Michael Schudson argues in *Advertising: The Uneasy Persuasion,* those selections often are not based on legitimate differences among products. From this essential comparability of competing products and from advertisers' need to differentiate one from

---

9. *Washington Post,* 29 May 1986, p. A12.

the other come a marketplace full of claims that are less than fully informative. Nonetheless, advertising not only cannot save a bad product, it can hurry its demise. When a product fails to deliver on its promises, customers do not purchase it a second time.

TO SUM UP

In this chapter we have examined some of the ways advertisers use claims and evidence to persuade us to purchase one product rather than another. This persuasive end is particularly difficult when, as is often the case, the advertisers' product differs little if at all from several others on the market. In addition, advertisers operate in extremely limited time and space. Many of the complaints registered against advertising arise from these limitations. Unless checked by regulation, advertisers tend to tell us what is good but not what is bad about their products, relying on our willingness to invest messages with meaning to induce us to hear stronger claims than those actually being made.

SELECTED READINGS

Arlen, Michael J. *Thirty Seconds*. New York: Farrar, Straus & Giroux, 1980.

Barnouw, Erik. *The Sponsor: Notes on a Modern Potentate*. London: Oxford University Press, 1978.

Clark, Eric. *The Want Makers: The World Advertising Industry—How They Make You Buy*. New York: Viking, 1989.

Ewen, Stuart. *Captains of Consciousness: Advertising and the Social Roots of the Consumer Culture*. New York: McGraw-Hill, 1976.

———. *All Consuming Images: The Politics of Style in Contemporary Culture*. New York: Basic Books, 1989.

Hine, Thomas. *The Total Package*. New York: Little Brown, 1995.

Ogilvy, David. *Confessions of an Advertising Man*. New York: Atheneum, 1980.

Schudson, Michael. *Advertising: The Uneasy Persuasion*. New York: Basic Books, 1984.

Schwartz, Tony. *The Responsive Chord*. New York: Doubleday, 1974.

Sethi, S. Prakash. *Advocacy Advertising and Large Corporations*. Lexington, Mass.: Lexington Books, 1977.

CHAPTER 8

Influencing Advertisers

Listerine was compelled to confess in its ads that it will not help prevent colds or sore throats.

Producers of a diet product were told that they could not show a thin Santa Claus who stated that he lost his job because he lost weight.

The appearance of an elderly schoolteacher was changed in an ad before it was permitted to air.

In this chapter we examine the regulatory and self-regulatory mechanisms that produced these changes. Chapter 9 shows how consumers can use these channels to influence news and advertising practices.

Regulation and Self-Regulation

Advertisers are influenced by formal regulation from government agencies and by agencies created by industry to preempt and forestall government regulation.

The Federal Trade Commission

The Federal Trade Commission (FTC) regulates "unfair methods of competition" (Section 5), "unfair or deceptive acts or practices" (Section 5), and "false advertising" (Section 12). The FTC's Bureau of Consumer Protection has issued a handful of guides to aid advertisers and the public in determining how certain types of products should be advertised and what techniques may be used. One guide discusses use of testimonials, for example. These guides are advisory, as are the FTC's opinions about the applicability of federal laws to specific cases.

The Trade Regulation Rules issued by the Bureau of Consumer Protection are, by contrast, legally binding. These rules govern what is and is not consid-

---

BOX 8-1

The Costs of False Advertising

Being charged with false advertising can cost a company millions of dollars, even if no fine is ever levied.

In an analysis of the effects of advertising regulation, the FTC said that when charges of false advertising have been brought against a company, its stock price has usually declined, often significantly.

The FTC study focused on 122 false-advertising cases between 1962 and 1985. In the cases settled by consent order, the companies' stock value lost an average of 2.5 percent in the five days after the announcement, the study found. In cases in which companies contested the FTC charges in court, but eventually lost, stock-price losses average 1.3 percent at the time of the complaint, 1.8 percent when the administrative law judge ruled, and 1.9 percent on final commission action.[a]

[a]"False-Ad Cases Can Be Costly," *New York Times*, 7 June 1988, p. 46Y.

---

ered an illegal practice. The Advertising Evaluation Section of the Bureau of Consumer Protection was set up in 1973 to oversee advertising and to review the substantiation of advertising claims. The staff of the Advertising Evaluation Section draws samples of televised and print ads for evaluation and also reviews complaints filed by the public.

When the FTC concludes that a complaint is worth pursuing, staff members will determine whether, in their judgment, the ad has violated the law. If so, they may seek voluntary assurance that the practice will be discontinued. Such an agreement is not legally binding, but if violated the FTC may reopen the case against the advertiser. When the case is serious or the advertiser stubborn, the FTC institutes formal proceedings. To halt these proceedings, the advertiser may sign a consent order stipulating the facts in the case, the findings of the commission, and the conditions accepted by the advertiser, and indicating that the practice will not be repeated. This order is legally binding.

If, instead, the advertiser wishes to contest the findings, a hearing is held before an administrative law judge who may dismiss all or some of the charges, issue a legally binding cease-and-desist order, or order corrective advertising. Either the FTC staff or the advertiser may appeal this decision to the five FTC commissioners. An advertiser who loses at this level may appeal to the federal court of appeals and, losing there, may appeal to the U.S. Supreme Court.

The appeal process may go on for years, during which the contested advertising practice may continue. For example, in 1965 the FTC told the producers of Geritol to eliminate the claim that the product combated "tired blood." Being tired is not a reliable indicator of iron deficiency. Nonetheless, Geritol reintroduced the claim in subsequent ads. The FTC sued and finally won in 1976. Geritol's maker, which had since switched advertising strategies, was fined $125,000 for noncompliance.

The use of corrective advertising to counter false impressions is a relatively new phenomenon. In 1971, the FTC demanded that the producers of Profile Bread devote one-quarter of one year's media budget to countering the impression that eating their product would produce weight loss. The corrective ad asked, in part, "Does Profile have fewer calories than other breads? No. Profile has about the same calories per ounce as other breads. To be exact, Profile has seven fewer calories per slice. That's because it's sliced thinner. But eating Profile will not cause you to lose weight."[1] Similarly, the producers of Domino Sugar were required to spend one-quarter of a year's budget to correct the impression that their sugar was a better source of energy than other brands.

In the first court test of the FTC's right to require corrective advertising, the Supreme Court let stand the U.S. Court of Appeals for the Second Circuit's order that the makers of Listerine mouthwash state in their next $10 million worth of advertising that "Listerine will not help prevent colds or sore throats or lessen their severity."

In the corrective advertising agreements, the FTC indicates the type of corrective language that is necessary, the dollar amount or percentage of the advertising budget to be spent on correcting the false impressions, and even the size of the ads and the outlets in which they will appear. This development has taxed the ingenuity of copywriters to incorporate the required disclosure without undercutting the ability of the ad to sell the product.

Appointees of the Reagan administration made three changes in FTC operations. Rather than focusing on abuses in an entire industry (such as funeral operations and used car sales), the FTC worked on a case-by-case basis. Second, the conditions required to establish deception were circumscribed. Whereas formerly the potential to mislead was considered deceptive, now a consumer acting reasonably in the circumstances must prove that an ad's representation, omission, or practice affected the actual buying decision. The FTC policy articulated in 1984 stated that "any representation, omission, or other practice that is likely to mislead the consumer acting reasonably under the circumstances to the consumer's detriment" was deceptive. Under the earlier definition, "any representation, omission, or other practice that has the capacity to mislead the consumer who is not sophisticated, wary, or cautious" constituted deception. Finally, the ground rules for substantiation of advertising claims were reframed. Inquiries are no longer conducted in public. Substantiation investigations are now revealed only upon completion. These changes shifted the burden of proof from the advertiser to the consumer.

This shift indicated the power of regulatory agencies to set their own course. Reagan's FTC Chair James Miller tried unsuccessfully to get Congress to redefine "deceptive acts or practices." Miller then offered the FTC, controlled by like-minded appointees, a statement of policy that supposedly analyzed the law of deception but actually narrowed FTC jurisdiction in ways consistent with his failed congressional initiative.

---

1. "Profile Bread's Well-Buttered Correction," *Consumer Reports*, February 1972, p. 64.

Deception is one of two practices over which the FTC has jurisdiction. The other is unfairness. In August 1994 Congress ended a decade-and-a-half dispute about what constituted unfair advertising by defining unfairness as "acts or practices that cause or are likely to cause substantial injury to consumers, which is not reasonably avoidable by consumers themselves and not outweighed by countervailing benefits to consumers or competition." From 1980 to 1994 Congress had not approved legislation reauthorizing the FTC because the House and Senate could not agree on the extent of FTC authority.[2] The impasse between the House and Senate originated in 1976 when an FTC inquiry seemed to be moving toward arguing that all children's TV advertising is unfair. The House took the position of the consumer groups, the Senate that of the advertising industry.

The Powers of Other State and Federal Agencies

The Food and Drug Administration (FDA) has the authority to recall products that it determines pose hazards to public health. The U.S. Postal Service can also obtain court injunctions barring companies from receiving mail orders. Additionally, states can sue corporations for consumer fraud. Outcomes of such suits include agreements not to market some products in some states. The case of Cal-Ban 3000, a so-called miracle diet product, is illustrative.

In ads in the pages of beauty magazines and tabloids, Cal-Ban 3000 was touted as a means of losing "up to 30 pounds in 30 days or your money back!" In July 1990, after documenting one death and numerous injuries, the FDA asked the company to recall it. But the FDA was not the first agency to act. In 1987, the U.S. Postal Service had obtained a court injunction barring the company from receiving mail orders for the diet product. The manufacturers responded by substituting an 800 telephone number. In 1989, the state of Iowa went to court against the product. The result was the company's agreement not to sell Cal-Ban 3000 in Iowa. Florida also moved to ban the sale. The company that produced the product, Health Care Products Inc. of Tampa, settled the civil suit against it in Florida by agreeing that it would never again sell the product in the United States. The company also paid a $1.3 million fine. In early July 1990, federal officials obtained a court order of their own barring both mail and phone sales of the product. This last action effectively ended the company.

Cal-Ban used guar gum, a commercial thickening agent found in some beverages and diet products. When combined with moisture, guar gum swells. The swelling inside the stomach was supposed to make the dieter feel full. While still marketed in an uncoated form, Cal-Ban could swell while in the throat, causing life-threatening obstructions. One Florida user died of complications from surgery to remove the swollen gum from his throat. A postal inspector estimated that before its demise, between $20 and $30 million of Cal-Ban had been sold.[3]

---

2. Christy Fisher, "How Congress Broke Unfair Ad Impasse," *Advertising Age*, 22 August 1994, p. 34.
3. Barry Meier, "Diet-Pill Death Raises Questions on F.D.A. Role," *New York Times*, 4 August 1990, p. 48.

BOX 8-2

AT&T v. Sprint

In summer 1990, the NAD found for AT&T and against Sprint. Sprint challenged an AT&T ad that read: "On average, MCI and US Sprint take over 50 percent longer than AT&T to set up a long distance call . . . and when you multiply that by the number of calls a large company makes a year, it comes out to hundreds of wasted work hours. . . ." NAD ruled that AT&T had supported the claim.

The National Advertising Division

The National Advertising Division (NAD) of the Better Business Bureau is industry's main mechanism for policing its own advertising. The NAD reviews all charges of deception in advertising brought by consumers and manufacturers, or submitted by local Better Business Bureaus. The NAD also monitors advertising on its own.

The NAD's own monitoring is the greatest source of complaints. Information released by the NAD indicates that 96 of the 100 leading advertisers have participated voluntarily in the NAD review process—either as advertisers or complainants.

The NAD evaluates all complaints received. If it concludes that the ad violates good advertising practices or contains falsehoods or inaccuracies, the NAD tries to persuade the advertiser to change or drop the ad. If the advertiser and the NAD cannot reach agreement at this level, either may appeal the case to the National Advertising Review Board (NARB). A panel drawn from the seventy-member NARB serves as a court of appeal at this stage, and a public member sits on each review panel.

The NARB members employed by a company that manufactures or sells the product being evaluated or a competing product may not serve on a review panel. Similarly, advertisers who represent a competing product are disqualified from serving on such review panels.

Figure 8.1 details the review and appeals process. Note that if the matter cannot be resolved by the NARB panel and the advertiser, the case can be referred to the Federal Trade Commission for further action. The industry would clearly prefer to resolve its own differences and respond to consumer dissatisfaction without government intervention. Indeed, the NAD and NARB were created to forestall restrictive legislation. Only 3 percent of the 3,200 cases reviewed in this process since the NAD's founding in 1971 have been forwarded to the FTC.[4]

In summer 1995, the NAD announced that it would begin monitoring advertising that appears on line. NAD asked on line services to provide it with cost-free access to the networks and the Internet. As with non-net ads, consumers and

---

4. Andrea Sachs, "NAD Turns Ad Monitor to Cyberspace," *Advertising Age*, 8 May 1995, p. 20.

BOX 8-3

Examples of NAD/NARB Decisions

Advertising Modified or Discontinued

Tonka Corporation, Minnetonka, Minn. (Jordan, Case, Taylor & McGrath—N.Y.), and Hanna-Barbera, Hollywood, jointly advertised the *GoBots: Battle of the Rock Lords* movie in the children's magazine *GoBots,* a practice the NAD's Children's Advertising Review Unit (CARU) found questionable because it could lead to "confusion between advertising and editorial content." Tonka agreed and said it would discontinue the practice.

Advertising Claims Substantiated

Ragold, Chicago (Tatham-Laird & Kudner), in television spots for sugar-free Velamints claimed, "You see, most Tic Tac and Life Savers are over 90 percent sugar." A visual depicted sugar being poured into containers. New York-based Ferrero USA, marketer of Tic Tac mints, challenged the ad on the basis that it implied that the Tic Tac container is filled to 90 percent of its capacity with sugar and that Velamints contain fewer calories. Ferrero provided tests indicating that Tic Tacs are only 65 percent sugar by volume and actually contain far fewer calories than Velamints. Ragold countered with tests indicating that Tic Tac contains 93 percent sugar by weight and that its sugar-free claim is distinct from a low-calorie claim. The NAD agreed that the Ragold claims were substantiated.[a]

[a]These examples of NAD decisions are reprinted with permission of the NAD.

---

competitors can contact NAD directly with complaints. And in a twist that acknowledges the growing importance of computer sites, NAD will now also take complaints through e-mail or through the Better Business Bureau's site on the Web (http://www.cbbb.org/cbbb).[5]

As with many self-regulatory moves, this one was inspired by discussions in Congress about regulating what appears on line. "NAD will be better than the government at regulating the Internet," said American Advertising Federation president Wally Snyder, "because they (NAD) can offer a service that is quicker, less costly, and voluntary."

Critics of this self-regulatory procedure point out that it is a post hoc mechanism—no action can be taken until a violation has occurred. Industry defenders respond that the outcomes of previous cases clearly show advertisers what sorts of tactics to avoid. One side argues that asking the industry to police itself is like asking the fox to guard the chicken coop; the other side responds that a member of the public now sits on all the NARB review panels and that the number of findings against advertisers attests that this procedure is not a sham. Critics

---

5. Ibid.

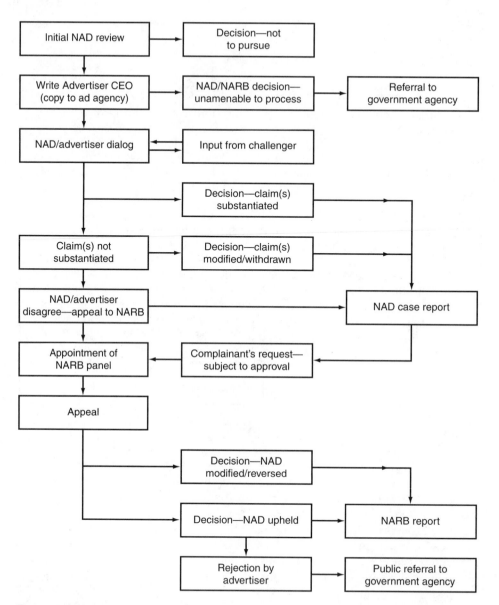

Figure 8.1   Steps in the NAD/NARB process (chart provided by the NAD/NARB and used with permission).

charge that the NAD/NARB procedure has no mechanism for meting out punishment or for correcting false impressions already created. Defenders concede this point, but argue that U.S. antitrust laws make it difficult for the board or the panels to levy punishments.

The National Association of Broadcasters

The National Association of Broadcasters (NAB) adopted a radio code in 1929 and a television code in the early 1950s. A code authority director and a limited staff were established in 1952. In the early 1960s, when the payola and quiz-game scandals such as the rigged *$64,000 Question* triggered fears of stringent new regulations, the staff was enlarged and the function of overseeing the two codes was combined under a single code authority director.

In March 1982, U.S. District Court Judge Harold Greene ruled that the section of the NAB code barring a sponsor from advertising more than one product in an ad shorter than 60 seconds violated the antitrust laws. The NAB responded by suspending enforcement of the advertising standards of the code. The code has not been reinstated. However, under pressure to clean up the broadcast airwaves, in June 1990, the NAB's board adopted voluntary guidelines. The guidelines urged that depictions of "physical or psychological" violence be responsible, that the details of violence not be "excessive, gratuitous, or instructional," and that violence for its own sake be avoided. The guidelines also recommended that "the use of illegal drugs or other substance abuse should not be encouraged or shown as socially desirable." The NAB statement reiterated that the guidelines were purely advisory and carried no enforcement mechanism.[6]

That stations and networks did not rush to air ads for contraceptives and hard liquor and did not solicit ads for palm readers and phrenologists in 1983 revealed the extent to which the NAB norms had been adopted by the industry. Indeed, in many instances the networks, whose screening of ads remains, impose more stringent criteria than the NAB. Also, the restraining power of public sentiment continues to operate.

The print media also have policies governing acceptance of advertised material, although these policies are less uniform than those governing broadcast ads.

Network Standards

Public sentiment acts as a powerful constraint on broadcast advertising. As a *TV Guide* editorial noted, "It doesn't take a fortune-teller to predict the result if broadcasters opted for making an easy buck: viewers would be up in arms."[7]

The extent to which broadcasters fear offending the viewing community was evident when in February 1987 all three national commercial networks refused a request by the surgeon general to air ads for condoms. Use of condoms could protect sexually active persons from transmitting the AIDS virus, argued the surgeon general; accordingly, broadcasters should air them. Arguing that such ads

---

6. Doug Halonen, "NAB Sets Standards for Cleaning up Airwaves," *Electronic Media*, 25 June 1990, p. 3.
7. "As We See It," *TV Guide*, 17 April 1982, p. A2.

are offensive to a significant part of the viewing audience, the networks initially refused.[8] Seven years later the climate had changed. Lovers in bed discussing condom use and an animated condom were features of the campaign sponsored by the Centers for Disease Control to reduce the spread of HIV infection. All four commercial networks and many cable networks and radio stations carried at least some of the spots. The network airtime donated was estimated to be worth $2 million.[9]

Each network is responsible for determining that its commercials meet its own standards. ABC, CBS, and NBC estimate that each receives 18,000 to 25,000 tapes a year. Only 1 to 2 percent are rejected outright.[10]

Because FCC regulations apply to the airwaves, which are publicly owned, but not to cable networks, some ads that have been rejected by the networks air instead on cable. USA Network estimates that it refuses about half as many commercials as do ABC, CBS, and NBC. So, for example, when the major networks rejected or required disclaimers on a Yoplait ad depicting supposed "news reporters" reporting on the heist of frozen yogurt, Vroman Foods simply took the ad and its $5 to $6 million account to cable television.[11]

The competition from cable is a factor in network standards. "In the past, it was easier to say no [to such ads]," notes Matthew Margo, vice-president for program standards at CBS in New York. "But in a more complex media world today, it's critical that people come up with solutions to get [the commercials] on the air. There is a lot at stake to turn down an ad today. That's millions of dollars in revenue down the drain."[12]

To insulate the reviewers from economic pressures, each network has separated its broadcast standards division from its sales and programming divisions. If the staff in the broadcast standards division reported to the sales division, for example, it might conceivably be subject to pressures from major sponsors. Instead, the broadcast standards division reports directly to top management.

Typically, an advertiser will submit the storyboards or shooting scripts for a set of commercials to all three television networks at the same time. If the commercial involves a demonstration, many advertisers will not wait for the network to ask for an affidavit from the producer testifying to the authenticity of the action in the commercial; they will supply this documentation and substantiation for any questionable claims when the storyboard is submitted.

The internal standards set by the three networks differ. Occasionally, a commercial will be accepted by one network, rejected by a second, and sent back for changes by a third. The type of changes broadcasters demand was revealed in testimony before the House Select Committee on Aging. A represen-

---

8. "Surgeon General Urges Ads on TV for Condoms in Combatting AIDS," *New York Times*, 11 February 1987, p. 1.

9. Jim Cooper, "Television Networks Air Condom PSAs," *Broadcasting & Cable*, 10 January 1994, p. 59.

10. Wayne Walley, "Network Ad Rejections: At What Cost?" *Advertising Age*, 9 April 1990, p. 22.

11. Ibid.

12. Ibid.

tative of NBC reported that "one editor recalls requesting a change in the portrayal of an elderly schoolteacher in a commercial message. The editor objected to the characterization of an excessively prim and unfashionable woman."[13]

Obstacles to Regulation

Problems Faced by Regulators

By acknowledging that audiences cooperate in acts of influence, we raise an important and troublesome problem for regulators. Once regulators admit that an ad may induce the audience to draw a false conclusion even though the ad itself is explicitly truthful, the regulators must examine the ad's implied content. Because that content resides not in the ad but in audience interaction with it, a regulator concerned with monitoring implied deception is forced to study the audience.

The audience of concern to regulators is the general public. The courts have characterized the general public as:

> that vast multitude which includes the ignorant, and the unthinking, and the credulous, who, in making purchases, do not stop to analyze but too often are governed by appearances and general impressions. . . . The ordinary purchaser . . . is not an "expert in grammatical construction" or an "educated analytical reader" and, therefore, he [sic] does not normally subject every word in the advertisement to careful study.[14]

Because the law was established to protect "the trusting as well as the suspicious,"[15] an ad can be deceptive if it deceives persons who are naive, uncritical, or even careless. Consequently, when a claim has two possible interpretations—one truthful, the other misleading—the advertiser can be found guilty of deceptive advertising.

In order to determine what an ad promises, the FTC and the courts must rely on the testimony of experts such as scholars who have studied certain types of advertising, consult surveys of consumers to determine whether or not they were deceived, and trust their own common sense.

In its review of a claim against the makers of Anacin, the court dismissed the testimony of two experts in marketing research and relied instead on tests of consumer reactions that the court called "the best evidence of what meaning consumers take from advertising." Customers had concluded from a television commercial for Anacin that the product was a superior analgesic. The ad claimed that "for pain other than headache, Anacin reduces the inflammation that comes with pain. These [Tylenol and Datril] do not. Specifically, inflammation of tooth extraction,

13. Congress, *Age Stereotyping*, p. 58.
14. *FTC v. Sterling Drug, Inc.* 317 F. 2d 669, 674 (2d Cir. 1963).
15. *FTC v. Standard Education Society*, 302 U.S. 112, 116 (1937).

BOX 8-4

A Claim by Any Other Name . . .

David Minton, Washington counsel for the Magazine Publishers Association, told the Senate Commerce Committee that "the cigarette firms, unlike producers of some foods and other products, do not claim that their brands are good for health. 'Cigarette advertising pictures things, cowboys, pretty girls [sic], and so on, but there is no claim,' he said."[a]

[a]Lawrence M. O'Rourke, "Tobacco Industry Flexes Its Muscles," St. Louis *Post-Dispatch*, 16 May 1982, p. 6F.

---

muscle strain, backache, or if your doctor diagnoses tendonitis, neuritis." The court concluded that the makers of Anacin had misrepresented its properties by claiming that their product was a superior analgesic to Tylenol. A permanent injunction was issued restraining the makers of Anacin from making such claims in other ads.[16]

Determining Deception

The FTC's own sense of what constitutes deception is sometimes so strong that it relies on its own judgment to determine that an ad is deceptive, rather than on expert testimony or survey data.[17] And the courts have acknowledged that the FTC is often better able than the courts to determine what is and is not deceptive.[18]

When a claim is implied but not explicitly stated, the NAD, the FTC, and the courts try to determine what is implied and whether that implication deceives. So, for example, in 1992 an ad for Eggland's Best claimed that clinical trials showed that eating a dozen of the firm's eggs each week as part of a low-fat diet would not increase serum cholesterol. "You can eat the eggs . . . and not increase your serum cholesterol" said the television ad. "They're special eggs from specially fed hens." The NARB agreed with the NAD that the ad "implied that the advertiser's eggs were uniquely capable of reaching the result found by [a University of Pennsylvania] study, when in fact the study . . . did not make any comparison between different brands of eggs." The panel recommended that the ad be pulled, and no claims about cholesterol effects "be made without the advertiser first assuring through appropriate testing that unintended claims were not heard by the audience." When the advertiser refused to comply with the recommendations, the case was forwarded to the FTC.[19]

---

16. *American Home Products v. Johnson and Johnson*, 3 Med. L. Rptr. 1097 (1977).
17. Ira M. Millstein, *The Federal Trade Commission and False Advertising*, 64 Col. L. Rev. 439, 469 (1964).
18. *FTC v. Colgate-Palmolive Co.*, 380 U.S. 375, 385 (1965).
19. Steven W. Colford, "Paper Tiger Litmus Test; FTC Gets Eggland's, Its First NARB Case," *Advertising Age*, 20 December 1993, p. 2.

An interesting situation arises when a deceptive claim is implied not by the ads currently on the air but by advertising that the audience remembers. Here the audience invests new ads with an old claim, and if the old claim was a powerful one, its residual power gives the maker of the product an unfair advantage in the marketplace.

For example, for almost 100 years, ads for the popular mouthwash Listerine claimed that the product prevented colds and sore throats. It does not, and its new ads do not claim that it does. But in 1977 the court upheld the FTC requirement that the next $10 million of Listerine's regular advertising include the corrective statement, "Listerine will not prevent colds or sore throats or lessen their severity." To justify its decision, the court cited evidence that six months after the challenged claim had been removed from the ads, 64 percent of those responding to a survey cited as the main theme of Listerine ads the claim that Listerine was "effective for colds and sore throats." Sixty percent concluded that Listerine was one of the best mouthwashes because of its effectiveness against colds and sore throats.[20] Some claims, then, are not in the current ad; they reside wholly in the audience's memory.

Effects of Stricter Regulation

Our discussion to this point may have created the impression that advertisers make any claims they think the audience will find persuasive, and continue to make these claims until challenged. Indeed, before 1971, the government regulatory system was reactive, not proactive, and corrective, not preventative. In 1971, however, the FTC began requiring that advertisers be able to prove claims about a product's performance, characteristics, quality, safety, effectiveness, or comparative cost. If the FTC challenges a claim, the advertiser has thirty days in which to provide proof.

Two unfortunate by-products of this stricter regulation of advertising have been claims that are more meaningless and information that is less specific. Fewer than half of the commercials sampled in one study were found to contain useful consumer information.[21] Although no one need bemoan the loss of misleading claims, the new ads are not exceptional either. Excedrin's makers used to contend that Excedrin was an "antidepressant." Now they claim it is more effective for pain "other than headache." Anacin's makers used to claim that it relieved pain faster than any other analgesic available; instead, the ads now claim that it is "better" and "stronger." Profile Bread used to claim that it promoted weight loss. Now it isn't advertised on television anymore. Ivan Preston identified the logic underlying this shift when he wrote:

> The effort to obtain information of greater quality and quantity has spurred tighter laws against false advertising, but the ad industry's response to them has brought

---

20. *Warner-Lambert Co. v. FTC*, 562 F. 2d 762 (1977).
21. Alan Resnick and Bruce L. Stein, "An Analysis of Information Content of Television Advertising," *Journal of Marketing* 41 (January 1977): 50–53.

something other than hoped-for improvements. . . . Why not discontinue using information, they asked themselves, and substitute a type of content not subject to being called deceptive. . . . The law may have achieved its goal of making more information nondeceptive, but only in conjunction with the sad yet perfectly legal fact that a lesser proportion of message content now is informative.[22]

What Advertisers May Not Say and Do

The mass media can be used to invest products with characteristics they do not in fact possess, and the potential consumer has no immediate way to test many of the claims in ads. Therefore, in the United States a number of rules and laws have been developed to combat deceptive advertising.

Limitations on Distortion

In 1914 Congress passed the Federal Trade Commission Act. Section 5 declares "unfair or deceptive acts or practices in or affecting commerce" to be unlawful. In Section 12 the act forbids false advertisements for "food, drugs, devices or cosmetics." False advertisements are defined in Section 15 not only as those containing "material" misrepresentations but also as those failing to reveal material facts about the consequences that may result from use of the advertised product.

In June 1986, the Federal Trade Commission charged the R. J. Reynolds Company with violating the law banning false and deceptive advertising. At issue was a print ad titled "Of Cigarettes and Science" that ran in twenty-five newspapers and magazines from February through June 1985. The ad, cast as an editorial, alleged that the results of a major, federally funded, national health study (the Multiple Risk Factor Intervention Trial or MRFIT) called into question the link between smoking and heart disease. The ad argued, "The controversy over smoking and health remains an open one."

But administrative law judge Montgomery K. Hyun ruled against the FTC, noting that the advertisement did not name any of the Reynolds's brands or discuss their attributes. Rather, Hyun said, it expressed the company's view on smoking and health. The ad did not lose its status as constitutionally protected speech, he went on, merely because it coincided with the company's economic interest.

The FTC indicated it would appeal the ruling. Matthew L. Myers, director of the Coalition on Smoking or Health (a private organization that had asked the commission to file the complaint), said the ruling "amounts to a license to lie to the American public."[23]

---

22. Ivan L. Preston, *The Great American Blow-Up* (Madison: University of Wisconsin Press, 1975), p. 276.
23. *New York Times*, 10 August 1986, p. 7E.

In June 1990, the issue was resolved. Under the settlement, R. J. Reynolds agreed in future ads not to misrepresent the results of the government study. During the four years of the controversy, however, the distorting information had stood. The tobacco company, in effect, had gained a four-year reprieve.

Determining whether an ad distorts is not as simple as it may at first seem. An examination of a number of advertising claims will illustrate when an ad is materially deceptive and when it is not.

Product Characteristics   The product seen in the ad must look and act like the real product that the consumer buys. The color of the product as shown in the ad must approximate the actual color; the advertiser cannot recolor the grape juice to make it look a deeper purple than it actually is, or retouch the milk to make it look whiter or the lipstick to make it look rosier. Color can be enhanced in products other than the one being sold, however. So, if the display in the ad shows chicken, the product being sold, on a plate with green beans, the advertiser can add color to the beans but not to the chicken.

The size of the product also must be represented accurately in the ad. An advertiser may not use a small soup bowl to make the amount of soup in the can seem more than it actually is. When the product is enlarged or visually distorted by camera angle, that fact must be disclosed. Often a product must be enlarged visually if the consumer is to appreciate its fine points, as with small articles of jewelry.

In such ads, the product's actual size will be noted, the fact that the picture is an enlargement will be made clear, and a picture of the jewelry in its actual size will probably be included somewhere in the ad.

Advertisers are not permitted to construct a special instance of the product for the sake of the commercial. The product shown in the ad must be comparable to the typical product being produced, and it must be sold under the same name advertised.

Product Performance   In a classic case of the deceptive use of a mock-up, the Colgate-Palmolive Company showed its Rapid Shave shaving cream softening sandpaper to the extent that the sandpaper could actually be shaved. The FTC received complaints from consumers who had tried to shave sandpaper with the product and had failed.

An investigation established that it was not actually sandpaper that was being shaved in the ad but glass lightly covered with bits of sand. The FTC challenged the ad. Colgate countered by arguing that sandpaper covered with Rapid Shave could indeed be shaved, but that the sandpaper was of such a fine quality that the television viewer would not be able to see that it could be. Hence, Colgate argued, shaving glass was a simulation of what the product could actually do.

Could the product enable a razor to shave coarse sandpaper, the kind of sandpaper suggested by the demonstration? No, Colgate conceded. Colgate said, however, that it had tested its claim on fine sandpaper, but had to use a mock-up suggesting coarse sandpaper because the fine sandpaper would simply look like flat paper on television.

In the course of the investigation, the FTC also learned that even fine sandpaper could not be shaved as quickly as the mock-up implied, but only after being soaked for a long time. In the commercial, Rapid Shave was applied and almost immediately the razor shaved the glass clean. The commercial did not indicate that it was taking place in a time span longer than that actually shown. Had it indicated that the elapsed time was ten or fifteen minutes, the FTC probably would not have challenged the ease and speed with which the shaving took place. The contest between the FTC and Colgate ultimately reached the Supreme Court, which ruled that when the point of the ad is to establish the reality of what is being demonstrated, the audience must be informed that a mock-up is being used.

This does not mean that viewers always see actual demonstrations on television. But when more time has elapsed in the course of a demonstration than that shown, that fact will be indicated in the ad. When a demonstration is a re-creation of what happened, the commercial is likely to disclose that fact. And when substitutions are made for products—when, for example, whipped potatoes are substituted for ice cream because ice cream would melt under the lights—the ad will not draw attention to any characteristic of the ice cream that might be misrepresented by the potatoes.

The nature of television makes it difficult to represent some products such as ice cream accurately. When captured by the television camera, for example, coffee looks muddy. Because coffee advertisers have legitimate reasons for wanting to show coffee in their commercials, advertisers are permitted to substitute something that looks more like coffee than coffee does. Ironically, use of the actual product instead of a substitute would in this instance distort and be deceptive. But the FTC banned the substitution of oil for coffee because it looked both darker and richer than actual coffee.

In order to differentiate their product from others, advertisers often offer demonstrations supposedly showing their product's comparative superiority. As a general rule both the FTC and the NAD require that such comparisons employ comparable products. So, for example, the NAD concluded that an advertiser could not compare its bias-belted tire with a competitor's lower-grade tire. Bias-belted tires must be compared with other bias-belteds, not with the lesser-grade bias-ply tires.

Similarly the NAD ruled that an extra-thick spaghetti sauce must be compared with the extra-thick sauce manufactured by the competitor, not with the competitor's regular sauce. In the ad in question, the advertiser's extra-thick sauce and the regular sauce of the competitor were poured through kitchen strainers creating an obvious but irrelevant demonstration of superiority for the advertised product.

Puffery   Advertising copy creates a world in which superlatives are commonplace. Products are "the very best," "the finest"; they produce "the cleanest, freshest washes," the "most beautiful," "softest" faces and hands. The systematic, habitual use of hyperbole has diluted the power of the advertiser's vocabulary. If everything is "the best," how is a genuinely superior product to be described?

In keeping with this penchant for exaggeration, advertisers tend to place adjectives before nouns and adverbs before adjectives. For example, a wine isn't simply "fine," it is "really fine wine." The tar in a cigarette is not "low" but "ultra low," and Hallmark and Nestlé make not the "best" but "the very best." This tendency conflicts with the need to make short, memorable claims. When adjectives and adverbs are pared from ad copy, it is often because the need for brevity has overcome the tendency toward hyperbole.

Most hyperbole is legally acceptable because it consists of subjective, nondocumentable, nonfactual opinions. Although I may taste a product touted for its fine taste and find the taste disagreeable, my opinion does not invalidate the claim in the ad. Taste is a matter of . . . taste. For legal purposes, esthetic and value judgments generally fall under the label "puffery." So I can claim that a paper napkin is "beautiful," that the soft drink on which you are gagging "tastes great," that cookies as hard as cement are as good as mother used to make; although you may disagree on all counts, I have made legally acceptable claims.

But a hyperbolic claim is not protected as mere puffery when it claims an attribute the product does not have. An ad cannot claim that a candy bar is the finest chocolate if it contains no chocolate. An ad cannot claim that oleomargarine is a dairy product. A puffed statement in an ad is in effect a nonfalsifiable claim. But if falsity cannot be proven, then neither can truth.

So what value does puffery have for the advertiser? The advertiser benefits when we take the subjective claim to have objective validity, when we assume that there are criteria governing the determination of the quality claimed and that someone is assuring us that the quality as claimed exists. Rather, puffed statements should be treated as bald assertions of superiority with no evidence to back them up.

For example, the NAD concluded that the claim "Europeans . . . love Kronenbourg" was an expression of the opinion of the manufacturer and "not subject to substantiation by objective research data," but that the claim "Europeans drink more Kronenbourg than any other bottled beer" was a factual claim requiring proof. When the advertiser provided sales figures from the European brewers' association confirming that Kronenbourg was the best-selling bottled beer in Europe, the NAD concluded that the claim had been substantiated and closed the case.[24]

An ad may not promise something a product cannot do, however, and the FTC now has the power to force advertisers to include statements remedying past deceptions in current advertising. That is why Hawaiian Punch told us in one series of ads what percentage of its product is fruit juice, and Listerine conceded in its ads that it does not prevent colds.

Fantasy   No reasonable person believes that a cleaning product comes with a giant who will clean your sink, or that its competitor releases a white tornado. The rationale for permitting such claims is the same as that permitting puffery—

---

24. "News from NAD" (press release), 15 May 1981, p. 10.

reasonable people do not believe such claims. The difficulty arises when some consumer believes the claims. If you believe that a support shoe will really enable you to walk on air, and buy the product expecting to be transported above the crowd, the ad has deceived you. Nonetheless, the law assumes that you should not have been deceived by the fantasy in the ad because its claim is patently ludicrous.

The NARB's treatment of the Chicken of the Sea claim that it was the "best" tuna illustrates the bounds of a claim based in fantasy. When Chicken of the Sea made the claim "in a whimsical jingle involving a mermaid" it was acceptable. When the mermaid was eliminated or deemphasized "thereby diluting the whimsical quality of the claim," and the claim "what's the best tuna—Chicken of the Sea" was juxtaposed with a visual of a government seal, the NARB concluded that the ad had the capacity to deceive. The ad's use of the seal, available to any seafood manufacturer who maintains the required quality, implied that Chicken of the Sea had government endorsement as the "best" tuna.[25]

Limitations Imposed by the Audience

The mass media are available to people of all ages and they address the whole public, not some specialized segment. Therefore, most ads accepted by the media (with the exception of political ads, to be discussed later) will not overstep what the media consider to be the standards of decency and taste of the audience. So, for example, the *Washington Post* rejects sexually explicit ads for X-rated films.

Children in Audiences   The presence of children in the audience also imposes special requirements on advertisers. In 1974, a National Advertising Review Board consulting panel concluded, for example, that "all product advertising must be 'child-proofed,' reviewed and evaluated from the standpoint of a child's interpretation of what he [sic] sees and hears."[26] So, for example, the Children's Unit of the NAD recommended that an ad showing a woman inside a dishwasher be discontinued after the Dallas Better Business Bureau reported that a 3-year-old child had allegedly climbed into an automatic dishwasher after viewing the ad.

The realization that children watch television at all hours of the day and night led the NAD to its conclusion that all ads should be childproofed.

Advertisers are conscious that ads shape children's attitudes by the environments shown in the ads as well as by the appeals made on the product's behalf. In response to the concern of the Children's Unit of the NAD, Dial-a-Story ads were changed to include the caution, "And kids, be sure to ask your parents before you call," to ensure that children would not be encouraged to use the telephone without parental supervision or consent.

---

25. NARB release, 30 January 1980.
26. "News from NAD," National Advertising Division Council of Better Business Bureaus, 15 April 1981, p. 1.

BOX 8-5

Ads on Children's Programming

In fall 1990, Congress passed a bill, to take effect in 1992, limiting commercials on children's television programs to $10\frac{1}{2}$ minutes an hour on weekends and 12 minutes on weekdays. The legislation also requires the FCC to evaluate the quality and quantity of children's programs when a broadcaster's license comes up for renewal.[a]

In fall 1995, federal records showed that in the years since the limit, one out of four stations had violated the rules. The FCC had fined forty-four stations, and admonished another ninety-eight.[b]

Sweden, Greece, Ireland, and Belgium have laws that limit or totally ban advertising during children's programs.[c]

[a]Nathaniel C. Nash, "White House Gets Bill to Cut Ads on Children's TV Shows," *New York Times*, 2 October 1990, p. A1Y.
[b]Paul Farhi, "Children's Advertising," *Washington Post*, 13 October 1995, p. A33.
[c]"EC Vote May Threaten Ads Aimed at Kids," *Advertising Age*, 11 December 1995, p. 4.

The language in advertising directed to children is also subject to special scrutiny. When research indicated that children do not understand the phrase "assembly required," the NAD recommended that advertisers simplify such language. "You have to put it together before you can play with it" was a recommended alternative.

Critics remain dissatisfied with advertising to children. Whittle Communications was widely criticized for making satellite dishes and playback equipment available to elementary and secondary schools that agreed to air its newscast, which carried advertising. In summer 1990, Consumers Union singled out a number of major advertisers for criticism, among them:

> Nike and Reebok International for using "emotional sells" in TV spots featuring celebrities; Hershey Foods Corp. and Colgate-Palmolive Co. and Procter and Gamble for candy and toothpaste ads, respectively, that resemble editorial matter; Campbell for giving schools sports equipment in exchange for soup labels; and PepsiCo for donating free products or sports equipment in exchange for vending machine placements."[27]

Taboos   If visitors from another planet were to analyze all of our commercials to determine what we are like as a people, they would conclude that we habitually speak in superlatives and view the purchasing of products as a solution to all our problems. Our visitors would also note that, despite our preoccupation with beauty, youth, sex, security, and social acceptability, we are also a remarkably prudish people. This prudery would be documented by ads that suggest a decided discomfort with speaking directly on the mass medium of television about

---

27. Judann Dagnoli, "Consumers Union Hits Kids Advertising," *Advertising Age*, 23 July 1990, p. 4.

the human body and its functions, and about the specific functions of products designed for use on taboo areas of the body. For example, ads for brassieres don't usually mention breasts. Similarly, ads for douches speak in a veiled fashion of "freshness" without indicating what is going to be made "fresher." "I don't know what 'freshness' is," notes ad critic Bob Garfield, "but it has to do with surf washing up on the beach."[28] Nor do ads discuss the actual contents of diapers. Instead, advertisers show their absorbency by pouring blue liquid into them. There are taboos in print as well. The *Wall Street Journal* was among the publications refusing an ad for a device to correct impotency.

Some products are advertised seldom, if at all, on television. For example, there are no nationally televised ads for birth control pills, but such ads do appear in print.

Our visitors could make a strong case for a claim that Americans are uncomfortable discussing bodily functions or specific portions of the anatomy, if televised ads were their only source of information. What would the visitors say when they hear the characters in a soap opera agonizing over whether one of the protagonists should have an abortion? Discussion of abortion in programming but no ads for contraceptives? No ads for abortion clinics? No ads for Planned Parenthood? They would wonder why programmers are more liberal than advertisers, or network censors more liberal about program content than ad content. That they are is evident in a remark by the executive creative director at the New York ad agency Kirshenbaun and Bond: "TV commercials have always been subject to far more scrutiny than programming." "I remember one commercial of mine being pulled off the air because it used the word *hernia*."[29] (But an episode of a sitcom, with Delta Burke as a U.S. representative, that showed and discussed condoms was not aired.)

One answer is that there is a difference between deliberate exposure to a program and inadvertent exposure to a commercial. A person who tunes in to watch reruns of *Dallas* presumably knows what to expect. We don't anticipate commercials and commercial content in the same way. Also, although many find it hard to believe, advertisers are loath to offend any segment of the consuming public. Because television is a public mass medium, children are watching it at all hours. Advertisers do not want to create ads that will make consuming adults feel awkward about the product. If a child sees an ad for a douche or a contraceptive and asks the adult questions that the adult would prefer not to answer, that adult is not going to respond with great affection toward the product or its sponsor.

Why then the treatment of such topics as abortion, incest, homosexuality, and rape on prime-time and afternoon television? In part, because the sponsor is somewhat insulated from that content. It takes a sophisticated consumer to blame the advertiser for the content of the sponsored program. Also, because such content increases audience size, it performs a useful service for the advertiser. In

28. Jane M. Von Bergen, "Now Advertisers Discuss What Mom Wouldn't Tell You," *Philadelphia Inquirer*, 19 February 1995, p. D1.
29. Stuart Elliott, "Madison Ave. Finds Courage to Ask: Want a Condom?" *New York Times*, 9 January 1994, p. 4.

BOX 8-6

What Would a Visitor from Outer Space Think?

Because of the absence of the word *vagina* in ads, interplanetary guests might mistakenly conclude that a "feminine hygiene deodorant spray" is a room deodorizer.

Because of the absence of the word *anus* in ads, they might conclude that we line, wrap, clean, or write about our toilets on toilet paper.

And what would they make of the oblique references in ads to "disposable, absorbent protection" offered by older actress June Allyson?

And what would Emily Post say when she found them setting dinner forks on our sanitary napkins?

---

short, the advertiser has more to gain than to lose by such discussion in programming, but more to lose than to gain by treatment of taboo parts of the body in ads.

Finally, creating ads that force the knowledgeable audience to invest them with meaning is strategically wise; making the audience an accomplice in the process of persuasion increases the likelihood that persuasion will occur. To decode euphemistic ads, the auditor or viewer is drawn into a participatory process highly advantageous to the advertiser. The viewer cannot resent the implied request to fill in explicit content, because the viewer probably is willing to acknowledge that discussion of the taboo subjects—in at least some of the environments in which people watch television and with at least some of the people with whom one watches television—could prove awkward. So euphemistic ads exist because it is to the advertiser's advantage.

When a broadcast ad campaign speaks directly, the very fact of direct address, free of conventional euphemisms, gains our attention. The radio campaign for OXY 5 and OXY 10 facial cleansers, for example, included the word *zits* in the copy; the ad asked, "Which would you rather have, a few extra cents or a few more zits?" The contrast between the announcer's intonation and the harsh slang word riveted the audience's attention.

Similarly, ads that violate advertising's unwritten rules about what may or may not be the visual focus of an ad may attract attention precisely because of that violation. The ad campaign for Calvin Klein jeans featuring then teenage movie star Brooke Shields was rejected by some stations and one of the networks. The ad prompted negative columns in newspapers, negative editorials, and hostile letters to the networks not because of the double entendre in the verbal message—after all, the double entendre with sexual nuances is a staple in "beauty product advertising"—but because its use of a teenage model delivering such lines and the camera angle focusing on her pelvis bluntly acknowledged teenage sexuality. By breaking the rules, the ad campaign gained quick visibility and became the topic of public discussion.

In August 1995, Calvin Klein's ads again created a stir and drew press attention, this time for "crotch shots" of young models with their underwear exposed under their Calvin Klein One jeans. "The ads' appearance last week on the sides of New York City buses prompted an outcry," reported the *Philadelphia Inquirer*.

BOX 8-7

The Power of Multinationals

Multinational manufacturers and multinational advertising agencies now have enlarged power to suppress public messages they do not like. In 1988 Saatchi &
Saatchi (formerly the world's largest advertising conglomerate) acquired the
Campbell-Mithun agency in the United States. The small agency was servicing antismoking ads for the Minnesota Department of Health, but Brown and Williamson
Tobacco Company was spending $35 million then with Saatchi to advertise Kool
cigarettes. The Minnesota account was only 3 percent of that, so Saatchi dropped
the health department. The parent firm had learned its lesson three months earlier
when one of the biggest advertisers in the world, RJR Nabisco, dropped another
Saatchi subsidiary because it had created a Northwest Airlines television commercial showing passengers applauding the airline's no-smoking policy. RJR Nabisco,
besides marketing food products, makes Camel, Winston, and Salem cigarettes.[a]

[a]Ben Bagdikian, "Global Media Corporations Control What We Watch (and Read)," *Utne
Reader*, July/August 1990, p. 88.

"Iona Seigel, director of a rape crisis center . . . told the New York *Daily News,*
'I've never seen anything as disgusting as this. It's unbelievable.'" Among the ads
triggering the controversy was one showing a blond girl on her back, her mini-
skirt raised to reveal a section of her panties.[30] Responding to the protests, Calvin
Klein withdrew the ads.

TO SUM UP

In this chapter, we have examined the complex relationships among government, industry, consumers, and advertising. We have demonstrated the eagerness
of industry to regulate itself when faced with the threat of government regulation.
Government and industry regulators often are faced with difficulties dealing with
claims that exist in the minds of the members of the audience but do not reside
explicitly in the advertising content.

   Existing regulation of advertising provides a sense of what advertisers may
and may not do, but unfortunately efforts to minimize deception have produced
an unintended result. Instead of producing ads with accurate but challengeable
information, the regulations have prompted many advertisers to minimize informational content and instead emphasize unprovable puffery.

   Audiences, however, are made up of potential consumers; the individuals
and groups making up these audiences have the power to influence advertising
and other media practices.

---

30. Roy H. Campbell, "Is Calvin Klein Over the Line?" *Philadelphia Inquirer*, 20 August 1995, p. H3.

A N A L Y S I S : Analyzing an Ad

In the brief space of three chapters on advertising, we have been able to touch only on a few of the questions that could be asked in a thorough analysis of an ad. Here we provide some of the other questions a person intent on critically analyzing an ad might ask.

What Type of Ad Is It?

1. Public service announcement?
2. Advertising an idea?
3. Advertising a service?
4. Ad designed to engender goodwill?
5. Political ad?
6. Ad for a product?

If the Ad Is a PSA

1. Did it appear in a space or time when it was likely to reach its intended audience?
2. Was it sponsored by a nonpartisan source?
3. Why was it aired or printed? What distinguishes it from PSAs rejected by this media outlet?

If the Ad Is an Idea Ad (pro-life or pro-choice, for example)

1. Who is the sponsor?
2. Did the sponsor incorporate for the purpose of sponsoring this campaign or have an identity independent of the campaign?
3. Why sponsor this ad? How does this ad serve the sponsor's self-interest?
4. Did the sponsor pay to air or place the ad?
5. How is the idea particularized or made concrete in the ad?
6. What is the intended audience of the ad? What cues in the copy or visuals reveal the identity of this audience? What does the ad want the audience to do? to think?
7. Does this ad exist to counter other ads or unpaid coverage about opposing ideas? If so, how successful is it in accomplishing this objective?

If the Ad Advertises a Service Rather Than a Product (for example, travel on a certain airline)

1. How is the service made concrete in the ad?
2. What is the intended audience for the service? How did the ad reveal the identity of its intended audience? What techniques did the ad use to increase the audience's desire for its service? What attempts were made to convert this want into a need?

If the Ad Is a Goodwill Ad

1. Is there a problem with the image or product that the ad is trying to overcome? If so, what techniques are used to overcome the problem?
2. By what channels did the problem come to public attention?
3. Does the ad explicitly identify the problem it is trying to overcome? If so, did the ad inadvertently make you aware of a problem you were not aware of before?
4. What if anything is the relationship between the product manufactured by the sponsor and the content of this ad (such as an ecology ad sponsored by an oil company)? If the relationship is nonexistent or minimal, does the sponsor provide a rationale for the existence of the ad in the ad itself?

If the Ad is a Political Ad

1. Is it sponsored by a committee associated with or dissociated from a candidate? by a political party?
2. Is it an attack ad or an affirming ad (attacking an opponent or supporting the candidate)?
3. Does the ad identify the party of the candidate? Why or why not?
4. Does the ad make explicit appeals to get you to register? to vote?
5. How long is the ad? Is it a "lift" taken from a longer ad? If so, what, if anything, is lost in the shorter version?
6. Is the ad consistent with unpaid coverage of the candidate? Has the ad incorporated newslike material about the candidate? actual news footage of the candidate?
7. Did the ad appear adjacent to content with which it was compatible?
8. Did the ad employ a no-tag tag? If so, what was the tag and how effective was it? If not, what form of disclosure was employed to reveal the sponsorship of the ad?
9. What is the audience for which the ad is intended? How is the audience mirrored in the ad?

If the Ad Is a Product Ad

1. Who manufactures the product? Can you learn the identity of the manufacturer from the ad? If so, how? If not, what strategic purpose is served by the absence of an identifiable manufacturer in the ad?
2. Is the trademark for the product used in the ad? Is it central to the ad? What does the trademark tell you about the product? How is the trademark integrated into the ad?
3. What is the unique selling point in this ad?
4. What are the redundant elements in the ad? Is this redundancy productive?
5. Is the product shown in the ad? Is it focal to the ad? What is being done with or to the product in the ad? What is this attempting to tell you about the product?

Audience

1. What is the intended audience—age? sex? ethnic background? religion? political affiliation? advertisers? elites? suppliers? distributors?
2. Did the ad appear in a time or place likely to reach the intended audience?
3. How does the ad mirror the intended audience? Does the ad imply special knowledge about wants and needs of this audience?

Ad Content (not all points apply to PSAs)

1. What is the central claim in the ad? Is this claim believable?
2. What evidence is marshaled in support of the claim? example? lay testimony? statistics? figurative analogy? literal analogy? expert testimony? Does the explicit evidence in the ad warrant the claim? What associations are used to prompt inferences about the sponsor or product? What are some of these possible inferences? Are they legitimate?
3. Does the ad position the product (or service, idea, candidate) in relation to others? If so, how?
4. What specific strategies are used to personalize the product (service, idea, candidate)? to adapt the message to the audience?
5. Does the visual content of the ad support, underscore, or echo the verbal content? If not, what is the relationship between the visual and the verbal? Is it a productive relationship?
6. Is the ad trying to reach a new audience (persuade them to buy or support) or is it trying to reinforce belief in those who already own the product or support the candidate?
7. Is anyone likely to be offended by this ad? If so, on what grounds? Does the ad offend publicly accepted standards of decency or taste? If so, why was it aired or printed?
8. How does the ad create recognition, differentiation, association, participation, and repetition?

Assumptions (values presumed in the ad)

1. What assumptions about society are embedded in the ad—about progress, consumption, political participation, racial harmony, multigenerational families, and so on?
2. What assumptions about the role appropriate to various types of persons—older persons, children, women, men, African Americans, Hispanics, Native Americans—inhere in the ad?
3. What assumptions about work or occupation are in the ad—about blue collar workers? professionals? professors? doctors? lawyers? working women as a class?
4. What assumptions about societal structures inhere in the ad?
   a. Households: what constitutes the normal family according to the ad? How many people? How many children? number of boys? girls? significant

others—grandma? Mrs. Olsen? milkman? Tony the Tiger? What is their relationship to other characters in the ad? Who gives advice? Who takes advice? Who extends approval? disapproval? What are the norms for appropriate behavior for different characters in the ad? What types of behavior can be initiated by some characters and not by others?

b. Medical establishment: Is the doctor ever anything other than an authority? Are health care and healing ever separate from consumption of a product? When the physician is female, will she be found in different circumstances and in different relationships from when the physician is male? Is the female doctor ever seen treating a male patient?

c. Religious establishment: If there is a rabbi, priest, or minister, what kind of a role does he or she play? How are religious symbols (or roles) used (nuns, monks, altar, candles, icon, and so forth)?

5. What assumptions are made about bodily processes—aging; euphemistic terms for parts of the body; body functions that are not identified?

6. What types of communication are legitimized in ads? What sorts of problems are revealed or concealed from other characters in ads? Are there things concealed from adults by children or from children by adults? Is duplicity sanctioned (for example, any pretext that a product made from a mix is really homemade)? Is one generation played off against another (grandma tells mother that if she bought the wrong thing it is granddaughter Susie's fault)? Does the product serve as a substitute for an expression of affection or some other form of communication? Does the ad advocate a particular type of communication, for example, preference for the telephone or writing a letter? If so, what are the special attributes of the preferred communication that are demonstrated in the ad?

7. How are politicians treated in nonpolitical ads?

Programming or Content Sponsored by an Ad

1. Is there a relationship between the content of the ad and the content of the sponsored program, for instance, an antidrug ad by a politician in an antidrug documentary or an ad for a beauty product in a woman's magazine?

2. Is the content of the program potentially offensive to any organized interest group? If so, is the advertiser aware of this? If so, why is the advertiser sponsoring the program?

Content Surrounding (contextualizing) an Ad

1. Do the programs or stories surrounding the ad provide a positive context for the ad? Do the ads surrounding this ad provide a positive context for the ad? Does the unpaid coverage of this product, idea, candidate, if any, provide a favorable context for this ad? If not, how does the ad adapt?

Media Mix

1. How much money is being spent on purchases of advertising space and time? How many ads have been purchased? Where? When? to reach what total audience?
2. Does the ad appear in the same form in other media? What changes are made in the ad in other media? How do you account for the changes? constraints in media? audience adaptation?
3. Do different ads for this product appear in different media?
4. Is the ad one in a campaign? Is it related to others in a campaign? What is the relationship?
5. Why did the advertiser choose this medium? What are the advantages and disadvantages in this choice? Are there important claims about this product, idea, service, or candidate that cannot credibly be made in this medium?

Pressure on Advertiser

1. Has the advertiser or manufacturer been subject to pressure from groups that disapprove of the product or the program/content sponsored by the product's ads? Have ads or sponsorship been altered in response to this pressure?
2. Has the advertiser altered the ad in response to a consent agreement with the FTC?
3. Have the networks, stations, newspapers, or magazines in which the ad appears requested changes in the ad? Were the changes made and how did the changes affect the ad's ability to convey its intended meaning?

Effect

1. Was this ad pretested? Was it altered as a result of pretesting?
2. Does evidence exist to document the effect of this ad or ad campaign on its intended audience? on an unintended audience? Was this effect positive or negative? Is the evidence of effect credible?
3. Can you construct a more effective version of this ad?

SELECTED READINGS

Advertising and Women. National Advertising Review Board, 1975.

Preston, Ivan L. *The Great American Blow-Up*. Madison: University of Wisconsin Press, 1975.

U.S. Congress, Select Committee on Aging. *Hearings on Age Stereotyping and Television*, 99th Cong., 1st sess., 1977 (available from Government Printing Office).

CHAPTER 9

How to Influence the Media

Short of running for political office or joining a congressional staff in order to change the laws, what can individuals or groups do to influence media practices? Here we examine the means of persuasion available to individuals, groups, social movements, and nongovernmental organizations to change the content or form of ads or news. We assume that an individual who is aware of all the available means of influence is better able to select and skillfully employ effective means. We proceed from the simplest to the most complex, from the easiest to the most difficult, and from individual action to actions by established organizations.

Individual Complaints

The function of the media is to deliver an audience to advertisers, and advertisers want to persuade the audience to buy their products. Therefore, the media and advertisers cater to their audiences and spend large sums of money analyzing audience preferences. Chapter 5 considered this economic basis of the audience-media relationship; Chapters 2 through 4 on news and Chapters 6 through 8 on advertising discussed the character of this relationship.

The relationship between audiences and the media dictates that something as simple as writing a letter can have an impact on a newspaper or a radio or television station. Because relatively few people write them, each letter to a media outlet has a disproportionate impact. Although media managers and advertisers know that people who write letters are not typical of the entire audience, they tend to assume that each letter represents a large number of viewers or readers. As the number of letters protesting any single item, episode, or ad increases, the tendency to assume there is substantial dissatisfaction increases. When the offending medium or program has provided a mechanism for publishing or airing dissident views, a letter can also publicize one's grievance to the outlet's audience. So, for example, *60 Minutes* airs selected comments from viewers as do the letters-to-the-editor columns in newspapers.

BOX 9-1

Mail and the Media

In both media [print and television] . . . letters which describe factual mistakes are read carefully; as is critical mail when it arrives in unprecedented numbers or when it is unexpected, dealing with topics that do not usually anger letter writers.[a]

[a]Herbert Gans, *Deciding What's News* (New York: Vintage Books, 1980), p. 231.

In summer 1986, NBC created a series of image-enhancing spots that gave television critics a national platform on which to air their grievances. The 30-second spots featured nine citizen-activists speaking their minds about television. These critics included Ralph Nader, National PTA president Ann Kahn, and the founders of Viewers for Quality Television. The spots were NBC's answer to critics' complaints that the networks fail to listen to or to air criticism of their performance. The following comments are among those included in the spots: "If you think television is doing anything wrong or having any kind of negative effect on your child, turn the damn set off for a while. Put the five-year-old in your lap and read him [*sic*] a book." "Even if television had nothing but perfect programs on it, I think it would be important for people to limit the amount of television that young children watch."[1]

The public's lack of awareness of the channels of complaint is criticized by both supporters and foes of the regulatory and self-regulatory processes. Even many in the advertising industry itself are not familiar with the National Advertising Division. In 1993 NAD issued eighty-seven decisions, an increase of 34 percent over the year before. Nonetheless, NAD's board decided the program needed its own advertising and hired a public relations director.[2]

Complaints about material appearing on network programs should be addressed to the network's audience services division in New York and to the community affairs director of the local station airing the material. This procedure pressures the people directly responsible for approving content at the network; at the same time, it magnifies the impact of the dissatisfaction by encouraging the local station, whose license is dependent on serving the local community, not to clear such material in the future. Because the network wants to keep its affiliates happy, expressions of dissatisfaction from local stations to the network are very persuasive.

Networks are responsible for what they air. Most of their programming and all of their advertising is internally prescreened and approved. When these internal checks work, they preempt objections. When they fail, and protest is mounted by dissatisfied viewers, the existence of these checks assures the public

---

1. *Washington Post,* 11 June 1986, p. B2.
2. "NAD Gets Boost From Gov't in Airline Case," *Advertising Age,* 14 March 1994, p. 16.

Phil Sokolof v. McDonald's

In 1966 Phil Sokolof had a heart attack. He was not overweight and considered himself physically fit. How had it happened? he wondered. The culprit turned out to be cholesterol. Sokolof vowed to wage a campaign against the cholesterol we ingest unmindful of its presence.

Sokolof had one asset the ordinary citizen lacks. As a building materials manufacturer, he had become a millionaire. By mid-1990, he had sunk $2.5 million of his own money into his campaign for change. In the process, he founded a group called the National Heart Savers Association.

In October 1988, Sokolof took out newspaper ads in more than a dozen daily newspapers indicting companies that created foods by using cholesterol-rich tropical oils. His targets included such corporate giants as Sunshine Biscuits, Quaker Oats, Nabisco Brands, Procter & Gamble, Keebler, Borden, General Foods, and Pepperidge Farms.

Media coverage followed. Public pressure mounted. Eleven of the companies substituted other oils for tropical oil. One company, Nabisco, held out. Sokolof turned his attention to that corporation in his second series of "Poisoning of America" ads. In June 1990, Nabisco too gave in.

By April 1990, Sokolof had settled on another target: the high-fat content of fast foods. His focus: McDonald's, the nation's leading fast-food marketer. His third phase of ads addressed McDonald's directly: "McDonald's, your hamburgers have too much fat!" The ads called on fast-food chains to lower the fat content of their hamburgers by 10 percent and urged readers, "If you agree, write or call now!" The ads listed McDonald's address and phone number.

Again he bought ads in the nation's major newspapers, including the *Wall Street Journal* and the *New York Times.* But $500,000 of his budget went unspent when the *Los Angeles Times,* the *Baltimore Sun,* and the *Chicago Sun-Times* rejected the ads. Because newspapers are privately owned, they may reject any ads they want. Presumably, these papers did not want to risk the wrath of one of the nation's larger advertisers.

By 1991, McDonald's was testing cooking french fries only in vegetable oil and noting that it had added bran muffins and low-fat yogurt and shakes to its menu. [By 1994 the use of vegetable oil was also under fire.]

In the course of his campaign, Sokolof's message has been magnified by appearances on the major morning talk shows, the news, and in stories in the nation's newspapers.

He explains his success this way, "I got the message to the people, and the people got the message to the food companies."[a]

[a]Judann Dagnoli, "Sokolof Keeps Thumping Away at Food Giants," *Advertising Age,* 9 April 1990, pp. 3, 63.

that the network is conscientious. These checks also provide a bureaucratic structure through which complaints can be channeled. Although network news is not formally screened and approved by a separate division, any material that appears on the news programs has been examined by various gatekeepers within the

McDonald's, Your Hamburgers Still Have Too Much Fat!
and Your French Fries Still are Cooked with Beef Tallow*

National Heart Savers Association
4601 South 76th Street
Omaha, Nebraska 68127
(402) 339-3813

Dear Friends:

High Cholesterol Kills!

Over 50% of the public have a cholesterol that is too high...
25% have a level that is dangerously high.

Deadly saturated fats are the major contributors to raising your cholesterol level. It is estimated that Americans consume two billion ounces of saturated fat per week, clogging arteries and leading to over 500,000 heart attack deaths every year!

Meat and dairy products make up over ¾ of your saturated fat intake. To lower your cholesterol, it is necessary only to alter some eating habits. A complete change of diet is not necessary. You can dramatically reduce your cholesterol level and potentially extend your lifespan. Eat smaller portions of leaner meats and lower fat dairy products.

High Cholesterol May Be Endangering Your Life!

To A Healthy Heart,
NATIONAL HEART SAVERS ASSOCIATION
Phil Sokolof, President

National Heart Savers Association ran full-page "Poisoning of America, Part III" ads nationally April 4. We called on McDonald's and other fast food chains to reduce the fat content of their hamburger by 10%, and eliminate beef tallow from their french fries, cooking them in heart healthy vegetable oils.

McDonald's didn't respond to our request. However, the public did respond by choosing to reduce their intake of saturated fat in fast food restaurants.

A May Gallup Poll was commissioned by Advertising Age magazine.
It measured the impact of our Poisoning of America, Part III "McDonalds, Your Hamburgers Have Too Much Fat!" ad, and other cholesterol awareness efforts.

TWO QUESTIONS ASKED WERE:

In the last month, have you read, seen, or heard any claims that a fast-food hamburger restaurant cooks its products in animal fat, which has an impact on the cholesterol level of users of its products?

31% of adult Americans — 57 million people — responded YES.

Those who had responded yes were asked: Have these claims caused you to increase or decrease your usage of fast-food hamburger restaurants in general?

38% of those Americans — 21 million people — responded YES, they had decreased their usage.

Hamburger Fat

Our original ad stated that McDonald's hamburger contains 21.5% fat, precooked.

McDonald's claims their hamburger has 19.5% fat, precooked. Laboratory tests conducted for the New York Times after our ad ran showed McDonald's hamburger ranged from 20.28% to 22.50% fat, after cooking.

As the industry leader, Hardee's has introduced a new hamburger, The Lean 1, with 17.5% fat, precooked.

**McDonald's
Burger King
Wendy's
French Fries

All Cooked
With
Beef Tallow!**

Beef Tallow in French Fries

McDonald's, Burger King and Wendy's still cook their french fries with beef tallow!

Hardee's is the only big 4 hamburger chain to cook its french fries in heart healthy vegetable oils.

THIS ADVERTISEMENT IS A PUBLIC SERVICE OF NATIONAL HEART SAVERS ASSOCIATION.

*Both references are applicable to Burger King and Wendy's.

Courtesy of National Heart Savers Association.

news bureau. Complaints about news content can be sent directly to the anchor or to the program's producer. A carbon copy of each complaint should be sent to the president of the offending media outlet as well, to increase internal pressures for change within the system itself.

BOX 9-2

How to Write an Op-Ed

The usual Commentary Page column is about 800 words—certainly it can be shorter, sometimes longer. It should be accompanied by your name, address, daytime phone number and Social Security number. (We pay a small honorarium to most contributors). . . .

Analyze the facts. Give us some insight. Help the reader draw some conclusions. . . .

Consider the piece to be an argument—lay out your central points in the beginning, then back them up with facts, anecdotes and illustrations. The opening few paragraphs must get the reader's attention, indicate what the piece is about, and—if at all possible—make the reader believe that he or she will be better off for having read it to the end.

Having something to say is the main aim: then you must be able to back it up. . . .

One word of caution, however: Pick that ammunition carefully. Don't include every possible example to prove your point. . . .

And now to my final point. Emotion. Even passion. We want it on our pages. . . .

One other thing to keep in mind: Remember the difference between a letter to the editor and a column. In general, if you want to respond to a particular story, editorial or another column—that's a letter. An article for the Commentary Page has to stand on its own.[a]

[a]Jane Eisner, associate editorial page editor, *Philadelphia Inquirer*, 26 November 1989, p. 7C.

A letter from an individual can also trigger industry-sponsored self-regulatory mechanisms. As we have indicated, self-regulatory agencies such as NAD monitor advertising and initiate action against ads that seem deceptive. Similarly, readers' advocates for individual newspapers and the National News Council arbitrate complaints from dissatisfied readers and viewers. These individuals and organizations give the individual consumer the ability to initiate the investigation of a deceptive ad or an unfair news item.

An individual letter can also spur action by government regulatory agencies such as the Federal Trade Commission (FTC) and the Federal Communications Commission (FCC). The FTC monitors ads, calling for proof of questionable claims, and initiates formal proceedings against ads that seem deceptive. The FCC superintends the use of the airwaves.

The ability of a single individual to produce change in broadcast content was clearly demonstrated when a young lawyer, John Banzhaf III, argued persuasively to the FCC that the Fairness Doctrine mandated the airing of anticigarette ads to counter procigarette ads on television. As Banzhaf's legal training proved, specialized expertise is a definite asset in dealing with either the FTC or the FCC.

An effective letter of complaint presupposes a knowledge of the standards the self-regulatory agency or regulatory agency applies, an understanding of the sorts of complaints it is authorized to handle, and of the avenues of redress it is able to exercise if a complaint is credible. In making a complaint, the audience member must clearly specify the time, location, date, and character of the offensive item.

In addition, such a letter should indicate either that the item violates the standards of the agency or that the standards ought to be broadened to include items of this nature. Three lines of argument are particularly effective when justifying a complaint: (1) the item or ad is inaccurate or deceptive; (2) the item or ad violates community standards or tastes; or (3) the news item is unbalanced or the ad is unfair (for example, it exploits negative stereotypes or capitalizes on the gullibility of children).

Group Pressure

Boycotts

What can a consumer do if the regulatory and self-regulatory mechanisms dismiss the complaint? Because the relationship among the consumer, the advertiser, and the media outlet is an economic one, the consumer can threaten a boycott of the advertised product or the sponsored program or both if the desired change does not take place. To make this threat credible, the consumer must have or be able to marshal a large number of like-minded people willing to carry out the boycott. As we shall see, the threat of a boycott often eliminates the need for an actual boycott.

Advertisers want to avoid boycotts for a number of reasons. First, negative publicity in the news is more believable than advertising and functions as negative advertising. In addition, if an advertising agency produces an ad that triggers a boycott—especially if sales begin to drop off or if the boycott seems so well-organized and widespread that it will create negative associations in the public's mind with the manufacturer's other products—it will lose the client's business. Consequently, the advertising agency is uniquely susceptible to pressure to change offensive ads. Groups of consumers can put pressure on the ad agency that produced the ad, the mass media outlet that carried the ad, or the manufacturer that produced the advertised product.

Similarly, groups can marshal members of the community to cancel subscriptions to an offending newspaper or turn off an offending news program. If this tactic works and the size of the audience declines, the media outlet's profits are threatened; it can no longer deliver the desired audience to the advertisers. Groups also can exert indirect economic pressure by persuading advertisers not to buy space or time from the offending media.

BOX 9-3

Roe vs. Wade

Pressure from a fundamentalist religious group prompted several advertisers to withdraw from *Roe vs. Wade,* a dramatization of the 1973 Supreme Court decision that legalized abortion, according to NBC executives. Some groups, particularly the American Family Association, led by the Rev. Donald E. Wildmon, urged viewers not to watch the film.

The attack on *Roe vs. Wade* sparked concern within the television and advertising industries because the film was considered to be of high quality and well balanced.

Richard Kostyra, media director for the J. Walter Thompson advertising agency, said some clients had withdrawn from the program, and commented, "I don't believe advertisers have a moral obligation to put their products on the line for the benefit of freedom of speech."[a]

[a]Jeremy Gerard, "Advertisers Withdraw from *Roe,*" *New York Times,* 11 May 1989, p. 15Y.

Legal Actions

Our ability to influence the media through legal action is constrained by the laws governing the agencies we seek to influence. Before 1966, only persons who had a clear economic stake in a case were able to intervene in the FCC licensing of a station. This changed with a challenge to the renewal of the license of WLBT, a Jackson, Mississippi, television station. In this case, the court ruled that "civic associations, professional societies, unions, churches, and educational institutions or associations" may contest an application for a station's renewal of license. This decision gave such groups legal standing on the grounds that "the holders of broadcasting licenses [must] be responsive to the needs of the audience."[3]

Notice that not all individuals or groups have legal standing. To have legal standing, an individual must be a member of a group that represents a substantial portion of viewers or listeners and has a legitimate and genuine interest in the station's performance in the community. The challengers in this case, the Office of Communication of the United Church of Christ, argued that although the city of Jackson was 45 percent African American, the station was not sensitive to matters of concern to the African-American population.

In response to this decision, a number of groups representing the interests of special segments of the audience focused their attention on the license renewal process. These included not only the pioneering Office of Communication of the United Church of Christ but also the National Association for the Advancement of Colored People (NAACP) Legal Defense Fund in New York, which seeks to increase minority involvement; Action for Children's Television in Newton

---

3. *Office of Communication of the United Church of Christ v. F.C.C.,* 359 F. 2d 994, 1002 (D.C. Cir. 1966), 425 F. 2d 543 (D.C. Cir. 1969).

Centre, Massachusetts; and the Mexican-American Legal Defense and Educational Fund in San Francisco.

Such groups are able to produce change not just through actual transfer of licenses but also by threatening that if change does not occur, they will intervene in the licensing process. For example, in 1969 an African-American coalition reached an agreement with KTAL-TV in Texarkana, Texas, under which news coverage, programming, and employment practices were altered. In return the coalition withdrew its petition to deny the renewal of the station's license.

Group legal action also has produced important changes in advertising. A group of law students calling itself SOUP (Students Opposing Unfair Practices) deserves credit for paving the way for the FTC's use of corrective advertising. In 1969 the students tried to intervene in the FTC case against Campbell Soup. Campbell's advertisers had placed marbles in the bottom of soup bowls to accentuate the solid ingredients in the soup. The students argued that a consent order that would stop the practice was insufficient to remedy the impression created by the false ads. The students proposed corrective advertising instead.

Although the FTC did not impose corrective advertising to resolve the case, it did acknowledge that it had the right to do so if a case warranted such action. The impact of SOUP testifies to the power of groups that understand the regulatory process. Its understanding of this process enabled SOUP, a group otherwise powerless and underfinanced, to bring about a major change in advertising.

Group action often is more effective than individual action, but group action generally requires specialized legal expertise and the resources to support it. Such groups are better able to establish that they have standing before the FCC. In the case of the FTC, where standing is not a prerequisite for consideration of a complaint, individual action is possible. But even here the ability of a group to establish that it represents substantial sentiment in the community is more compelling than a comparable claim by an individual.

Group legal action is not effective in influencing the press except in the area of advertising. The press is not licensed and has important First Amendment protections from government interference. Nongovernmental legal action against the print media is limited almost entirely to the enforcement of the libel laws. In extreme cases, such as the suit brought by Carol Burnett against the *National Enquirer*, this avenue can be very effective; the financial judgment against the tabloid in this case was large.

To the consternation of some, ABC News agreed to an out-of-court settlement with Philip Morris and R. J. Reynolds in response to lawsuits brought by the cigarette companies over allegations made on ABC's *Day One* that cigarettes were "spiked" with added nicotine in the manufacturing process. In what the *New York Times* referred to as "an extraordinary act of contrition," ABC News agreed to apologize twice during prime time as well as pay legal expenses, estimated to be near $3 million. Said ABC senior vice president Patricia J. Matson, "There was a mistake. We corrected it."[4] The role of legal action in influencing the news is discussed in Chapter 4.

---

4. Mark Landler, "ABC News Settles Suits on Tobacco," *New York Times*, 22 August 1995, pp. A1, D6.

BOX 9-4

National Association of Talk Show Hosts

Taxpayer Action Day was organized by the Council for Citizens Against Government Waste, a Washington lobby that claims 400,000 members.

The National Association of Talk Show Hosts mailed out flyers about the protest to 300 of its members. Some of them supported the protest on the air, such as Bob Grant, the host of *The Bob Grant Show* on WABC radio, New York City, which Arbitron says has 126,000 listeners, and Mary Beal, host of *The Morning Magazine* on WNSS, Wichita, with about 50,000 listeners.

Their reasons for supporting the protest are not entirely public spirited. Neil Myers, a host of NBC's Talknet shows, said: "Some of these people are in a numbers game. They are looking to grab headlines. . . . The campaign against giving Congress a raise was a perfect marriage between public interest and the dramatization of hosts. It got covered in *Time* and *U.S. News & World Report* and seemed to galvanize everyone."

Talk-show-driven protests can be effective. A talk station, FM New Jersey 101.5, coalesced voter resentment against Jim Florio, the governor of New Jersey, because of a record tax increase that he pushed through the legislature in 1990. That protest generated 800,000 signatures on a petition seeking to provide a mechanism for recall of public officials and legislation by initiative and referendum.[a]

[a]Wayne King, "Tax Protest, Fueled by Talk Shows, Is Getting Steamed Voters Organized," *New York Times*, 26 October 1990, p. A12.

Those bringing action against a business or government make themselves vulnerable to the possibility of libel suits, however. In Suffolk County, New York, a real estate developer sued nine civic organizations and sixteen individuals for running an ad in a local paper objecting to the developer's plans. They also produced a leaflet and a flier telling citizens to attend a hearing at the town meeting. When the town board rejected the developer's plan, the real estate concern brought suit. In cases like this, even if the defendants win, their legal costs will have exceeded $10,000. University of Denver law professor George Pring notes that such suits are not usually brought with the aim of winning damages. Rather, they are intended to deter such actions in the future.[5]

Promoting Self-Regulation

Groups that understand the relationship between government and industry can also effect change by exploiting industry's desire to avoid government regulation. As we have noted, increased self-regulation of the broadcasting and the

---

5. *Washington Post*, 19 July 1986, p. A23.

BOX 9-5

Controlling Controversy

Networks appreciate controversy for its ability to attract viewers, but they like it best when the controversy is uncontroversial. When the system works, according to Kathryn C. Montgomery, an assistant professor of film and television at UCLA and author of *Target: Prime Time,* political and social issues are shaped "to conform to the institutional demands of network television. Important societal conflicts are extracted from the public sphere and injected into entertainment programs, where they are reduced to problems for individual characters." The result: "Controversial issues are consistently and carefully balanced within each program so that one clear argument cannot be discerned."[a]

But in spring 1989, in response to letters from angry television viewers, such major advertisers as Coca-Cola, McDonald's, Chrysler, General Mills, Campbell Soup, Ralston-Purina, and Sears canceled commercials on television programs because of material cited as offensive in viewer complaints. Typical of such grassroots protests was a campaign by Terry Rakolta of Michigan who charged that the Fox Network series *Married . . . with Children* was offensively vulgar and shown at a time when children easily could watch it.

A number of factors contributed to a climate encouraging grassroots protest. Under economic pressure, all three networks cut back staff in their standards and practices divisions; the Hollywood writers strike of spring 1989 shortened the time between program production and broadcasting, increasing the chances that potentially offensive material would air; technological improvements allowed viewers to tape broadcasts of offensive programming and cite specifics they find objectionable; and concerned heightened about the vulnerability of U.S. children to violence and drugs.

Montgomery argues that corporate takeovers of all three networks in the preceding five-year-period created a climate in which a new protest movement could flourish: "The reason the standards and practices divisions were working in the first place is because they were actively managing the advocacy groups. Then the ownership changed, the staffs were cut back, and all that institutional memory was lost. Of course, the advertisers have that institutional memory."[b]

[a]Walter Goodman, "How the Viewers Work Their Will on Commercial TV," *New York Times,* 24 April 1989, p. 18.
[b]Bill Carter, "Sponsors Heed Viewers Who Find Shows Too Racy," *New York Times,* 24 April 1989, p. 14.

advertising industries is often prompted by industry fear of government regulation. By arousing industry fears that the government is about to regulate some facet of their operations, viewers or readers can prod industry to adopt its own preemptive regulations.

For example, the now defunct NAB Television Code allowed as much as 16 minutes of commercials during children's Saturday morning programming, but permitted only 9.5 minutes during prime time. The Massachusetts-based organization, Action for Children's Television (ACT), charged that this difference unfairly exploited children. The FCC responded to this charge by hinting broadly that if broadcasters did not limit the amount of children's advertising, the FCC would. Subsequently, the code was amended to set a ceiling of 9.5 minutes per hour on the commercials in children's shows.

Industry is aware of the power of self-regulation to forestall government regulation. Had the broadcasting or advertising industry regulated cigarette advertising, it might have been spared the anticigarette commercials and ultimately the television ban on cigarette advertising. The FCC actually cited the existence of the newly created National Advertising Review Board to justify dismissing arguments by TUBE (Termination of Unfair Broadcasting Exercises) for an FCC-established Code of Advertising Standards for Television Advertising and an Advertising Advisory Board.[6]

Pressure from an Established Organization

Individuals may persuade advertisers and manufacturers that a sizable part of the audience opposes an ad or news practice by protesting through a respected, legitimate group recognized by the public, the media, and advertisers. The arguments of such an established organization will be widely aired and readily accepted even by people not affiliated with the organization.

The PTA is one example. When the PTA takes a stand on advertising, particularly if the stand pertains to children's advertising or to the effects of ads on children, that stand is likely to bring about the desired change. The PTA is newsworthy according to the criteria described in Chapter 2. It has a track record of being newsworthy and is perceived as speaking for a substantial segment of the news outlet's audience—parents, teachers, taxpayers, children, and other people interested in education.

In August 1976, the national PTA placed television programming on probation for the amount of violence shown, and announced a national effort to monitor televised violence. If the level of violence did not decline significantly, the PTA indicated, it would consider sponsoring a boycott of those products advertised in the violent programs. Kodak, General Foods, General Motors, and Sears were among the companies that announced their support for the efforts to reduce violence in programming, an announcement that piggybacked on the newsworthy PTA statement and that garnered favorable national publicity for these manufacturers. By the end of 1977 a number of "violent" shows had been canceled "in a major concession to anti-violence crusaders."[7] Here it was not an actual boycott of products but the threat of a boycott by a nationally respected organization that produced results. In 1978, the PTA expanded its monitoring to include "offensively portrayed sexuality."

---

6. *Adoption of Standards Designed to Eliminate Deceptive Advertising from Television*, 32 F.C.C. 2d 360, 372–374.

7. "ABC: Laughing All the Way with Its New Schedule for Prime Time," *Broadcasting*, 2 May 1977, p. 23.

BOX 9-6

It's Not What You Know but Who You Know

Organized letter-writing campaigns are discounted by the journalists, but letters from officers of major national organizations are taken into account and are apt to be answered by an executive. If sent to a magazine, they may be published in the letters section.

Interest-group pressure appears to be effective when it obtains political support, in Congress or elsewhere; when it threatens advertisers and local television stations; and when it is persuasive to the journalists. However, pressure from powerless groups is ignored.[a]

[a]Herbert Gans, *Deciding What's News* (New York: Vintage Books, 1980), p. 265.

BOX 9-7

Viewers for Quality Television— How Many Letters Are Enough?

"Once upon a time viewers just sat quietly and watched," said one network executive who has been the recipient of tens of thousands of letters in the last few years and who asked, fearing more mail, that his name not be used. "Now they write. They write a lot." Dorothy Swanson, founder of the Virginia-based Viewers for Quality Television, which coordinates efforts to save television shows, commented, "They believe they can influence what's on their television set. Look at *Cagney & Lacey*." She was referring to the first of the grassroots campaigns to save a series. In 1984 CBS announced cancellation of the program about two women police detectives because of poor ratings. CBS received 20,000 letters over the next three months saying the program had fine writing and realistically portrayed working women; *Cagney & Lacey* was renewed.

But letters alone are not enough to return a show to the air. For instance, the ratings for *Cagney & Lacey* rose sharply during the summer between its cancellation and renewal, partly because it ran in a different time slot and partly because of publicity generated by the write-in campaign.

But Swanson and network executives say an avalanche of letters can influence a close call. In early 1987, CBS took *Designing Women,* a comedy about four partners in an Atlanta decorating firm, off the air indefinitely without actually canceling it. Harry Thomason, executive producer of the program, asked Swanson to ask the 1,500 members who receive her monthly newsletter to encourage their friends to write to CBS. The network received 50,000 letters, and *Designing Women* went on to become the highest-rated CBS comedy. It stayed on CBS through the 1992–93 season and then went into syndication. In 1994, Lifetime bought 162 episodes and exclusive rights to evening airing.[a]

"The more common these crusades become, the sooner they will kill the effect," Thomason said. "A mere 50,000 letters isn't as impressive anymore."[b]

[a]"Lifetime Acquires 162 Episodes of *Designing Women* Television Program," *Mediaweek,* 7 March 1994, p. 29.
[b]Lisa Belkin, "Viewers Pens Can Be Mightier Than the Ax," *New York Times,* 18 June 1987, p. 24Y.

A group will be less effective if its economic self-interest is obvious to the audience. Although the PTA has a self-interest in the quality of education, changes in programming or advertising produce no direct economic benefit to its members. By contrast, efforts by Mobil Oil Company to alter broadcast and print stereotypes of Arab sheiks and efforts by the Tobacco Institute to alter the way the media cover the dangerous effects of smoking have been less effective, because their economic self-interest is apparent.

Financial resources are critical if a group plans to use paid channels (advertising) to influence unpaid channels (news coverage). When, for example, the Tobacco Institute took out ads reprinting news items that, in its judgment, were underplayed in the print press, and placed them in elite media like the *Columbia Journalism Review,* it was attempting to influence media decision makers directly by arguing that journalists had violated their own norms of balance and fair play. When such ads appear in the popular press, they suggest that the audience should be more critical in its consumption of news items on such an issue. This strategic use of paid media is not available to resource-poor groups.

Pressure from a Social Movement

Social movements are more loosely organized than groups such as the PTA. In their early stages, social movements lack the structure to disseminate information efficiently; they often lack identified leaders whose opinions are accepted by the media as representative of the opinions of the movement as a whole.

Social movements seek to produce specific changes in society. They also attempt to create awareness of issues, generate audience identification with their cause, and have their leaders recognized as spokespersons for larger constituencies not formally identified with the movement.

Social movements need to capitalize on journalistic norms and routines to accomplish these objectives. Ideally, they become part of someone's beat, their leaders are perceived as newsworthy by the media, their concerns become ongoing news themes, and their spokespersons are quoted on controversial issues affecting their constituencies.

As we have indicated in our discussion of age stereotyping in Chapter 6, the media are powerful purveyors of societal attitudes. African Americans and women, aware of this power of the media, have sought to increase their representation among newspeople. The civil rights and women's rights movements assume that female and African-American reporters are more sensitive to racism and sexism and also assume that their presence is a symbolic statement of support for these movements.

Changing the portrayal of women and minorities is also seen as a means of altering societal attitudes about these groups. The same arguments were made by the members of the movement for the rights of the elderly, in arguing that mandatory retirement and age discrimination had deprived such older reporters and commentators as Pauline Fredericks and Eric Sevareid of their network jobs and

---

BOX 9-8

Neighbor to Neighbor Versus Procter & Gamble

Neighbor to Neighbor is a citizen group organized to change the U.S. policy toward El Salvador. In 1989, the group began to focus its attention on coffee producers who use Salvadoran coffee beans.

Neighbor to Neighbor created an ad indicting Procter & Gamble for brewing "misery and death." Narrated by actor Ed Asner, the ad showed an overturned coffee mug spilling blood instead of coffee. Twenty-five stations in New Orleans, Kansas City (Missouri), Cincinnati, and New York rejected the ad. When the CBS affiliate in Boston aired the ad, Procter & Gamble responded by pulling $1 million in commercials from the station.

Neighbor to Neighbor countered by picketing N. W. Ayer, the advertising agency that holds the Procter & Gamble account. "Ayer, there's blood on your hands," read the picket signs.

Although most U.S. coffees use Salvadoran beans, the ad campaign targeted Folgers because it is the country's best seller. Neighbor to Neighbor next planned to picket stores that carry the coffee. By May 1990, the boycott begun in November had yielded minimal results. Stores in some college towns had dropped the brand. Red Apple markets in Manhattan agreed that it would not provide Folgers with end of the aisle displays and would not feature Folgers in its ads.

"Boycotts are 'economic blackmail'" says a Procter & Gamble spokesperson. "We can't buy time in New York because of the chilling effect of P & G and Ayer's action," said a Neighbor to Neighbor leader.[a]

[a]Judann Dagnoli and Lauri Freeman, "Coffee Boycott Boils," *Advertising Age*, 21 May 1990, p. 6.

---

that older persons are underrepresented and often caricatured when they do appear in ads.

The potential impact of movements is seen in the dramatic changes in advertising that occurred as a result of the pressure of the women's rights movement, pressure that triggered industry self-regulation. The National Advertising Review Board, an industry-based board set up to monitor truth and accuracy in advertising, issued a report titled *Advertising and Women* in 1975. That report acknowledged that "the more vocal critics of advertising as 'sexist' are younger, better educated, more articulate women who often are opinion leaders. On the average, they have more discretionary income. As their numbers increase (with increasing educational and job opportunities), their challenge to advertising will probably become greater, unless constructive action is taken."[8]

Political pressure and economic self-interest allied to produce ads in which women no longer appeared simply as housewives and mothers but also in their roles in business, the professional world, and community affairs. The board

---

8. *Advertising and Women*, Report of the National Advertising Review Board, 1975, p. 6.

offered a checklist of principles to be used by advertisers to determine whether their ads treated women in an appropriate fashion.

The power of both respected institutions such as the PTA and large social movements such as the women's rights movement resides in their ability to speak for a large number of consumers who might be persuaded to boycott products or programming if the demands of the movement or institution are not met.

Creating Legislative Pressure

State Level

Both the state and federal governments exercise considerable control over commerce, including advertising. Action by state governments often precedes federal action and, ironically, creates an incentive for industry to acquiesce to federal legislation. One instance occurred in July 1965 when Governor Nelson Rockefeller signed an act requiring a health warning on all cigarette packages sold in New York State. "If there was anything the cigarette companies wanted less than federal regulation," explains A. Lee Fritschler in *Smoking and Politics*, "it was state requirements that health warnings appear. This could have meant as many different labels as there are states, creating an obvious marketing problem."[9]

Federal Level

Congress can exercise enormous power over the government regulatory agencies, which were created by and can be modified by congressional legislation, are funded by congressional appropriations, and are overseen by congressional committees. In addition, high-level government appointments, including appointments of FCC commissioners, must be confirmed by the Senate.

Actual congressional action is not always necessary to produce change in the media. For example, on February 3, 1971, the FTC asked Congress to require that all print advertising for cigarettes carry a health warning. On April 15, seven of the nine largest cigarette companies began voluntarily including health warnings in all print ads.[10]

But when Congress is affronted by the actions of a regulatory agency, it is capable of strong action. In the mid-1960s, for example, without consulting key members of Congress, the FTC bowed to pressure from anticigarette forces and issued a notice of rule making requiring a health warning on all packages of cigarettes and in all cigarette advertising. Both houses of Congress held hearings on

9. A. Lee Fritschler, *Smoking and Politics: Policymaking and the Federal Bureaucracy* (Englewood Cliffs, N.J.: Prentice-Hall, 1975), p. 121.
10. Ibid., p. 165.

BOX 9-9

Where to Write to Comment or Complain

National Advertising Division
Council of Better Business Bureaus
845 Third Avenue
New York, N.Y. 10022
(212) 754-1320

Federal Trade Commission
Pennsylvania Avenue at Sixth Street, N.W.
Washington, D.C. 20580
(202) 326-2180

Federal Communications Commission
Consumer Assistance Office
1919 M Street, N.W.
Washington, D.C. 20554
(202) 632-5050

Networks and Cable Companies

ABC
Capital Cities / ABC, Inc.
77 West 66th Street
New York, N.Y. 10023-6298
(212) 456-7777

CBS
CBS, Inc.
51 W. 52nd Street
New York, N.Y. 10019
(212) 975-4321

NBC
General Electric Building
30 Rockefeller Plaza
New York, N.Y. 10112
(212) 664-4444

Showtime, The Movie Channel
Showtime Networks, Inc.
1633 Broadway, 37th Floor
New York, N.Y. 10019
(212) 708-1600

MTV, Nickelodeon, VH-1
1515 Broadway
New York, NY 10036
(212) 258-7800

HBO, Cinemax
1100 Avenue of the Americas
New York, N.Y. 10036
(212) 512-1000

TBS, CNN
Turner Broadcasting System
P.O. Box 105366
Atlanta, Ga. 30328
(404) 827-1700

CBN
Christian Broadcasting Network
CBN Center
Virginia Beach, Va. 23463
(804) 424-7777

ESPN
The Sports Network
ESPN Plaza
Bristol, Conn. 06010
(203) 585-2000

PBS
Corporation for Public Broadcasting
901 E Street, N.W.
Washington, D.C. 20004-2037
(202) 879-9702

the FTC action. The resulting legislation removed the FTC's rule-making powers concerning cigarette advertising and negated the FTC rule.[11]

The battle over cigarette advertising heated up again in summer 1995 when President Bill Clinton proposed regulations to be enforced by the Food and Drug Administration that would specify that any publication with more than 15 percent of its readers under the age of 18 would be able to run only informational ads on cigarettes. The proposed regulations would also affect billboards, coupons, promotional giveaways, and displays in stores. Billboards touting cigarettes would, for example, not be permitted within 1000 feet of schools. Sporting events could be known by the parent company's name, for example the R. J. Reynolds Championship, but not by the name of a brand of cigarettes. The effects of the proposed regulations would be significant. An FTC report indicates that cigarette industry spending in 1993 on print and billboard cigarette advertising exceeded $500 million or 9 percent of the money the cigarette companies spent on marketing. The proposal would also require that the industry fund a $150 million ad campaign urging teenagers not to smoke.

Clinton argued for the regulations by noting, "Teenagers don't just happen to smoke. They're victims of billions of dollars of marketing and promotional campaigns designed by top psychologists and advertising experts. These campaigns have one inevitable consequence: to start children on a lifetime habit of addiction to tobacco."[12]

The tobacco companies immediately went to federal court to sue to stop the plan. By doing so they increased the controversy and hence the newsworthiness of the proposal magnifying the visibility of the FDA claim that the nicotine in cigarettes is an addictive drug. Aware that placement of cigarette ads in publications such as *Seventeen* would arouse critics, the cigarette industry has avoided such placement. In October 1995, R. J. Reynolds removed Joe Camel—the controversial carton icon—from billboards in response to pressure from those opposing advertising to children.[13]

TO SUM UP

This brief consumer's guide to influencing the mass media describes how otherwise powerless individuals or groups can exploit the complex relationship among government, industry, and audience to influence advertising and news coverage. In some cases individual action is effective; in others, group action is necessary.

Established organizations have a distinct advantage over social movements; resource-poor groups also operate at a significant disadvantage.

---

11. PL 89-92 (1965), U.S. Code, sec. 1331. For a discussion, see Fritschler, *Smoking and Politics*, pp. 118–120.
12. Anthony Ramirez, "Advertising," *New York Times,* 14 August 1995, p. D6.
13. Melanie Wells, "RJR Pulls Star Joe Camel," *USA Today*, 27-29 October 1995, p. 1.

An understanding of journalistic norms and routines, regulatory and self-regulatory procedures, and the legal process enhance the likelihood that a rhetorically sophisticated but resource-poor group will succeed.

In those instances when change can occur only through legislation, individuals may be forced to gain influence as members of congressional staffs or to run for office. Groups can support candidates for public office sympathetic to their points of view. Therefore, in the following chapters, we focus on the use of media to elect politicians.

A N A L Y S I S :   Constructing a Dissemination Strategy

In Chapter 4 we spoke of the principles and processes involved in influencing news media. In the last chapter we noted avenues consumers can use to effect change in media practices. Here we combine the principles of these chapters in a checklist of steps useful in creating strategies to influence the media.

Following is an outline of steps in constructing a strategy for disseminating a message through the mass media. These steps are appropriate for individuals, citizen groups, news managers, and political consultants.

Step I: Isolating the Message

Distill the essential message to be communicated from the ocean of information, and draw together essential support material (forceful, dramatic evidence in support of your claim or position).

Step II: Defining the Intended Audience

What the audience is expected to do with information often determines target audience. Reach all the essential people but only the essential people with the message. (Prepare to answer the questions, "Why is this on my desk and not on the desk of the assignment editor?" "Why is this on my desk when I don't write about this subject?") Determine if the message will pass through more than one pair of hands if it accomplishes its objective.

Consider who possible target audiences are for this message—employees of a cabinet department? other government employees? members of Congress? scholars interested in this subject? ordinary citizens affected by this policy? residents of particular localities? anyone else?

Step III: Determining the Newsworthiness of the Message

Consider whether you will have to pay to disseminate this message, and whether it can be communicated as soft news if it will not be used as hard news. Decide if it can be made newsworthy by piggybacking off other news, holding it for a slow news day or for dead news time, releasing it in a newsworthy setting, or releasing it through a newsworthy person.

Step IV: Determining Factors Constraining Release

Factors that may affect release of a news item include a congressional dead-line, a public promise by a supervisor, someone wanting to see it buried, or someone wanting to see it released and heavily publicized.

Step V: Selecting Appropriate Channels

In deciding the channels through which to release information, consider which channels best reach the target audience. Does your media list contain all relevant outlets (all publications reaching target audiences, all specialized publi-cations that cover this subject, all outlets in a particular locality)? Have all pos-sible channels been considered (press releases to county papers, radio feeds to rural America for use in pre-drive time)? Is the form of the message compatible with the selected channels? Different channels may require different forms. Is the language of the message compatible with the channel—popular language to popular channels, technical language to specialized channels? If the message is transmitted by phone or given in response to phoned inquiries, the information should be stored in a manner that lends itself to quick, clear retrieval. Responses to inquiries by phone or stories that must be transmitted by phone to meet dead-lines should be written down.

Is the message to be released to selected outlets or mass-released? Decide if you should use the elite media such as the *New York Times* to draw the attention of the other media, and if you should use one medium (such as radio) to sensi-tize others (for example, print and television) to your message.

Determine whether your message is part of a larger message.

Step VI: Adapting the Message to the Channel

Each channel imposes constraints on the messages it relays: *format* (*The NewsHour with Jim Lehrer,* national network news, *Face the Nation,* or the *New York Times*); *deadlines* (morning or evening papers, drive-time radio); *content* (weeklies or dailies, audio, print, visual, or audiovisual content); and *cost* (costs in equipment and personnel to carry this message).

These constraints influence message construction. Television news is a visual medium (consider the talking head versus the visual aid; the effects of location), and it is an *audio*visual medium (the brilliant statement might be mumbled, stumbled, and fumbled). Television news deals in 1- to 1.5-minute units, so try to write the quotable quote, the single synthetic sentence that digests the debate. It is also a medium favoring the dramatic, the confrontational; it often includes upbeat human interest stories at the end of a program. Also, what is not news today may be recast as news tomorrow (newsworthiness is a function of what else is newsworthy that day).

Television also includes interview shows (*Today, Face the Nation, The NewsHour with Jim Lehrer*) and televised documentaries. Other appropriate me-dia might be radio news spots or all-news radio, newspapers (chains, national, or county), the wire services, and specialized publications.

Step VII: Monitoring Your Success or Failure

In reviewing the success or failure of your dissemination effort, ask again what was covered and why? Future messages should be adjusted accordingly.

SELECTED READINGS

Fritschler, A. Lee. *Smoking and Politics: Policymaking and the Federal Bureaucracy.* Englewood Cliffs, N.J.: Prentice-Hall, 1975.

Krasnow, Erwin G., Lawrence D. Longley, and Herbert A. Terry. *The Politics of Broadcast Regulation.* 2d ed. New York: St. Martin's Press, 1982.

Sethi, S. Prakash. *Up Against the Corporate Wall: Modern Corporations and Social Issues of the Seventies.* Englewood Cliffs, N.J.: Prentice-Hall, 1971.

Simons, Herbert W. *Persuasion: Understanding, Practice & Analysis.* 2d ed. New York: Random House, 1986.

CHAPTER 10

Political versus Product Campaigns

Conventional wisdom says that candidates for political office are now sold to the electorate like cigarettes or soap. There is some truth to the claim. Both manufacturers and politicians develop mass media campaigns to persuade us to act as they wish. Both manufacturers and politicians seek to create name recognition and employ differentiation, association, audience participation, and repetition to communicate their messages. Both rely on campaigns that are centrally coordinated by people issuing many messages—or a single message to many media—across an extended period of time, in order to accomplish a specific objective. Both condense their messages into slogans.

But politicians are not soap or cigarettes, and the campaigns for products and politicians have contrasting functions, values, regulations, and financing. In this chapter we focus on these differences to indicate the peculiar limitations operating on those who would influence the outcome of a political campaign; we also show the resources available to them. By contrasting political and product campaigns we hope to increase understanding of both.

Using the Media

A political campaign's use of media is more *short-lived and more intense* than a campaign on behalf of a product. We may see the ads for a specific product, such as Ivory Soap, for decades. As long as the product holds a share of the market the manufacturer considers acceptable, the product will stay on the market. We use soap all year, so advertising for soap appears year-round. A political campaign is more akin to an ad campaign for a seasonal product, such as a brand of Christmas tree ornaments.

A political campaign is relatively short. Only rarely does a candidate for statewide office begin to air commercials more than three months before the election. Usually, ads appear in the last four to six weeks, and the number of ads increases as the date of the election approaches. By contrast, a three-month campaign for a product would be a very short campaign. Often producers spend more than three months just testing the product and then spend additional time testing the commercials that will market the product. The short duration of the typical political campaign is one of the campaign's major liabilities, because it is difficult to create or change attitudes in a short period of time. Consequently, candidates are announcing earlier than they once did, and speculation about likely contenders begins the day after each inauguration.

Creating an Image

The image for a product can be created more easily than the image for a politician because politicians bring to office a documentable past. Often the campaign attempts to capitalize on that past by stressing that experience has prepared the candidate in specific ways for the office sought. But the past can be a liability too. A politician with no previous elected experience can attempt to frame that lack of experience as an asset by creating an "outsider" image, but experience that isn't in the record cannot be fabricated. A politician—even a vice-president—with a shady past may find that it returns to haunt him or her. By contrast, if the product doesn't taste the way potential consumers would like, the manufacturer will determine that fact in product testing and reformulate the product. The product can be repackaged more easily than the candidate can.

Targeting the Audience

The politician wants to reach potential voters. In most states that audience includes unregistered voters until the registration books close. But once the deadline has passed, the politician can effectively discount those who are not registered to vote. In a primary in which only registered Democrats can vote for a Democratic candidate, the various Democratic candidates will focus their attention on reaching registered Democrats. The politician also focuses on voters who can be swayed to vote for him or her. When it is possible to separate one from the other, the politician is unlikely to target advertising to those committed to an opponent.

The politician often focuses attention on different age groups from those important to the commercial advertiser. For example, children and teenagers are prime audiences for the commercial advertiser. For the politician, these audiences are comparatively insignificant because they can't vote. By contrast, the politician will focus more attention on the older segment of the audience than will the commercial advertiser. As we age, the likelihood that we will vote increases. Persons over 65 cast proportionately more votes than their percentage of the population would suggest. The commercial advertiser is interested in those who are likely to spend money to purchase a product; the politician is interested in those who are likely to cast a vote.

BOX 10-1

From MTV to Product Ads to Political Ads

Since the advent of Music Television (MTV) and its popularity, the style of music videos has become standard in the advertising industry. These techniques began to be used in advertising on MTV that blurred the line between programming and commercials. Judith McGrath, MTV's Senior VP creative director, commented: "It's almost hard to tell one [video] from the other [commercials]."[a] Music videos used many techniques that originated in commercials (after all, videos are commercials), but commercials have adopted many of the techniques that were introduced in videos.

This new style soon found its way to other cable stations and networks, usually in an attempt to reach a younger audience. *Miami Vice,* originally conceptualized and sold as "MTV Cops," used music and MTV-style editing.[b] Harriet Seitler, MTV vice-president of marketing, stated: "Just look at commercials on *Miami Vice* and you'll see we've changed the way people watch TV."[c]

The quick intercutting central to this style is not predictable; it requires the full attention of the viewer. Hence, it is more challenging because it requires viewer participation in order to form it into a narrative, much like an enthymeme. Viewers read their own emotions and dramas into the intercuts. In this way, the dramas created become more emotionally binding than those concocted for viewers by advertisers.

John Pettegrew views MTV and MTV-like commercials as a result of post-modernism. He believes that non-narrative style is adapted to a generation of non-narrative viewers (they watch many shows at once, do other things while watching television, randomly channel surf, and so on). He also contends that replacing logical argument with a series of images creates an emotional connection to the product.[d]

By contrast, Alex Abrams, author of *Late Bloomers: Coming to Age in Today's America,* argues that advertising that is too much like MTV "doesn't reflect who this generation is, nor does it reach Generation X. . . . There's a significant number of older advertising people trying to do advertising for a generation that they don't understand."[e]

[a]Jennifer Pendleton, "Chalk Up Another Victory for Trend-Setting Rock 'n' Roll." *Advertising Age,* 9 November 1988, p. 160.
[b]Pendleton, p. 160.
[c]Lenore Skenazy, "Explosive Promos Ignite MTV," *Advertising Age,* 28 September 1987, p. 75.
[d]John Pettegrew, "A Post-modernist Moment: 1980s Commercial Culture & the Founding of MTV." *Journal of American Culture,* 15 (Winter 1992): 57–65. Cited material on p. 60.
[e]Laurie Freeman, "Advertising Mirror Is Cracked: Generation X Sees Ad World's Projected Image, and Isn't Buying." *Advertising Age,* 6 February 1995, p. 30.

Nonpolitical commercials are rarely broadcast to reach lower-income groups. Although people with lower incomes are less likely than their more affluent counterparts to vote, Democratic politicians, particularly liberal Democrats, routinely aim advertising at these groups. Often this advertising includes appeals to register and to vote as well as messages designed to persuade the audience to

The impact of this style is recognized. In 1986, for example, the American Sewing Association won the Cable Television Advertising Bureau's $25,000 Grand Prize for a 90-second MTV-like music video aimed at increasing interest in sewing and achieved a "national presence that they never could have done traditionally for the same price."[f]

Similarly, automotive advertising has exploited many of the techniques of music videos in selling entry-level cars. In 1987, for instance, Pontiac used these techniques to sell the LeMans. Quick intercuts of a band in concert, cars, and "sultry scenes such as a woman who shrugs off an oversize shirt to reveal her swimsuit as she runs past her LeMans at the beach" were seen as music plays in the background.[g] Chevrolet claimed that these advertisements were copied almost directly from their own "Heartbeat of America" campaign.[h] Pontiac, however, added a 25-campus MTV tour to their campaign that included an expanded 210-second music video.[i]

MTV commercial director Stu Hagmann admits that MTV has influenced television commercials, but the use of these techniques concerns him: "The techniques become the message—and I think that's too bad."[j] Joe Saltzman, chairman of the Broadcasting School at the University of California, expressed concern about wider use of these techniques, particularly on political issues. He argues that when style and image replace substance, intelligent discussion and decisions become impossible:

> Rational discussion becomes the first victim when these subjects are subverted to simple, one-dimensional images: a tasteless picture of someone's genitals, a drug-induced death, a twitching fetus, the American Flag. These powerful images overwhelm anyone's argument unless he or she can come up with equally gripping images to seduce the American public to another point of view. When public discussion of issues that go to the heart of a democracy is reduced to image and catchword, the very survival of the U.S. as a free society is in jeopardy. Citizens become conditioned to respond to the facial stereotype, to the symbols they trust or fear, and they become incapable of understanding and acting on real debate and questioning. They even grow to resent such discussion, wanting instead a quick fix, a fast image, an easy-to-grasp phrase.[k]

[f]Ronald B. Kaatz, "Creativity and Clutter," *Marketing & Media Decisions,* 22 (May 1987): 109–110. Cited material on p. 110.
[g]Raymond Serafin, "MTV Inspires Pontiac's Ad Effort in '88," *Advertising Age,* 21 September 1987, p. 84.
[h]"Chevrolet Exec Nips at Ads for Pontiac," *Advertising Age,* 21 September 1987, p. 84.
[i]Serafin, p. 84.
[j]Pendleton, p. 160.
[k]Joe Saltzman, "Style vs. Substance," *USA Today,* January 1989, p. 87.

vote for the liberal Democrat. So voting power is a great equalizer in political advertising. It means that persons who otherwise are not the focus of product advertising will become the target audience in some sorts of campaigns.

Earlier we noted that the typical commercial was set in an upper-middle-class or upper-class environment. Nonpolitical ads do not show poverty, slums, incorrigible despair. Product ads affirm the basic health of the economic system by creating a world in which people live comfortable, pleasant lives. The only discomforts the people in these ads experience easily can be remedied by purchase of a product.

By contrast, the politician out of power wants to indict the status quo and pin the blame for the ills of the system on the incumbent. These indictments are most effective when they are visually underscored. Consequently, the candidate will tape ads in slum housing to establish that the incumbent's promises of change have been unfulfilled. Political ads will also feature testimony from the disenchanted—those who are unhappy at the way in which government is being run. Political ads are able to feature the poor, the unemployed, and those who are ill, and ads attacking incumbents are prone to do just that. Ads for liberal candidates, in particular, will include the disadvantaged, who are otherwise seldom seen on television except on an occasional segment of the evening news.

Political ads are also more likely to include persons with regional dialects because their presence is a signal to the corresponding regional or ethnic group that the candidate has support from their peers. In order to reach the widest audience possible, commercial advertising, by contrast, tends to employ characters who speak standard American English with a general American accent.

Both candidates and manufacturers want to reach their target audiences in a cost-efficient fashion. It is generally easier for the manufacturer to meet this objective than it is for the politician, because the ways in which the electorate is segmented for electoral purposes do not always lend themselves to cost-efficient purchase of media space.

For example, a candidate who is running for governor in Connecticut can only reach viewers in Fairfield County if time is purchased on New York television stations; Fairfield County is part of the Greater New York Metropolitan Area for broadcasting purposes. But over 80 percent of the money spent on New York television advertising will reach New Yorkers who cannot vote in Connecticut. This means that, all things being equal, a candidate who is well known in Fairfield County has an advantage. Such a candidate can focus the media budget on buying television time in the central Connecticut cities of New Haven and Hartford, reaching primarily Connecticut voters. But the candidate who is unknown in Fairfield County must decide whether becoming known there is of sufficient importance to warrant spending 80 cents of every dollar reaching nonvoting out-of-staters (see Figure 10.1).

The competition for media time is particularly fierce in those markets that serve many states simultaneously. For example, Philadelphia stations also reach voters in Delaware and New Jersey; Washington, D.C., stations reach Maryland, the District of Columbia, Virginia, and a slice of West Virginia. Because audiences are accustomed to being addressed by those who want them to purchase an accessible product, they run the risk of responding as one Virginia resident did when she told a pollster that she planned to vote for Jay Rockefeller—who was running for the governorship of West Virginia.

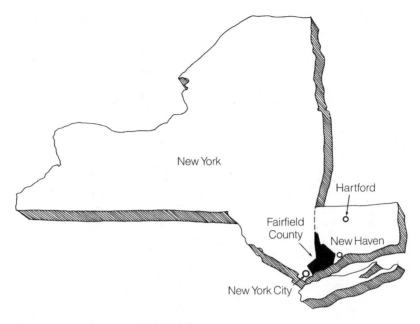

Figure 10.1 Outline of Fairfield County.

Economic versus Political Values

Ads for products argue that buying is a good thing; ads for politicians argue that voting is good. Ads for products assume that purchasing products makes us as individuals happier. Ads for political candidates assume that involvement in the political process makes the world a better place. In the world of political ads the system works. Ads do not argue for overthrow of those they oppose but for action within the system—voting. In political ads, problems exist but can be solved. Incumbents tell us that they have worked to solve the problems and have actually produced solutions. Those out of office point to problems that remain unsolved and offer solutions. Both types of ads affirm that problems are manageable and ought to be addressed from within the system by voting for one candidate or another. In ads for products, problems exist but these problems too are solvable. Here the solution is found, not in voting, but in purchasing.

Both political ads and ads for manufactured products affirm that we are able to function as agents of change. We can buy the product that produces the whiter smile. We can vote for the politician who will turn the economy around. Consequently, both types of ads are fundamentally optimistic. Their outlook is positive.

Suppose, instead, that the world is filled with unsolvable problems. Suppose, for example, that wars are not winnable, that the federal deficit is intractable, that we are plagued by problems that do not lend themselves to political solutions within the system. If all this were true, then why worry about which candidate ought to be elected? All are equally powerless. Political ads must affirm that we can be agents of change, that voting causes change, that politicians in office can make a difference, that problems are solvable. In the process of affirming these premises, political ads reinforce our belief in our political system.

Regulation

The laws governing political and product ads differ in important ways.

Censorship

Networks are free to recommend changes in product ads and often do so when, in their judgment, the ads are inaccurate, are in poor taste, or embody negative stereotypes. In contrast, it is illegal to censor a political ad. Consequently, material that would never be heard or seen in a commercial ad can be included in a political ad.

Similarly, political ads may employ words found to be "obscene, indecent, or profane," although commercial ads and programming may not. In 1978 the Supreme Court upheld the FCC's right to impose sanctions on a radio station that broadcast George Carlin's monologue about words that cannot be used on radio and television.[1] But in 1980, presidential candidate Barry Commoner was allowed to air a political radio commercial that included one of the prohibited words in Carlin's monologue: *bullshit*. "Bullshit" said the ad. "What? Reagan and Anderson—it's all bullshit."

What protects a station, then, from a libel suit claiming that a person or organization was defamed by a political commercial or statement made during access secured as a result of an equal-time request? In Fargo, North Dakota, in 1956 such a situation arose. A candidate for the Senate requested and received equal time on WDAY-TV. During the time secured by the equal-time request, the candidate charged that a prominent union, the North Dakota Farmers Union, was controlled by the Communists. The union responded by suing both the station and the candidate. The North Dakota Supreme Court held, and the U.S. Supreme Court affirmed, that stations could not be considered legally responsible for untrue or libelous statements made in such a circumstance. Because Section 315(a) of the Federal Communications Act forbids the censoring of remarks by candidates, the station could not be held accountable.

Occasionally, the results offend. "This commercial is not suitable for small children because abortion is not suitable for America," said the ad broadcast on July 3, 1992, on the superstation TBS. Pictures of three happy infants appear with

---

1. *FCC v. Pacifica Foundation et al.*, 3 July 1978 in 3 Med. L. Rptr. (Washington: Bureau of National Affairs, Inc., 1978), p. 2553.

the label "Choice A." Next: bloody fetuses tagged: "Choice B." Then Republican Congressional candidate Jimmy Fisher states, "When something is so horrifying that we can't stand to look at it, then why are we tolerating it? Pro-choice is a lie. This baby wouldn't have chosen to die. Vote Jimmy Fisher July 21 and stop the killing." In April 1992 another pro-lifer won the Republican primary in Indiana's 9th Congressional district with similar ads.

Within hours of the broadcast, the call-in lines at talk shows in Atlanta began ringing. Some expressed outrage. Others said that it was about time the effects of abortion were displayed. Still others asked the question, Why do they let pictures like that on television?

The simple answer is that the First Amendment guarantees freedom of speech. The Federal Communications Commission has placed some limits on broadcast political speech, but not many. A station that has accepted ads from one candidate must accept them from her opponents. A station may refuse an ad for a bona fide candidate for federal office only if it is too long or too short for the time purchased, if it fails to indicate the name of the sponsor, if it has technical problems (for example, the sound breaks up in the middle of the ad), or if it is "obscene." A candidate cannot invoke free speech rights, for example, to show a copulating couple, even in the missionary position.

Even if a station manager knows that an ad by a federal candidate is unfair, factually inaccurate, or offensive to part of the community, she must air the ad. The need for the protection was evident in the early days of radio when station owners simply refused all ads by candidates they personally opposed. Who would you trust to determine when political speech is fair and accurate? In essence, the FCC and the courts have answered, "In an open marketplace of ideas, we trust the public."

The results seem ironic to some. Where the stations and networks police product ads vigilantly, political ads are untouched. So if an aspirin ad says that it reduces headache pain more quickly than its competitors, the viewer can fairly assume that the claim was not fabricated in a Madison Avenue backroom. And if the accuracy of a product ad is questioned, the Federal Trade Commission can look into it, requiring corrective advertising if needed.

Not so with political ads. So, for example, a political ad can claim to be showing a "fetus" or "child" aborted in the third trimester when what is in fact being shown is a child stillborn during that period. How would a viewer know? If the press is doing its job, as newspapers around the country increasingly are, an "adwatch" will detail the facts. When the press is asleep at the switch, as it largely was until 1989, the voter must either turn investigative reporter or fall back on a lifetime's worth of judgment calls.

The courts have also held that candidates have a right to access. "It is the purpose of the First Amendment," wrote the Court in the famous Red Lion case, "to preserve an uninhibited marketplace of ideas in which truth will ultimately prevail, rather than to countenance monopolization of that market, whether it be by the Government itself or a private licensee."

The protections afforded broadcast political speech have broadened the latitude of discourse in ways that have variously offended liberals and conservatives.

In 1972 the FCC protected the right of J. B. Stoner, a state office seeker in Georgia, to say in an ad that "The main reason why niggers want integration is because niggers want our white women." Only a clear and present danger of imminent violence would justify tampering with political speech, reasoned the commission. The ruling was justified by the guarantee of free speech even for claims that are abhorrent.[2]

Equal Time

If stations could effectively deny airwave access to candidates they opposed, or provide blocks of free time to candidates they supported with no responsibility to other candidates, the broadcast media would become dominant power brokers in the political arena. Section 315 of the Federal Communications Act guarantees that broadcasters who open their facilities to one legally qualified candidate must give equal opportunities to the other legally qualified candidates. To be legally qualified, a candidate must have announced for the office and have met the legal requirements asked of those seeking the office. So, if one candidate is given five minutes of time at no charge, then other legally qualified candidates for the same office must also be given five minutes of equivalent time each. If one candidate has been permitted to buy time on a station, all other legally qualified candidates for the same office also must be permitted to buy time. The equal opportunity provision does not mean that a station must give all candidates free time if one candidate has purchased time; that purchase simply entitles other candidates to purchase equivalent time.

Right to Access

The Supreme Court has also held that candidates have "an affirmative right to access to the broadcast media." This ruling, handed down in July 1981, was the result of a challenge by the Carter campaign to network denial of the right to purchase 30 minutes of prime time in December 1979. ABC and NBC had rejected the request outright. CBS had offered two 5-minute time slots instead. Under the new ruling a broadcaster can deny access only if the requested purchase would substantially disrupt programming. The candidate may then appeal that decision to the FCC, which is empowered to determine whether or not to order that the ad run. If the station refuses an FCC request to air the ad, its license can be revoked.

Prior to this ruling, the FCC simply required stations to discuss controversial issues (the Fairness Doctrine) and to grant equal time to all qualified candidates if any one candidate was given or permitted to purchase time (Section 315). Writing for the Court in 1981, Chief Justice Warren Burger argued that "it is of par-

---

2. "FCC Won't Block Racist Ad in South," *New York Times*, 4 August 1972, p. 37.

ticular importance that candidates have the opportunity to make their views known so that the electorate may intelligently evaluate the candidates' personal qualities and their position on vital public issues before choosing among them on election day."[3]

How then is it possible for presidential debates among two or three major contenders to take place? The debates between Richard Nixon and John Kennedy in 1960 occurred because Congress had suspended Section 315 to permit them to occur. The debates between Gerald Ford and Jimmy Carter in 1976, between Ronald Reagan and John Anderson and Reagan and Jimmy Carter in 1980, and between Reagan and Walter Mondale and George Bush and Geraldine Ferraro in 1984 were possible under a 1975 ruling of the FCC that held that such debates were bona fide news events and, as such, exempt from the equal opportunity requirement.

To be considered a bona fide news event, the debates must be sponsored by an outside organization (in 1976, 1980, and 1984, the League of Women Voters; in 1988 and 1992 by the Presidential Debate Commission), must be planned without the involvement of the broadcast media, and must be covered live and in their entirety.

Some other news formats are also exempt from the requirements of Section 315. Bona fide newscasts and interview shows, such as *Meet the Press,* are exempt. A news conference scheduled by the candidate and considered newsworthy by the broadcaster is also exempt if it is covered live and in its entirety.

Campaign Objectives

For the politician there is only one day that really counts; for the product one day is as good as another, but sooner is better and often is best. A politician wants us to cast a vote on election day and to cast that vote for him or her. The politician also wants to mobilize that percentage of the electorate that occasionally works in a campaign, if that is possible, and to translate as much support as possible into money and volunteer time.

The manufacturer wants us to buy the product, sooner rather than later, and often—if that is possible. The manufacturer wants those of us who have purchased the product to recommend it to our friends and, when the occasion arises, to purchase it again. In that sense the manufacturer and the politician are alike: both benefit if we become walking advertisements for them.

But "election day" for the manufacturer—the day on which we can vote to buy or not to buy the product—comes more frequently than it does for the politician. This poses a major problem for the politician; in a sense, he or she is trying to persuade us to take action, an important action that will benefit us, but to delay taking the action until a specified day and specified times within that day.

---

3. Fred Barbash, "Court Eases Candidates' Access to TV," *Washington Post,* 2 July 1981, pp. 1, 4A.

It may rain that day. We may be ill. We may be out of town. We may forget to vote. The manufacturer is not plagued by rain, our illness, our business trips, or our forgetfulness in the same way the politician is because we have repeated opportunities to buy the product.

Voting versus Buying

The manufacturer will make the product available to us in a convenient location, or by phone or mail whenever possible. Ideally, the product intrudes on our normal pattern of activity. We go to the supermarket and there the product is, advertising itself to us from the shelf. But voting occurs in places most of us do not routinely visit—an elementary school or a municipal building. So the facts of a single election day and the special voting place complicate the job of the person who wants us to vote for a certain candidate.

Voting against a product is easier than voting against an elected official. If you buy a product and are dissatisfied, you can complain to the retailer, the manufacturer, and various consumer protection agencies. You can refuse to purchase another, attempt to get your money back, or discourage your friends from buying one. But what can you do when the politician you elect proves to be inept? The next chance you will have to vote "no" will be the next election, unless you are governed by a charter that permits recalls; even then the recall process is time consuming, costly, and usually unsuccessful.

Criteria for Victory

The criteria for victory are different in elections from those in campaigns for products. If a manufacturer's product is fourth or fifth in the market compared with competing products, that level may be cause for rejoicing. A company can do very well financially by holding 5 or 6 percent of the market for a specific product. Many manufacturers earn a lot of money with a comparatively small share of the market because the market is large enough to be shared profitably. Consequently, there are more winners in campaigns to sell products than in elections.

Dove, Dial, and Irish Spring can all make a profit, but Bob Dole, Steve Forbes, Phil Gramm, and Bill Clinton cannot all be president at the same time. Placing fifth in a field of candidates where the person with the most votes wins means that you have lost. There is no consolation prize.

In most elections the person who wins the majority of votes cast gets the office, and the rest are losers. But an advertiser can lose entire segments of the audience, even alienate those who won't buy the product, yet the product may make a healthy profit. In contrast, the candidate needs 51 percent plus 1 of the vote in most instances and cannot, as a result, afford to write off as large a percentage of the audience as the manufacturer can.

We refer to "as large a share of the audience" because, like the manufacturer, the candidate does in effect write off a portion of the audience in most cases. It is unlikely that a voter who dislikes Candidate A, is committed to Candidate B, and has a high level of information about both candidates will be persuaded to vote for Candidate A. Such persons are classed as "hostile" and written off in most campaigns. If that class of hostile voters makes up over 51 percent of the electorate, Candidate A is usually advised to withdraw rather than to attempt the impossible.

Unpaid Coverage

A candidate is likely to obtain more unpaid coverage than a product unless the product is in trouble. Candidates both profit and suffer from the media coverage of political campaigns. There is no such thing as an election that is not newsworthy; some elections are simply *more* newsworthy than others. A mayoral contest in a small town is newsworthy to the town paper and may receive coverage in county papers as well. The mayoral contest in a large city like Baltimore will receive coverage not only in the Baltimore media but also in Washington, D.C., because the city is large and because how it is governed has an impact on the area surrounding it.

In the nationwide presidential election, the nominees of the two major parties cannot avoid the attention of the media, and if they attempt to avoid it, their attempts at avoidance will be covered.

On the other hand, it is rare to see much news at all—or favorable coverage when coverage occurs—of a corporation, an industry, a manufacturer, or a product. For example, we read a lot about savings and loans in 1990. Most of the coverage focused on the need for the federal government to come up with billions of dollars to back Federal Deposit Insurance Corporation (FDIC) guarantees. The coverage started from the admitted premise that something was wrong.

However, overall, the news coverage of corporations and their products is almost nonexistent compared with the coverage of the typical political campaign.

Quality

Reporters are assigned to cover specific candidates and become experts in matters pertaining to that candidate; reporters are not assigned to cover specific products unless there is a problem, such as a recall or malfunction. Consequently, there will be more routine investigative reporting about candidates and their campaigns than about products and their campaigns.

Endorsements

The endorsement of a powerful newspaper can save a candidacy, as it did in 1978 when the *Baltimore Evening Sun* endorsed Maryland gubernatorial candidate Harry Hughes and salvaged his foundering campaign. Candidates typically translate endorsements by newspapers into paid advertisements by multicopying the endorsement and distributing it as a flier, paying to have it reprinted as a newspaper ad, reading it in a radio ad, or crawling it across the television screen in a commercial. There are few equivalents for products. When *Consumer Reports* ranks products, for example, it does so with the stipulation that the results may not be used in the products' ads.

Financing

A candidate must not only get you to buy the product—to vote—but also must raise money; a manufacturer has the money to create the product and does not advertise for contributions but rather to get you to buy the product. Presidential candidates who accept matching funds from the government must also accept a ceiling on expenditures. Manufacturers face no such limit.

In 1971 Congress enacted the Federal Election Campaign Act, amended in 1974. The enactment of this law required that candidates running for the presidency or for Congress report campaign contributions and expenditures, "limited the amount of money that could be collected and spent, made public funds available for presidential contenders, and established the Federal Election Commission to administer and enforce the law."[4] Subsequently, the Supreme Court upheld limits on the campaign contributions of individuals and groups other than the candidate and upheld the limits on spending by candidates who accepted public funds. In 1992 both George Bush and Bill Clinton accepted public funds and the resulting spending ceilings. Independent candidate Ross Perot did not. As a result, in the general election, Clinton and Bush were limited to spending the $55.2 million each received in federal support while Perot could spend as much as he wished.

The Court also permitted spending on a candidate's behalf by groups independent of the candidate. This provision gave rise in 1988 to such groups as Americans for Bush and the National Security Political Action Committee. The most famous ad of the campaign, the "Willie Horton" ad, was a PAC ad. PACs were less active in the presidential campaign of 1992.

In contrast, there is no limit on the amount of money a manufacturer may spend on behalf of a product and no limitations on the sources the manufacturer may tap to raise money—provided, of course, that the money is raised legally.

The Federal Election Campaign Act, as amended, was designed to minimize the influence of large anonymous contributors on government policy. The disclosure requirements were designed to ensure that the public would know to whom the candidates were indebted, personally and economically. The existence of these regulations makes it possible for news reporters to determine which industries are contributing more heavily to one candidate than another and to correlate politicians' voting behavior with the sources of their campaign financing.

---

4. Herbert Alexander, "Rethinking Reform," in *Campaign Money* (New York: Free Press, 1976), pp. 1–2.

BOX 10-2

Election Deadlines: Politicians Pay More for Ads

An audit released by the FCC disclosed that during the first half of 1990, television and radio stations in Cincinnati, Dallas-Fort Worth, Philadelphia, San Francisco, and Portland (Oregon) charged political candidates significantly more than other customers to broadcast advertisements.

The FCC said that at 80 percent of the television stations and half of the radio stations it had audited, candidates paid more for broadcast time than other customers during virtually every time period of the day, including the vital slots before the evening news programs. At one unidentified station, candidates paid $4,000 for 30-second spots leading into the evening news, while other advertisers paid as little as $575 for such airtime; in another city, candidates paid an average of $6,000 for a 30-second spot, while other advertisers paid an average of $2,713.

Broadcasters attacked the report, and television executives said the higher prices paid by political candidates were legitimate. The issue concerns distinctions between rates for "fixed" and for "preemptible" airtime. Fixed rates, which are higher and are the sort politicians usually demand, guarantee that an advertiser's message will be broadcast at a particular time. A preemptible time spot allows a station to replace the scheduled ad at the last minute in favor of another who is willing to pay a higher price.

"Stations overbook time," said Richard Cerucci, vice-president and general sales manager for KRON-TV in San Francisco, which is owned by the Chronicle Publishing Company. "All our other advertisers accept preemptibility. But the politicians come here and say they don't want to be treated like that. If someone wants to go in and not be preempted, they usually pay top of the line."[a]

Fearful that overcharging for political ads would become an issue at license renewal time, stations rolled back their rates in response to FCC findings, dropping their prices for political advertisements by 20 to 30 percent.[b]

[a]Edmund L. Andrews, "F.C.C. Broadcast Data Show Politicians Pay More for Ads," *New York Times*, 8 September 1990, pp. 17, 19Y.
[b]Randall Rothenberg, "Usual Flurry of Election Ads Becomes Blizzard This Year," *New York Times*, 21 October 1990, p. 20Y.

Candidates are given a financial break in their purchase of broadcast media time by the Section 315 requirement mandating that, for forty-five days before a primary or for sixty days before a general election, charges for commercial time purchased to air political material may not exceed the lowest rate charged by the station for that class of time. This regulation puts political ads on the same economic footing as the ads of the largest advertisers who purchase huge blocks of time at a discount.

In 1970 the FCC added the Zapple Doctrine to its list of requirements for broadcasters. The Zapple Doctrine gives all legally qualified candidates the right to the same access to purchased time as any one political candidate. If a station sells time to one candidate, comparable time must be made available to opposing candidates who want to purchase it and can afford the purchase.

Many of the regulations we have discussed protect the public's access to political information. Because broadcasters are corporate entities whose existence is predicated on making a profit, they are naturally inclined to limit the amount of time made available to candidates at a rate below the normal selling rate; they are naturally reluctant to preempt a show like *E.R.* that produces high advertising revenues for a political broadcast that produces minimal revenue. The Zapple Doctrine and the affirmative right-to-access rules are designed to ensure that the corporate desire to maximize profits will not significantly impede the public's right to political information.

TO SUM UP

In this chapter we have examined the ways in which the politician's use of media differs from the manufacturer's. In the process we have touched on some of the unique constraints that govern the financing, creation, transmission, and reception of political messages. In the final chapter we will examine the ways in which the political candidate manipulates the media.

SELECTED READINGS

Jamieson, Kathleen Hall. *Dirty Politics*. New York: Oxford University Press, 1992.
————. *Packaging the Presidency*. New York: Oxford University Press, 1996.

CHAPTER 11

News and Advertising in the Political Campaign

The U.S. political process has produced few candidates whose images when in office differed shockingly from their campaign images. A candidate knows she or he cannot entirely control the news coverage of the campaign. Because differences between the image projected in commercials and the actual behavior of the candidate are likely to be exposed in campaign reporting, commercials cannot stray too far from the truth about the candidate without great risk. Indeed, major campaign goals are creating a positive, electable image of the candidate, ensuring that the image is communicated consistently throughout the campaign, and that it is underscored by news coverage.

To accomplish these ends, the campaign staff attempts to: (1) control news coverage by controlling media access, setting the media's agenda, and creating credible pseudo-events; (2) blur the distinction between news and commercials in order to increase the credibility of the commercial's message; (3) exploit the linguistic categories reflecting criteria for newsworthiness and the conventions of news presentations through which journalists view campaigns; (4) insulate the candidate from attack; and (5) enlist the help of journalists in responding to attacks.

Controlling News Coverage

Particularly when a candidate seeks the presidency, it is unlikely that serious character flaws or past misdeeds will evade public scrutiny. If a candidate's commercials create the image of a quiet, reasonable individual but the politician hurls ashtrays when unhappy with staff work, a disgruntled or indiscreet staff member is likely to point out the disparity to journalists. If the candidate is a womanizer but the campaign stresses his image as a good family man, reporters are likely to find out and, in one way or another, convey the contrast to the public.

Journalists have always been aware of discrepancies between image and actuality. Until recently, however, an unwritten journalistic code said that if the private activities of politicians did not affect their conduct in office, they ought not be made public. During the 1982 centenary celebration of Franklin Delano Roosevelt's birth, reporters focused attention on this changed standard by telling us that during FDR's four terms as president, the news media hid the disabling effects of his polio from the public. An article in the *Washington Post,* for example, noted that in 1932 the press corps made no mention of FDR's fall when during a speech in Georgia, the podium that was supposed to be bolted to the floor as a brace slid forward. The same article reminded readers that "although he spent most of his waking hours either in or near a wheelchair, no photograph of this chair ever appeared in the papers or magazines during his lifetime."[1] Nor did newspeople reveal FDR's long-lived involvement with Lucy Mercer.

Similarly, reporters have known which members of Congress drink excessively, but such reports did not appear in the nation's newspapers until a stripper known as the "Argentine Firecracker" leapt from Wilbur Mills's car into the Washington Tidal Basin. This scandal was made public in an era in which investigative reporting revealed that one president lied about the Vietnam War, while another lied about his involvement in Watergate, and in which Theodore H. White's *Making of the President, 1960* legitimized an inside view of campaigns that focused on personal details about the candidates, their families, and the campaign decision-making process.

In this environment Senator Gary Hart's relationship with a young, attractive model became a focus of news coverage in the 1988 presidential primaries. After Hart dared the press to put a tail on him, promising that they'd find that he lived a dull life, the press did just that. Pictures of him aboard a luxury boat followed. On his knee was the model. In his hand, a drink. At an end: his presidential aspirations.

Candidates obviously want to minimize journalistic access to information that might contradict the image their campaigns are trying to convey. Strategies employed in this effort are examined in Chapter 4. Yet candidates are constantly being tripped up by news coverage of events they themselves supposedly controlled.

For example, on a cattle round-up, calculated to stress his masculine, Texas background, 1990 Republican gubernatorial candidate Clayton Williams commented to the assembled reporters that one should treat the advent of poor weather the way one should treat an inevitable rape—just lie back and enjoy it. The remark created a furor and raised questions about Williams's sensitivity to issues of special concern to women.

A candidate can also benefit from the image created by the media. Media focus on the Bushes' dog, Millie, added a dimension of humanity and warmth to President Bush's persona that would have been denied him if the dog had not become a media favorite. Socks the cat played a comparable role for Bill Clinton.

---

1. Hugh Gregory Gallagher, "FDR's Cover-up: The Extent of His Handicap," *Washington Post,* 24 January 1982, p. D4.

BOX 11-1

A Pollster's View

Patrick H. Caddell, pollster for President Jimmy Carter and other Democratic candidates, discussing Ronald Reagan's tightly regulated contacts with the press during the 1980 presidential campaign, said:

> The Reagan campaign has set a model. I would never be involved in another presidential campaign where the candidate was openly accessible to the press. As a campaign operative, this makes it easier for me. As an American citizen, I shudder to think what people like me would do. It's terrible for the country.[a]

[a]From *The Permanent Campaign* by Sidney Blumenthal, cited in the *New York Times*, 3 March 1983, p. 8Y.

In order to increase the probability that what we see and hear in the news will be consistent with the campaign theme, politicians employ all available strategies for manipulating the press. We illustrate how these strategies have been used in past campaigns and demonstrate the incumbent's advantage in manipulating media.

Controlling Media Access

As we noted earlier, public officials routinely control press access as best they can. The issue becomes particularly sensitive in times of international crisis or war.

Setting the Media's Agenda

As Maxwell McCombs has argued persuasively, the news media do not tell us what to think as much as they tell us what to think about. From the thousands of events and persons that satisfy basic news norms, some move to the top of the media agenda. For example, from September through December 1994, the story that topped the news agenda with a total of 444 minutes of coverage on ABC, CBS, and NBC weekday evening news was the restoration of Haiti's president Jean Bertrand Aristide and the ouster of the military junta. The Republicans preparing for power in the 104th Congress was second with 273 minutes of coverage.[2]

Agenda-setting theory suggests that the public's sense of what problems need attention is affected as much by media coverage as by personal experience. Public opinion in turn influences political action. So, for example, in 1994 the crime rate was dropping. Violent crime was down as well. Yet polls reflected

---

2. *Tyndall Report*, January 1995, p. 3.

public concern about crime. So, President Clinton expanded the section of his State of the Union address to respond to the upswing in public concern. That concern itself may have been driven by overreporting of crime in local news.[3]

Because only a small number of issues can sustain public interest at the same time, the agenda-setting capacity of the media is limited. An issue, in other words, moves up the agenda at the expense of other issues. So, for example, news coverage of the federal deficit, the Persian Gulf War, and the recession influenced how important the public thought each issue was. But the issues themselves competed for public attention. As an issue gained prominence, it drew converts from other issues. The agenda is a zero-sum game.[4]

The more personal experience an individual has with an issue, however, the less likely it is that the media will set that person's agenda.

On any given day the president exercises more control over the news agenda than do most other public officials in the United States. An incumbent, particularly an incumbent president, has more control over setting this agenda than a challenger.

Media focus on one topic can displace others. For example, in summer 1990, the press focus on the unfolding crisis in Iraq displaced headlines about President Bush's nomination of a candidate to be a Supreme Court Justice whose stand on abortion could not readily be discerned.

Creating Credible Pseudo-Events

Politicians routinely create pseudo-events, staged events designed for media coverage. In the last decade, reporters have become more skeptical of politicians—particularly since Joe McGinniss's *The Selling of the President, 1968* revealed the extent to which Richard Nixon had been packaged by media consultants in 1968. As a result, the artificial nature of such events and their explicit goal of media coverage are now pointed out by newspeople almost as a matter of journalistic honor.

Blurring the Distinction Between News and Commercials

Voters report that their voting decisions are more influenced by what they read, see, and hear in news, documentary, and public affairs programming than by what they gather from commercials. Such research is flawed by its reliance on self-report data. I am not likely to admit that I am influenced by something as crass and manipulative as a commercial when I can say instead that I was influ-

---

3. See Maxwell McCombs and Dixie Evatt, "Los Temas y los Aspectos: Explorando una Nueva Dimension de la Agenda Setting," *Comunicacion y Sociedad* 8 (1): 7–32.
4. Jian-Hua Zhu, "Issue Competition and Attention Distraction: A Zero-Sum Theory of Agenda Setting," *Journalism Quarterly* 69 (1992): 825–836.

enced by a more socially approved channel, like the news. In addition, it is likely that most of us are unaware of the primary channels influencing our decisions. In addition, channels influence each other, making it impossible to distinguish the influence of one from that of the others. Nevertheless, the mandated disclosure or tag reminds us that the source of the message is self-interested.

As a result, campaign commercials often are made to look as much like news as possible. Commercials may use actual news footage as San Francisco's former mayor Diane Feinstein did in the 1990 California gubernatorial race when her ads included a news clip of her announcing the murder of her predecessor. The news clip underscored Feinstein's theme: Tough and Caring.

Campaign commercials also use production techniques identified with news coverage. Cinéma vérité techniques such as handheld cameras and natural lighting give the commercials the look of documentaries, for example. Formats we identify as those of public affairs programs also invest commercials with the credibility of news.

Print ads can also capitalize on the credibility of news sources by reprinting and distributing favorable media coverage of the candidate or by reproducing newspaper editorials endorsing the candidate. Alternatively, attack ads feature negative news clips about the opponent. Most of the attack ads used by the Clinton campaign against George Bush in 1992 employed a succession of brief clips of Bush speaking. Appended to the clips was documentation that Bush had failed to keep his promises.

Slice-of-life commercials also resemble news clips. These commercials walk the viewer through part of the candidate's day, permitting voters to eavesdrop on exchanges with important people, overhear warm human exchanges with constituents or would-be supporters, and see the candidate with family. The difference between such a commercial and a comparable news item lies in who controls the editing process. The commercial will not show the candidate making a mistake, being manipulated by staff, or exhibiting characteristics inconsistent with the image being projected in the other paid media. The news clip might well show all three.

In order to blur the distinction between news and commercials, the political ad will often bury its mandated disclosure at the bottom of the last frames, thus minimizing the likelihood that we will recall that what we heard or saw was sponsored by the campaign. In addition, campaign managers encourage us to remember advertised content as news content by placing their ads adjacent to news and public affairs programming. In summary, then, politicians deliberately blur the distinction between news and ads by placing their ads near news and employing newslike formats and newslike or news content in the ads themselves.

A candidate can attempt to obtain news coverage that will serve as advertising as well as news by creating a pseudo-event that plays both in news and as advertising. In 1988, for example, Republican presidential contender George Bush appeared at a rally surrounded by police. At the rally, one officer gave the vice-president the police shield of the officer's son, a police officer killed in the line of duty. The scene was replayed in news as well as Bush ads.

CASE STUDY 11-1

The Adwatch

Those of us who study how politicians and the press communicate with voters are occasionally chided by our colleagues in the news media for being chronic complainers who haven't a clue about how to reform the practices we criticize. For reasons that I will explain in a moment, that diagnosis rings more true for one of us than it once did.

Throughout the 1988 presidential campaign—the one that gave us the misleading ads featuring Willie Horton and the Boston Harbor—Jamieson expressed concern that reporters were focusing more on the political strategy behind the ads than on the accuracy of the claims presented.

On *Meet the Press* and in an op-ed in the *Washington Post,* she suggested either the revival of the nonpartisan private watchdog group, the Fair Campaign Practices Commission, or alternatively that reporters themselves evaluate the fairness and accuracy of the ads.

Although Jamieson has been credited with prompting the adwatches that later characterized print coverage of the 1990 elections and print and broadcast reporting in 1992, the idea did not catch on until syndicated columnist David Broder embraced it in a column following the 1988 campaign.

Her actual contribution was different. Although she believed that adwatches were needed, as the presidential campaign progressed in fall 1988, she came to realize that they had to be done very carefully. A participant in a focus group had alerted her to this when what she recalled of a network newscast analyzing an ad was not the debunking words of the reporter but the ad itself. That ad showed Democratic nominee Michael Dukakis in an armored tank as words running across the image alleged that he had opposed virtually every weapons system developed since the Second World War. Lost on the focus group member was reporter Richard Threlkeld's statement that Dukakis was on record favoring some of the weapons the ad said he opposed.

Subsequent testing confirmed that when network reporters showed ads on the full television screen, while verbally commenting on their distortions, viewers remembered the ads better than the corrections. The implication for the proposed adwatches was clear: They could amplify, rather than undercut, the influence of deceptive advertisements.

Because we believe that a first premise for scholars and doctors alike should be to do no harm, for the next two years, graduate students at the University of Pennsylvania's Annenberg School and Jamieson experimented with techniques for criticizing ads without magnifying their power. They finally came up with a formula that worked. In brief, when reporters showed the ad running on a television set rather than showing it full screen, when they identified it on the screen as an ad and superimposed print corrections over it, the ads impact dropped and that of the reporter's commentary rose.

With help from the MacArthur Foundation and CNN, we further tested our results and produced illustrated guidelines to show television producers how to put them into practice. In the primaries of 1992, CNN adopted the formula. The National Association of Broadcasters distributed the guidelines and an illustrative tape to its members at the group's annual convention in spring 1992, and in the general election of that year CNN, ABC, NBC, and CBS each used some version of our formula.

Of course, the real utility of such strategies lies not in pointing out distortions to news audiences, whose numbers are comparatively small, but in preventing politicians from creating deceptive ads in the first place. Adwatches also help candidates who are the object of misleading ads because they can use the corrections of the adwatches in counteradvertising.

That's what happened in 1992. "George Bush is running attack ads," noted the unseen announcer in a 1992 Clinton ad. It went on to quote from news reports that outlined errors in the Republican attack ads.

Following the 1992 election, campaign consultants acknowledged that the adwatches had affected how they operated. "It was a terrible feeling when I used to open the [New York] Times and they used to take my commercial apart, or watch CNN and watch them take it apart. . . . I think these reality checks made our commercials less effective," observed Harold Kaplan, an adman for the Bush-Quayle campaign, during a conference at the Annenberg School after the election.

Noted Mandy Grunwald, advertising director for Bill Clinton's campaign, "I spent more time talking about economics and the latest statistics from the Bureau of Labor statistics and the Bureau of Census than I thought a creative person ever would in her lifetime." She said that she and the policy analysts in the campaign talked constantly about whether or not a particular statistic could legitimately be used in an ad.

Naively assuming that adwatches were here to stay, our research team at Annenberg muttered in self-congratulation, "Scholarship can make a difference." But as advertising on health reform flooded the airwaves in early 1994, we learned that we were wrong.

Between September 8, 1993 and July 15, 1994, Joseph N. Cappella and Jamieson studied news media coverage of $50 million in advertising designed to influence voters to urge specific legislators to vote for or against certain elements of health-care reform. Less than 10 percent of the reporting on these advertisements examined their fairness or accuracy. Instead press commentary focused on the political strategy behind them, analysis of little use to citizens trying to make sense of the controversy over access and choice in the health-care debate.

Moreover, two of the four networks that had faithfully followed some version of our formula for adwatches in 1992 were commenting on the strategy of the ads as they aired them full screen. Some of the other practices we had criticized were back as well. Several ads on health reform received more free exposure on news shows than they had when aired as ads in regular programming.

The lapse wouldn't matter if the ads had been accurate, but an analysis of 73 of those broadcast and 125 printed during the period of our study revealed that more than half of those aired and more than a quarter of those printed were unfair, misleading, or deceptive.

In good soldierly fashion, we documented the demise of adwatching, the return of news coverage that focused primarily on strategy, and the escalating inaccuracy of the ads. Then in July we sat down with reporters at the National Press Club in Washington to talk about what we had found.

(continued on next page)

We discovered that changes in press practice after the 1988 presidential campaign were driven by a pervasive belief that both reporters and the candidates had failed the electorate. No such sense filled discussions of the health reform debate. As important was that many who had done the adwatches in 1992 were now covering beats other than health care. And those who covered both no longer had adwatches as part of their explicit assignment. In other words, the practice of adwatching had not been institutionalized.

Reports of our findings in the *New York Times* and the *Washington Post* and an op-ed in the *Washington Post* didn't prompt a rush of adwatching either. Any effect that our recent study has had on reporting about ads has occurred on the margins. National Public Radio and *The NewsHour with Jim Lehrer* have shifted from strategy-based discussions of health reform ads to coverage that includes analyses of accuracy. ABC did one news segment addressing the truthfulness of the ads. And when the Health Insurance Association of America (HIAA) released a new set of "Harry and Louise" ads the week after our conference, the reporters who had attended ignored them. Because earlier ads featuring the yuppy couple obsessing about weaknesses in the Clinton plan had garnered more than five minutes of free airtime on national newscasts and more than 700 press mentions in the previous eleven months, this silence did represent a change. As one of the reporters who attended the conference told me, a tree fell in the woods, and no one reported it.

Our six months of analyzing media coverage of the health reform debate made a difference only if impact is measured in millimeters rather than miles. In retrospect we made two major mistakes, focusing on reporters rather than on their bosses and failing to reinforce good adwatching with praise. Had we persuaded assignment editors of the utility of adwatches in 1992, these editors and producers could easily have reinstituted adwatches on health reform in 1994. And where we were quick to criticize reporters for inadequate treatment of ads in 1988, we were slower to praise the adwatches of 1992. Reward might have invited repetition or at least a discussion with editors about the merits of reviving the adwatch form. In short, as scholars of communication, we forgot the lessons of sociology and psychology.

Exploiting Media Concepts of the Political Process

Like the rest of us, journalists see the world through language that limits what can be seen and how it will be interpreted. Some terminology used to describe the political process illustrates journalistic concepts of political campaigns and political candidates and also illustrates the criteria for newsworthiness discussed in Chapter 2.

The Campaign The media tend to see political campaigns as contests. The contest is described in battle metaphors, sports metaphors, or a combination of the two. If the electoral process is viewed as a game, it has contending sides, rules, and a goal.[5] Sports metaphors enable reporters to describe vividly the stages of the process (early primaries are the first innings or the first quarter), the intensity of the struggle (two outs in the ninth with the runner at bat, third down in the last quarter), the stakes (Super Bowl Sunday, the World Series), and the outcome (touchdown, home run).

Battle metaphors enable reporters to describe the staff and volunteers as troops, the primary as a battleground, the strategy as a process of mapping out options, and the outcome as analogous to such memorable names as Armageddon or Waterloo. Strategic options include a holding action, a retreat, a withdrawal, a first strike, or a preemptive strike. The outcome can be defeat, victory, or a rout. Candidates can declare a truce, sign an armistice, sign a peace treaty, declare war, or continue hostilities. Reporters can also dip into the biblical past to resurrect images of David and Goliath or, in the case of feuding among ideological kin, Cain and Abel. In 1988, for the first time in recent history, metaphors of the campaign as war occurred more often than sports metaphors.

When candidates campaign by attacking rather than advocating they invite the press to describe the campaign in military terms. So rarely did either presidential candidate say a kind word about his opponent that, in both the campaigns of 1984 and 1988, reporters took time in the presidential debates to ask those who sought the nation's highest office whether they could find something positive to say about their opponents. The axiom in contemporary campaigns has become, if you can't say something nasty about your opponent, don't say anything at all.

The metaphors in which the press and politicians discuss politics reflect and reinforce the view that "campaigning" is an extended search and destroy mission. As the fall 1988 campaign approached, Bob Shieffer of CBS News asked Republican consultant Stu Spencer, "What kind of a campaign is this going to be? Spencer replied, "No prisoners taken." At the campaign's end, reporter Thomas Oliphant adopted the language of combat to plead with editors and reporters to control their obsession with campaign tactics. "If there's a lesson in 1988," he said, "it takes the form of an appeal to editors. . . . 'Stop me before I kill again.' We do like to do the tactical pieces, the horse race coverage. . . . Don't let us. Ruthlessly cut it out."

In 1988 the game and sports metaphors that had framed political discussion for two decades were displaced by words of war. The 1992 campaign was battle as usual. As the superpowers disarmed in spring 1992, the candidates armed. Politicians and their advisers described the "strategies" and "tactics" of their "campaigns" as if they were generals engaged in "attack" and "defense," prepared to "outflank" and "outmaneuver," dreading defeat and hungering after

---

5. For an excellent analysis of the function of metaphors in press coverage of the 1972 Democratic presidential campaign, see Jane Blankenship, "The Search for the 1972 Democratic Nomination: A Metaphoric Perspective," in *Rhetoric and Communication*, ed. Jane Blankenship and Hermann G. Stelzner (Urbana: University of Illinois Press, 1976), pp. 236–260.

victory in the "battle" for the presidency. Jesse Jackson criticized Clinton's comments on sister Souljah as a "sneak attack." Ross Perot said he had experienced "saturation bombing" of his character. A senior White House aide bragged that the Bush attacks had "wounded" Perot. "Strap on the helmet, put on the flak jacket, full speed ahead," proclaimed Clinton's communications director George Stephanopoulos.

The press cast politics as war by other means as well. Allegations about extramarital affairs were dubbed "bombshells." Clinton organized a "squadron" of defenders to respond. The attacks preceding Super Tuesday "shellshocked" the Clinton campaign. Meanwhile, Senator Bob Kerrey "divebombed into the state with a strong attack." Jerry Brown was the "kamikaze" candidate with whom Clinton had to deal. Bush was engaged in an "anti-Perot blitz." Effective ads were labeled "killers" and "hand grenades." Political susceptibilities were termed "land mines."

The language of war invites us to see "campaigns" as a series of "tactical maneuvers," not as a discussion of the problems facing the country and the best means of dealing with them. Winning, not finding the most practicable solutions, is the goal of the campaign as war.

Such a framework invites public cynicism. At the same time it obscures the relationship between the "campaign" and governance. The language of war traffics in the Manichean dualities of allies and enemies, the United States as savior against Saddam Hussein as Satan, the candidate of the rich versus the candidate of the rest, the champion of morality and middle-class values against the scoundrel bent on destroying everything we hold dear.

By conceiving of the candidates as adversaries without common ground, the language of war focuses on areas of conflict and ignores categories of consensus. Lost in the focus on the politics of maneuver and attack in 1992 was the fundamental similarity between Clinton and Bush's policies toward the republics formerly identified as the Soviet Union. Yet it is precisely the areas of agreement that ultimately make governance possible. In a two-party system, lawmaking and other forms of collective action are the by-products of forms of compromise and conciliation unforecast by scorched earth campaigns.

The rhetoric of bullets and ballistics directs our attention to attacks and their effectiveness not to expositions of the differences and similarities among the candidates' policy proposals. In the process it reduces press coverage of the "campaign's" most informative discourse to two meaningless questions: "Who won and lost the debate?" and "What was the debate's single decisive moment?"

The Candidates   In the linguistic world of the news media, there are front-runners, contenders, minor candidates, and also-rans. The criteria employed by reporters to determine to which category a candidate ought to be assigned vary from campaign to campaign. Before the campaign finance law required that a candidate qualify in twenty states to receive matching funds, the presidential candidate with the most and the earliest "wins" was considered the front-runner. The new finance rules changed the criteria. To be a serious contender and not a minor candidate, a candidate has to qualify for matching funds.

Front-runners and contenders receive more news coverage than do minor candidates and also-rans, and the type of coverage they receive differs. Also-rans are treated as human interest oddities. Their stands on issues are not probed; their chances of winning are not pondered. It is assumed they are going to lose.

Once classified a contender, a candidate is subject to comparison with past political figures. Is this candidate glamorous, dynamic, wealthy? Or cold, sneaky, untrustworthy? Like Roosevelt, Kennedy, Reagan, Nixon? Is this a common man like Truman? Or an innovator, a communicator, like FDR? Is this a bookish, intellectual candidate like Wilson or Stevenson? Democrats compare Republicans with Hoover and Nixon; Republicans respond by tarring Democrats as Carteresque.

Candidates try to act so that journalists will associate their actions with those of admired historical figures such as Lincoln and FDR. They also identify with those people, places, and actions that the intended voters stereotype positively, and divorce themselves from those we negatively stereotype.

So, for example, in his successful 1990 campaign for the Democratic nomination for Cook County board president, Richard Phelan sits at a *"Cheers"*-like bar, and tells how his parents *"sacrificed"* to enable him to study at *Notre Dame*. He worked at *"a one-lawyer firm,"* he says and built it into one of the largest in the Midwest. *"The boys in the backroom"* carp about his success, he notes, but adds that that is because he plans to work *for the taxpayers* and not the *professional politicians*.

When a candidate succeeds in sculpting an image consistent with a stereotype, it begins to play out in press coverage. For example, a report in the *Washington Post* described the 1990 Republican Texas gubernatorial nominee this way:

> Williams, a West Texas millionaire oilman, is the most colorful political character to appear on the Lone Star scene in years. He brags about his fistfights, loves to drink beer, rides horses in his TV commercials, designs his swimming pools in the shape of cowboy boots, paints all his possessions, including two airplanes, in the maroon and white colors of his beloved Texas A & M Aggies, says he wants to double the state's prison capacity and get more criminals "pounding rocks," and talks wistfully about Texas the way it was when his Daddy was around.[6]

But stereotypes can cut two ways. When Williams refused to debate Democratic nominee Ann Richards, she told the press, "You can't pretend to be John Wayne and run from a girl."[7]

---

6. David Maraniss, "In GOP Race, Money Takes Lead," *Washington Post*, 10 February 1990, p. A7.
7. *Dallas Morning News*, 17 August 1990, p. 18A.

CASE STUDY 11-2

Campaigns as Seen Through Their Slogans or Themes

The essence of a well-conceived political campaign is distilled in its advertising; the essence of its advertising is distilled in a slogan or theme reflecting the campaign's core by answering the questions, "Why is this candidate running?" and "Why should I vote for this candidate?"

In the 1960 presidential campaign, for instance, Richard Nixon and his vice-presidential running mate Henry Cabot Lodge summed up their campaign in the slogan, "Nixon–Lodge: They Understand What Peace Demands." The advertising slogan revealed that unlike Lyndon Johnson, John Kennedy's running mate, Lodge was a central part of the argument for the election of Nixon. Kennedy's slogan, "Leadership for the 60's," did not mention Johnson and, except for a millisecond glimpse of LBJ's picture on a placard in a televised ad designed both to build name recognition for Kennedy and to create a bandwagon for the Democratic ticket, LBJ was conspicuously absent from national televised advertising. By contrast, Lodge—his height dwarfing Nixon—not only was featured in the still photograph that closed each Republican ad but also starred in a series of ads. What the 1960 ads reflect is the respective functions of Lodge and Johnson in the campaign. Lodge appeared in nationally aired ads because he strengthened the ticket throughout the country. Johnson's value was primarily regional; consequently, as a campaigner, he concentrated his time on rallying the South behind the Democratic ticket.

The Nixon–Lodge slogan also indicates that the campaign stressed the comparative advantage the Republican ticket offered in foreign policy from Lodge's U.N. ambassadorship and Nixon's vice-presidential experience. Consistent with the campaign theme, televised ads for Nixon translated questions of domestic policy into questions of foreign policy. In one ad, for example, a disembodied voice asked, "Mr. Nixon, what is the truth? Is America lagging behind in economic growth?" Nixon, seated on a desk, assures the viewer that the U.S. economy is healthy, and adds, "This is the kind of economic growth we must have to keep the peace." Each ad closed with the tag "Nixon–Lodge: They Understand What Peace Demands."

Consistent with his theme, Kennedy's opening statement in the first Kennedy–Nixon debate focused the election on domestic questions:

> In the election of 1860, Abraham Lincoln said the question was whether this nation could exist half-slave or half-free. In the election of 1960, and with the world around us, the question is whether the world will exist half-slave or half-free, whether it will move in the direction of freedom, in the direction of the road we are taking, or whether it will move in the direction of slavery. I think it will depend in great measure upon what we do here in the United States, on the kind of society that we build, on the kind of strength that we maintain.

Kennedy asked that we get the country moving again. By contrast, Nixon stressed that we were stronger than ever and that the Republicans had kept the peace:

> There is no question but that we cannot discuss our internal affairs in the United States without recognizing that they have a tremendous bearing on our international position. There is no question but that this nation cannot stand

still; because we are in deadly competition, a competition not only with the men in the Kremlin, but the men in Peking. We're ahead in this competition, as Senator Kennedy, I think, has implied. But when you're in a race, the only way to stay ahead is to move ahead.

Each campaign had created a theme and a slogan consistent with the background and perceived strengths of its candidates. Kennedy's service in the Senate had provided no real foreign policy experience. Consequently, he stressed domestic affairs. Nixon could have stressed domestic affairs, but with the country in a recession, he had a stronger case if he stressed what was, for that ticket, a strength as well as Kennedy's weakness—foreign affairs. The theme chosen by Nixon explains Lodge's importance in the campaign and why he appeared in televised ads. Ads were created that recalled memorable moments from Lodge's U.N. service— his challenge to the Soviets over the presence of bugging devices in a U.S. office, for example.

An effective campaign slogan tells the audience what a vote for the candidate means, and it sums up the content of the candidate's advertising. In addition, an effective campaign slogan cannot be used to attack the candidate, and it is believable to voters.

Telling the Audience What a Vote Means

George Wallace, former governor of Alabama, was a potent force in the 1968 presidential election, where, running as a third-party candidate, he won almost 10 million votes. Wallace might have been a decisive factor in the 1972 presidential campaign had he not been shot and incapacitated during the Maryland primary campaign. His message in each of his tries for the presidency was simple and direct: "Send Them a Message."

A vote for Wallace was a message. But what was the message? In 1968 his commercials asked whether you were satisfied seeing your dollars sent to unsympathetic regimes, whether you were satisfied with crime-ridden neighborhoods, whether you were satisfied with seeing your children bused miles from home in order to attend school? If you were not, a vote for Wallace signaled your dissatisfaction.

Wallace's anti-big government, anti-intellectual, anti-bureaucratic appeals prefigured those that Jimmy Carter would successfully parlay into victory in 1976. In his speeches, Wallace wondered aloud what bureaucrats packed in those big black briefcases and speculated that if you opened one of them you'd probably find the *New York Times* and a peanut butter sandwich. According to Wallace, pointy-headed bureaucrats couldn't even park a bicycle straight, yet dared to meddle in the lives of working people. These statements revealed that the "them" of the slogan were the Washington establishment and federal bureaucrats. By framing the election as a contest of "us" (Wallace and his supporters) against "them" (the Washington establishment), the slogan provided a symbol consistent with the other rhetoric of the Wallace campaign.

Because the press labeled Wallace a spoiler and speculated on whether he would capture enough of the vote to send the 1968 election to the House of Representatives, Wallace needed to insulate himself against the suggestion that a vote

(continued on next page)

for him would be wasted. The slogan accomplished this goal. The reason for supporting Wallace was not necessarily to get him elected but to send a message to the person elected and to other elected officials—that Wallace's constituency must be taken seriously and accommodated. A slogan like LBJ's in 1964, "The Stakes Are Too High for You to Stay Home," would not work for a candidate who was not regarded as having a serious chance of winning. LBJ's slogan is the sort useful only to a candidate who has a realistic chance of becoming president. "Send Them a Message" enabled Wallace to redefine the meaning of voting. A vote for Wallace might not elect him (although Wallace never discounted that possibility); rather, the message the vote carried would affect the behavior of those elected.

A campaign slogan can send a subtle, even unintended message. In his campaign for the position of mayor of Los Angeles, Tom Bradley, an African-American former police officer, used the slogan "He'll Work as Hard for His Paycheck as You Do for Yours." The slogan was a message to whites that he would represent both whites and African Americans and a message to those who feared he would sell out the city to welfare recipients that he believed in the work ethic. According to Jeff Greenfield (one of David Garth's associates and now an ABC news personality), what the media adviser in the Bradley campaign and his associates were trying to say with the slogan was: "(a) Yorty [Bradley's opponent] wasn't working for his salary, (b) Bradley would earn the job of mayor, (c) Bradley understood the premises of the work ethic and was no permissive open-the-treasury welfare enthusiast, (d) Bradley understands how hard you, the typical voter, work for your paycheck because he is one of you."[a]

Bradley won in a landslide. The slogan was a prism through which the campaign could be viewed: it provided a reason to vote against Yorty and a number of reasons to vote for Bradley; it reassured voters who required assurance; and it identified Bradley with an important subsection of his audience—workers. The ads in the campaign were consistent with the slogan. They stressed Bradley's accomplishments and in the process demonstrated that in the past he had worked hard for his paycheck and had worked for things the voters supported.

Summarizing the Campaign's Advertising

The slogans used in the Kennedy and Nixon campaigns of 1960 offered reasons for voting for the ticket. Slogans can be directed against the opposing ticket as well. Lyndon Johnson's 1964 presidential campaign slogan was "Vote Johnson November 3. The Stakes Are Too High for You to Stay Home." The slogan implies a special urgency about the 1964 election. If "you" stay home and do not vote for Johnson, catastrophe may result. The slogan also reveals the campaign's concern that projections of a Johnson landslide would lull Johnson supporters into complacency. If all of Goldwater's supporters voted and most of Johnson's supporters stayed home, Goldwater could win the election. In a campaign with a slogan about the urgency of voting, we would expect to find commercials advocating voting. In the Johnson campaign, for example, a commercial showed a man with an umbrella

[a]Jeff Greenfield, *Playing to Win: An Insider's Guide to Politics* (New York: Simon & Schuster, 1980), p. 85.

plunging through a downpour to get to the polls. The ad said, "If it rains on November 3, get wet. The Stakes Are Too High for You to Stay Home."

Just as the commercials run on behalf of Nixon and Kennedy in 1960 were summarized by the slogans of each campaign, so, too, the slogan used by the 1964 Johnson campaign previewed and summarized the thrust of the ads run for Johnson. In 5-minute commercials Johnson argued that, like other presidents before him, Republicans as well as Democrats, he was committed to keeping the peace. The implication, of course, was that Goldwater was not.

The famous daisy commercial made that implication explicit in the minds of auditors who read into an otherwise benign ad the conclusion that it was "trigger-happy," "shoot from the hip" Goldwater who would blow the little girl up. The ad did not explicitly make that claim, but simply showed a child in a field picking daisies as she counts from one to ten, slightly out of sequence, a sign of the genius of the ad's creator Tony Schwartz, who realized that children rarely count linearly. As the child reaches "ten," a voice from one of the satellite launch countdowns intones "Ten, nine, eight . . ." When the voice reaches "zero," the girl is replaced on the screen by an exploding bomb, and we hear Lyndon Johnson's voice saying that we must learn to love one another or we will surely perish. The tag then appears as the announcer's voice declares, "Vote Johnson November 3. The Stakes Are Too High for You to Stay Home." The tag prompted the audience to read Goldwater into the ad.

Other ads more explicitly provided the evidence that the daisy commercial left implicit. One ad for Johnson noted that Barry Goldwater had described the nuclear bomb as "merely another weapon." The announcer's incredulous voice then repeats, "Merely another weapon?" The ads for Johnson also argued that the stakes were too high domestically. One ad showed a Social Security card being torn apart as the announcer informed the audience that even William Miller, Goldwater's running mate, had claimed that electing Goldwater would mean the end of Social Security as we know it. A series of visually compelling production ads insinuated that Goldwater could not be trusted with the presidency. One of these ads purported to show the auction of the Tennessee Valley Authority, a dramatic illustration of Goldwater's suggestion that the TVA be sold. Another showed a model of the map of the United States suspended over water. As a saw loudly severed the eastern seaboard off the map, the announcer reminded the audience of Goldwater's statement that perhaps "we ought to cut off the eastern seaboard and let it float out to sea." "Can a man who would say that really be trusted to serve all the people, justly and fairly?" the ad asked. The Johnson campaign aired ad after ad to reinforce the same claim—that a vote for Goldwater was a risky exercise in a high-stakes venture. The ads raised voters' anxiety about Goldwater's stands on issues and then reduced that anxiety by assuring viewers that a victory for Johnson would avert such catastrophes.

Some slogans are too imprecise to accomplish any of these purposes. In 1984, Democrats Mondale and Ferraro campaigned on the slogan "Mondale: Ferraro: Fighting for Your Future." Neither the slogan nor the advertising to which it was attached revealed the nature of that future. The same problem plagued the 1988 Democratic slogan "The Best America Is Yet to Come." Not only did that tag fail to define the future America but it also was a slogan equally applicable to the Republican ticket.

BOX 11-2

Spending by PACs

"Charles Keating, Jr., principal owner of the failed Lincoln Savings and Loan Association, channeled more than several hundred thousand dollars in campaign contributions to five U.S. Senators. Dubbed the 'Keating Five,' the senators intervened as a group in April 1987 on Keating's behalf with government regulators who were examining alleged violations by Lincoln Savings. It took another two years for examiners to finally seize Lincoln—a delay that will cost taxpayers an estimated $1.3 billion. When Keating was asked whether his contributions influenced political figures to take up his cause, he responded, 'I want to say in the most forceful way I can: I certainly hope so.' " [a]

Common Cause used this case to lobby for reform. The postcard reproduced on page 323 was part of this campaign.

[a]*Common Cause Magazine*, January/February 1990, p. 43.

Responding to or Preventing Attack

The prime function of an attack is to discredit an opponent. This is usually accomplished by casting suspicion on an opponent's campaign theme or by raising doubts about an opponent that can be corroborated by news channels. The danger in attacking an opponent is that the politician attacking, rather than the opponent, will be discredited.

Fear of backlash limits the attacks in a typical political campaign. A politician who violates our standards of fair play invites the judgment that she or he is not to be trusted with the office sought. But fear of backlash restrains behavior only when the person attacking is identified with the candidate running for office. The rise of independent political action committees removes this powerful constraint from the electoral process because, by law, PACs must function independently. Thus, it is possible for a PAC to attack one candidate without creating a backlash against the candidate who benefits from the attacks. Consequently, those attacked by an independent political action committee seek to link the PAC to the opponent.

If this can be done successfully, then any backlash resulting from the attack will hurt the opponent. If the reaction hurts only the PAC and not the politician who benefits from the attack, there is no restraining force controlling attacks because no one accountable to the electorate is held responsible for them. So, for example, the most controversial political ads of 1988, those featuring furloughed murderer Willie Horton, were sponsored not by the Bush campaign but by a pro-Republican Political Action Committee.

In general, candidates who are ahead in the polls and who anticipate winning by a comfortable margin do not usually attack their opponents. An attack invites reply and media coverage of the reply. This legitimizes the opponent and

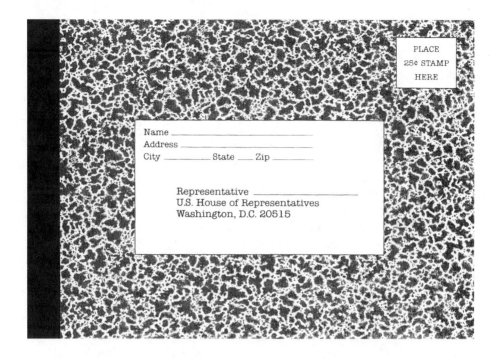

Name _____

Address _____

City _____ State ____ Zip _____

Representative _____
U.S. House of Representatives
Washington, D.C. 20515

PLACE
25¢ STAMP
HERE

Take the Keating Test.

Dear Representative _____ :

Will you support the key reforms necessary to clean up congressional campaigns and end influence-money abuses like the Savings & Loan scandal involving Charles H. Keating Jr., the "Keating Five" Senators and $1.3 million in political donations? Take the Keating Test!

YES NO

☐ ☐ **DO YOU AGREE** that "soft money" contributions must be banned to prevent "fat cat" contributors, like S&L owner Charles Keating, corporations and labor unions from making contributions of $100,000 or more to support presidential and congressional candidates?

YES NO

☐ ☐ **DO YOU AGREE** that limits on sky-rocketing campaign spending must be established to stop the never-ending chase for campaign contributions that sends Members of Congress running to private interests like Charles Keating and the PACs for political money?

YES NO

☐ ☐ **DO YOU AGREE** that political action committee (PAC) contributions to congressional candidates must be dramatically reduced to prevent special interests, like the S&L industry, from contributing huge amounts of influence money to Members of Congress?

YES NO

☐ ☐ **DO YOU AGREE** that alternative campaign funds must be provided to ensure that "clean" campaign resources, such as public matching funds and low-cost mailings, are available so Members of Congress aren't dependent on influence-seekers?

YES NO

☐ ☐ **Will you support and fight for these reforms necessary to end influence-money abuses like the "Keating Five" Affair and restore the credibility of Congress?**

Sincerely,

_____

PRINTED BY COMMON CAUSE • 2030 M STREET NW • WASHINGTON, D.C. 20036

Reprinted by permission of Common Cause.

provides the opponent with media access. Counterattack is a legitimizing strategy that tacitly assumes comparable stature. Why would a politician waste time attacking someone who was totally inconsequential and no real threat to the politician's election?

Last-Minute Attacks

Not surprisingly, the sorts of attacks that have difficulty withstanding journalistic scrutiny tend to appear late in a campaign. In such circumstances the political system works for the attacker and against the candidate attacked. Because stations may not censor political ads, the burden of proof falls on the person attacked. If a lie is carefully worded, the burden of establishing its falsity can divert the time and attention of the attacked candidate's top-level campaign strategists who, in the final days of a campaign, ought to be concentrating on getting out the vote. In such circumstances, a well-financed campaign with a skilled media consultant has at least the chance of placing responsive or counteractive ads on the air. A poorly financed campaign must rely on the investigative tendencies of reporters and the sympathies of columnists.

When the Fair Campaign Practices Committee was still functioning, an injured candidate could appeal to it for a determination of whether an ad was fair or not. Newspeople then reported the complaint and the resolution. No functioning independent national group now exists to police the fairness of campaign tactics.

The difficulty in dealing with last-minute attacks is compounded by the fact that an attack ad can run for a full day or more before the attacked candidate knows about it. Once alerted to its existence, the campaign staff must spend time securing a copy. Additional time is required to document its falsity. If the attack campaign includes many ads, the burden is increased proportionately.

If the candidate decides to use a news conference to expose and reply to the attack ads, schedules must be cleared, an appropriate location secured, and the media alerted—all of which take time. Meanwhile, the candidate's staff must develop a strategy to counter the ads. Under such pressure, strategic errors are likely to occur. Perhaps the candidate will be panicked into refuting ads that have reached few voters. Such a move enlarges the opponent's audience. Perhaps the candidate's rebuttal will seem histrionic and discredit him or her. Finally, given the time pressure, there is a danger that even if they are exposed as false by journalists, the attack ads will have reached more people than the rebuttal. There may not be time for a backlash to build against the attacker, and the sight of two candidates battling it out over the truth of the ads may drive voters to a third candidate not contaminated by the controversy.

Exploiting Blunders

At some point in their political lives, most public figures have said something they regret. These blunders are often newsworthy not only because they reveal a previously unknown fact but also because they express a candidate's position succinctly. In 1976, presidential candidate Reagan made the mistake of attaching a specific figure to the amount of money that could be cut from the federal budget. The gaffe was a headline writer's dream: "The Ninety Billion Dollar Blunder." The statement was newsworthy not simply because Reagan was newsworthy as a candidate but also because it was brief, concise, specific, concrete, and dramatic. It haunted Reagan through the rest of the campaign.

When a prominent candidate makes this sort of slip, it receives news coverage. By incorporating reminders of the gaffe in attack commercials, the candidate's opponents can keep the charge alive and make it a focal factor in voting decisions. The "revolving-door prison furlough program" ad that the Republicans aired against Democratic nominee Michael Dukakis drew its power from the furlough of Willie Horton during Dukakis's term and from Dukakis's resistance to public calls for change in the law and his refusal to meet with Horton's victims or to apologize to them.

When an attack ad replays an opponent's blunder, it is often to make the mistake concrete for the audiences. For example, in a 1976 commercial Gerald Ford reminded workers gathered around him that Carter had promised to lower taxes for those below the median income and raise taxes for those above the median income. But the median income in this country turned out to be lower than Carter had imagined. Ford then said that he didn't think the people surrounding him needed to have their taxes raised.

When the blunder is not a concise synthetic statement but part of a long rambling answer to a question, it cannot be used as effectively either in news or in an ad. A commercial that opens in the middle of an opponent's sentence or cuts from the sentence before it is finished invites us to conclude that the statement has been taken out of context. This saved Ronald Reagan from hearing replays of his 1976 statement that he might order the use of troops in Rhodesia (now Zimbabwe). The statement came in the middle of a long, rambling, involved answer that did not lend itself to use in an opponent's commercial. Instead, the Ford campaign assumed audience familiarity with the statement and created an ad that warned "Governor Reagan couldn't start a war. President Reagan could."

Attacks Legitimized by the Media

News and ads are not the only outlets for, or sources of, attacks in political campaigns. Editorial cartoons, political columns, and comic monologues are among the other sources of attacks over which a candidate exercises no direct control and which are especially difficult for a candidate to counter effectively.

A political attack in a comic strip is effective because it appears in a context that does not ordinarily provoke critical responses. We expect to be entertained, so we relax our guard. The same is true of the political humor in Jay Leno's monologues. Audiences laugh and, in the process, accept the premises underlying the jokes. Occasionally, when a comic strip becomes too blatantly political, the editors will move it from the comic section to the editorial page, as was done with Al Capp's "Li'l Abner" in the 1960s and with Garry Trudeau's "Doonesbury" in the

1980s. Occasionally, newspapers drop "offending" cartoons altogether or selectively delete them when the message proves distasteful or controversial.

The nature of humor is such that a cartoonist or a comedian will tend to reinforce existing attitudes rather than create new ones. When audiences fail to laugh at a certain type of joke, that joke is quickly dropped. This ensures that Jay Leno will underscore, not initiate, attacks.

Editorial cartoonists have more latitude than any other source in the broadcast or print industry. Because their content is primarily visual, they are not readily subjected to tests for truth that, as we have indicated earlier, are most suited to assessing verbal statements of factual propositions. So, for example, when one editorial cartoonist wanted to make the claim that Reagan's secretary of the Interior was not interested in protecting wildlife, he showed James Watt at a desk with Bambi's stuffed head decorating the wall. The claim in the drawing, which can be comprehended in seconds, is stronger, clearer, and more damning than any of the columns of ponderous prose that defended a milder version of the same claim in deadly—and probably unread—detail.

The effectiveness of such cartoons poses problems for attacked candidates. If a candidate is attacked in an editorial, a newspaper column, or an opinion editorial (op-ed), he or she may appeal to the newspaper for space to respond. Unlike the broadcast media, newspapers are under no legal obligation to permit reply. Nonetheless, most newspapers will give an aggrieved party who has been directly attacked space in an op-ed or in the letters-to-the-editor column. The controversy adds excitement to the paper and holds readership. Presenting both sides creates a sense that the newspaper is fair and responsive to the interests and needs of the community, so it is in the newspaper's self-interest to permit a person attacked in its pages the opportunity to respond. But there is no effective way to respond to an editorial cartoon.

The national syndication of cartoons and columns means that when an attack occurs or misinformation is published, the impact is widespread. A column by nationally syndicated *New York Times* columnist William Safire will reach some audience in every major city in the country. Someone attacked by Safire who wants to respond to a column and does not have access to the syndication service will have to deal directly with hundreds of op-ed page editors across the country.

Editors occasionally refuse to print a regular column when, in their judgment, it has overstepped professional boundaries. Jack Anderson's free-wheeling columns, on occasion, failed to appear in the *Washington Post,* for example. Columnists also police themselves. When Anderson learned that vice-presidential candidate Thomas Eagleton had not been convicted of drunken driving as Anderson had claimed, he admitted the error and apologized. It is difficult to determine what damage was done by the false charge.

Enlisting the Help of Journalists

The material used in attacks against a candidate is often culled from the public record. The most accessible channels that preserve the public record are often the print and broadcast media. Consequently, any political figure has a vested interest in accurate reporting about his or her activities. If uncorrected, misinterpretations by journalists can be resurrected for use against a candidate.

Reporters have access to those who have followed the careers of both candidates and to the public record of both candidates' activities, as reported by journalists in past stories and broadcasts. Thus, it is often a reporter or columnist who is in the best position to determine the accuracy of an attack. Because interpreting the meaning of a candidate's voting record is a complex process involving analysis of many substantively meaningless procedural votes, it is often the knowledgeable columnist or reporter who alerts the public that, although an attack is a technically accurate report of a procedural vote, it misrepresents the actual position of the attacked candidate.

So, for example, nationally syndicated columnist George Will evaluated charges made by senatorial aspirant Bruce F. Caputo against incumbent senator Daniel Patrick Moynihan and concluded: "Caputo asserts that Moynihan 'voted against capital punishment.' Moynihan favors capital punishment for certain crimes. There has been no direct vote on capital punishment since Moynihan entered the Senate. Caputo is referring to procedural votes that reveal more about the parliamentary context at the time than Moynihan's views on the subject."[8]

When candidates believe they have been unfairly attacked, they often attempt to enlist the aid of the media in combating the attack. Journalists can be drawn into the campaign as arbiters of the truth or falsity of attacks by the attacker, by the person attacked, or by the interchange itself.

After the 1988 campaign, academic conferences around the country raised the question, "Why had the press not pointed out the distortions and the false inferences invited by the 1988 presidential candidates' ads?" Among these were the implications of a Dukakis ad that George Bush would all but eliminate Social Security, and the implications of a Bush ad that Dukakis had released a large number of first-degree murderers to kill and rape again.

Newspapers responded by printing the texts of 1990 ads in their entirety and then documenting the facts as the reporters knew them. For example, when an ad for Texas Democratic gubernatorial candidate Ann Richards claimed that her opponent had "mountains of debt," the *Dallas Morning News* boxed the following information: "The Midland entrepreneur has borrowed extensively over the years to develop his oil, ranching, and long distance telephone enterprises. And he has seen his net worth fall by almost two-thirds since 1982, according to a review of his business dealings by the *Dallas Morning News*. Still, the *News* puts Mr. Williams' net worth at about $116 million, concentrated in oil and gas properties."[9]

For the first time in 1992, the advertising of a presidential campaign was "policed" for fairness and accuracy by both print and broadcast reporters. The most systematic work was done by Brooks Jackson of CNN. On NPR Andy Bowers led analyses of radio, an important move because the most serious distortions of the campaign were found in the final weeks on local radio. Eric Engberg of CBS and Jackson of CNN performed yeoman service in locating and analyzing the radio ads on television.

---

8. George Will, "The Things Bruce Caputo Says," *Washington Post*, 28 February 1982, p. B7.
9. *Dallas Morning News*, 17 August 1990, p. 18A.

Reporters approved of press coverage of ads. Of the reporters surveyed, 77 percent approved of these policing efforts.[10] One television newsperson told Times Mirror that the debunking of the ads "is the primary reason why no Willie Horton ads or their cousins have appeared in this campaign. Our coverage is keeping the bastards honest."[11] "We'll need a Teddy White to come along later to see if those who planned commercials really sat around worrying about whether we'd criticize them or not," another editor told the surveyors.[12]

Political commercials also reveal their creators' perception that material culled from news reports constitutes credible evidence. Hard-hitting attack spots quoting an opponent's stand are often insulated from journalistic attack by their use of actual quotations from newspaper articles or television coverage to document their claims.

Tests of Credibility Applied by Journalists

Journalists are uniquely sensitive to changes in a candidate's position.[13] Consistency is one of the categories reporters use to test a candidate and a campaign. If the candidate is a prominent one or the election an important one, the meaning of the change in position will be probed. Throughout his 1988 presidential bid, George Bush repeated the promise, "Read My Lips: No New Taxes." When in summer 1990, he concluded that new tax revenues were in fact needed, the switch in positions provided fodder for editorial cartoonists and dominated three days of broadcast and print coverage.

Journalists focus so tightly on consistency because it is easy to test and because it lends itself to the behind-the-scenes-of-the-campaign perspective with which reporters are comfortable. By focusing on inconsistency, newspeople provide credible evidence for opponents to use in attacking the inconsistent candidate.

Charges of inconsistency can be damaging for a reason implied in the closing statement of an ad that Democrats for Nixon ran in 1972 against George McGovern. The ad asked, "Last year . . . this year . . . what about next year?" The tactic is commonplace in races at all levels. In spring 1990, Republican gubernatorial contender Clayton Williams aired ads asking how one could know where his fellow Republican aspirant Ken Hance actually stood. The ad opens with blurry pictures. The announcer intones, "There are two candidates for governor who can't seem to agree on anything." The ad proceeds to document their contradictory stands on issues. As the pictures come into focus, the announcer notes, "The trouble is . . . they're both Ken Hance." If a candidate has changed position on important issues in the past, what assurance have we that the candidate will not change on those issues that make him or her attractive to us?

---

10. "The Press and Campaign '92: A Self-Assessment," *Times Mirror Center for the People and the Press.* December 20, 1992, p. 7.

11. Ibid.

12. Ibid.

13. Donald R. Matthews, "The News Media and the 1976 Presidential Nominations," in *Race for the Presidency,* ed. James David Barber (Englewood Cliffs, N.J.: Prentice-Hall, 1978), p. 67.

How Has New Technology Changed Politics?

The Internet has made it possible for voters to locate candidate speeches, press releases, and position papers on line. At the same time, citizens with computer access can locate press accounts from around the country, talk politics with other citizens, and, on occasion, exchange messages with the candidates and office-holders themselves.

Quick access to large bodies of information will make it easier for reporters to check on the consistency of candidate messages; at the same time, access will make opposition research less costly.

The World Wide Web (WWW) is not simply a way to retrieve information and graphics on line; it is also interactive. And it is growing at a rapid pace. By mid 1996, estimates of the number of Web Sites ran from 90,000 to 265,000.[14]

The Web was created by scientists at the European Particle Physics Laboratory in Geneva, Switzerland, to make it possible for scholars to collaborate on line. By 1992, candidates were making use of the linking capacity of computers. Voters could query the Clinton campaign for information, for example. As we write this, readers can gather information about President Bill Clinton's policies as well as those of Republican nominee Senator Bob Dole by visiting their Web sites.

Faxes have also proved to be a powerful political tool. Those with computers can generate fax material and fax to thousands of numbers directly from the computer. Some credit a fax campaign with derailing the so-called Conference on the States, a conference planned to reassert states rights. Fearful that the conference would be a staging ground for rewriting the Constitution and perhaps put in place global government, some conservatives mobilized small business owners and stay-at-home mothers among others. "A national fax network founded by Detroit-area sales representative Karen Mazzarella to fight Clinton's 1993 tax package mushroomed during the health-care debate and tripled to more than 100,000 people while fighting the Conference of the States," reported the *Washington Post*. "The movement is closely allied with talk radio."[15] Supporters report faxing information to sympathetic talk show hosts who urge listeners to call or write those in power.

How Has Television Changed Politics?

Television has changed politics by changing the way in which information is disseminated, by altering the way politics happens, and by changing our patterns of response to politics. By giving the electorate direct access to the candidates, television diminished the role of the party in the selection of the major party nominees. By centering politics on the person of the candidate, television accelerated the electorate's focus on character rather than issues.

---

14. Trip Gabriel, "The Meteoric Rise of Web Site Designers," *New York Times,* 12 February 1996, p. D1.

15. Dale Russakoff, "No-Name Movement Fed by Fax Expands," *Washington Post,* 20 August 1995, pp. A1, A22.

Television has altered the forms of political communication as well. The messages on which most of us rely are briefer than they once were. The stump speech of one to two hours that characterized nineteenth-century political discourse has given way to the 30-second spot ad and the 10-second sound bite in broadcast news. Increasingly, the audience for speeches is not that standing in front of the politician but the viewing audience that will hear and see a snippet of the speech on the news.

In these abbreviated forms, much of what constituted the traditional political discourse of earlier ages has been lost. In fifteen or thirty seconds, a speaker cannot establish the historical context that shaped the issue in question, cannot detail the probable causes of the problem, cannot examine alternative proposals and argue that one is preferable to others. In snippets, politicians assert but do not argue.

Because television is an intimate medium, speaking through it required a changed political style that was more conversational, personal, and visual than that of old-style stump oratory. Reliance on television means that increasingly our political world contains memorable pictures rather than memorable words. And words increasingly have been spoken in places chosen to heighten their impact. "We have nothing to fear but fear itself" has given way to "Let them come to Berlin" and "Mr. Gorbachev, tear down this wall." Schools teach us to analyze words and print; in a world in which politics is increasingly visual, informed citizenship requires a new set of skills.

Recognizing the power of television's pictures, politicians craft televisual, staged events called pseudo-events designed to attract media coverage. Much of the political activity we see on television news has been crafted by politicians, their speechwriters, and their public relations advisers for televised consumption. Sound bites in news and answers to questions in debates increasingly sound like ads.

Political managers, termed "handlers" in 1988, spend large amounts of time ensuring that their clients appear in visually compelling settings so that the pictures seen in the news will reinforce those seen in ads. In debates, candidates recall those staged pseudo-events.

By focusing on mainstream values, television mainstreams its viewers. Heavy viewers of television differ from light viewers in some politically relevant ways. The likelihood that a character in a prime-time program will be the victim of a crime is higher than it is in real life. Heavier viewers believe that they are more likely to be victims of crime than they actually are. Heavy viewers are also more conservative in their views about the socially appropriate response to crime. They are, for example, more likely than light viewers to favor heavy sentences and use of the death penalty. Heavy-viewing conservatives and heavy-viewing liberals are more likely to agree on how to respond to crime than are heavy- and light-viewing liberals.

But whereas heavy viewing makes liberals more conservative on crime, television's legitimation of government response to social problems draws conservatives closer to a more liberal view of the value of government solutions to social problems.

The quantity, quality, and audience for televised information about politics is changing. In the mid-1980s an increase in the quality of political programming on the Public Broadcasting Service and the rise of cable meant that the amount of substantive political information available on television increased.

The rise of cable meant that specialized audiences could now be addressed directly by candidates. What had been a broadcast medium, reaching a large undifferentiated mass audience, was increasingly becoming a narrowcast medium, reaching smaller, more homogenous audiences. What was once true only of radio and direct mail became true of television in the mid-1980s. Spanish-language cable reached Hispanics in large numbers; MTV reached young voters. Whereas broadcasting dictated that political messages speak to concerns that transcended our differences, the narrowcasting of cable meant that the special concerns of special segments of the audience could now be addressed.

But whereas the limited number of broadcast channels meant that reporters could easily eavesdrop on and criticize candidate ads, the narrowcasting available on over 100 cable channels makes this increasingly difficult.

What Forms of Communication Shaped Voting Decisions?

In the new pool system of exit polling, in 1992 each network was permitted to ask proprietary questions. CBS asked what had helped voters make their voting decisions. The answer was: debates (60%); talk shows (45%); conventions (25%); political advertising (23%). Note that with the exception of talk shows television was the primary conduit of the information gotten through these sources of influence.

The good news in 1992 was that public attention to politics was up. The third and final presidential debate, hampered by the fact that it began at 7 P.M. EST, a time that made it very difficult for West Coast viewers to watch, reached over 90 million viewers, a total that does not include those who watched on PBS, C-SPAN, or CNN. That is an audience approaching Super Bowl level. As important, the final debate attracted more, not fewer, viewers than the earlier debates, a fact consistent with the Times Mirror finding that voters made up their minds late that year, with 24 percent deciding their vote in the final week.[16]

By available accounts the general election presidential campaign of 1992 was helpful to the electorate and an improvement over the campaign of 1988. A panel back survey of the electorate conducted by the Times Mirror Center for the People and the Press found 77 percent of the respondents saying that "they had learned enough during the campaign to make an informed choice among President George Bush, Governor Bill Clinton, and independent candidate Ross Perot.[17] In 1988, 48 percent found the debates helpful; in 1992 that percentage had risen to 70.

---

16. "The People, the Press and Politics Campaign '92," *Times Mirror Center for the People and the Press,* 15 November 1992, p. 5.
17. Ibid. p. 1.

The public was less pleased with the performance of the press; 36 percent gave campaign coverage an A or B grade, up slightly from the 30 percent in 1988. Of particular note is that 35 percent thought the press was unfair in its coverage of Bush.[18] Public dissatisfaction led nationally syndicated columnist David Broder to observe that "the press is on probation just as [are] the politicians who were elected. . . . The attitude that was out there all year, the anger, the frustration in the public that fueled this year's politics did not disappear overnight on Election Day. It's there as a challenge to Clinton and to all of the members of Congress and it's there as a challenge to us."[19]

Although exit polls reported that talk shows were second only to debates in the help they provided voters, "nearly one in five voters could not evaluate their conduct in this campaign."[20] The problem in evaluating the meaning of either of these responses is that, for some, talk shows indicate the radio call-in programs hosted by such emerging opinion leaders as Rush Limbaugh; for others, they mean Larry King.

The importance of talk shows is that in this format voters are able to talk to candidates. Inclusion of voters in the second presidential debate was a similarly empowering move.

Image versus Issues; Character versus Positions

Scholars have wasted a lot of time trying to distinguish between messages that relate to candidate's images and messages that relate to candidates' stands on issues. The problem, of course, is that almost every message says something that can be interpreted as an issue and tries to enhance the candidate's credibility, hence, image. It is more useful to recognize that stands on issues produce an image and that such "image" questions as trustworthiness and competence often are issues.

A more useful distinction separates the character or natural temperament/disposition and relevant biography of the candidate from the specific legislative action the candidate proposes. So a candidate might demonstrate her compassion, a facet of character, by indicating her strong support for Aid for Dependent Children, a policy position or stand on an issue. Since the early seventies, voters have been telling pollsters that the character of the candidates is more important to them than the candidates' policy positions or stands on issues.

The Comparative Relevance of Character and Stands on Issues

In the 1960s and 1970s the electorate learned that judging a candidate on stands on issues was not a reliable predictor of his or her conduct in office. Some candidates acted against voter expectations: Lyndon Johnson, elected in 1964 as

18. Ibid., p. 4.
19. Election debriefing, Annenberg School for Communication, University of Pennsylvania, 12 December 1992.
20. "The People, the Press and Politics Campaign '92," p. 3.

the peace candidate, escalated the war in Vietnam. Some presidents proved unable to meet their objectives. John Kennedy did not succeed in translating his campaign promises into law; only after his death did his successor secure passage of some of Kennedy's key initiatives. Jimmy Carter, elected to bring the budget into balance and lower inflation and unemployment, had not accomplished these goals by the end of his first term. Bill Clinton failed to make good on his campaign promise to deliver a health-care reform plan that could be financed by cost-savings in the existing system.

In this period, one campaign stood out for accurately forecasting a president's positions and accomplishments. Ronald Reagan campaigned promising a defense buildup and tax cuts and produced both.

Meanwhile, the character of a candidate seemed increasingly important in judging performance in office. Whether a person was truthful and trustworthy were focal concerns of those probing the failures of Johnson's handling of the Vietnam War, Nixon's handling of Watergate, and Clinton's handling of Whitewater; whether a person was competent was central to those probing the failures of the presidencies of Ford and Carter; whether a person was candid about his health was of concern to those who learned of Kennedy's Addison's disease only after his death.

What can and does television tell us about issues and the character of presidential candidates?

Determining Which Issues Are the Likely Focus of a Campaign In their own ads, in debates, and in news clips, candidates reveal their popular past positions and conceal their unpopular ones. At the same time, candidates reveal the unpopular past positions of their opponents. Public opinion polls and focus group tests (analysis of the response of small groups to various messages) help campaigns determine which issues will resonate with which voting group.

When an issue is controversial but, nonetheless, beneficial to one side or the other, that issue is more likely to be raised in the ads and news coverage of a Political Action Committee (PAC), not in the candidate's own messages. As we noted in the previous chapter, a PAC is a group of like-minded citizens formed to advance a specific interest and unaffiliated with a party or candidate. A PAC contributes to candidacies and produces messages consistent with the self-interest of its members. Most major corporations have formed PACs as have a number of ideological groups.

The Center for Responsive Politics in Washington, D.C., is among the groups monitoring the flow of PAC money. As telecommunications policy was being discussed in Congress, the center reported that long-distance (telephone) PACS had given $1.7 million in the 1993 through 1994 session, cable interests had put up $1 million in PAC funds, and the regional Bell operating companies had contributed $3.1 million to various members of Congress.[21]

After interviewing twenty-five former members of Congress about the influence of PAC money, reporter Martin Schram concluded that "Members were in

---

21. *Capital Eye*, 15 April 1995, p. 4.

rare agreement on one seldom-spoken fact of legislative life: Special interests are generally most successful at achieving their goals in Congress on matters that are relatively minor and unimportant to the general public and thus ignored by the news media—but that can be of multimillion-dollar importance to a single corporation, or entire industry, or other special interest."[22]

When an issue hurts both candidates or both parties, as the savings and loan crisis did in 1988, it will be raised by neither side.

In general, at the presidential level the party affiliation of the contender has accurately predicted the likely positions on certain issues. Republicans will, for example, favor less government intervention and less taxation but will support greater defense spending than will Democrats.

In general, the issues on which news, advertising, and debates will focus are those advanced by major party nominees. Although in 1988 over 100 citizens filed the appropriate papers to be considered bona fide presidential contenders, public discussion focuses, with few exceptions, on the Democratic and Republican parties' nominees and on the issues they consider important.

Issues of general concern will receive treatment in the mass media; issues of less national concern or highly specialized issues will be treated in specialty publications and broadcasts. For example, those interested in a candidate's monetary philosophy are more likely to find such information on *Wall Street Week in Review* or in the *Wall Street Journal* than on the *NBC Nightly News* or in *USA Today*. Specific environmental policies are likely to be treated in magazines devoted to the subject.

Because television is a visual medium, the messages produced on it are more likely to speak to issues that lend themselves to visualization. This means that crime and environmental pollution are more likely to be the subject of political ads and of news coverage than is the national debt or international liquidity.

Determining Which Facets of Character Are the Likely Focus in a Campaign   The character defects of the most recent president are likely to shape the criteria by which the character of the candidates is judged. After Nixon's resignation, Carter won election campaigning as a candidate who would never lie and who would provide a government as good as its people.

Societal norms shape the criteria we set for candidate character. In the 1950s and 1960s, a divorced candidate was weakened by that fact. During their presidential runs, divorce was raised as an issue against Adlai Stevenson and Nelson Rockefeller. By the 1980s being divorced no longer carried a social stigma, and the country elected its first divorced president, Ronald Reagan.

The press and public are in the process of determining which facets of character are relevant to governance. In the 1988 primaries we learned that having smoked marijuana in one's youth was not a disqualifier. In the Texas gubernatorial campaign of 1990, we learned that the press and public consider it inappropriate for a candidate for governor to have purchased the services of prostitutes

---

22. Martin Schram, *Speaking Freely: Former Members of Congress Talk about Money in Politics* (Washington, D.C.: Center for Responsive Politics, 1995), p. 93.

in his youth. In 1992 those who voted for Clinton seemed to say that a candidate's past infidelity was acceptable if it was not ongoing and his wife had remained with him in spite of it.

Any form of hypocrisy, any discrepancy between private behavior and public, political statement, is likely to be scrutinized by the press. As a result during the primaries of 1992, two facets of Bill Clinton's past preoccupied the press: his failure to serve in Vietnam and his alleged affair with a nightclub singer.

The Interplay of Influence: Issues and Character in Ads, News, and Debates

Ads

There is more issue content in many ads than in broadcast news. The typical television viewer gets most of his or her political information from ads. A number of factors minimize the ability of ads to convey useful issue information. Conveying useful information is not the goal of the advertising. By stressing issues that will benefit them, candidates' ads attempt to set the issue agenda for the campaign. Because ads are partisan sources of information, they are poor sources of primary political information. Ads suppress information that would hurt their candidate; ads occasionally take evidence out of context; ads occasionally invite false inferences.

Political ads for bona fide candidates for federal office are not subject to tests of fairness or accuracy by those broadcasting them. A political ad for a bona fide candidate for federal office must meet only four tests: (1) it must have a discernible disclaimer disclosing its sponsor; (2) it must fit the time purchased; (3) it must meet the technical standards of the broadcast outlet; (4) it may not be obscene.

If a station has sold advertising time to one candidate in a race, it must make comparable time available for sale to all other bona fide candidates for that race. Because candidates must pay for most ad time, we are more likely to see ads for those who are wealthy or able to raise more money than their opponents. At the presidential level, in the general election, this advantage is muted by equal federal financing of both major party candidates.

Ways to Compensate for or Counter These Limitations

1. The best way to protect oneself against distortions in advertising is to seek out alternative forms of information. The best-informed voters are those who combine television viewing with newspaper and magazine reading. Because candidates often respond to the distortions of ads in press conferences, viewing news helps obtain the "other side."
2. In debates candidates are directly accountable to a press panel and to their opponents. Some questions of accuracy can be resolved by attentive debate viewing.

3. Concern about the distortions in attack advertising has prompted calls for legislation. Opponents of these proposals argue that they violate the Constitution's protections of free speech. Proposals include: (a) requiring that attacks be made by a candidate in person speaking in an ad; (b) providing free response time for a candidate attacked by a PAC ad; (c) requiring that shortly after an ad begins airing, the sponsoring candidate hold a press conference to respond to questions about it.

News

Viewers tell pollsters that their voting choices are more influenced by print and broadcast news than by ads. This finding, however, may be the by-product of our human tendency to report that we are influenced by approved sources and uninfluenced by presumably manipulative sources. There is no dispute that when news coverage of a candidate is consistent with that candidate's ads and debate performance, the power of the candidate's message is magnified.

Several factors may minimize the ability of news to communicate useful issue information. For over a decade, scholars have consistently found that broadcast and print journalism focus not on issue content of campaigns but on strategic intent of the candidates, the outcome of their strategies, and on who is winning or losing. This focus on the "horse race" and "game plan" displaces discussion of other matters.

In addition, candidates attempt to control the news agenda. When they succeed, the news agenda and their ads are similarly focused, employ similar pictures, and use much the same language.

When network newscasts do focus on issues, some of their news norms minimize the impact of their discussion. For instance, news is only news once. Once a story on an issue has aired or been printed, it is unlikely to be re-aired. The problem occurs when a distortive ad repeatedly makes a false claim that is only corrected or contextualized a single time in news. A problem occurs as well when the attention of parts of the public has not yet focused on the campaign at the time at which the issue is covered.

Another news norm problem is that it is the job of reporters to cover the story, not to make it. Accordingly, reporters focus on the issues preselected by the candidates. However, reporters are willing to set the agenda for discussion of character and to probe any discrepancies between candidate character and accepted social norms.

Ways to Compensate for or Counter These Limitations
1. Gather information from multiple news sources and multiple media.
2. Determine what issues are relevant to you and seek out forms in which those issues are likely to be addressed.
3. Begin paying attention to news and debates in the early presidential primaries when news coverage is likely to treat emerging issues in depth.
4. Use computers in libraries or at home to retrieve early news stories of importance in contextualizing candidate claims. Often newspapers carry careful studies of the biography and record of a candidate early in the primaries.

Debates

In a national election, debates are the single most useful form of information available to voters. In debates, a large viewing audience has the opportunity to compare the candidates and their positions. Debates provide the only direct comparison available in most campaigns. The results are beneficial to every segment of the viewing audience from the least to the best educated. After each presidential debate, surveys have shown that viewers could more accurately identify and report the candidates' positions on the major issues debated.

There are several factors that minimize the ability of debates to communicate useful information on issues. First, the candidates' desire to protect themselves from gaffes leads them to (1) seek a panel of reporters on the expectation that reporters will ask predictable questions; (2) negotiate a format that includes only short answers on the assumption that all possible questions can be anticipated and short answers prepared; and (3) negotiate a format that denies reporters the ability to follow up their questions on the assumption that inconsistencies and inaccuracies are less likely to be exposed if there are no follow-up questions.

Second, the press panelists tend to ask questions of more interest to a knowledgeable reporter than to an information-seeking voter. This flaw was remedied in the 1992 campaign when in the Richmond debate actual citizens drawn from the Richmond community asked questions directly of the presidential candidates.

Third, press coverage tends to reduce debates to one decisive moment. This focus distracts from information in the debate about the candidates and their positions. These supposedly decisive moments include "There you go again." "Do you remember when you said, 'There you go again?'" and "Senator, you are no John Kennedy." They also include Clinton's claim in the first 1992 debate that George Bush's attacks on his patriotism betrayed Bush's father's memory. In the 1950s, Senator Prescott Bush had objected to the tactics of Senator Joseph McCarthy.

Fourth, the press focuses on the strategic intent of the candidates and on who won or lost the debate. There is no intelligent way to judge a win or loss. More important is that the focus on winning and losing displaces other more useful discussions of what could be and should be learned from debates.

Ways to Compensate for or Counter These Limitations

1. The well-informed voter will be able to spot errors and inconsistencies.
2. The well-informed voter need not rely on commentators to determine what was and was not significant in the debate.
3. The well-informed viewer will not let debate coverage determine what is useful but will instead ask what issues and traits of character are important and will seek out that information systematically.

TO SUM UP

In this chapter we have examined the complex interaction among the candidates and the media in campaigns. One medium can be used to contextualize the content carried by another; for example, a print reporter may determine the accuracy of charges contained in a broadcast ad. Alternatively, an ad such as the anti-Nixon Watergate ads run by McGovern may take articles published in a print form and employ them in a televised ad.

We also noted the interplay of news and advertising across the various media. Ads become the subject of analysis in news, and items in the news become the content of ads. In the process, the well-financed candidate has the ability to take his or her case directly to the American people in ads, but even as this right is exercised, it is subject to the scrutiny of the news media.

Finally, we have shown some of the ways in which politicians manipulate the news in their attempts to impose a consistent image of themselves and their campaigns on all media outlets. This chapter illustrates the systemic and commercial character of the U.S. mass media. Political communication includes both news and advertising. As news, political activities are shaped by the criteria for newsworthiness and the conventions of news presentation. In advertising, candidates, like products, must achieve name recognition; differentiate themselves from their competitors; create identification with and participation by target audiences; associate themselves with admired persons, activities, and values; and use repetition to overcome audience resistance.

In political communication, news and advertising interact in an unusually significant way. News coverage can make a candidate credible, reinforce the messages in political ads, and protect her or him against certain kinds of attacks. As a result, politicians seek to blur distinctions between news and advertising; campaign managers create pseudo-events to attract media coverage; and news footage or newslike content and formats are used in political advertising.

Journalists, with their special access to information and their credibility as investigators, evaluate the claims in political ads and serve as a corrective to deceptive and misleading advertising. Conversely, through ads candidates can respond to news coverage and influence how audiences react to news items.

National and state political candidates cannot be elected without the credibility conferred by news coverage or without the images created through advertising. As a result, the costs of political campaigning have increased. Political advertising is expensive, as are the services of professionals with the expertise to influence news coverage. In one sense, mass media have made political communication more efficient—the cost of reaching each voter has decreased—but they have also made politics a game successfully played primarily by the affluent and the media savvy.

A N A L Y S I S :   Political Ads and News

Many of the questions found at the end of the chapters on news and advertising can be asked also of the political use of ads and news. Here we include some additional questions that pertain specifically to advertising and news in political campaigns.

Determining Who Is Newsworthy

What criteria are governing which candidates are receiving news coverage? Are some candidates receiving more coverage than others? Are some candidates receiving more coverage in one medium than in others? If so, why? How are the candidates using the conventions and routines of news coverage to secure news coverage? Are some candidates doing this with greater skill than others? Are reporters reporting these efforts at manipulation?

Determining What Is Covered

Are the candidates' ads a subject of news reporting? If so, what is the focus of such stories? (cost? claims? evidence? fairness? image? media consultants?) Is one candidate more clearly setting the agenda for the media than others? What agenda is being set for voters by the media? Are they focusing on issues that favor one candidate over the others? Are the media focusing on some primaries and not others? If so, why? Which candidates are benefiting from this focus? Has the nature of coverage changed during the campaign? Has the quantity of the coverage increased, decreased, or remained the same as the campaign has progressed? What interpretation has been placed on each announcement of candidacy and each statement of withdrawal? Are journalists acting to determine the truth or falsity of charges in the campaign? If so, to what effect? Has any candidate invoked libel laws, equal opportunity, or right to access? If so, to what effect? If this is a statewide campaign, a congressional or senatorial campaign, has it received coverage in the national media? If so, what of significance or interest to a national audience is being credited to this campaign?

Relationship of Candidates and Reporters

Compare the treatment of reporters by each campaign. Are they better fed and housed, more courteously treated in one campaign than others? If so, what effect, if any, is this having on media coverage? Are some journalists being given preferential treatment? If so, to what effect? Are some reporters being punished by the campaign for unfavorable coverage? If so, what form of action is the punishment taking? restricted access? undesirable accommodations? What are the ongoing themes in the coverage of this campaign? (horse race? appearance versus reality? consistency?)

The Image of the Candidate

Is the image projected by the candidate consistent? If not, what are the discrepancies and what accounts for them? Is the image projected in person consistent with the image in ads? in news? Are some of the candidates more visually appropriate for televising than others? If so, what impact is that having on the campaign? on reports about the campaign? Has the image of the candidate altered over time? If so, why and to what effect? Is the presence of a media consultant an issue in this campaign? If so, what is the consultant saying about his or her role in the campaign? Is the media consultant helping or hurting the candidate? What are the adjectives used most often by the media to describe this candidate? Is an independent political action committee running ads to create a positive or negative image about one of the candidates? If so, to what effect? How are the candidates reacting to the PAC?

Candidates' Ads

Are candidates using ads to contextualize news? Are materials from news reports functioning as evidence in ads? Have ads been a subject of news reports? If so, did the coverage help or hurt the candidate? Is the candidate using attack ads? If so, are they truthful and fair? If so, are they airing throughout the campaign, at specific points in the campaign, or at the end of the campaign? How does the pattern of airing attack ads affect their impact in this campaign? Will these ads provoke a backlash? If so, why? If not, why not? Are these attack ads responding to other attacks? If so, is the response legitimizing the attack of the opponent? How are the ads creating recognition, differentiation, association, participation, and repetition?

SELECTED READINGS

Barber, James D., ed. *Race for the Presidency: The Media and the Nominating Process.* Englewood Cliffs, N.J.: Prentice-Hall, 1978.

Blumenthal, Sidney. *The Permanent Campaign: Inside the World of Elite Political Operatives.* Boston: Beacon Press, 1980.

———. *Pledging Allegiance: The Last Campaign of the Cold War.* New York: Harper Collins, 1990.

Cannon, Lou. *Reporting: An Inside View.* Sacramento: California Journal Press, 1977.

Cramer, Richard Ben. *What It Takes: The Way to the White House.* New York: Random House, 1992.

Crouse, Timothy. *The Boys on the Bus.* New York: Random House, 1972.

Edelman, Murray. *The Symbolic Uses of Politics.* Champaign: University of Illinois Press, 1967.

———. *Politics as Symbolic Action: Mass Arousal and Quiescence.* New York: Academic Press, 1971.

Graber, Doris A. *Verbal Behavior and Politics.* Champaign: University of Illinois Press, 1976.

Hart, Roderick P. *The Sound of Leadership.* University of Chicago Press, 1988.

———. *Seducing America: How Television Charms the Modern Voter.* University of Chicago Press, 1994.

Herbers, John. *No Thank You, Mr. President.* New York: W. W. Norton, 1976.

Jamieson, Kathleen Hall. *Packaging the Presidency.* New York: Oxford University Press, 1984.

———. *Eloquence in an Electronic Age.* New York: Oxford University Press, 1988.

————. *Dirty Politics: Deception, Distraction, and Democracy.* New York: Oxford University Press, 1992.

Nelson, Michael. *The Presidency and the Political System.* Washington, D.C.: Congressional Quarterly, 1984.

Patterson, Thomas E. *The Mass Media Election: How Americans Choose Their President.* New York: Praeger, 1980.

————. *Out of Order.* New York: Alfred A. Knopf, 1993.

Sherrill, Robert. *Why They Call It Politics.* New York: Harcourt Brace Jovanovich, 1979.

Windt, Theodore O. *Presidential Rhetoric: The Imperial Age 1961–80.* Dubuque, Iowa: Kendall-Hunt, 1980.

————. *Presidents and Protesters: Political Rhetoric in the 1960s.* Tuscaloosa: University of Alabama Press, 1990.

Index